GAELIC GRAMMAR

containing

THE PARTS OF SPEECH

and

THE GENERAL PRINCIPLES OF PHONOLOGY AND ETYMOLOGY

with

A CHAPTER ON PROPER AND PLACE NAMES

by

GEORGE CALDER, B.D., D.Litt.

Lecturer in Celtic, University of Glasgow

GAIRM PUBLICATIONS
Glasgow
1990

The original edition was published in Glasgow in 1923. A
photographic reprint was published by Gairm Publications in 1980.

Reprinted 1996

ISBN 0 901771 34 1

Printed in Great Britain by Martins the Printers Ltd
Berwick upon Tweed

GAIRM: Leabhar 84

DO

M' OILEANAICH

A THA, 'S A BHA, 'S A BHIOS

INTRODUCTION.

"GRAMMAR," says Professor Bain, "is a science—or nothing." Grammar, one may add, is the description of a language, as Geography is the description of a country. The rules of Grammar rest on use and wont, and on induction from observed facts ; and the examples are illustrative, not exhaustive. In dealing with fading usages, however, like dual **dà**, fuller illustrations are desirable ; and in intricate combinations like article with noun, preposition with pronoun, and the verbal system, exhaustive treatment is the only satisfactory course.

Attracted by Celtic philology, and following in the footsteps of Zeuss, international scholars have since his time, in increasing numbers, studied Old Irish ; and the mass of material being manageable, they have produced many admirable grammatical works, which, though differing widely in aim and importance, throw much light upon modern Gaelic.

Comparatively little has been done in this restricted field since Stewart published his grammar, a great work, which evoked the admiration of O'Donovan. The time seems ripe for an attempt to lay before the Gaelic-speaking public the main results of modern scholarship ; and in order to save the time and energy of teachers, the editor has set down, in grammatical order, facts that have constantly emerged and engaged his attention as a teacher of Gaelic during the last decade.

These pages contain some matters not hitherto treated adequately or at all in Gaelic grammars. The time has come for dealing with philological changes, compound nouns, proper names, and the compounding of verbs with preverbs, of nouns with prenouns, of nouns with suffixes ; and the use and derivation of enclitics and particles.

While these topics will interest pupils who have made some progress in the language, the Grammar may be also used with advantage in the hands of a skilful teacher for the instruction of junior pupils.

The noun forms, the adjectives, the numerals, the pronouns, the prepositions, the prepositional pronouns, and the verb forms may be learnt by the youngest pupil, with this added advantage, that he may at the same time read and assimilate the examples which may be found suited to his state of advancement.

The Editor makes grateful acknowledgements to Professor Fraser and to Mr. Calum Macpharlan for having read part of the proofs.   The sheets have been looked over also by Mr. Neil Shaw and Mr. James MacLaren, and thanks are due to them for pointing out some errors.   The Editor is greatly indebted to the Rev. Dr. J. King Hewison for the loan of the pastoral visitation roll (MS.) of the Rev. Dr. MacLea, minister of Rothesay, 1760-1824, containing all the names and surnames in the parish.   Finally, the Editor has much pleasure in acknowledging his obligations to Principal Sir Donald MacAlister for the great interest he has taken in the work from first to last, and for many helpful suggestions.

An Comunn Gàidhealach has generously given a grant of £100 to the Editor to aid him in producing the work.

GLASGOW,
    May, 1923.

CONTENTS

PAGE

Authorities quoted or referred to.

(The quotations are given usually without alteration.)

A' Choisir—A 'Choisir-Chiùil, The St. Columba Collection of Gaelic Songs, Paisley.

Am Bìobull—Editions 1888 and 1902.

Am Fear-Ciùil, F.C.—Am Fear-Ciùil, Poems, Songs, and Translations, by Donald MacKechnie, Edinburgh, 1910.

An Gaisgeach—*v.* D. B.

An t-Òran.—The Gaelic Songster, An t-Òranaiche, le Gilleasbuig Mac-na-Ceàrdadh, Glasgow, 1879.

Arab.—Sgeulachdan Arabianach, Tales from the Arabian Nights, translated into Gaelic, Inverness, 1906.

Aur.—Auraicept na n-Éces, The Scholars' Primer, ed. George Calder, B.D., Edinburgh, 1917.

Bedel—Leabhuir na Seintiomna, le Uilliam Bedel, London, 1684. An Tiomna Nuadh, le Uilliam O Domhnuill.

Book of Deer—The Spalding Club, ed. Dr. Stuart, 1869.

Brah. Seer—The Prophecies of the Brahan Seer, by Alexander Mackenzie, F.S.A. (Scot.), Stirling, 1909.

C.G.—Caraid nan Gaidheal, A choice selection of the Gaelic Writings of the late Norman MacLeod, D.D., Edinburgh, 1899

C.R.—The Celtic Review, 1904-1916, Edinburgh.

C.S.—Common Speech.

Catm.—Leabhar Aithghear nan Ceist.

Claig.—*v.* D. B.

Clar.—Clarsach an Doire, le Niall Macleoid, Duneideann, 1883.

Collect. Reb. Alb.—Collectanea de Rebus Albanicis, the Iona Club.

Còmhraidhean—Còmhraidhean an Gaelig 's am Beurla, by Rev. Duncan MacInnes, Edinburgh, 1880.

Cos.—Teagasg nan Cosamhlachdan, leis An Urramach Domhnull Iain Mairtinn, M.A., Edinburgh, 1914.

Cuairt.—Cuairtear nan Gleann, 1841.

D.B.—The Spiritual Songs of Dugald Buchanan, ed. Rev. Donald Maclean, Edinburgh, 1913.

D. Ban—The Gaelic Songs of Duncan MacIntyre, ed. George Calder, Edinburgh, 1912.

Dineen—Foclóir Gaedhlige agus Béarla, An Irish-English Dictionary, by Rev. Patrick S. Dineen, M.A., Dublin, 1904.

Dr. Johnson's Journey—A Journey to the Western Islands of Scotland in 1773, by Samuel Johnson, LL.D., reprinted, Paisley, 1908.

F. M.—Annals of The Kingdom of Ireland, by The Four Masters, edited by John O'Donovan, LL.D., M.R.I.A., Dublin, 1851.

F. T.—Folk Tales and Fairy Lore, in Gaelic and English, by Rev. James MacDougall, ed. Rev. George Calder, B.D., Edinburgh, 1910.

Fois—Fois Shìorruidh nan Naomh, le Mr. Richard Bacster, Edinburgh, 1908.

Forbes—Gràmar Dùbailt Beurla 'us Gàelig, le Iain Foirbeis, 1843, ed. altera, 1848.

Gillies—A Collection of Ancient and Modern Gaelic Poems and Songs, Perth, 1786.

Gillies Gr.—The Elements of Gaelic Grammar, by H. Cameron Gillies, M.D., London, 1902.

Guth na Bliadhna, 1904...

H. B.—Faclair Gàidhlig air son nan Sgoiltean, le Dealbhan, Camus-a-Chorra (Herne Bay), 1902.

H. S. D.—Dictionarium Scoto-Celticum, A Dictionary of the Gaelic Language, by The Highland Society of Scotland, Edinburgh and London, 1828.

H. S. Report—Highland Society's Report.

Ir. T.—Irische Texte, von Ernst Windisch, 1880-1905.

J. W.—John Wesley, Memorial Papers of Rev. John McCallum, 1911.

Kirk—Bìobull, 1690.

L. & W.—Life and Work, The Magazine of the Church of Scotland

L. C.—Leabhar nan Cnoc, le Tormoid Macleoid, D.D., Greenock, 1834.

L. nan G.—Leabhar nan Gleann, by George Henderson, Ph.D., Edinburgh, 1898.

Là Bhr.—v. D. B.

Laws—Ancient Laws of Ireland, vol. VI., Dublin, 1901.

MacCallum, A. K.—Laoidhean agus Dain Spioradail, Glasgow, 1894

MacCor.—Gu'n d' thug i Spéis do'n Àrmunn, sgeul le Iain Mac Cormaig, Stirling, 1908.

Maclagan MSS.—Gaelic MSS. collected by Maclagan, deposited in Glasgow University Library.

Mart. Donegal—The Martyrology of Donegal, Dublin, 1864.

McA.—A Pronouncing Gaelic Dictionary, by Neil M'Alpine, 8th edition, Edinburgh, 1881.

McB.—An Etymological Dictionary of the Gaelic Language, by Alexander MacBain, M.A., Inverness, 1896. Roman numerals refer to McB.'s Grammar.

McD.—Eiseirigh na seann Chanan Albannaich, le Alastair Donullach, 8th edn., Edinburgh, 1892.

McKay—Easy Gaelic Syntax, by J. G. McKay, London, 1899

Ml.—*v.* Thesaurus Palaeohibernicus, a collection of Old Irish Glosses Scholia, Prose and Verse, by Stokes and Strachan, Cambridge, 1901.

Mòrachd Dhé—*v.* D. B.

Munro—A Practical Grammar of the Scottish Gaelic, by James Munro, Edinburgh, 1843.

N. G. P.—A Collection of Gaelic Proverbs and Familiar Phrases, ed. Alexander Nicholson, M.A., LL.D., Edinburgh, 1881.

O'D. Gr.—A Grammar of The Irish Language, by John O'Donovan, Dublin, 1845.

O.M.—An t-Ogha Mor, le Aonghas Mac Dhonnachaidh, Glascho.

P. H.—The Passions and the Homilies from Leabhar Breac, by Robert Atkinson, M.A., LL.D., Dublin, 1887.

Ped.—Vergleichende Grammatik der keltischen Sprachen, von Holger Pedersen, Goettingen, 1909, 1913.

Poetry of Badenoch, The—ed. Rev. Thomas Sinton, Inverness, 1906.

R. B., Red Book—Red Book of Clanranald, Reliquiae Celticae, edd. Macbain and Kennedy, Inverness, 1894.

R. C.—Revue Celtique, Paris

Reliq. Celt.—Reliquiae Celticae, by Rev. Alexander Cameron, LL.D., edd. MacBain and Cameron, Inverness, 1892.

Ross—Orain Ghàëlach, le Uilleam Ros, Edinburgh, 1902.

S.O.—Sar-Obair nam Bard Gaelach, ed. John Mackenzie, 1841.

Stewart—Elements of Gaelic Grammar, by Alexander Stewart, 3rd edn., Edinburgh, 1876.

Stewarts—Cochruinneacha Taoghta de Shaothair nam Bard Gaëleach, by Alexander and Donald Stewart, A.M., Duneidin, 1804.

Teachd.—An Teachdaire Gaelach, May, 1829—April, 1831.

Thur.—Handbuch Des Alt-Irischen, von Rudolf Thurneysen, Heidelberg, 1909.

Turner—Comhchruinneacha do Dh' Orain taghta Ghaidhealach, le Paruig Mac-an-Tuairneir, Duneidionn, 1813.

Uist Bards—The Uist Collection, ed. Rev. Archibald Macdonald, Glasgow, 1894.

Waifs—Waifs and Strays of Celtic Tradition, London, 1889-1895.

Wb.—*v.* Ml.

Z. C. P.—Zeitschrift fur Celtische Philologie, Halle.

ABBREVIATIONS.

a., acc.	= accusative		**m., mas.**	= masculine
abs.,abstr.	= abstract		**M.G.**	= Middle Gaelic
act.	= active		**n., nom.**	= nominative
adj., adjj.	= adjective, adjectives		**N.**	= Norse
A.S.	= Anglo-Saxon		**N., N.S.**	= North, North and South
art.	= definite article			
Br., Bret.	= Breton		**O.G., O.I.**	= Old Gaelic, Old Irish
			O.H.G.	= Old High German
cf.	= confer, compare		**p., pass.**	= passive
Corn.	= Cornish		**part.**	= participle
comp.	= comparative		**p. p. p.**	= perfect participle passive
cpd., cpds.	= compound, compounds			
Cym.	= Cymric		**pf.**	= perfect
d., dat.	= dative		**p., pl.**	= plural
			poss.	= possessive
E., Eng.	= English		**pres.**	= present
e.g.	= exempli gratiâ, for example		**pro.**	= pronoun
			rel.	= relative
f., fem.	= feminine		**Sc.**	= Scots, Scottish
fut.	= future		**s., sing.**	= singular
G.	= Gaelic		**Sk.**	= Sanskrit
g., gen.	= genitive		**subj.**	= subjunctive
Gaul.	= Gaulish		**v., voc.**	= vocative
Ger.	= German		**W.**	= Welsh
Gk.	= Greek		*****	= a hypothetical original form
Goth.	= Gothic			
I.G.	= Indo-Germanic		**ᶜ**	= causing aspiration
ib.	= ibidem, in the same place		**+**	= plus, together with, immediately followed by
Ind.	= Indicative			
Inf.	= Infinitive		**=**	= equal to, pronounced as
Ipf.	= Imperfect			
Ipv.	= Imperative		**γ**	= spirant g
Ir.	= (Modern) Irish			
L.	= Latin			

A Gaelic Grammar.

§ 1.   **THE ALPHABET.**

The Alphabet consists of 18 letters :—

    Five vowels,   **a, o, u, e, i.**
    Twelve consonants,   **b, c, d, f, g, l, m, n, p, r, s, t.**
    And a breathing,   **h.**

Of these symbols, **h** has not been considered to be a letter, but merely a breathing, and it is used :—

(1) as a mark of aspiration : e.g. a bh*ó*—*his cow* § 19, 2.
(2) as indicating a trace of a lost word or inflection : e.g.
    Ni **h**-eadh—*It is not, no* ;
    beul na **h**-oidhche—*the mouth of the night, the gloaming* :—
    Ross 44.   §48, 2.

O.G. used in foreign words the letters k, q, x, y, z, which are now considered superfluous.

    k and **q** are represented by **c, x** by **cs, y** by **i** and **e, z** by **s.**

The consonant **p** is lost in original Gaelic words: e.g.
    athair *father* ; Lat. **p**-ater
    ca-**p**-era-x, cáera, caora f. *a sheep*, Lat. caper, E. heifer
and **p** appears in words of foreign origin only : e.g.
    pòsda *married*, Lat. sponsa
    pìos m. *a piece*
    pòg f. *a kiss*, Lat. **p**ac-em
    sà**p**air, sà**p**hair *sapphire*, L. sapphirus §49.
All consonants may be aspirated §19.

§ 2.   **I.—DIAGRAM OF VOWELS.**

The traditional division of vowels is into broad and slender.

    a, o, u are broad ;   **e, i** are slender.

This division is not only convenient but fundamental. It is presupposed by the law of infection §6 ; and the pronunciation of all consonants (except labials §2, II. 2, §51) depends upon it.

Vowel sounds are very numerous in Gaelic. They are dealt with in some detail § 35-§ 41. Here the following diagram shows that the slender vowels are formed forward in the mouth along the soft palate towards the teeth: the broad vowels are formed from the back roof of the mouth down to the lower part of the throat, in the following order :

ì, é, è, ù, ó, ao, à ò, e.g.

sìth f. *peace* ; séid *blow* ; feuch *behold* ;
dùn m. *fort* ; mór *great* ; gaoth f. *wind* ; dà *two* ; bròn m. *sorrow.*

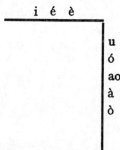

II.—CLASSIFICATION OF CONSONANTS.

1. Liquids : **l, m, n, r.**

    Of these only **m** takes the sign of aspiration, e.g.

    a **m**hac—*his son*

but **l, n, r,** are also distinctly aspirated in pronunciation :

    o là gu là—*from day to day*
    o neart gu neart—*from strength to strength* :—Ps. lxxxiv. 7
    a réir—*according to,* § 60

o aspirates a following consonant, §200 ;

gu does not so aspirate, § 195.   Hence the pronunciation of **là** and of **neart**, when they are governed by **o** is different from the pronunciation of **là** and **neart** when they are governed by **gu** v. §58, §59.

2. Mutes :

	Tenues.	Mediae.	Aspirates.
Labials,	(p)	b, m	ph (=f), bh, mh (=v)
Dentals,	t	d	th (=h), dh (=y & γ)
Gutturals,	c	g	ch, gh (=y)

The labials (in which **m** is included) have only one sound. All other consonants have a broad and a slender sound and are hence called mutable.

3. Spirants: **f, s,** and the aspirated mutes.

Diagram of Consonants.

Name.	Stops.		Spirants.		Liquids.		
	voiceless	voiced	voiceless	voiced s (= z)	nasal		
Dentals	t	d	(th), s	aspir- ated d	n	l	r
Gutturals	c	g	ch	aspir- ated g	n before g		
Labials	(p), b		f, ph	aspirated m			
				aspir- ated b	m		
Breathing			h initial (f)h and nil (s)h and nil (t)h and nil				

§ 3.   **GROUPING.**

The grouping of vowels results in a diphthong or a triphthong § 42, § 47.

A diphthong or triphthong is in pronunciation the sounding of one vowel after another or of a succession of vowels with no intervening consonant § 65.

A consonant group is pronounced with no intervening vowel, but cf. § 66.

Word groups are pronounced as a single expression.

Examples of word groups are :—

1. Substantive groups :

a. Article and noun, § 88
    an t-each—*the horse*
    an cù *the dog* =angcù
    an duine *the man* =annduine, annuine
    an òigh *the virgin* =annòigh.

b. Noun and adj., § 91
    each bàn—*a white horse*

c. Article, noun and adj., § 92
    an t-each bàn—*the white horse*

d. A substantive which itself governs another noun in the genitive, remains in the nominative after a governing noun :

   Fhuair thu onoir fir Alba—*You got the esteem of Scotsmen* :—S.O. 49ᵇ26

   ri smaointinn bean t' àilteachd—*by thinking of a woman of thy beauty* :—Ross 87

e. A noun or preposition may govern a clause :

   do bhrìgh an leanabh a bhi air chall—*because the child was lost* :—Cos. 130

   Tha dearbh-bheachd agam nach bi bàs . . . comasach **air** sinne a sgaradh o ghràdh Dhé—*I am persuaded that death will not be able to separate us from the love of God* :—Rom. viii. 39

For substantive groups governed by a preposition, and distinct from cpds., § 101, 2, v. § 185, 5

II. Verb groups, whether of the older synthetic class like
    bhuailinn—*I used to strike*
    bhualamaid—*we used to strike*
or of the more recent analytic class like
    bhualadh sinn—*we used to strike*
gather round them preverbs and suffixes into a single expression for tense and mood § 155.

   An tog e ?—*Will he raise ?* =anndog e
   Cha tog e—*He will not raise* =chadog e
   Gu'n tàinig e—*That he came* =gunndàinig e

III. Word groups form a sentence. The normal order is : Verb, subject, object, adverb, or clauses.

   Cha do chum (verb) mi (subject) ni sam bith (object)

an cleith air an rìgh (clause complementary to object)—
I kept nothing concealed from the King :—Arab. iii. 30.

Interrogative Particles and Pronouns and occasionally phrases like

mu dheireadh—*at length* :—ib. 30
aig an uair àraidh—*at the appointed time* :—ib. 31

begin the principal sentence ; and in subordinate sentences phrases of time like an uair—*when*, are used as conjunctions.

Co aige a tha fhios dé na duilgheadasan troimh an robh aig an duine ud r'a dhol **mus** b'urrainn dha ruigheachd air a' chaoraich chaillte—*Who knows the hardships that man had to go through before he could reach the lost sheep* :—Cos. 99

The poets allow themselves considerable latitude in the order of words and clauses :

'N uair bha mo chupan sòlais làn—*When my cup was of joy full* :—Clarsach 90

Ged bhiodh dearcan 'us ùbhlan Air gach fiùran a' fàs— *Though berries and apples Were on every branch growing* :— ib. 117

'S bhur dùthaich na fàgaibh— *And your country do not leave* :—ib. 127

Bhur sìnnsirean dh' fhàg i Mar dhìleab— *Your ancestors left it As a legacy* :—ib. 127

Ri 'n daoine cho càirdeal— *To their people so kind* :—ib. 128

Cha robh gaisgeach Nach robh mo shonas ris cho làn—*There was no hero But my happiness was as full as his* :— ib. 137

'S iad air do bheatha 'n tòir—*And they of thy life in pursuit* :— ib. 146

The order is changed for emphasis :

Ach Iain cha robh tighinn — *But as for Iain he was not coming* :—Mac-Cor. 86.

§ 4.   ELISION.

At the beginning or end of a word one letter or more, whether vowel or consonant, may be dropped.

I. Vowels :

1. An unstressed initial vowel is frequently elided in pronunciation, thus :—is tric is pronounced 's tric—*it is often*

an uair ='n uair—*when*

anns an ='san, a's—*in the*

ann do =ad, 'nad—*in thy*

aig an ='gan—*at the*

'n aghaidh labhairt an sgriobtuir—*against the teaching of Scripture* :—Turner 75

'n t-sùil bu bhlàithe gun ghaise—*the warmest unflinching eye* :—Turner 92, 20

The words should, however, be fully written in prose. The use of the apostrophe, except in cases established by universal usage, is to be discouraged.

2. Elision of an unstressed final vowel takes place before a stressed initial vowel in a following word :

do iarr is pronounced dh' iarr ; with proclitic, gu'n d'iarr e—*that he asked*

do fhaod =dh' fhaod ; gu'n d' fhaod e—*that he might*

bu fheàrr =b' fheàrr ; gu'm b'fheàrr—*that 'twere better*

mo òglach =m'òglach—*my lad* (m' lad)

do òglach =t' òglach—*thy lad*, § 114

The pronouns—mise, tusa :

Bidh mis' ann an Gearr-Loch,
Bidh tus' an Cinn-tàile nam bó—
I shall be in Gare Loch,
You will be in Kintail of the Kine :—Ross 49

Elision of a final letter or syllable in a stressed word is caused by distance from the stressed syllable. The vowel of the gen. sing. fem. of a stems is seldom preserved beyond the second syllable, sometimes not beyond the first :

le neart feirg' agus gaisgidh—
by force of anger and valour :—Turner p. 92, 18

3. Omission of a his ; a her ; a relative : § 4 II., 3

II. Consonants are elided (or assimilated § 8, § 9) in a few often-used words :

1. The art. nom. fem. **a'** may be elided after a vowel :

'S cò **mhàthair** nach biodh ann an teinn—
And who is the mother that would not be in anxiety :—
Clarsach 58, §8, 1

ag elides **g** before consonants in a verbal noun forming a participle § 187 :

a' bualadh—*a-striking*

but **g** remains before vowels (and sometimes also before gutturals) :

ag òl—*a-drinking*

'g cur aoibhneis anns a' chridh'—*putting joy in the heart* :—Metr. Ps. xix. 8

The full forms, e.g. ag gairm—*calling*, ag call—*losing*, are to be preferred to a' call, a' gairm, because the use of an apostrophe is unnecessary.

ag mo becomes **'gam, a'm'** ;

'S a gaol **a'm'** mhealladh o m' chéill—
And her love wiling me out of my wits :—D. Ban 204, 114

a'm is used for **agam** :

An té bha dùil **a'm** bhi laighe dlùth rium—
She I hoped to have by my side :—Clars. 74

Tha fios **a'm** nach bithinn fo ghruaim—
I know that I would not be gloomy :—ib. 107

Is fhios **a'm**—*I know it* :—MacCor. 20

Cha robh dùil **a'm**—*I had no expectation* :—ib. 19

2. **do** and **de** are sometimes reduced to **a**: or **do** is aspirated :

do : Cas **a** shiubhal garbhlaich— *A foot to tread the wilds* :
—D. Ban 254, 23

Cha strìochdadh do dhìlsean
A luchd mì-ruin tha beò—*Thy kindred would not yield to enemy that lives* :—ib. 208, 22

'S coslach do'm aodach **a** bhi tana—*My garments are likely to be thin* :—ib. 226, 54

de : gu'm b'e diùgha **a** bhuill **airm** e—*It was the worst of war weapons* :—ib. 8, 95

dh'aon rùn—*with one consent* ;

dh'aon bharail—*with one mind* ;

a là agus **a dh**'oidhche — *by day and by night* :—Stewart 128

3. **ag, do, de,** the possessive adjj. **a** *his,* **a** *her,* and the relative
pronoun **a** *who,* are sometimes omitted, their force being established partly by the meaning, and partly by the initial letter
of the following word :

ag : 'N àm bhi **b**uachailleachd nam bó— *At the time of*
     herding of the cows :—An t-Òran. 271

     Anns an fheasgar bha sinn aobhach **G**abhail òran—
     In the evening we were joyous, a-singing songs --—ib.
     'S lurach mo Mhàiri **b**leoghann na spréidh—
     Lovely is my Mary a-milking the kine :—ib. 259

do : Thàinig mi **D**hun-éideann **a dh** 'iarraidh leannain—
     I came to Edinburgh to seek a lover :—D.Ban 16, 5
     Cha téid thu **B**had-odhar— *Thou shalt not go to Badour* :
     ib. 218, 27
     'N uair a théid mi **G**hlascho—*When I shall go to*
     Glasgow :—ib. 254, 29

de : De'n fhuil as airde **s**hliochd Dhiarmaid—*Of the best*
     blood of the race of Diarmid :—ib. 102, 55
     bharr, for **a** bharr, **de** bharr—*off*
     chum, for **a** chum, **do** chum—*unto*

a *his* : Pilleadh an t-aingidh o **s**hlighe—*Let the wicked*
     turn from his way :—Esech. xxxiii. 11.
     Ciod e ainm ? *What is his name* ?—Mòrachd Dhé 1.
     Sgeul as cruaidhe ri **c**hluinntinn— *A tale which is very*
     hard to listen to :—S.O. 153ᵇ30

a *her* Geug fo bhlàth o **b**arr gu talamh— *A Sapling in*
     bloom from its crop to earth :—D. Ban 200, 45 ; cf.
     § 114, 6

a relative, originally **do** § 116
     Càit 'eil am beachd **c**huir neart am chridh' ?
     Where is the thought that put strength in my heart ?—
     A. K. McCallum
     An ann a' cumail bruidhne riumsa **th**a thu ?—*Is it*
     bandying words with me you are ?—Waifs iii. 119

4. The conjunction **co, cho** *so, as,* has suffered the elision
of a nasal : G. comh, W. cyf.

§ 5   SYNCOPE.

1. When the vowel of a post-tonic syllable is suppressed and the consonants fall together, the result is syncope. The main stress is on the first syllable. A secondary stress, in trisyllabic words, falls on the third syllable. The second syllable, being thus pronounced at first rapidly or indistinctly, finally disappears, and is no longer written § 95, 5, (a), (b) :

> abhuinn f. *river*, g.s. aibhne for abhuinne ;
> baile m. *town*, g.p. bailtean for bailetean ;
> mì-mhodhail *unmannerly*, mlomhail ;
> caismeachd f. *march*, cais-im-theachd.

2. In dissyllables, syncope fuses the two syllables, and causes increase of stress (when a single preverb is suppressed, being diphthongised), or a long vowel :

> gu'n tabhair e, gu'n toir e—*that he will give* ; latha—
>   *day*, là ; comhair—*presence*, còir ; a rithis—*again*,
>   a rìs ; fhathast *yet still*, (fo-deacht-sa) ; fòir—*help*
>   *thou*, fo + reth, § 184, 80
> Trod chàirdean (charaidean)—*The scolding of friends* :—
>   N.G.P. 373

3. When a consonant is suppressed before another, one of which must be a liquid, the result is **compensatory lengthening** of the vowel. The suppressed consonant may be :

> **n**   deud m. *tooth*, L. dent-is, cf. ceud § 143, lùchairt § 18,3, § 76,3
> **d**   sgeul m. *tale*, W chwedl
> **g**   deur m. *tear*, W deigr
> **t**   eun m. *bird*, L. penna, § 132, c.f. § 62

§ 6.   VOWEL INFECTION.

A vowel now or previously existing exerts an influence backward on (or infects) the vowel in the syllable immediately preceding. § 32. Thus :—**ri tu,**—*against thee*, **do tu**—*to thee* compounded become **riut, dut, duit** § 48

1. A slender vowel infects a previous broad vowel.

-i- In Gaelic the final **i** of the gen. sing. of **o** stems, § 76, disappears at the end of the word, but maintains its influence by infection in the word itself :

Latin				Gaelic :	
	n.s.	templ-u-m	*temple*,		teamp-u-ll
	g.s.	templ-i	*of a temple*,		teamp-ui-ll
	n.s.	equus	*horse*		each
	g.s.	equi	*of a horse*		eich

Latin	n.s.	cat-us	*cat*	cat
	g.s.	cat-i	*of a cat*	ca-i-t
	n.s.	vir	*man*	fear, *ver-os
	g.s.	vir-i	*of a man*	fir
	d.s.	vir-o	*to a man*	O.G. fiur

In leinibh, g.s. of leanabh m. *child*, both syllables are infected, cf. eile *other*, O.G. aile §95, 5 (c).

Pògadh an leinibh air sgàth na banaltruim—*Kissing the child for the sake of the nurse* :—N.G.P. 338

An example of the d.s. in **o** is **cionn** in the phrase **os clonn**, a stereotyped dat. which appears in : Is phàidheadh d'a **cinn**—*And pay him back for it*:—S.O. 148ᵃ34 : an example of the acc. pl. is, **feara,** vir-os, an acc. pl. which is sometimes used as nom. pl. : and also as the regular voc. pl., **a fheara**—*o men*:—MacCor. 52.

-e- The final -**e**- of the gen. sing. of fem. -**à**- stems § 78 infects a previous syllable :   α ο υ   εⁱ

Latin	n.s.	planta *scion*	Gaelic :	clann f. *children*
	g.s.	plantae *of a scion*		cloine *of children*

2. A broad vowel infects a previous slender vowel :

-**a**- caochladh m. *change, variety* :   O.G. com-im-chlód
      feòlmhor *fleshy* : feòil + mor
-**u**- sùil f. *eye* g.s. sùla : *sūl-ōs

3. Conversely, a broad stressed vowel depalatalises a following unstressed slender vowel § 32.

§ 7.   THE ACCENTS AND THE STRESS.

I. 1. The grave accent is placed on long vowels thus :
      à, ò, ù, è, ì

   e.g. fàsach *desert* ; òr *gold* ; lùth *agile strength* ; fèath *a calm* ; fìon *wine*

2. The acute accent is used to express the close or forward sound in **ó**, and in **é** :

   e.g. có *who*? cóig *five*, fóid mòna, *a peat*, bóid *vow*, glé *clear*, céir *wax*, gréine *of sun*

The use of the written accent is limited to long vowels when they are stressed. The accent is not omitted in writing, unless the stress has left the long vowel and shifted to another syllable.

In all unstressed syllables a long vowel is shortened, e.g. teaghlach m. *household* : teach +slūagh ; and unstressed final vowels tend to become **-a-,** e.g. cha, mugha § 7 iii.

II. The accent is written when the stress coincides with a long vowel.

The syllable immediately before the stress, and the syllable immediately after the stress, is weak and tends to disappear.

Every word (except the definite article, simple prepositions, monosyllabic conjunctions, and adverbial particles) has a stress. The stress falls on the first syllable of the word, or on the second. The stress falls on the first syllable of every stressed word except :

1. Verbs preceded by imperfectly compounded preverbs, in which case the stress is upon the second syllable, e.g.

gu'n **do bhuail**—*that he struck*; but the Ipv. and the Inf., e.g. buail, *strike thou*, bualadh *striking*, are always stressed on the first syllable.

2. Imperfect noun or adj. compounds. A perfect compound is stressed on the first syllable, e.g.

bàthaich m. *byre*, bà-thaigh, bó +tigh § 100, § 101
còmhdhail f. *meeting*, seanfhacal m. *proverb*, mìorun m. *ill-will* ;
casbheart, caisbheart, càiseart f. *footwear* ;
caismeachd f. *march* (for cais-im-theachd)

An imperfect compound is usually stressed on the second part, but a minor stress may rest on the first part of the compound, especially if it be dissyllabic :

am peacadh gin m. *original sin* :—Am Fear-Ciùil 222
bealbhan-ruadh *a species of hawk*   fear-casaide *accuser*
cas-chrom *crooked spade*   do-dheanta *impossible*

3. Diminutives in -**an**, -**ag**, which were accented in O.G. -án, -óc, are still stressed almost equally with the stressed syllable :

eachan m. *pony*   fearan m. *manikin*
ealag f. *cygnet*   sgalag f. *farm-servant*.

Prepositional and adverbial expressions like **ar aon**—*along with*, **air son**—*for*, **car son**—*why*, **a bhòs**—*on this side*, **a bhàn**—*down*, **a mach**—*out, away*, **a mhàin**—*only*, **an nochd**—*to-night*,

a nùas—*down*, **a nis**—*now*, **a ris**—*again*, are written in two words to indicate that the stress is always on the second; except **gidheadh**—*nevertheless*, which is written as one word and stressed on the second. Expressions like these are more properly written as one word when the stress falls on the first syllable, e.g. ciamar *how*.

In certain long **amorphous** compounds, the stress falls upon the last, or upon the penultimate, word:

eadar-dhà-shian—*between-two-blasts*, eadarra'hian
Beinn-eadar-dhà-loch—*Benderloch*
Dia-eadar-dà-oin—*the day between-two-fasts*, Diardaoin *Thursday*
Eadar-dà-chaolas—*Edderachillis*

III.   The Shifting of the Stress.

The loss of stress upon a pretonic syllable is occasionally followed by the loss of the syllable:

a chum, chum *to, unto* : O.G. dochum
bagair *threaten* : imb-ad-gair § 184
casaid(e) f. *complaint, accusation* : L. accusatio § 175
cha *not* : O.G. ní co n-, M.G. nocho, nocha § 144, 2
dé ? *What is* ? : O.G. cote, cate § 119
dragh m. *trouble* : O.G. indráigne *detriment*
mu, ma *about* : O.G. imma § 199
maille ri *with* : O.G. immalle fri (imb-an-leth frith)
mar *as* : O.G. amal, Cym. mal § 198
mearal m. *error* for iomrall § 68
mugha m. *loss, destruction* : O.G. immudu
nighean f. *girl* : O.G. ingen (by Svarabhakti inighean) § 68, 1
'san *in the*, for anns an
sòr *hesitate, grudge, shun* : ess-od-ro-soim § 184, 110
nèarachd f. *happiness*, from (mo ge)near-acht § 143
has lost two unaccented pretonic syllables.

In the case of the five irregular verbs :—O.G. **at-beir, at-chí, do-beir, do-gní, fo-gheibh,** the stress is normally on the second syllable, that is, the stress falls not on the preverb but on the stem of the verb. The preverb, being thus pretonic and unstressed, ceases to be pronounced, and disappears, leaving the aspirated initial consonant of the stem still to attest the influence of the preverb, cf. § 153, 1

(Berid) **beiridh mi**—*I shall bear*, is a simple verb, without preverb, and remains unaspirated; with gu'n, gu'm beir mi air, *that I will overtake him*; while (do-bheir) **bheir mi**—*I shall give*, is a compound which has lost its unstressed pretonic preverb, and is therefore aspirated. But after the interrogative, negative, and conditional particles (§ 144 et seq.) prefixed to verbs, viz., **an, am**; **cha, cha n-**; **na'm, na'n**; **nach, gu'n,** the stress moves upward from the stem of the verb and rests upon the preverb:

e.g. O.G. fo-gheibh—*he gets*, is stressed on the verbal stem; the pretonic preverb **fo-**, being unstressed, ceased to be spoken, and the result is that **fo-** has dropped off, leaving the prototonic stressed stem **gheibh**—*he gets*. But when one of the above enclitic particles introduces the verb, the preverb is resumed, and receives the stress: **am fo-gheibh** ? *will* or *does he get* ? The word is "darkly bound," the last syllable (the stem) having lost the stress, falls off, leaving **fo-gh,** which is infected by the slender following vowels, and becomes **fo-ei-gh, faigh: am faigh** —*will he get* ?

Similarly O.G. ro-bói, -robe, with proclitic particle, becomes in G. gu'n ro-bh; do ro-gni, becomes gu'n d'rinn; at-beir becomes gu'n abair; do-beir, gu'n tabhair (or gu'n *toir*); at-chì, gu'm f-aic (with prothetic **f.**)

IV. In compound proper names certain first elements, mostly monosyllabic, are seldom or never stressed, even though the syllable was originally long § 107, 12, § 112, 4:

1.			
aber-	*confluence*	dùn-	*castle, fort*
abhainn-	*river*	eaglais-	*church*
allt-	*burn, cliff*	gleann-	*glen*
àth-	*ford*	inbhir-	*confluence*
bàrr-	*top*	loch-	*lake*
beinn-	*peak*	poll-	*pool*
bun-	*base*	sgùrr-	*peaked hill*
camus-	*bend*	srath-	*strath*
ceann-	*head*	teampull	*stone church*
cinn-	*at head*	tìr-	*land*
cill-	*at cell*	toll-	*hole*
cnoc-	*hillock*	tom-	*hillock*

| dail- | *dale* | dàil *meeting* | torr- | *hill* |
| druim- | *back, ridge* | | tulaich- | *knoll* |

      Dun-éideann—*Edinburgh*
      Roinn-Lìothunn—*Point of Lyon* :—S.O. 45[a]7

2. The honorific prefixes **mo** *my* ; **do, t'** *thy* are unstressed, unless by elision they coalesce with the proper name :—
      cill-mo-Chalmaig— *Kilmachalmaig*
      cill-mo-(Ædan)- Aodan— *Kilmodan.*   § 112, 3 ;
        § 121, 1, 2

3. **maol** *tonsured, bald* : O.G. máel
    maol when unstressed is often confused with **mo**, but the former is more liable to initial aspiration :
      Cill-maoil-rubha *Kilvary* (MucCairn).

    Through aspiration, assimilation, and loss of stress **maol** is occasionally reduced to -**a**-, -**e**- :
      Cill-maoil-rubha— *Killarrow* (Islay).

4. **suidhe**—*seat* or *locus* of a saint :
    Suidh(e) -Bhlain (Kilblane)
           -Cathan (Bute)
           -Donnain (Kildonain)
           -Ghuirmein (Glenmoriston)
           -Innen (Kilwinning)
           -Maree (Applecross)
           -Mhercheird =Mhaoil-Erchaird (Glenurchart).

5. **Suidhe + maol**- :
    Seemirookie : St. Roque (Dundee), cf. St. Rollox, Glasgow
    Simon Rollock's kirk (Boroughmuir) : *id.*
    Simmer-lu-ag (Clova) : Lu-gaid § 112, 6
    Summer-eve (suidhe-maoil-rubha)

6. **aiseag** m. *ferry*, Aiseag-ma-Rui (Skye)
    Cil-maol-rubha— *Kilmaree* (Loch Slapin)
    tobar m. *well*, tobar-maol-rubha Tobar-ma-Rui (Skye).

§ 8.   **ASSIMILATION.**

    When two or more consonants come together, the tendency to ease in pronunciation causes a change in one or more of the consonants so that they either approximate to, or become identical with, one another.

1. Approximation of the assimilating consonants:—
   -**n**- of the Art. §87 becomes -**m**- before labials and is as-
     similated and disappears before aspirates except
     -**fh**- § 89
     An is still used before aspirates in Uist, an chàisg f. *Easter*.
   -**n**- of **an** as a Rel. Pro. §115 ; §116, 2 : as Interrogative
     Proclitic §144 ; as a Conjunction, gu'n §145, 1, mu'n
     §219, na'n §145, 5 becomes -**m**- before labials.   Proclitic
     agus is reduced to '**gus**, **a's**, **is**, '**s** ; **an do** becomes **na** :
   Far **na** dh'àraicheadh na gaisgich—*Where the heroes were
     reared* :—C.R. v. 85
     do is scarcely heard before the verb in : gu'n ghabh
       mi—*that I took*
     cha *not*, before vowels **cha n**- : O.G. ní co n- ;
   The -**n**- is assimilated before consonants, except -**t**- which it
     eclipses § 144, 3 ; and **f** which it aspirates § 16, 5
       cha tug e, *he did not give*—often misspelt cha d'thug e
       § 13, 3
     mur *unless* : O.G. manip § 145, 4
     nic *grand-daughter* : nighean mhic

2. Identity of the assimilating consonants, to take only recent
   examples § 13 II. :

n to **l**	colainn f. *body* g.s. colna, colla
n to **s**	cosmhuil *like* : con-samhuil, L. similis
n to **g** (c)	eugsamhuil *unlike* : an-con-samhuil
n to **t**	aotrom *light* : an-trom § 150, 5
n to **th**	cothrom *equilibrium* : com-trom
ngbh to **m**	cumail f. *keeping* : congbhail f., v. n. of con-gab
g to **s**	Sasunn *England* : Sasgun *Saxon* :—D. Ban 20, 13
lt to **ll**	coslach *like*, colsach § 11, coltach, collach
rl to **l**	§ 64
lls to **s**	§ 62

§ 9.   **DISSIMILATION.**

1. Dissimilation of joined consonants :
     ceirsle, ceirtle f. *clew* : ceircle, L. circul-us
     arsa for alsa : O.G. olse
     curta E. *curst*

br- for mr-
gr- for dr- § 61

2. Dissimilation of separated consonants in the same word:
> boirionnach m. *woman* : boinionnach
> biolaire f. *watercresses*, O.G. biror, W. berwr
> cànail f. *speech*, cànain
> iolair f. *eagle*, W. eryr
> lànail m. *couple*, lànan
> luramachd, loramachd f. *nakedness* : lomnochd.

3. Dissimilation in phrases:
> far rium *with me* : mar rium
> Feill Fairc f. *Epiphany* : Feill Failc
> ri leathad *down* : le leathad :—F.T. 232, cf. § 203, 4

§ 10.   REDUPLICATION.

The repetition of a word (or part thereof) has always been a feature of the Gaelic language, e.g.

1. The first personal pronoun pl.—sinne *we*, arises from sinni, sisni, snini, sní-sni § 121, 3

2. The prepositions:
> an—*in* : ann an neamh—*in heaven*
> co—*to, unto* : chugam, chu-cu-m,—*unto me*
> do—*to* : a dh' Eirinn—*to Ireland*

3. The adjective:
> motha, momha (with o nasalised)—*more*, from mo-mho, mo-mo, compar. of mór-mór, e.g.
> 'S cha mhotha tha mi 'g a thuigsinn— *And no more do I understand it* :—Am Fear-Ciùil 330

4. Words and phrases that give point and elegance to prose and poetry, e.g.
> trèan-ri-trèan—*corncrake*, Ir. traona, O. Ir. tradna
> aon is aon—*one by one*
> a h-aon seach aon—*one by one*
> beag is beag—*little by little*
> beag air bheag—*little by little*
> bho cheann gu ceann—*from end to end* :—MacCor. 61
> ceum air cheum—*step by step* :—Am Fear-Ciùil 259

ceart no cearr—*right or wrong* : ib. 240
cinn air chinn—*heads on heads*
fear an déidh fir—*man after man, one by one* :—MacCor. 60
fear is fear }
neach is neach }—*man by man*
mion air mhion—*little by little, piece-meal*
o choille gu coille—*from wood to wood*
o thaobh gu taobh—*from side to side*
teann ri teann—*at close quarters*
Thàinig is thàinig e, uair is uair—*He came and came, time
     and again* :—Am Fear-Ciùil 333
thairis is thairis—*over and over* :—MacCor. 67
Chaoin is chaoin e—*He wept and wept* :—MacCor. 105
Fiorom-farum chon is dhaoine—*Confusion of men and
     dogs* :—Gillies 82
Leigidh iad air cimith-comith—*They set upon it kim-
     kam* (*awry, any way*) :—ib.
Chuag a's gug-gùg aic'—*The cuckoo and her note* :—
     Stewarts 123, 12, cf. § 86, 5

§ 11.   **METATHESIS.**

In a number of words the sequence of articulations is changed
in order to facilitate pronunciation, and certain letters are
transposed, e.g.

adhlaic *bury thou* : O.G. Inf. adnacul
altach m. *grace* (at food) ;   O.G. adtlugud, attlugud,
     atlugud
am feasd, *for ever*; O.G. i fecht-sa
an dràsda, *now*; O.G. a tráth-sa—*this time* : more
     correctly, as pronounced, a drasda
asgall m. *armpit*, a form of G. achlais, L. axilla
asgnadh m. *ascending* : O.G. ascnam (ad-com-snf) § 184
baist *baptise thou* : O.G. baitsim, L. baptizo
Beurla f. *English, speech* : O.G. beul-re (cf. luibh-re,
     buidh-re)
ceunda *the same* (in Lewis), for ceudna
coisir f. *choir* : L. *chorus*
coisrigeadh m. *consecration* ; O.G. coisecrad, L. conse-
     crat-io

B

coltach *like*, from colsach, coslach :—D. Ban 449

comraich f. *protection, sanctuary* : O.G. comairce §65

dìsle *more faithful*, compar. of dìleas

dreangad *a flea* : O.G. dergnat

drisleach *glittering* : dial. for drìlseach

dusileag for duileasg m. *dulse*

dùdlachd f. *first of winter* : dùldachd and dùbhlachd

easbuig m. *bishop* : L. episcopus

easbaloid f. *absolution* : L. absolutio

éisdeachd f. *listening* : O.G. éitsecht (en-tóis § 184)

éisg, éisgear m. *satirist* : O.G. èces

éiteag f. E. *hectic stone*

faisge *nearer*, compar. of fagus

fàistine f. *prophecy* : O.G. fàit-sine

fhathast *yet* : O.G. fo-decht-sa

firmidh *he must*, imiridh, H.B.

fòtrus m. *refuse*, for forts, D.Ban 178, 296

fuaidne f. *peg*, fuaidhne, pl. fuaintean (Uist)

fuasgail *open thou*, O.G. f-uaslaicim (od-ess-lécim)

fuilear, fulair f. *enjoining* : O.G. furáil, S.O. 148ᵇ27

ilimeag, for imleag f. *navel*

ilimich, for imlich *lick*

ìlse *more lowly*, compar. of ìosal

imrich *flit* : O.G. immirce, dial. irimich

iormall for iomrall m. *error*

iorram m. *boatsong*, Ipv. iomair *ply, row*

luramadh m. *fleecing*, for lomradh

loistean E. *lodging*

magairle m., O.G. macraille, L. testes

mislean m. *sweet grass* : milis

muin(i)chill m. *sleeve* : muilchinn

pàisde E. *page*

préisg *preach thou*

reul, reult f. *star* : O.G. rétglu

sneaghan, snioghag, snioghan dial. for seangan m. *ant*

siormag, silimeag, seamrag f. *clover*

spaisdear, spaidsear m. *saunterer*, L. spatior

susbaint f. *substance*

uailse *nobler*, for uaisle, compar. of uasal

§ 12. PROJECTION OF CONSONANTS.

I. Besides nasals § 13, the last consonant of an unstressed often used word is sometimes projected upon a closely connected stressed word immediately following :

1. The **t** or **d** of the article :

an **t**-each m. *the horse,* an **t**-suil f. *the eye,* an **t**-ì, tì m. *the person,* an **t**-é, té f. *the woman,* hence té f. *woman ;* an **d**-eigh *the ice,* hence deigh f. *ice ;* an **d**-éideag, **d**-éiteag f. *the pebble, hectic*(stone), hence déideag ; an **d**-ala—*the other,* hence an dara—*the second ;* an **d**-ala n-ai—*the other of them,* hence an darna—*the second.*

an deanntag f. *the nettle,* for an d-neanntag.

2. The **s** of the preposition anns an, 'san, *in the* :

a steach, '**s**teach (acc.) *into the house, within* : O.G. teach a stigh, '**s**tigh (dat.) *in the house, inside*

Thoir t'aidhe *take thy heed,* for thoir do aidhe ; O.G. óid, ùid, McB.

3. In a few proper names, **mac** *son,* projects the final **c** which eclipses the following consonant, and the pretonic unstressed *ma* of *mac* is dropped, e.g.

MacDhomhnuill	*Macdonald,*	Ma Connel	*Connel*
MacMhuirich	*Murdoch,*	Ma Cuirich	*Currie*
MacThomhais	*Thomson*	Ma Comhais	*Cosh*
Mac-a-Phearsain	*MacPherson,*	Ma Cerson	*Carson, Corson*
Mac Isaac	*MacIsaac,*	Ma Cisaac	*Kessack*
MacAoidh	*Mackay*	MacCaoi	*Kay, Caie*

II. The converse process is retraction § 13 when initial -**c**-, -**t**- of the proper name is retracted and assimilated to the -**c**-, -**t**- of mac, sanct :

Mac Cathal	*MacAll*	§ 111
Mac Constantin	*MacAuslan*	§ 110
Sanct Tanoch	*St. Enoch*	§ 112, 9

Retraction occurs seldom with common nouns § 13, § 17 but there are examples :

an eanntag f. *the nettle,* from an neanntag §12, 1

an eumhann m. *the pearl,* from an neamhain f., Ir. neamhunn

§ 13.   **NASALISATION.**

In words originally ending in a nasal, the nasal may be transported or projected to a closely connected following word.

I. Before vowels : the nasal appears as **n**

>   ar **n**-athair—*our father*

The **n** of the art. **an** is permanently transported and nasalises —**a nis** ; O.G. indossa, ind-or-sa—*this hour, now.*

The projected **n** of the preposition air (O.G. iar n- § 188, 3) remains in several petrified phrases :

>   An là iar-**na** mhàireach—*the day after to-morrow, to-morrow* : Arab. ii. 5
>   Is ann uidh air **n**-uidh a thogair na caisteil—*It is step by step that castles are built* :—cf. F.C. 316
>   àill air **n**-àill—*willingly or unwillingly* :—Fois 50
>   iochd air **n**-achd—*willy-nilly*

The **n** of **an** *in*, **an** *from*, is similarly transported in **nasgaidh** *gratis* ; O.G. **a n-aisge**—*as a gift* **noir** m. *east,* **a n-oir**—*from the east* : air

The rel. eclipse remains in os **n**-aird *publicly*, os **n**-iosal *secretly*

Iad fudh 's n-iosal sileadh dheur—*They secretly shedding tears* :—Ross 18

And in **na'n** *if* ; O.G. dia n-, which is the rel. with the preposition **de,** § 145, 5

The transported -**n**- after **dochum n-** is retracted §12, II. and remains attached to the preposition in the form **thun** (also **chon**) ;

>   thun an taighe so :—Arab ii. 67
>   thun na luinge :—ib. 43
>   thun na coise :—ib. 48, but cf. §210, Ir. T. iv. xiv.

II. Before consonants :

1. The liquids and **s** tend to assimilate the nasal :—

am miann	*their desire,*	pronounced	a miann
an làmh	*the hand*	,,	a làmh
an nead	*the nest*	,,	a nead
an raoir	*last night*	,,	a raoir
an saoghal	*the world*	,,	a saoghal

2. In the case of **f** instances occur where **f** is changed by the nasal into **v** (bh), e.g.

> ainbheach m. *debt* (McA.) from ainfhiach §150, 4 ;
> **gu bhfeil, gu bheil e**—*that it is* : O.G. fil, feil ;
> a **n**-fos, a **bh**fos, a **bh**os—*on this side*
> a **n**-fàn, a **bh**fàn, a **bh**àn—*down*

§ 14

A mute suffers *eclipsis* when its radical sound is suppressed by a preceding nasal. The eclipsing nasal reduces the mute to a weaker mute of the same origin ;   otherwise the nasal disappears.

1. **p, t, c** become **b, d, g**, but only in pronunciation. § 150, 5a

> Dh' aontaich mi gu'm **pò**sainn i—*I agreed that I would marry her* :—Arab. i. 28

> Mur a **pò**s mi fo Challuinn— *Unless I marry before Christmas* —Clarsach 142

> Gu'n **t**oir iad glòir do bhur n-athair—*That they may glorify your Father* :—Math. v. 16

> Co d'an **t**oir iad cìs—*To whom they shall pay tribute* :—Là Bhr. 390

> Na measaibh gu'n **t**àinig mise do bhriseadh an lagha— *Think not that I am come to destroy the law* :—Math. v. 17,

> cf. go **dt**ainic :—Kirk's ed. 1690. Eclipsis of **c**, § 14, 3 (b).

2. Instances occur (Skye) of the projected **n** of the acc. sing causing eclipsis in spelling :

> Cha n'eil beachd dhomh gu deimhinn gu'n cuala mi aon **nd**uinne riamh roimhe—*I don't think I have ever before heard a single individual* :—MacCor. 54

3. In many instances *eclipsis* has been misunderstood, and frequent (a) misspellings—some of them (b) permanent—have resulted :

> (a) Cha **d' thug** (tug) iad oladh leo—*They took no oil with them* :—Math. xxv. 3, § 144, 3
>
> > Cha **d' théid** (téid) mi do'n ghleannan—*I shall not go to the dell* :—Ross 47

anns gach àite do'n déidheadh (téideadh) e—*Everywhere he used to come* :—Cos. xix.

(b) Cha deic (cha n-tecte)—*It is not lawful; convenient* :—McB.

Cha deic luathas na h-earba gun na coin a chur rithe—*The speed of the doe is excessive without sending the dogs at her* :—N.G.P. 95 (where the sentence is mistranslated, cf. McKay 53, L.C. 147).

Angeartair (an ceart uair)—*just now* :—Munro 148

Tobar na geann (tobar nan ceann)—*well of the heads.*

b, d, g become *mb, nd, ng* in certain dialects. In this series which alone in O.G. is eclipsed in writing, only the nasal is pronounced : **ng** however, is pronounced as in English *king*

tìr na m(b)eann—*the land of the mountains*

Moch an (d)e, moch an n-e—*early yesterday*

Na (= an do) ghabh thu e ?—*Did you take it* ?

Cha n-urrainn n(d)uinn—*We cannot.*

Ghlac iad an n(d)uine—*They seized the man.*

Meangail *crafty* ; seang *slender*

fa-near, thoir fainear —*observe, consider* —from O.G. fo-fera—*causes,* (with infixed pronoun) fo-d-fera, fo-dera —*causes it,* often used as a noun, § 86, with the meaning *reason, cause*

The present form and meaning of this last example have developed from a (further) infixed relative pronoun causing eclipsis, § 11, fa-ndeara ; but sometimes **fá** is mistaken for the past of **is** (cf. fá neasa). Cad fa ndeara dhuit sain do dheanamh—*Why have you done that* ?—Dineen p. (289).

To the above nasal is prefixed in error an infixed -s- :

Gu'n d' fhàs mo ghaol maireann,

'S e sìr-thighinn fos-near dhomh ni's mo—*My love has grown lasting. It keeps coming to my thoughts evermore* :—Ross 48

§ 15.

Some unstressed words nasalise following initial vowels, but do not uniformly eclipse following initial tenues or other initial consonants.

I. Inflected words :

1. Plural possessive pronouns (old genitives pl.) § 121, 4

ar n- }
m- } *our*
    bhur n-
    'ur n-
    bhur m-
    'ur m- } *your*
    an
    am } *their*

    an athair—*their father*
    am màthair—*their mother*

Ni bheir air bhur **n**-anam cràdh no leòn—*A thing that will bring upon your soul anguish or hurt* :—Là Bhr. 344

ar ceann-feadhna mòr prìseil—*Our great beloved chief*:—S.O. 151ª42.

2. The def. article nasalises the nom. sing. fem., and the gen. pl. mas. and fem., of initial vowel stems §89 ; and in some districts eclipses following initial tenues and mediae in nom. and acc. sing. mas. §14, 2, and the gen. pl. mas. and fem. §16, 7

    Mor chuideachd nan tarbh—*the multitude of bulls*:—Ps. lxviii. 30

    Donnchadh nam Pios—*Duncan of the cups*:—L. nan G. 300

§ 16.

II. Uninflected words causing eclipsis :

1. Conjunctions.

    gu—*that, so that.* Is cinnteach gu'n tig e—*It is certain that he will come.*

    mu—*before.* Mu'n tug e cheud bhoinne de thràghadh—*Before it yielded its first current of ebb* :—S.O. 47ª27

    na—*if.* Na'n tigeadh e—*should he come* :—S.O. 46ᵇ8

    o, bho—*since.* O'n ghabh (do ghabh) an t-aibhisteir greim dhith—*Since the adversary got a hold of her* :—S.O. 46ᵇ40

2. The negative particle **an**- assimilates the written nasal **n** to a following **t, c, an**- thus becoming **ao**- and **ou**-, and reduces **t, c** to **d, g** in pronunciation § 150, 5

3. The interrogative particle **an** causes eclipsis.

    An e sin Ailean mo ghràidh—*Is that my dear Allan* ?
    An tig thu an diugh ?—*Will you come to-day* ?—A'Choisir 2
    Na (an do) thuit e ?—*Did he fall* ? C.R. v. 84

4. The preposition an—*in*
    An Albain—*in Scotland*
    am prioba na sùl—*in a twinkling* L.C. 40
    cuir an céill—*declare*
    ann an tòir air—*in pursuit of*

5. The negative **cha** projects a nasal before a vowel or **f** pure, aspirating the latter :
    Cha n-iongnadh leam—*I do not wonder* :—H.B.
    Cha n-fhan i bho'n tí—*She will not keep from tea* :—An t-Òran. 259
and reduces the dental tenues to mediae :
    Cha téid mi do'n ghleannan—*I shall not go to the Dell* : Ross 47.
    Cha toir e seachad an rìoghachd—*He will not give up the Kingdom* :—Cos. 28
and aspirates gutturals and labials § 25

6. The relative pronoun **an** :
    Gach àit an téid thu—*Every place you come to*:—A' Choisir 2
    The relative causes nasalisation regularly by analogy also in the indicative mood in **is tu** = is du ; and subj. gur tu, cf. § 13. The nasalisation of **tu = du** after -**adh**, e.g. **dh'fhaodadh tu,** is due to the same cause.

7. The acc. sing. and gen. pl. of the art. causes eclipsis in some districts § 15, 2 :
    Chunnaic mi an duine = a n(d)uine—*I saw the man* :—cf. Cor. 54
    creag nam beann = nam (b)eann—*Crag of the peaks* or *kids* (Blackmount)
    Achadh nan cat—*Auchnagatt* (Aberdeenshire)

8. Intruded nasal § 63

§ 17.   DENASALISATION.

Denasalisation occurs when an original nasal is dropped, leaving little or no trace.

I. In conversation denasalisation, which may be called the converse of eclipsis, takes place in certain dialects § 59 :
    a (n) duine m. *the man*
    a (n) taillear m. *the tailor*

annsa *preferable* (ausa) innis *tell* (fi-ys)
anns—*in the* (as) uinnlean *elbows*
anrath m. *distress* (aara)
annlan m. *condiment* (aulan)
cainnlean *candles* (cailan)
e fhéin, mi fhìn, become ● he, mi hi (Lochalsh).
Rù, rà, Ridire!—Ross 84, for rùn, ràn—*a very
splendid secret*:—Aur.

§ 18.

II. In literature the following instances of Denasalisation are
noteworthy :

1. The prep. **an** with the Art. d.s. **anns an** becomes—a's,
' sa,' as, ast :

a stigh, *in the house*
a steach, *into the house*
a' s t-earrach, *in the spring*:—N.G.P. 5, 62
Is bochd am fear nach faigh a leòir a's t-Fhoghar—*He is
a poor man who won't get his fill in Autumn* :—N.G.P.
219; 20
'S a' gheamhradh—*in the winter*.

2. The prepositional prenoun and preverb **com**-
cothrom m. *equipoise* § 147, 1
coguis f. *conscience* § 184, 31

3. *Nouns* :
initial—
blas m. *taste* ; O.G. mlas
brath m. *betrayal* ; M.G. mrath, Inf. of mairnim
brug m. *hostel* ; O.G. mruig
uibhir f. *number, quantity* : L. n-umer-us
medial—
ifrinn (ifirn, iutharn) f. *hell*, L. infern-um
iar-ogha m. f. *great-grandchild* : O.G. iarm-ua
lùchairt f. *palace* : O.G. longphort *haven, camp*, whence,
Longford, Luncarty
rùbail f. *rumple* :—Am Fear-Ciùil 327
eanntag f. *nettle*, an neanntag f. *the nettle*
eumhann m. *pearl*, an neamhain f. *the pearl*, Ir. neamhunn § 12.

4. *Conjunctions* :

    muna *unless*, becomes mur :   mur 'eil—*unless it be*
         § 145, 4
    f assimilates a nasal :—
         na'm *if*, becomes na :   Na faigheadh e—*If he should*
         find :—Cos. xix.

5. *Verbs* :

    bleagh *milk*, Ir. bliginn :   O.G. mligim
    bleith *grind* :   Inf. of O.G. melim
    bagair *threaten* :   imb-ad-gair.

6. *Adjectives* :

    blàth *warm* :   O.G. mlaith
    breachd, breac *speckled* :   O.G. mrechd

7. Instances of internal denasalisation :

    iongantas m. *wonder*, igadas (Skye) § 68, 3

   In place names Còthan for Comgan :

    An cladh Chòthan rugadh mise — *In Kilchoan was I*
         born :—S.O. 145[b]6
    Orasa Cholasa— *Oransay of Colonsay* :—C.S., go hOransaigh
         Cholbhansaigh :—R.B. Reliq. Celt. ii. 164.

8. n pronounced r after c, g, m, t, § 59

§ 19.   ASPIRATION.

Aspiration is a weakening in pronunciation, a change in
the radical consonants from being stops in the breath to spirants;
or a change from a stronger to a weaker spirant. The aspiration
of a consonant is caused by a preceding word or word-group
§ 3, which ends, or originally ended, in a vowel.

1. A single consonant, flanked by vowels, is aspirated.

2. A consonant, originally doubled, or forming one of a
group, resists, or tends to resist aspiration.

-h- is written after a consonant as the sign of aspiration
instead of the older dot or *punctum delens* placed above the
consonant to indicate aspiration § 1, 1 :

    'na sheasamh ='na seasam—*in his standing*

The sign of aspiration -h- is written after all the aspirated consonants, except **n, l, r,** where it is omitted, e.g.

o neart gu neart—*from strength to strength.*

The mutes and **mh** become spirants ; **sh** is reduced to a breathing, a shùil *his eye* ; **fh** is silent, except in

fhuair *he got*
fhéin *self*
fhathast *still,* where the **h** sound persists.

Féin *self,* is generally aspirated, **fhéin,** in conversation.

§ 20.

1. **so** *this,* **sin** *that,* **sud** *yon,* **gach** *every,* and the emphasising particles, -**sa,** -**se,** -**san,** are exempt from aspiration ; and all unstressed words, except **do** *to,* when used as a preverb § 142, and **do, de,** compounded with pronominal elements (where they are in stressed syllables) e.g.

a dh'iarraidh, **dha, dh**eth

2. The consonant groups **sb, sg, sm, sp, st** are not aspirated :—
do spiorad—*thy spirit.*

3. Final **l** prevents aspiration of a following dental **t, d,** e.g.
sgoil-dannsa—*a dancing school.*

4. Final **n** prevents aspiration of a following dental, liquid or s : (**d, t, n, l, r, s**) e.g.
sean sluagh—*old people.*

5. Homo-organic mutes do not aspirate one another except in recent compositions :

(1) Gutturals :
dro**ch c**ù—*bad dog* :—HSD. ; droch chù :—HB.
Is iomadh mìle dro**ch c**òmhdhail—*There's many a thousand evil happenings* :—S.O. 147[b]s except :
deagh *good,* which always (ex. § 20, 2) causes aspiration :
deagh-ghean *good-will*

(2) Dentals :
leitir, lei**th-t**ir—*half country, slope*
Stei**dh-d**òchais—*ground of hope* :—C.G. 471

Bha rìgh na dùthcha cosmhuil ra chuid daoine—*The king of the country was like his men* :—L.C. 44

A' cheud—*the first*, sometimes aspirates a following dental, especially in cpds. :

Rinneadh an ceud dhuine Adhamh 'na anam beò—*The first man Adam was made a living soul* :—1 Cor. xv. 45 ; so ed. 1902

Toiseach ceud-thoraidh d' fhearainn—*The first of the first fruits of thy land* :—Ex. xxiii. 19, so ed. 1902

Sean daoine a chunnaic an ceud thigh—*Ancient men that had seen the first house* :—Ezra iii. 12, so ed. 1902

'S e an ciad thaom de'n taigeis as teotha dhith—*The first squirt of the haggis is the hottest* :—N.G.P. 230

Though the tendency is towards aspiration, the old usage survives :

Chaidh an ceud talamh thairis—*The first earth has passed away* :—Rev. xxi. 1 ; thalamh, ed. 1902

Cha do ràinig e gu ruig a' cheud triùir—*He attained not to the first three* :—2 Sam. xxiii. 19, 23 ; so ed. 1902

ars' a' cheud te a labhair—*said the first woman that spoke* :—Arab. i. 68

An tusa an ceud duine a rugadh—*Art thou the first man that was born ?*—Job xv. 7 ; so ed. 1902

An ceud duine o'n talamh, talmhaidh—*The first man is of the earth, earthy* :—1 Cor. xv. 47 ; ceud dhuine, ed. 1902

air a' cheud dà là—*on the first two days* :—F.T. 48

A' cheud does not aspirate a following initial -s- :

Fhuair mi a' cheud sealladh dheth—*I got the first glimpse of him* :—Cuairt. 27, 61

bu, § 27, (M.G. bud) having ended originally in **d** does not aspirate a following dental :

Ged bu toigh leam riamh iad—*Though I ever loved them* :—D.Ban 410, 45

Bu dùrachdach a leannainn iad—*Eagerly would I follow them* :—ib. 50

(3) Nasals :

Coimeas m. *comparison* : com-mes

gun meas *without reputation* ; tamh-neul *trance* :—Ps. 121

Tha mi gun meas 'sam bith air—*I do not respect him at all.*

(4) Labials :

    sip-péin =sibh fhéin :—Munro 70 : O.G. sib-fadéisne
  Except :
  aspirated labials :
    dearbh-bheachd f. *assurance*
    dearbh-bhrathair m. *brother-german*

§ 21.

The vocative particle **a** aspirates the initial consonants of all nouns and adjj. except § 20, 2

The vocative particle **a** is repeated with nouns in opposition :

    A Mhàiri, **a** chuilean mo rùin—*O Mary, O puppy of my love* :—L.C. 15

The voc. particle **a** is (a) assimilated before vowels, (b) omitted before the possessive pronouns, which remain unaspirated :

    (a) amadain—*Thou fool*:—Math. v.22
    (b) " Mo dheagh bhean," arsa mise, " cha dean thu sin idir—" *My good woman," quoth I, " you shall not do that at all* ":—Arab. i. 29
    " Mo thighearna," arsa mise—" *My Lord," said I* :—ib. 116

but **o** is sometimes substituted for omitted **a** :
    O mo Dhia—*O my God* :—Ps. lxxi. 4, 12.

The def. art. aspirates the initial consonant (including **s** pure, **sl, sn, sr** ; but excepting **sb, sg, sm, sp, st,** § 20, 2) :

1. of all mas. nouns in gen. and dat. sing. except **t, d, n, l, r,** § 88

A noun is sometimes rendered definite by governing a possessive group, and thus causes aspiration like the art :

    Is iomad òglach chinne t'athar—*There's many a warrior of thy father's clan* :—S.O. 41ª29

2. of all fem. nouns in nom., acc., and dat. singular, § 89, except fem. nouns with initial **t, d, n, l, r,** § 20, 4

3. The rel. pronoun **a** aspirates initial consonants of verbs :

    Is mall **a mh**arcaicheas am fear **a bh**eachdaicheas— *Slowly rides the man who observes* :—N.G.P. 270

4. also **ma** *if* :—

    Ma theicheas tusa—*If thou flee* :—Arab. i. 57

    Agus ni sinn so, **ma cheadaicheas** Dia— *And this will we do, if God permit* :—Heb. vi. 3

    Ma **gheibh** e fios—*If he get information* :—Arab. ii. 4

    Ma **mholas** gach eun a thìr féin—*If every bird praise its own land* :—S.O. 145ª17.

§ 22.

Nouns indefinite, except § 20, 4, and *e.g.* **ceud**—*a hundred* § 98, 10, aspirate the gen. pl. of nouns indefinite, § 92, 3

Mas. nouns aspirate adjj. in gen. sing. ; nouns definite aspirate also in the dat. sing. ; and mas. **o** stems aspirate in nom. pl. besides, § 92, 3.

Fem. nouns aspirate adjj. in nom. and dat. sing. § 92, 1.

Aon, *one* (and **gun** *without*) aspirate all initial consonants, except § 20 1, 2, 4.

§ 23.

A'cheud *the first* § 20, 5 ; **dà** *two*, aspirate all consonants except § 20, groups 1 and 2. **Trì, ceithir** regularly aspirate **ceud** *a hundred*, which was a neuter noun in O.G. § 98, 6

In O.G. **trì, ceithir**, aspirated neuter nouns :

    Air luingeas mòr nan trì chrann àrd—*On the great ships of the three tall masts* :—MacCor. 96

Traces of this use remain in m. and f. nouns : e.g.

    'S tha thu shliochd nan trì Cholla— *And thou art of the race of the three Colla* :—S.O. 42ᵇ5

    Trì gheatacha—*three gates* :—Rev. xxi. 13 (ed. 1807).

    A thrì bhliadhna an àma seo—*three years at this time* :—H.B. p. 970

    Tha dhà no tri chearcan aig bana choimhearsnach dhuinn — *A neighbour of ours has two or three hens* :—Am Fear-Ciùil 135

§ 23.

    mi *I*, is aspirated after **cha** and **bu** :

    cha mhi—*it is not I*

    bu mhi—*it was I* :—Waifs III. 12

tu *thou*, is always aspirated in the accusative, and generally in the nominative, except :

(1) after a verb ending in **s** :

Is tu thilg a' chlach air a' chaisteal—*What a stone you threw at the castle* :—N.G.P. 294

(2) after a homo-organic consonant like the verbal terminations in **-dh** :

foillsichidh tu thu féin—*Thou wilt reveal thyself*
Shaoileadh tu gu'n robh an saoghal a' caoidh—*You would have thought the world was weeping* :—L.C. 94.

§ 24.

The pronominal possessives—**mo** *my*, **do** *thy*, **a** *his* ; the prepositions, **de** *of*, **do** *to*, **fo** *under*, **gun** *without* (v. aon), **mar** *as*, **o, bho** *from*, **roimh** *before*, **troimh** *through* ; and the intensive particles **glé** *clearly*, **ro-** *very*, aspirate a following consonant.

§ 25.

Cha aspirates all initial consonants except dentals § 16, 5 :

1. Gutturals :

Cha chadal 's cha tàmh—*It is not sleep, it is not rest* :— L. nan Gleann 166
Cha cheil mi—*I shall not conceal.*
Cha ghabh sin deanamh—*that cannot be done.*

2. Labials :

Cha phill e uaith—*He will not turn from it* :—Ps. cxxxii. 11
Cha bhean sibh ris—*Ye shall not touch it* :—H.B.
Cha mhac mar an t-athair thu—*You are not a son worthy of your father* :—H.B.
Cha mhair iad leth an làithean—*They shall not live out half their days* :—Ps. lv. 23

3 and **s**: cha seas e—*He shall not stand* :—Is. viii. 10; Dan. xi. 17

But in later works **s** is aspirated :

Le snaim cho dian cha shnasaichinn—*With a knot so strong I would not bind myself* :—Ross 21.

Before **f** pure, **cha** aspirates, retaining its nasal, § 16, 5 :
    Cha n-fhaod mi—*I may not.*

The preverbs **do**, **ro**, aspirate the Perf. of verbs.

do, being pretonic and unstressed, is omitted, and the aspiration remains :
    bhuail e—*he struck*

After a conjunct particle, e.g. **gu'n**, **do** is resumed :
    gu'n do-bhuail e—*that he struck* § 7 iii.

The preverb **ro** aspirates : O.G. Perf. rigni, ro-gni, **gní** *does*, rinn *he has done* ; and **bha**, the Perf. of **tha** in the conjunct gu'n **robh**—*that he has been.*

§ 26.

By analogy aspiration is extended to other verbs, some of which have no moveable preverb :
    thig *come thou*
    thoir *give thou*
    théid *he comes*
    thàinig *he has come*
    thug *he has given.*

All these are deaspirated and nasalised by a preceding **gu'n** § 7 iii.

§ 27.

As, is *is*, rel. of **is** aspirates **f** : an duine as **fheàrr**—*the best man* : but confusion has arisen because of the identity in form of **is**—*it is*, and **is, as**—*which is.* In O.G. the latter causes aspiration, the former does not. Hence the erroneous forms : am fear as **feàrr** leam—*the man I prefer.* Is **fhiach** leam—*I value, I condescend* :—H.B. and often in N.G.P.

    Bu aspirates all consonants except dentals **t**, **d** § 20, 5 (2)
        fear bu **mhòr** rath— *A man who was of great prosperity*
            :—Stewart, p. 100
        Bu mhi, bu tu—*It was I, it was thou* :—Stewart, p. 100
        'S e 'n ceòl bu **bhinne** chualas—*It is the sweetest music that has been heard* :—D. Ban 406, 15
        Cha bu **gheamha** leam—*It would be no compensation to me* :—H.B.
        Bu **tiugh** an t-uisge a nigheadh a aodann—*Thick would be the water that washed his face* :—N.G.P. 72

Bu **d**ual da sin—*That was his birthright* :—ib. 71 § 20,5 (2)

Far 'm bu **ch**àirdeil fuaim an gàire—*Where friendly was the sound of their laughter* :—An t-Òran. 270

Bu **sh**earbh leam éisdeachd ris—*I found it intolerable to listen to him* :—H.B.

but **bu** is not itself aspirated :

Ged **bu** toigh leam riamh iad—*Though I always liked them* :—D. Ban 410, 45 § 20, 5, (2)

Aspiration may be initial, medial, or final.

§ 28.

The above remarks apply to initial aspiration ; but the two principles hold good in medial aspiration. The difficulties fall to be dealt with in O.G. Unaspirated consonants between vowels formed originally part of a group of consonants § 19

A simple example of the rule is :

Togail *raising* ; from to-od-gabail : the single vowel-flanked consonant **b** in **gaball** is aspirated and disappears leaving the end syllable **gall** ; but the **g** remains unaspirated, having been originally part of the consonant group **dg**, and thus **g** was supported by **d** (which is assimilated and disappears).

Medial aspiration is in Gaelic now limited to nominal, adjectival, (and a few verbal) compounds.

§ 29.

I. In perfect compounds the second member of the compound is aspirated. In the older compounds the aspirated consonant disappears :—ceann fhionn, ceannion *whiteheaded*, teaghlach (teg + sluagh) *family*, òircheard *goldsmith*, eilthir (eile + tìr)—*a foreign land* § 100.

II. In imperfect compounds, subject to exceptions § 20, 2, 3, 4 :

1. A noun aspirates a following noun in the gen. pl :
cailleach-chearc f. *hen-wife* :—Waifs iii. 113

cf. the common use of aspirated gen. pl. without the art.

An sin thàinig dithis bhan—*Then came two women* :—
1 Kings iii. 16

2. A noun aspirates an adj. or another noun in the gen. sing., in the cases where the uncompounded adj. would be regularly aspirated, e.g.

> Coilich-dhuibh—*of a blackcock, blackcocks* § 103, 1
> làin-mhara—*of a full tide*

3. An adj. preceding a noun aspirates the noun :

> dubh-fhocal—*a dark saying* :

except in phrases like :—

> as ùrar fonn—*of freshest land* :—D.Ban 42, 2
> is daichile pearsa—*of the handsomest person* :—ib. 216, 8,
> fear bu mhòr ràth—*a man who was of great prosperity* :—
> § 93 (1)

4. All adjj., compounded and uncompounded, except *gach, iomadh,* and *liuthad,* aspirate a following noun or adj. :—

> ciùin-gheal *calm and white* ; a h-uile dhaoine *all men* ;
> gach duine *every man.*
> Nach iomadh ceum gòrach a sheachnadh iad—*Is it not
> many a foolish step they would avoid* :—Cos. 20.

uile when preceded by **gach** sometimes does not aspirate the singular—

> **a h-uile duine** *every man.*

5. A verb preceded by a noun, adj., or prep. is aspirated : beò-ghlac—*take alive*; dlùth-ghabh—*embrace*; deann-ruith —*run at full speed*; cùl-shleamhnuich—*backslide*; grad-bhris—*burst thou*; eadar-mhìnich—*interpret*; tur-chaillte—*entirely lost* § 152, 6

6. The negative particles :—**do-** *ill,* **mi-** *mis-,* **neo-** *un-,* and the intensive particles—**so-** *well,* **ion-** *fit for,* **bith** *ever-,* **ath-** *again* aspirate regularly a closely connected following word.

An-, am-, amh-, ain-, aim-, aimh-, do so irregularly.

7. The omission of a closely connected non-aspirating word may cause aspiration in the following remaining word owing to the removal of the non-aspirating influence :

> O.G. **ní co n-**, M.G. **no co n-**, becomes in G. **cha n-**

O.G. -**ta**, G. **tha** Gur truagh a ta mi. cf. Tha mi gu truagh—
  I am sad
Cho fada agus a bha, cf. Fhad 'sa' bha e—*while he was*

8. Final aspiration is regular, e.g. in verbal nouns in **ad** :
  moladh *praising*

§ 30.   **DEASPIRATION.**

Deaspiration takes place, often with (a) metathesis, (b)
palatalisation :
  (a) fàistine f. *prophecy* : fàith
    iongantas m. *wonder* : in-gnáth-as
  (b) blàthaich *warm thou* : blàitich

§ 31.   **PALATALISATION.**

A consonant is preceded and followed by vowels of the same
quality or timbre § 6

The rule is expressed in Gaelic :
  Caol ri caol, agus leathann ri leathann— *A slender to a
  slender, and a broad to a broad.*

The palatal pronunciation of a consonant is indicated by
the presence of a slender vowel, generally -**i**- on one side of the
consonant : v. the examples under Infection § 6.   The gen. sing.
of -**o**- and -**a**- stems is palatalised.

Apparent diphthongs ending in -**i**- are in many cases only
indications pointing to a following palatalised consonant.

§ 32.   **DEPALATALISATION.**

Depalatalisation is the opposite process.   Here a broad
vowel takes the place of a slender vowel and indicates the broad
pronunciation of the consonant.

Depalatalisation, which is not frequent in Gaelic, results
from two main causes :

1. Weak pronunciation of slender vowels :—
    amharus m. *doubt* : am-ires
    aobhar m. *cause* : ad-ber
    asal f. *ass* : also aiseal, L. assellus
    atharrach m. *alteration* : O.G. aitherrech

caochladhm. *change* : O.G. com-im-cló-ed
cruadal m. *hardness, hardihood* : cruaidh-dál *hard-meeting*
feòlmhor *fleshy* : feòil f. *flesh,* mòr *great*
flàth m. prince : O.G. fláith
foras (forfhais) f. *enquiry* : for-fios
fuaghal m. *seam* : fuaigheal, O.G. uagaim
lonach *greedy* : O.G. loingthech *gluttonous* § 184

2. Difficulty in pronouncing palatalised consonants, especially -r- :

feum m. *need* ; M.G. feidhm
gàirdean, gaoirdean m. *arm* ; pronounced gaordean
ioras *down* (air and los)
leann, lionn m. *ale* ; O.G. lind, linn
leum m. *leap* ; O.G. léim
rud m. *thing* ; O.G. rét
ruith f. *running* ; O.G. riuth
sneachda m. *snow* ; O.G. snechte
sònrach *special* ; O.G. sainred-ach
urad f. *quantity* ; O.G. eret
ùrnuigh f. *prayer* ; O.G. er-ni-guide § 184

3. A few Perf. Pass. Participles preserve the original ending **-te,-the** without causing Infection in the previous syllable, and thus form an exception to the rule : Caol ri caol agus leathann ri leathann : § 31

cleachte *accustomed*	mùchte *smothered*
crochte *hung*	nochte *stripped naked*
deante *done*	olte *drunk*
glacte *caught*	togte *lifted*

4. In an example of *tmesis* :

O'n a dh' éigh iad rium cabar 's mi còrr—*Since they called me tattler* :—S.O. 38ª35

'**s mi** is introduced between the members of the cpd. cabar-corr m. *superfluous rafter* without causing depalatalisation.

§ 33.   **PROTHETIC f.**

1. An inorganic **f** is placed before the vowel of a stressed syllable in the following instances. The practical effect is to

distinguish clearly whether the word is aspirated or not, and thus to make the sense more intelligible.

f-abhra *eyelid*

f-adadh m. *kindling*

f-aghaid f. *hunting* : L. agitatio

f-agus *near*

f-aic—*see thou*

f-aicill f. *caution*

f-ailbhe f. *ring*

f-àile f.m. *smell*

f-àilleagan m. *hole of ear*

f-àinne f. *ring*

f-air, assumed as the unaspirated base of thoir—*give thou*

f-airgneadh m. *hacking* : O.G. orgun f.

f-airich—*observe thou* : aire

f-airleas m. *object on skyline*

f-airslich—*baffle*

f-aithir m. *shelving beach*

f-alcag f. *common auk*

f-allus m. *sweat*

f-alman, failmean m. *kneecap*

f-an—*stay thou*

f-aob m. *excrescence* : Ir. odb

f-aod—*may, can*

f-aodail f. *goods found by chance*

f-aoisg—*unhusk thou* : O.G. aesc

f-arbhalach m. *stranger,* cf. arrabhalach

f-arspag f. *seagull*

f-ar-aon—*together, also*

f-arradh m. *vicinity*

f-às—*grow thou*

f-asair m *harness*

f-asdadh m. *hiring, binding*

f-asdail f. *dwelling*

f-asnag f. *corn-fan*

f-eadh m. *length, extent*

f-éile f. *charm*

f-eòraich—*ask thou*

f-eud—*may, can*

f-eudail f. *cattle, treasure*

f-iuthaidh *arrow, weapon*

f-obhannan m. *thistle*

f-oidheam f. *idea, inference* : Am. Fear-Ciùil 230

f-othail f. *confusion*

f-radharc m. *vision*

f-uachd f. *cold*

f-uaigh—*stitch, sew thou*

f-uar *cold*

f-uasgail—*open thou*

f-uath m. *hatred*

f-ulair, f-urail f. *enjoining*

f-uras—*easy*

The process still continues in words like

f-aithnich *recognise*

f-eagal m. *fear*

f-iolaire f. *eagle*

f-os a chionn *above him*

f-urrainn f. *power*

2. Conversely, initial f is lost in the following :

    aileas m. *shadow*

    aiteag f. *shy girl* : faiteach *cautious*

    aitheamh f. E. *fathom,* O.W. etem, W. edaf, L. patere

eaman m. *stump* : feaman *tail*
eothanachadh m. *languishing* : feodaich *decay*
ri *against* : O.G. and in cpds. frith
uinneag f. *window* : M.G. fuinneóg, N. windauga

§ 34. PROTHETIC -s-

To a few words, mostly with initial **p**, an inorganic -**s**- is prefixed :

s-bann, s-pann m. *band, hinge*
s-parraban, bannaban m. *forehead bandage*
s-mug m. *snot* : L. muc-us
s-geilb f. *chisel* McA.[2] (W. Ross)
s-nèip *turnip*
s-pàirneag (Là Bhr. 1st ed. 385) bàirneach f. *barnacle* : L. bernaca, W. brenig
s-pluig *snot, icicle* : s-cluig ? McB.
s-préidh f. *cattle*, W. praidd *flock, booty*, L. praeda
streap *climb*, Ir. dreapainn, O.G. dreppa *ladders* : 3s. pf. threap e—*he climbed.*

A few words coming from Latin through Welsh substitute -**s**- for initial -**f**- :

sòrn m. *flue of a kiln*, L. furnus, W. ffwrn
srian f. *bridle*, L. frenum, W ffrwyn
sroghall m. *whip, lash*, L. flagellum, W. ffrewyll
sùist f. *flail*, L. fūstis, W. ffust
sleuchd *prostrate*, L. flecto, the G. long vowel may be due to L. plēcto

Conversely initial **s** is lost in :

beach, speach f. *wasp*, L. vespa ; con(n)as-beach, coinn-speach, connspeach f. *wrangling* or *dog bee*, McB., Gk. σφήξ *wasp*, Ir. earc-bheach f. *hornet-bee*
lamban m. *milk curdled by rennet* : slaman
mìog f. *a smile, smirk*, (σ)μειδάω
mùr *countless number* : smùir, smùrach m. *dust*
téid—*will go*, § 184, 16
tuar *food*, E. store

§ 35. OF THE SOUNDS OF THE LETTERS.

I.

Vowels.

All vowels may be long or short.

No vowel is written doubled. A doubled vowel generally results in a long vowel :—fo-od-gar, fògair *expel.*

The long vowels are accented : the short vowels have no mark to distinguish them.

bàs m. *death.*	bas f. *palm of hand.*
càraid f. *pair*	caraid m. *friend*
càs m. *difficulty*	cas f. *foot*
dòigh f. *manner*	toigh *agreeable*
gèadh m.f. *goose*	geadh m. *iron rod*
lòn m. *food*	lon m. *elk*
mò *more*	mo *my*
rìs *again*	ris *to him*
tùr m. *sense*	tur *entirely*

All long vowels may have the grave accent as exemplified above ; and two vowels **ó, é,** may have the acute accent also, e.g.

bó f. *cow*   té f. *woman*

mòr *great,* is also pronounced mór § 39

§ 36.

A has four sounds :

1. open   **à** màla f. *bag,* càth f. *chaff*
   a mala f. *eyebrow,* cath m. *battle*

2. close before **dh, gh,** nasal **ao, oe**
   adhbhar, aobhar m. *cause,* ladhran f. *hoofs,*
   lagh m. *law,* adharc f. *horn,* magh m. *field*

3. before **ll, nn,** nasal **au**
   clann f. *children,* fann *week,* gann *scarce*
   rann f. *part,* adhlaic *bury*

4. unstressed and obscure like **e** in Eng. *water :*
   an *the,* ar *our,* ma *if*

§ 37.

U has one sound :

> ù : ùr *new*, dùr *dull*
> u : ugh m. *egg*, ulag f. *block*

§ 38.

I has three sounds :

1. open   ì Eng. *me* : mìn *smooth*
           i Eng. *feet* : min f. *meal*
2. close   i Eng. *tight* : tigh m. *house*
3. before ll, nn :
         mill *destroy*, binn *harmonious*, cf. § 58
4. unstressed and obscure :
         Eng. *in* : is *is*

§ 39.

O has four sounds :

1. open   ò Eng. *fore* : òr m. *gold*, dòchas m. *hope*
           o Eng. *rot* : dochann *punish*, grod *rotten*
2. close   ó Eng. *cold* : bó f. *cow*, bóid f. *vow*, dobhran m. *otter*
           o Eng. *tome* : lomadh m. *stripping*
3.   ò Sc. *shune* : fòghlum m. *learning*, ròghnaich *choose*
           o Eng. *sow*, *bough* : fogharadh m. *harvest*, roghainn
             choice
4. before final ll, nn, m :
           o Eng. *brown*, fonn m. *land*, donn *brown*, toll m.
             hole, tonn m. *wave*, com m. *cavity of chest*

In unaccented short syllables (ə) has the sound of a, ao (short), or i. i with a broad vowel has these sounds also, cf. § 66

§ 40.

E has nine sounds :

1. Long open è, eu, which becomes dipthongised into -īa north of Lochs Linnhe and Leven and the Grampians.

Examples of difference in pronunciation :—

South	*North.*
beuc *roar*	biac
beul m. *mouth*	bial

South.	North.
breagh *fine, handsome*	briagh
breug, f. *a lie*	briag
cè, ceath m. *cream*	cia
ceudna *same*	ciadna
ceus m. *flocks of wool*	cias
crè f. *clay*	criadh
dean *do*	dian
deuchainn f. *trial*	diachainn
dreuchd f. *office*	driachd
easgaidh *willing*	iasgaidh
eulaidh, ealaidh m. *stalking*	ialadh
feuch *try*	fiach
feun m. *cart*	fianaidh, fianach *peat cart*
feur m. *grass*	fiar
feusag f. *beard*	fiasag
gèadh m. f. *goose*	giadh
greusaiche m. *shoemaker*	griasaiche
leud m. *breadth*	liad
leug f. *jewel*	liag
leus m. *torch*	lias
mèanan m. *yawn*	mianan
mèith *fat, sappy*	miath
meud m. *size*	miad
meur m. *finger*	miar
nèarachd, nearachd f. *luck*	niarachd § 143
neul m. *cloud*	nial
reub *tear*	riab
sè, sèa, *six*	sia
sèap *sneak off*	siap
seud m. *hero*	siad
seum, sèam *enjoin*	siam
sgeul m. *tale*	sgial
sgeun m. *frightened look*	sgian
sglèat m. *slate*	sgliat
sgreamh m. *loathing*	sgriamh
sleugaire m. *sly dodger*	sliagaire
smeur f. *bramble, anoint*	smiar
speuc *diverge*	spiac

The following are unchanged :

    deud m. *tooth*

    eud m. *jealousy, zeal*, and in many places, iad *they*= eud,
       but N. iadach m. *jealousy*

    eug m. *death*

On the other hand **ceud** *hundred* is nearly always pronounced
ciad, and -**deug** *-teen* nearly always -**diag**.

2. *close* **ē** (é)

beuban m. *anything mangled*	feumach *needy*
beud m. *hurt*	(in some parts fiumach)
beum m. *stroke*	feumail *needful*
beur m. *point*	geum m. *low*
beus f. *moral qualities*	geur *sharp*. N. giar
breun *foetid*	leum m. *leap*
ceum m. *pace*	speur m. *sky*
ceus *crucify*	reul f. *star*
creuchd f. *wound*	treubh f. *tribe*
eur *refuse*	treud m. *flock*
feum m. *need*	treun *strong*

3. *close* **e**

  (a) before -**s** (old -ss)

cleas m. *feat*	fleasgach m. *young man*
deas *right*	freasdal m. *providence*
eas m. *waterfall*	seas *stand*
easbuig m. *bishop*	seasg *dry*
feasda *for ever*	teas m. *heat*
feasgar m. *evening*	treas *third*

except leas *need* in **ruig a leas**

  (b) with a voiced stop :

beag *small*	feadan m. *whistle*
beadradh m. *fondling*	freagair *answer*
breab *kick*	geadas m. *pike*
eadar *between*	leag *throw down*
eag f. *notch*	teagamh m. *doubt*
eagal m. *fear*	teagasg m. *teaching*
eaglais f. *church*	

But -**e**- remains open before -**d**- normally :

cead m. *permission*	cread m. *groan*
nead m. f. *nest*	

§ 41.　Short open **e** :—

The breaking of **e**.

The vowel **e** is written as **e** very rarely, e.g. leth m. *side*, teth *hot*, but mostly as a digraph -**ea**- between a slender and a broad consonant. The digraph retains its original pronunciation of open **e** before single consonants (except -**l**-), e.g. **fear** m. *man*, **bean** f. *woman* (but **eala** f. *swan*). But when -**ea**- occurs before -**nn**- or any consonantal group containing -**l**- or -**r**-, the voice, in preparing to pronounce the consonantal group, throws the stress forward from -**e**- to -**a**-, e.g. **fearr** *better*, and the **e** is then said to be broken, and it becomes -**ia**- in pronunciation. The slender consonant preceding the digraph (except it be a labial) also exerts an influence upon the digraph, e.g. it absorbs some of the original vowel, the -**i**- of -**ia**-, in **ceann** m. *head*.

The breaking of **e** is completed in Ireland. In the Highlands the change is still proceeding.

4. **ea** *open* **e** :—
In the following instances -**e**- is
　(a) unbroken :—

bean f. *woman*	fearann m. *land*
bean *touch*	gean m. *good humour*
beatha f. *life*	gearan m. *complaint*
bleath *grind*	leabhar (levar) m. *book*
breac *speckled*	lean *follow*
breamas m. *mischief*	leathann *broad*
breath f. *judgment*	leat *with thee*
cead m. *permission*	meanbh *small*
ceap m. *block*	mear *active*
ceathramh *fourth*	mearachd f. *mistake*
cheana *already*	nead m. f. *nest*
cleatha f. *goad*	nèamh m. *heaven*
cnead m. *sigh*	peathraichean f. *sisters*
creathall f. *cradle*	sean *old*
eanchainn f. *brains*	sreath m. *row*
fear m. *man*	streap *climb*

　(b) broken :—

5. **ea** *into* **ia** :—

bealach m. *pass*	eallach f. *burden*
bealaidh m. *broom*	(d)ealtag f. *bat*

bealltuinn f. *Beltane*
beann f. *peak*
beannachd f. *blessing*
bearn f. *gap*
cealg f. *treachery*
ceann m. *head*
ceannaich *buy*
ceard m. *craftsman*
cearr *left*
ceart *right* S.O.40^b2
ceatharnach m. *trooper*
dealachadh m. *parting*
dealan m. *lightning*
dealbh m. *picture*
dealt f.m. *dew*
deanntag f. *nettles*
dearrsadh m. *glare*
Eabhra m. *Hebrew*
eala f. *swan*
ealadh f. *skill*

earrach m. *spring* S.O.47^ay
earraid m. *tip-staff*
earann f. *part*
feannag f. *hooded crow*
fearn f. *alder*
feàrr *better*
geal *white*
geamhradh m. *winter*
gearr *short*
gleann m. *glen*
greann m. *scowl*
leann m. *ale*
leannan m. f. *lover*
meall *deceive*
meann m. *kid*
sealbh m. *possessions*
sealg f. *hunting*
searbh *bitter*
speal f. *scythe*
teann *tight*

(c) in process of transition from unbroken to broken :—

beachd f. *opinion*
beartach *rich*
ceanalta *mild*
cearc f. *hen*
cearcall m. *hoop*
cleachd *accustom*
creach *raid*
dearbh *certain*
dearc f. *berry*
dearc *see*
dearg *red*
dreach m. *shape*
each m. *horse*

earb m. *roe*
earball m. *tail*
fearg f. *anger*
leac f. *stone*
leanabh m. *child*
leapaichean f. *beds*
neart m. *strength*
seach *beyond*
peacadh m. *sin*
sneachd m. *snow*
teachdaire m. *messenger*
tearc *rare*
tearnadh m. *escaping*

In the mouths of older speakers **ea**, in many of the examples in (b) and (c), remains unbroken.

6. **ea** *into close* **i** :—

meas m. *fruit*   measa *worse*

But meas m. *judgment*, measg *mix*, meadhon m. *middle* have this sound and also the sound of open **e**.

Do mios siad gur nar dhóibh—
They thought it was a shame for them :—Red Book, 196
Ionnis go tainic an namhuid na miosg astech orrtha—
So that their enemies came into their midst :—ib. 206

7. **ea** *into open* **io**—before -**bh**-, -**mh**- :—
deamhan m. *demon* S.O.40ᵇ25   eabhag f. *hawk*
leabhar (leor) m. *book*   treabhadh m. *ploughing*
sleamhuinn *slippery* has this sound and also the sound of open **e**.

8. **ea** *into* **iu**—(**u** like **u** in Hull) before -**gh**- :—
leaghadh m. *melting*   teaghlach m. *household*
A similar sound in N. Inverness-shire is heard before -**ng**- :—
seangan m. *ant*   teanga f. *tongue*
sreang f. *string*

but in many districts these nouns preserve open **e**.

9. **ea** *into* **iau**—before -**dh**- :—
feadh m. *extent*, adv. *among*   bleaghann f. *milking*
feadhainn f. *some*   meadhg, meòg f. *whey*
                       (or into **iu**)

also before -**ll**-
geall *promise thou*   steall f. *spout*
seall *look thou*   leann m. *ale*, O.G. lind

§ 42.   DIPHTHONGS.

A diphthong is a vowel group caused by Infection §6, or by the loss of a consonant.

Of the two vowels forming a diphthong, one is sonantal, the other consonantal.

The sonantal vowel preserves its characteristic vowel sound undiminished, the consonantal vowel is to a large extent or wholly spent in modifying its consonant.

Diphthongs are either rising or falling according as the consonantal vowel rises from or falls to its consonant or consonantal group.

ceart *right*, and many examples of unbroken -**e**- are falling diphthongs.

ceart represents broken -**e**- and the rising diphthongs.

The rising diphthongs are not numerous in Gaelic, being fully represented by :—eo, io, iu.

The falling diphthongs are :—

ài	ai
éi, èi, ēu §40	ei
ìa	ia
ìo	io
òi	oi
	ua
ùi	ui

§ 43. RISING DIPHTHONGS.

In rising diphthongs the first element is -e- or -i-

-eo- -eo- beò *living*, eòlas m. *knowledge* ;
but older speakers sometimes pronounce the -e- with an even or an accented stress.

In long monosyllables like ceò m. *mist*, teò *warm*, the vowel -e- is occasionally heard, but never in short syllables :—

> deoch f. *drink*

-io- -io- occurs only in short syllables and with the sound of -iu- :—

> diombach *displeased* iolach f. *shout*
> fionn *white*

In words like cionta m. *guilt*—ciunta, acc. pl. of cin, g.s. cinad *sin*, the -i- is consonantal.

-iu- -iu- occurs in a few examples in short syllables :—

> iubhar m. *yew-tree* iuchair f. *key*

In long syllables like :—

> tiùgh *thick* diù m. *refuse*

the -i- is consonantal, but with occasional instances in which it is heard as a vowel. It is entirely consonantal in short syllables :

> fliuch *wet* siubhal m. *walking*

§ 44. FALLING DIPHTHONGS.

In falling diphthongs the second element is -i-, -e-, or -u- ; of these the first vowel -i- is by far the most frequent.   The digraph -ao- is not pronounced as a diphthong, but as a vowel, § 2 I.; and -ea- has been already dealt with §41.

-ài- **-ài-**

This diphthong is heard most clearly pronounced when the -i- precedes a labial, e.g. làimh d.s. f. *hand*, or a silent final palatal, e.g. fàidh m. *prophet*, L. vātes.

The second element becomes consonantal when followed by :—

    (1) any other consonant except the classes above :—

        fàisg *squeeze*   fàsg
        tràill m. *slave*   N. þrael

    (2) an added syllable :—

        fàidhean *prophets*   fà:iean
        gàire f. *laughter*   gà:re
        Màiri *Mary*   Mà:ri

    (3) The diphthong tends to maintain itself when it is the result of recent contractions owing to the loss of **dh-, gh-, th-** :

    bràighe m. *brae*, O.G. bràge *neck*, whence locative brágaid, contracted bràid, which probably occurs in *Breadalbane*.
    bàich m. *byre*, bàthaich : bá + thigh

§ 45. **-ai-**

-ai- The second element -i- of the short diphthong is most clearly pronounced

    1. when followed by a labial :—

        caibdeal m. *chapter* : L. capitulum
        caibe m. *spade*
        caibeal m. *chapel* : L. capella
        caime f. *crookedness*

    2. **-ai-** is also heard as a secondary stress on a vowel originally long :—

        ìomhaidh f. *image* : L. imāgo
        iomarbhaidh f. *struggle*, O.G. immarbág

3. **-ai-** is further the result of contraction :—

faigh *get* : fo-gaib
maighstir m. *master* : L. magister
saibhlean *barns*, sabhal m. *barn* : L. stabulum
saighead m. *arrow* : L. sagitta

Before all other consonants the pronunciation is **ae, oe** :—

aigentach *spirited*	cainnt f. *speech*
ailse f. *cancer*	gailbheinn f. *rough hill*
aingeal m. *angel*	gaire *near*
aire f. *notice*	gairm f. *call*
airidh *worthy*	gaisge f. *valour*
aithreachas m. *repentance*	maide m. *stick*
aisig *restore*	paidir f. *pater (noster)*
aiteann m. *juniper*	saill f. *fat*
	tanaiste m. *next heir*

§ 46.   **-ei-**

1. **-ei-**

The pure sound of **-i-**, the second element in this diphthong, is rare, but it is heard in :—

sgeimhleadh m. *skirmish*   sgeim f. *foam*
eipistil f. *epistle*

Before palatals the **-i-** is contaminated into **-ae-, -ao-** :—

greigh f. *herd* : L. greg-is   ministeir—*of a minister*
meigh f. *balance*

In long diphthongs pure **-i-** sounded before labials is rare :—

sgéimh f. *beauty*

-i- before linguals and palatals is frequent with contamination of consonant :—

déidh, an déidh *after* : W. diwedd *end*
déine f. *eagerness* : dian *eager*
féidh *deer* : O.G. fiadach *hunting*

-i- is consonantal in words like :—

mèise *of a plate*, me:se
éiginn f. *force*, eg:in

-ia-

2. **-ia-**

Both elements of this falling diphthong are pronounced with a nearly equal stress.

-**ia**- short before a labial -**a**- is pure :—
fiamh m. *awe*
before palatals -**a**- is contaminated :—
fiar *crooked* : W. gwyr
iar *west* : *eperon

-**īa**- long before labials -**a**- is heard pure :—
sliabh m. *moor* : but
ciall f. *sense* is pronounced ciaoll
fiadh m. *deer* is pronounced fiaodh

-io-

3. **-io-**

In this falling diphthong when the -**i**- is short, the -**o**- is heard before labials :—
liob f. *lip*

Before linguals and palatals the -**o**- is faint or quiescent :—
biodag f. *dirk*
biorach *pointed*
crios m. *girdle*

When the -**i**- is long, -**o**- is heard pure before labials :
ìobairt f. *sacrifice* : aith-od-ber
slìob *stroke*

Before linguals and palatals -**o**- is contaminated with the sound of the following consonant :—
dìol *pay*   fìor *true*
cìosnaich *put under tribute*

-oi-

4. **-oi-**

In a short -**oi**- diphthong, -**i**- is heard before labials :
soipean m. *wisp*, soibheusach *well bred*
Before linguals and palatals the -**i**- is contaminated, as in troigh f. *foot*. In oidhche f. *night*, stress is thrown on -**i**- ;

c

-ɪ- is consonantal in coileach m. *cock*, doire f. *grove*, toic f. *wealth*

In a long -ōɪ- diphthong, -ɪ- is heard before labials :—
dhoibh *to them*   ròib f. *filth*

-ɪ- before linguals and palatals is contaminated :—
dòigh f. *manner*   òigh f. *virgin*

-ɪ- is consonantal in words like :—
còir *just*, W. cywir :   *com-ver-us
fòid f. *clod*
mòid *the more*
bòidheach *pretty* : buaidh

-ua-

5. -ua-

In this falling diphthong the -ua- represents original -ō- : sluagh, slōgh m. *host*, pl. slòigh ; the -u- is open, and the stress is from uə to even or nearly so, especially on the diminutive -an § 7 ii. 3.

Before labials :—uapa *from them*, uabhar m. *pride*

Before linguals and palatals :—
cuan m. *ocean*   tuadh m. *axe*
fuar *cold*

-uɪ-

6. -uɪ-

The second element -i- is heard :

(a) In a short diphthong before labials :—
luibh m.f. *herb*   suipeir f. *supper*
ruibh *to you*

Contaminated with following lingual or palatal :—
buidheann f. *troop*   ruigheachd f. *reaching*
muic *pigs*

-ɪ- as consonantal :—muir f. *sea*, fuil f. *blood*

(b) In a long diphthong -ūi- :

(1) before labials :—
lùib f. *fold, bend*

(2) before linguals and palatals :—
    sùigheag f. *strawberry*
-i- as consonantal :—
    cùil f. *corner*   sùileag f. *little eye*

The -i- only is heard in words like :—
    tarruing f. *pulling*
    còmhnuidh f. *dwelling*
and in some dialects :—
    suiper f. *supper* § 95, 5 c

§ 47. TRIPHTHONGS.

The last element of a triphthong is -i-, which before non-quiescent linguals or palatals often ceases to be a sonant and becomes consonantal.

The first element of a triphthong is -e-, -i-, or -u-. -a- does not occur as first element except in the trigraph -aoi-. But -ao- is always a simple vowel sound § 36; and therefore -aoi- is at most a diphthong, which is also spelt -éi- :—

    aoibhinn, éibhinn *joyous*

In words like :—
    aois f. *age*   caoineadh m. *weeping*
-i- is consonantal, and -aoi- results in a simple vowel sound.

Triphthongs consist of mixed rising and falling diphthongs, the rising and falling elements of which tend to become consonantal; and the quality of the principal vowel is modified in close syllables. But it is to be noted that all the vowels of the triphthongs can sometimes be distinguished, especially in the mouths of some of the older speakers who practise slow and careful enunciation.

With -e- as first element consonantal.

-eoi-   Before labials, final -i- remains sonant :—
        leòib *of a shred*, leòb m.

    Before linguals and palatals -i- becomes consonantal :—
        eòin *birds*, eun m.   geòidh *geese*, gèadh m.
        deòir *tears*, deur m.   meòir *fingers*, meur m.
        feòir *of grass*, feur m.   § 76, 3

-iùi- *With -i- as first element.*

Both rising and falling **-i-** are consonantal :—
ciùil *of music* : ceòl   § 76, 3
siùil *of a sail* : seòl
fliuiche *more wet*—often becomes fliche.

But in spliuig f. *discontented face*, the second **-i-** is sonant from analogy with diminutives in **-ig** § 78

When the first **-i-** is long it does not become consonantal :—
fiaire *more awry* : fiar, W. gwyr
diaigh *after* : di-saig-im

-uai- *With -u- as first element.*

Before a labial all the vowels are clearly sounded :—

| uaibh *from you* | fuaim f. *sound* |
| uaimh f. *cave* | |

Before linguals and palatals **-i-** of **-ai-** is consonantal as in :—
gluais *move* ; uair f. *hour*, L. hora ; or modified to -ao-, -ae- :—

| cruaidh *hard* | luaithe *quicker* |

§ 48.

1. **-H-** is a short voiceless breathing emitted by the vocal organs placed in position to produce any of the vowels.

The effect of **-h-** is heard in the strong escape of breath preceding short stressed voiceless stops :—

cat m.	*a cat*	pronounced	cah-t
slat f.	*a rod*	,,	slah-t
boc m.	*buck*	,,	boh-k
sop f.	*wisp*	,,	soh-p
ceap m.	*block*	,,	ceah-p

This **-h-** has never been written in literature.

2. **-h-**, appearing regularly before stressed vowels, represents certain lost letters :—

-b- gur h-e, gur h-ann—*that it is he, that it is there*, cf. M.G. co rop fír sin (co rap, rup, rob, rab, rub)—*that it may be true.*

-c- na h- (from *nach* used in M.G. with infixed pronoun) Na
h-abair—*Do not say.*

-d- Gu ma h-e—*That it might be he.*
O.G. co mbad, co mad : gu madh e.

-s- ni h- (from *nes, *ne est). Ni h-eadh—*Is is not.*
a *her* (Sk. tásyāh) a h-athair—*her father.*
na *the* (def. art. g.s.f., n.p.) na h-aoise—*of the age,*
na h-eòin—*the birds.*
di *day*, L. dies : Di-h-aoine (*day of fast*) *Friday,* an dara
(regarded as an -o- stem), an dara h-aite—*the second
place.* § 64
a h-aon *one,* a h-ochd *eight,* without a noun. § 98.
gu, (from co-s, qo-s)
(a) adv. :—gu h-olc *badly,* gu h-àraid *especially.*
(b) noun :—làidir gu h-obair—*strong to labour.*
ri *to against* (from fris, fres § 142) :
ri h-uchd gabhaidh—*facing danger.*
ri h-urnaigh—*engaged in prayer.*

-t- le (from leth *side*):—trom le h-àl—*heavy with progeny* :—
Is. xl. 11

le h-aithreachas—*with repentance.*

§ 49.   *Indo-European -p-*

Original -p- is lost in Gaelic. The loss took place so early that
no clear case of a symbol, e.g. h, representing -p-, is adduced.
Proofs of its loss are abundant :

1. before vowels :—

alt m. *joint,* Goth. falpan, Gk. δι-πλάσιος *double.*
arco, in cpds. § 184.
athair m. E. *father,* L. pater, Gk. πατήρ, Sk. pitrí.
eadh m. *space, time,* Gaul. cand-etum *space of 100 ft.,*
Gk. πέδον *the ground, earth* ; L. op-pidum *town,* cf.
ion-ad m. *place,* *eni-pedo
eun m. *bird,* L. penna *wing,* peto *seek,* Gk. πτερόν *wing,*
πέτομαι *fly*
iasg m. E. *fish,* L. piscis, Goth. fisks, W. pysg
ibh *drink,* L. bibo § 184
ileach, O.G. ildathach *many coloured, variegated,* iol-
prefix meaning *many,* Gk. πολύς, Sk. pur-ú

iodh-lann f. *cornyard*, O.G. hith, W. yd *corn*, Sk. pi-tu
    juice, drink, food ; +lann *enclosure*, O.W. lann, W. llan
ire, f. *progress, state, degree of growth*
    O.G. hire *wider*, Gk. περᾶ, L. perindie *over to-morrow*
uchd m. *breast*, L. pectus
uiridh, an uiridh *from last year*, Gk. πέρυσι, πέρυτι, Sk. parút
ula f. *beard*, pl. ulachan, Gk. πύλιγγες *curly hair*, Sk.
    pulaka *erection of the hairs of the body*
ùr *fresh new*, O.G. húrda, L. pūrus

also the place name Éire f. *Ireland*, M.G. Hériu, W. Iwer-
    ddon, Gk. Πιέριος

2. before consonants :—

làmh f. *hand*, W. llaw, A.S. folm, L. palma, Gk. παλόμη
làn *full*, liòn *fill*, L. plenus, Gk. πλήρης
làr m. E. *floor*, W. llawr, A.S. flōr *house floor*
leathann *broad*, W. llydan, Gk. πλατύς
luath *swift*, E. *fleet*, cf. L. pluit, *it rains*, Gk. πλέω *I sail*
raithneach, raineach f. *fern, brake*,
    W. rhedyn, Gaul. ratis, *prati: Lit. papártis

3. between vowels :—

air =O.G. for *upon* § 142, § 188
caora f. *sheep*, O.G. caera : *qapero, L. caper *goat*, Gk.
    κάπρος *boar*, N. hafr, E. *heifer*
crò m. *anything circular, sheep cot*, W. craw : *krapos :
    AS. hrof, N. hrof *a shed*, E. *roof*
fo = *upo § 142
saor m. *carpenter* : *sapero, L. sapio

-ep-

air =iar n- *after* : *epero-m § 188, 3
feamainn f. *sea-weed*, Ir. feam m. *the stump* on which it
    grows, dim. feaman m. *tail, rump*, Sk. vapati *strews,
    scatters, sows*
teth *hot*, L. tepens, Sk. tapant-

-epō-

in the termination of fìr-ean *just*, W. iawn, Goth. ibns
    even, O. Corn. eun-hinsic gl. justus, c.f. cam-hinsic

4. medially (a) before -n-, -s-, -t- :

-pn-

cuan m. *ocean* (O.G. =*haven*), N. hofn

suan f. *sleep*, W. hun : * sopnos : L. somnus, Gk. ὕπνος

teine m. *fire*, W. tân, O.W. tafnah *heat*

-ps-

lasair f. *flame*, W. llachar, Gk. λάμψω

uasal *noble*, W. uchel, Gk. ὕψι, ὑψηλός

-pt-

cachdan m. *vexation*, cachd f. *bondmaid*, W. caeth *slave* :
    L. captus, capta

riochd m. *form, personation*, W. rhith *species* : *prptu,
    Gk. πρέπω

seachd *seven*, W. saith, L. septem, Gk. ἑπτά

uachdar m. *upper surface*, M.W. uthyr, *oup-tero   § 139

(b) after -l-, -r-, -s- :

-lp-

cilleorn m. *urn*, O.G. cilornn, W. calwrn *pail*, L. calpar,
    Gk. κάλπη *urn*

col m. *sin*, W. cwl, L. culpa

moladh m. *praising*, W. mawl, moli, Gk. μολπή, μέλπω

-rp-

caor f. *berry*, cf. Gk. καρπός *fruit*

corran, Ir. carran m. *reaping hook*, L. carpo, Gk. καρπός

searr f. *sickle*, W. sèr *bill-hook*, L. sarpo, Gk. ἅρπη

-sp-

sian m. *foxglove*, L. spionia, W. ffion *digitalis*

sine f. *teat*, bó triphne *cow of three teats* ; N. speni *teat*,
    Sc. spean *to wean*

sonn m. *cudgel, hero*, W. ffòn, Gk. σφήν *wedge*, E. *spoon*

§ 50.   **CONSONANTS.**

The tenues **c, t, p.**

Following initial tenues is a slight emission of breath almost
amounting to **-h-**, e.g.

còir f. *justice*, tana *thin*, pìob f. *pipe*

In O.G. and Ogham, which had no -**p**-, the formula B + H = P (-b- cum aspiratione pro -p-, ponitur) was recommended in order to produce the difficult non-Gaelic sound -**p**- :—Aur. 432

This aspiration disappears, and the pure tenues emerge in certain combinations : am pìobaire m. *the piper*, iompachadh m. *conversion* ; and in the consonant groups—**cn-**, **cr-** ; **tn-**, **tr-** ; **pr-** ; **str-**, § 59

The mediae are pronounced like tenues :

(a) Medial

  g = **c** agadh m. *stammering*
     magadh m. *mocking*
     togail f. *lifting*
  also after -**s**- :—
     sgian f. *knife*
     measgadh m. *mixing*
  d = **t** fadadh m. *kindling*
     madadh m. *mastiff*
     sadadh m. *beating*
  b = **p** obair f. *work*
     pìobaire m. *piper*
     sgròbadh m. *scratching*

(b) Final

  g = **c** bog *soft*   rag *stiff*
     lag m. *hollow* thig *come thou*
  d = **t** rud m. *thing*
     sud *yon, yonder*
  b = **p** cab m. *mouth*
     pìob f. *pipe*

§ 51.   **THE LABIALS.**

The labials **p**, **b**, **m**, **f**, and their corresponding aspirates are immutable, i.e. they have no distinction of broad and slender sound ; they are, however, distinguished in Ireland.

P.

1. -**p**- sounds like Eng. -**p**- :—pill *return*, poll m. *pool*
  -**ph**- sounds like Eng. -**f**- :—
   làn a' phuill—*The full of the pool* ;
   gu'n phill mi MacPhàill—*that I turned MacPhail* :—S.O.
    150[a]18

B.

2.   **-b-** initial, is voiceless : baile m. *a town*
      medial and final, like -p- :—cabar m. *horn*, sgrìob *scrape*
  -bh- initial, like Eng. **-v-** : bha mi *I was*, bhuail e—*he struck*

Medial   (a) like Eng. **-v-** : leabhar m. *book*, aobhar m. *cause*
        (b) silent or with a close sound like Eng. **-w-** :—gobhal
        m. *fork*, cobhar m. *foam*

Final   like Eng. **-v-** or **-a-** :—marbh *dead*.   In Lorn, mara.

M.

3.   **-m-** initial and final, sounds like Eng. **-m-** :
      mac m. *son*, ceum m. *step*

  -o- before final **-m-** in monosyllables becomes diphthongised
    into **-au-, -ou-** :—

    com m. *cavity of chest*   tom m. *hillock*
    lom *bare*   trom *heavy*

  -mh- initial and final, like Eng. **-v-**, but it strongly nasalises
    the following vowel :—
    a mhàthair f. *his mother*,
    a' deanamh m. *doing*, in some dialects, a' dean**o**

  -mh- medial, like Eng. **-u-** strongly nasalised :
    (a) **-amh-** like Eng. **-au-** :—
    amhlair m. *dolt*, amhluadh m. *confusion*
    geamhradh m. *winter*, samhladh m. *likeness*
    sglamhruinn f. *scolding*
    (b) silent, with a nasalisation of the vowel :—
    amh *raw*, còmhradh m. *conversation*

§ 52.   **F.**

  -f- like Eng. **-f-** :—faigh *get*, fìor *true*, fòid f. *turf*
  -f- appears as the aspirate of :
    (a) **-sv-** :—*svolnestu-s, solus m., soillse f. *light*, follas m.
      publicity ; soirmeil, foirmeil *brisk*, E. *swarm* : O.G.
      siur f. *sister* (Sk. svásr, Ger. schwester), Ir. a fiur,
      G. a phiuthar *his sister* § 85, 4
    (b) **-p-** :—feòdar m. *pewter*, feucag f. *peacock*
    (c) **-b-** :—f-é-in (bud-é-sin) *self*

In dialects, -**f**- is substituted for :—

(a) -**bh**- :

initially : fo'n (=bho'n =o'n) a chaidh e—*since he went*
far (=bharr) a dhòigh—*out of his mind*

medially : Far (=tabhair) dhomh sin—*Give me that* ;
fafann m. *breeze, surmise* (tabhann, to-sven).

(b) -**th**- : fairis for thairis :

Chaidh an craicionn dlùth a chur fairis—*The skin was put
close over the wound* :—L. nan Gleann 153, 2 ;
thuair, for fhuair *got*.

Feadair *Theodore* (Strathglass)

-**fh**- is silent except in fhathast *still*, fhéin *self*, fhuair e *he got* ;
where -**h**- is still sounded   § 21

§ 53.   **THE GUTTURALS.**

C.

1.   Initial -**c**-, broad, like Eng. **c** (k) *come, curb* :—
càil f. *appetite*, cùl m. *back*

-**c**- slender like Eng. **k** (c) in *kin, keep* :—
cìr f. *comb*, cìs f. *tribute*

2.   In medial and final position, when -**c**- is derived from O.G.
-**cc**-, the first -**c**- is aspirated in G, and -**c**- so derived is pronounced
-**chk**-.   -**c**- in G. is pronounced -**k**- :

Medial **c** (cc) = **chk**   acain f. *moan*
bacadh m. *hindrance*

Final   **c** (cc) = **chk**   airc f. *distress*
boc m. *buck*
cnoc m. *hill*
mac m. *son*
olc *evil*
taic f. *support*
torc m. *boar*

but **c** = **k** in chunnaic mi—*I saw* (O.G. ad-chondairc),
ionnraic *just* ; oirdheirc *famous*

Final   **chd = chk**   beannachd f. *blessing* §
                            bochd *poor*, from -gt, § 184, 7
                            teachd f. *coming* § 176

      chd (pt) § 49, 4

      -ch- broad, like Sc. *loch* :—

Initial   chaidh mi—*I went*
                chuala mi—*I heard*
                chunnaic mi—*I saw*

Medial   achadh m. *field*
                rachadh—*he would go*

Final   lach f. *duck*
                a mach *out*
                nach e ?—*is it not* ?

      -ch- is heard also as a glide before **c** (=cc) :
                boc (bochk) m. *buck*

      and as O.G. **ch** before **d** (=k) :
                bochd (bochk) *poor*, from -ght

      -ch- slender, like Eng. *hue, hew* :—

Initial   chì mi—*I shall see*
                an tìr chéin—*in a far country*

Medial   oidhche f. *night* ; seiche f. *hide* :
      also nithean (=nichean) m. *things*

Final   sìthich *pacify*, dreach an fhithich—*the look of the raven*

      also bitheanta (=bicheanta) *continual*
            gu bràth (=brach) *for ever*
            bruith (=bruich) *boil*
            ith (=ich) *eat*

      -ch- is heard also as a glide before **c** (cc =q) =k :—
                mic (=michk) *sons*

  In Colonsay and Tiree final **-dh = -ch** :—

        chaidh e—*he went*
            aghaidh *face*
            ra theinidh—*on fire*
            as a léinidh—*in his shirt* :—Am Fear-Ciùil 137
            bithidh e—*he will be* (also in Islay)

60

§ 54.   **G.**

-g- broad, like Eng. -g- in *go, lag* :—gabh *take*
-g- slender, like Eng. -g- in *give, get* :—gin *produce*
-gh-, -dh-, broad like a flat voiced -ch-

Initial   a'ghrian f. *the sun*, ghabh *he took*, dhà *two*

Medial   foghar m. *autumn*, maghar m. *bait*, seadhail *in-
            telligent*

Final   bualadh m. *striking*
            marbhadh m. *killing* :

-dh- in this termination is often silent, ràdh m. *saying*.
Following a broad vowel -dh- is generally -g-, but -k in Inverness, -u- in Suth. Following a slender vowel -dh- is -ch- § 53, 4
or silent. Silent also in, e.g. cridhe m. *heart*, fàidh m. *prophet*,
though it forms a radical consonant of the word.

-gh- -dh- slender, like Eng. -y- in *yes, yonder* :—

Initial   ghéill e—*he yielded*   dheth—*of him*
            gheibh e—*he will get*   dh'iarr e—*he asked*

Medial   bòidheach *pretty* ; fuigheall m. *remainder*

The same sound, **y**, is heard before broken **e**, and unstressed
e preceding a long vowel :—

each m. *horse*, earb m. *roe*, geal *white*
beò *living*
ceò m. *mist*
geòidh *geese*

§ 55.   **DENTALS.**
                                      T.

Initial -t-   broad, no corresponding Eng. sound : t', tog *raise*
          -t-   slender, varies in pronunciation from Eng. -t- in
                question to Eng. -t- in *quit*
          -t-   after -n- is Eng. -t-, bantraich f. *widow*
          -d-   slender has, in medial and final positions, the same
          sound as -t- :

Cha téid mi idir idir ann—*I shall never never go*
Cha n-fhidrich an sàthach an seang—
The well-fed will not consider the lean :—H.B.

Initial -**th**- is like Eng. -**h**- in *house* :—thig *come*
Medial and
Accented -**th**- is sometimes like -**ch**- § 53, 3
Medial and
Final -**th**- is silent—suitheach *watery* ; tìtheach *intent on* ;
maith *good* ; sìth f. *peace* ; silent also in **thu** *thou*

§ 56.   **D.**

-**d**- broad like Eng. -**t**-, -**dt**-, between E. *dare* and
tare :—dol m. *going*
-**d**- slender § 55
-**d**- after -**ch**- (-**chd**) § 53 : -**dh**- broad § 54

§ 57.   **S.**

1. -**s**- broad, like Eng. **s** in *sea, mystery* strongly stressed :—
saor *free*, asal f. *ass*

(a) in short syllables a strong hiss :—cas f. *foot*, bas f. *palm*

(b) in long syllables a voiced **z** :—càs m. *misfortune*, bàs
m. *death* ; or after a diphthong :—uasal *noble*.

Òran na Gàsaid—*Song of the Gazette* :—D.Ban 392

In final position **s** is followed by **d** in some districts :—
solusd m. light ; dorusd m. *door* ; a rithisd *again* ; brist
break

2. -**s**- slender like Eng. -**sh**- in *show* :—sin *that*, bris *break*, sìos
down

-**s**- followed by **l**,-**n**,-**t**, with a slender vowel is slender : so
this, sud *yon* are always slender.

-**s**- followed by **b, g, m, p, r**, is always broad whether the
vowel be broad or slender :—
smèid *nod* ; is *is*, is always broad.

-**s**- aspirated is like Eng. -**h**- in *him* ; sheas e—*he stood*, shrann
e—*he snorted*

-**s**- is never aspirated before the consonants **b, g, m, p, t** :
sbàirn, spàirn f. *effort*, sgàin *burst*, smachd m. *authority*,
spionnadh m. *strength*, stéidh f. *basis* § 20, 2

-**s**- is silent, after -**t**- of the art. by aspiration :—
an t-sùil f. *the eye*, an t-slighe f. *the way*,
deireadh an t-saoghail—*the end of the world*

62

-s- epenthetic is often heard in pronunciation between -r-
and -t-, e.g. ceart *right* = cearst ; and occasionally between -r- and -d-, e.g. ceàrd m. *artificer*

In some dialects the -r- is entirely supplanted by -s-, e.g.
òrd m. *hammer* is pronounced òsd (Uist).

§ 58.   **LIQUIDS.**

Broad closed monosyllables ending in -ll-, -nn-, and in doubled
(or originally doubled) -m- diphthongise their vowels into -au-,
-ou- :—

> ball m. *member*
> com. m. *cavity of the chest*

When the word is lengthened either by inflection or composition,
diphthongisation ceases, unless the final liquid be strengthened
by position :—

> Gall m. *Lowlander*, but
> Gallach *Lowland* (short)
> Gallda *Lowland* (long)

L.

-l- broad.

> initial : no corresponding sound in Eng. :—laogh m. *calf*,
> làmh f. *hand*, slat f. *rod*, dlùth *near*
>
> medial : eallach f. *load*, mullach m. *top*

The Glug Eiggach—*the isle of Egg cluck* ; when -l- is sounded
like -w- :—mullach a' chladaich—*top of the beach*, like Muwach
a' chwadaich. When

> final : broad -l- is doubled or supported by another
> consonant :—call m. *loss*, mall *slow*, alt m. *joint*
>
> Aspirated, as in Eng. *loom, fool* :—
>
> initial : labhair e—*he spoke*, cas lom f—*a bare foot*, mol—
> *praise thou.*
>
> medial : bealach m. *pass*, mulad m. *sadness*
>
> final : àl m. *brood*, òl *drink thou*

-l- slender, like Eng. -ll- in *million* : lì f. *colour* ; linn m. *image* ;
> doubled in medial and final position : milleadh m.
> *injury*, pill *return thou*

Aspirated, like Eng. -l- in *limb, fill* :—

> leig liom—*let me alone* ; a linn—*his age* ; air an t-sliabh
> —*on the hill* ; mil f. *honey*

-l- is put for -n- :—

> clach-liobharraidh f. *whetstone*, for clach-shniaraidh :—
> Turner 81 § 62
> Skeulan for Sanc' Eunan (Aboyne) § 112, 9

§ 59.　　　　　　N.

-n- broad.

> initial : naisg *bind*, nuadh *new*
> medial : connadh m. *fuel*, donnal m. *howl*

Final -n- is doubled and -a- is dipthongised in stressed position § 58 : fann *faint*, tha e ann—*he is there* § 51, 3 ; but not in polysyllables, e.g. a' fannachadh (= a' fanachadh) m. *fainting*.

> aspirated, no corresponding sound in Eng. :—
> shnàmh e—*he swam*
> a' bhean nuadh-phòsda f. *the bride*
> mo nàire—*shame !* fan—*stay thou*

-n- slender, like Eng. -n- in new :

> initial : neamh m. *heaven*, neart m. *strength*
> ni m. *thing*, nigh—*wash thou*
> medial : teinne f. *tension*, binne f. *melody*

In some dialects -n- is unaspirated in aithne f. *knowledge*, duine m. *man*, teine m. *fire*, eileain—*of an island* ; air mo mhuin— *on my back*

> Aspirated :
> sin e—*that is he* ; mo neart—*my strength* ;
> ni e—*he will do* (for dogní)

-n- before -g- is a single sound like Eng. -ng-, or -ng-k-, broad or slender, according to its vowel. In some dialects a final -g- is hardened to -k- :—cumhang *narrow* ;

> or -n- is dropped and the vowel nasalised, e.g. meanglan m.
> *branch*, especially before d, l, n, r, s :
> a duine m. *the man*
> a taillear m. *the tailor*, = a daillear

annlan m. *condiment*
innis—*tell thou*
ànrath, m. *distress*
annsa *preferable* § 17

-n- following **c, g, m, t**, is by § 18 pronounced like -r- :—cnoc
m. *hill*, gnìomh m. *deed*, mnathan *women*, tnùth m. *envy*,
an t-snatha—*of the yarn*

-n- is unvoiced

medially 1. before -fh-, or original -fh- : buain-idh—*he will
reap*; cluain-idh—*he will hear*
2. before or after -th- : leithne *broader*, cruith-
neachd *wheat*
3. before or after medial -ch- : eanchainn *brains*,
aithrichean *fathers*

§ 60.

1. -r- broad, initial, has two sounds, both trilled (the second less
strongly) like Eng. -r- in :
(a) *rude* (with tongue point trilled), e.g. ruadh *red* ;
(b) *rod* (advanced), e.g. rabhadh m. *warning*, ceartas m.
justice, ràdh m. *saying*
medial : earrach m. *spring*, tarruing—*pull thou*
final -r- (usually -rr-) is strongly trilled—e.g. feàrr *better*,
tòrr m. *heap*

2. aspirated :
mo shròn—*my nose* ; a rosg—*his eyelid* ; anns an t-sruth
in the stream ; thraogh an abhuinn—*the river ebbed* ;
rannsaich iad—*they ransacked* ; ruith e—*he ran* ; fear
m. *man* ; mearachd f. *error*

3. slender :
fad thrì làithean—*during three days*
a rìgh—*her king*
àite réidh m. *level place, clear space*
duine reamhar m. *a fat man*, mirr m. *myrrh*

4. aspirated :
a rìgh—*O King !*
bean reamhar—*a fat woman*
Réidhtich i am bòrd—*She cleared the table*
Rinn e—*He did*

In corc f. *knife* and coirce m. *oats*, -**r**-, distinguished as broad
and slender in Uist, is in other districts not so distinguished.

5. -**r**- is unvoiced
    1. before original -fh- : iarr-aidh *asking*
    2. before -th- : cothrom m. *opportunity*, caithream m.
       battle shout, comharradh m. *a mark*, O.G. comartha

§ 61.   **INTERCHANGES OF CONSONANTS.**

-**c**- for -**p**- :—§ 49, 4

cailleach f. (nun) *hag*	L. pallium
càisg f. *Easter*	pascha
clòimh f. *wool*	plūma
cùbaid f. *pulpit*, dial. bùbaid	pulpitum
cuithe f. *pit, snow-wreath*	puteus
curpur m. *purple* (Lewis)	purpur
cartan m. *flesh-worm, crab*	Ir. partàn *crab* (Islay)
cuilse E. *pulse* (Islay)	

-**cu**- for -**wh**- :—
    cuidheall f. E. *wheel*
    Cuigse f. *Whigs*
    cuip f. *whip*

-**d**- for -**c**- :—dalma, calma *brave*

-**g**- for -**p**- :—
    grunnasdan, grunnasdal m.   prounasg m. *brimstone* H.S.D.

-**g**- for -**y**- (-j-)—geòla f. E. *yawl*, N. jula

-**b**- for -**p**- :—
    òb m. *creek, bay*.   N. hóp, hence place-name Ob-an

-**f**- for -**b**- : fos *yet, still*, O.G. beus

-**f**- for -**bh**- ; fair *fetch thou*, jussive fut. of tabhair

-**f**- for -**m**- : far rium = mar rium

-**f**- for -**p**-, through misunderstanding of aspiration :—
    fùdar m. E. *powder*
    peucag, feucag, eucag f. E. *peacock*
    Thubhairt beul an **ràfaird** rium—
    The voice of report told me :—S.O. 286[b]13

-**p**- for -**f**- :—
    plod m. *a fleet*, N. floti
    plùr, flùr m. *flower, flour*

punntainn, punnainn, funntainn f. *benumbment with cold* or *damp*, Sc. fundy *funny*

-p- for **-b-** ;   through misunderstanding of eclipsis :—
Bìoball, pronounced and sometimes written Pìoball m. *Bible*
campar m. *vexation*, Sc. cumber
plangaid f. *blanket*
bùlas m. *pothook*, pùlas, fòlais
conversely bundaist m. E. *poundage, grassum*

-p- for **-t-** :   cuspunn, cusmunn, E. *custom* :   cuspair *mark*, E. *customer*

-ph- for **-f-**, through misunderstanding of aspiration :—
phill *turn*, for fill.   The perf. with do—gives rise to a third stem, till

-b- for **-m-** :—
braich f. *malt* :   O.G. mraich
brath m. *betrayal* :   O.G. mrath
brugh m. *hostel* :   O.G. mrug
breac, *speckled* :   O.G. mrechd

-b- for **-w-** :—barant :   E. *warrant*
bathar :   E. *wares*
buaic :   E. *wick*
buinn :   E. *win*

-b- is intruded in :—
criombanach *niggard* :   crioman, creim
domblas m. *gall*, O.G. do-mlas
lamban m. *milk curdled by rennet* :   slaman
lombair *bare*, O.G. lommar

-m- for **-b-** :—
bealaidh m. *broom*, also mealaidh, mealaich
binid f. *rennet*, minid
boile f. *rage*, moile f. *impatience*
buntàta m. *potato*, muntàta
mealag f. E. *belly*

-mh- for **-nn-** (merely a matter of spelling) :—
comhlach for connlach f. *straw*
comhspoid for connspoid f. *wrangle*
cramhlach for crannlach m. *tulchan calf*
damhsa for dannsa m. *dance*

-nn- for **-mh-** :—
    connsaich for comhsaich *dispute* § 184, 86
-nn- for **-ng-** :—
    cumhann, cumhang *narrow*
    fairsinn, for-seng, *over slender, broad, wide*
-s- for **-t-** :—through misunderstanding the effect of the def.
    art. :—
    sabaid, tabaid f. *brawl*, sreud, treud m. *flock*
    séist, séis m., téis f. *melody*
    sìde f., tìde m. E. *tide, weather*
-t- for **-s-** :—in **rt** pronounced **rst** §57 v. below
-t- intruded :—
    prefixed   aillse, t-aillse f. *spectre*
    medial   ceirtle f. *clew of thread*, L. circulus
               fairtlich *baffle* § 184, 53
               airtneal m. *weariness*, M.G. forrnel
-t- for **-h-** :—tabh m. *ocean*, N. haf
               tapadh m. E. *hap*, miothapadh *mishap*
               talla m. E. *hall*
-t- for **-v-** :—tàrlaid f. *slave*, E. *varlet*
-s- for **-h-** :—sainnseal m., E. *handsel*
               seicil E. *heckle* : Am F.-Ciùil 320
-s- for **-ch-** :—seanns, seamhas m. *luck*, E. *chance* : S.O. 40[a]1
               seipeal f. E. *chapel*
-s- for **-j-** :—Semeuca *Jamaica* D. Ban 340, 11
s- lost : dìosg *barren* : di-sesc
-g- for **-d-** :—
    initial : geal f. *leech*, deal f.
            géibheann f. *fetter*, deubhann f. *horsefetter*, deubh f.,
                deubh-leum (McA.), dì-leum H.B.
            greallag f. m. *swingle tree*, dreallag f.
    final : cosg *spend*, cosd
-g- for **-t-** :—
    greis *a while*, treis, O.G. treimse *a period*

§ 62.

-l- for **-r-** :—
    biolaire f. *cress* : O.G. biror § 9, 2
    cuilm, cuirm f. *feast*
    eilitriom m. *bier*, L. feretrum

eilthir, oirthir f. *coast*
gairneal, E. *garner*, Sc. garnell, girnell *a meal chest*
glinn, grinn, *pretty*
iolair *eagle*, W. eryr
tailgneachd, tairgneachd f. *prophecy*
Griogail, Griogair *Gregor* cf. § 9, 1, 2

-l- for -n- :—
　a null *to the other side*, M.G. a nunn : an + sund *from here*
　bàirleigeadh, bàrnaigeadh m. E. *warning*
　cànail, cànain f. *speech*
　coinlein, cuinnean m. *nostril*
　lànail, lànan m. *couple*
　a' Ghearmailt *Germany*, cf. an Eadailt *Italy*

-l- disappears :—
　aisling, aisinn f. *dream*
　eisleach, eiseach f. *crupper*

-ll- disappears with compensatory vowel lengthening § 5, 3 :—
　deillseag, déiseag f. *slap, blow*
　soillse, sòise f. *a bolis, ball of fire*
　but boillsgeadh m. boillsgeachd f., boisge f. *brightness*
　from one -l- : L. fulgeo
　and aillse f. *fairy*, confused with aibhse f. *spectre*
　aillsich—*tell fairy tales, exaggerate*
　aibhseach *awful*, aibheis f. *abyss*

-bh- for -l- (-ll-) :—
　allsadh, abhsadh m. *clewing sail*, N. halsa
　allsporag, abhsporag f. *cow's throttle, stomach*

-d- for -l- :—the Islay pronunciations—
　dà, for là m. *day*　　　　　　dàn, làn *full*
　dàidir, làidir *strong*　　　　daogh, laogh m. *calf*
　dàmh, làmh f. *hand*

-d- for -n- :—
　deanntag, neanntag f. *nettle* § 17, § 14

§ 63.　　　　　　　　　**N.**

-n- for -l- :—
　leanabh, leanaban m. *child*, O.G. lelap
　munachag, mulachag, f. *kebbuck* ; spùinn *spoill*, for spùill

-n- for -m- :—
　màn or màm *mole, boil*, McEachan's Dict.

-n- for **-r-** :—
    bruan m. *fragment*, O.G. bruar
    an eanar, an earar—*the day after to-morrow*
    fiolan, fiolar m. *fly, earwig*
    gartan E. *garter*
    iomchan, iomchar m. *carriage, behaviour*
-n- for **-t-** :—
    cunnradh m. *covenant*, O.G. cundrad, L. contrāctus
    sléisne for sléisde *of thigh*
-n- is (a) pronounced, or (b) disappears nasalising its vowel,
or (c) is entirely omitted in :—
    banrìgh f. *queen*
-n- is intruded in :—
    buntàta m. *potato*   planc m. *plack*
    puinsean m. *poison*
  and in the place-names in Eng. :
    Colasa *Colonsay*, Orasa *Oronsay* § 18, 7

§ 64.

-r- for **-l-** :—
    caisil-chrò *bier*, Ir. cosair-chró : √ ser
    barraidh, baillidh m. *bailie, factor*, R. Donn, Ed. 1829, Ind.
    bruadar, bruadal m. *dream*
    Féill Fairc, Féill Failc f. *Epiphany* : fairc *wash thou*,
        O.G. folcaim, W. golchi
    in dara, ind ala *the second* § 48, 2
    mar (with loss of initial syllable) *as*, O.G. amal   § 198
    soirgheas m. *good voyage* = soilgheas : so-loingeas § 150, 8
-r- for **-n-** :—
    baraltrum, banaltrum f. *nurse*
    boirionn *feminine*, boirionnach m. *woman*, Ir. boinearn,
        Gk. βανά, γυνή
    doras fhios agam, donas etc.—*I don't know*, cf. gun norradh
        cadail—*without a wink of sleep* :—Arab. I. 76 ; II.
        53, 113
    m'aram fhéin, m'anam fhéin—*by mine own soul*
    mur, mu'n *unless* § 145, 4, cf. Ir. Luimneach *Limerick*
-r- is often assimilated before **-l-**, **-n-** :—
    atharla f. *heifer*
    atharnach, athainneach f. *red land*

beurla f. *English*
comhairle f. *counsel*
earlachadh m. *preparation of food*
fairtlich, fàillich *baffle*
mèirle f. *theft*
òirleach f. *inch*
ùrlar m. *floor*, unnlar (McA.)

Add the proper name Mac Calphuirn *Mac Alpine* § 111

-r- is sometimes epenthetic :—

bratàllion *battalion* (D.Ban 392, 13 C)
briosgaid f. *biscuit*
gus na phrill iad—*to which they returned* :—Gillies 260
grath-muinge, gath-muinge m. *mane*
mulardach, muladach *sorrowful*
mùrla *coat of mail*, sgrud, sgùd, *cluster* :—Claig. 106
trog *lift*, Manx troggal, but cf. tog § 184, 36

§ 65. THE PARASITIC OR (IN SANSCRIT) THE SVARABHAKTI VOWEL.

(*i.e.*, The " Voice-attachment," " vowel-portion," or glide vowel).

Svarabhakti is the development in the spoken language of a non-radical or inorganic vowel from the voiced sound of the preceding consonant, resulting in a repetition of the preceding vowel.

Tulach gorm m. *Green hill*, is in Scottish C.S. spoken and written as Tullochgorum (more correctly Tullochgorom).
The Svarabhakti or glide vowel occurs—

I. Between words, *i.e.* in sandhi or composition external to the word ; and

II. Between letters of the word, *i.e.*, internal.

I. External Svarabhakti—

an-a-lasda *insipid*   ban-a-mhaighstir f. *mistress*
an-a-moch *late*   aon-a-chat deug *eleventh cat*
an-a-ceart *unjust*   àr-amach *battlefield* : àr + magh
an-a-ghràdhach *doting*   ball-a-gheal *white topped*
cach-a-leth, cachliath, cachaileth f. *swing-gate* :—F.C. 319
ceanna-bhaile m. *chief town*:—Arab. 66 y.

dall-a-bhrònach *blind and sorrowful*
morghan m. *sea-sand, gravel*, moroghan
morbhach f. *land liable to sea flooding*, morobhach
sean-a-ghobha m. *old smith*
sean-a-mhathair f. *grandmother*

II. In Internal Svarabhakti, a full vowel is developed, having a level or an accented stress ; but it is seldom written :

Gheibh thu deiseil uisge teith dhomhsa a chum g'um fairig mi mi-fhéin— *You shall prepare hot water for me that I may bathe myself* :—Arab. ii. 47.

The Sv. vowel is, however, in some instances written regularly :
banachag f. *milkmaid*, for banchag
gnìomharra *deeds*, for gnìomhradha, pl. of gnìomhradh m.
iarunn m. *iron*, O.G. iarn
meiligeag f. *peapod*, for meilgeag
muinichill m. *sleeve*, for muinchill
muinighinn f. *trust*, for muinghinn
ocar m. *interest on money*, W. ocr, N. okr
seanachas m. *conversation, story*, for seanchas
suiridhe f. *wooing*, M.G. suirge
cf. imrich f. *flitting*, O.G. immirge, immirce.

The Svarabhakti vowel does not count in scansion, but there are a few exceptions :

Gur mairg a bhiodh 'san ubaraid— *Pity him who would be in the fray* :—S.O. 150ᵇ11.

Thu air an déiric anns gach àit— *Thou dependant upon charity everywhere* :—Clarsach 7.

In W., however, monosyllables like pobl · m. *people*, ffafr f. *favour*, teml f. *temple*, ofn m. *fear*, may be sung as dissyllables—pobol, ffafar, temel, ofon :—Hymnau a Thônau, p. ix.

§ 66.

Svarabhakti causes a repetition of the syllabic vowel, or parent sound, with two exceptions :—

(a) **io**, with Sv. **ao**, e.g. iomlan *perfect*, iumaolan ; iomchuidh *fit*, iumaochuidh ; ionmhuinn *beloved*, iunaomhuinn.

(b) **ui**, with Sv. **i**, e.g. buirb *of fierce*, burib
doilgheas m. *sorrow*, duligheas § 150, 8
guirm *of green*, gurim
luirg *of a track*, lurig

§ 67.

The consonant groups producing Svarabhakti are :—

1. A liquid followed by a labial, -**g**-, or -**ch**- :—

   -**l**- calpa m. *calf of the leg* = calapa
   Alba f. *Scotland*, Alaba
   dealbh m. *image*, dealabh
   tilg *throw*, tilig
   calma *brave*, calama
   salchar m. *filth*, salachar

   -**n**- cainb f. *hemp*, cain(a)ib
   banbh m. *fallowland*, banabh
   ainm m. *name* ain(a)im
   seanmhathair f. *grandmother*, sean 'amhair
   eanghlas f. *gruel*, eanaghlas
   eanchainn f. m. *brain*, eanachainn

   -**r**- borb *rough*, borob
   tarbh m. *bull*, tarabh
   dearmad m. *neglect*, dearamad
   lorg f. *staff*, lorog
   carghus m. *Lent*, caraghus
   dorch *dark*, doroch

2. -**m**- before liquids, -**ch**- and -**s**- :
   imlich *lick*, imilich and (with metathesis) ilimich
   imnidh f. *care*, iminidh
   iomradh m. *mention*, iumaoradh
   timcheall m. *circuit*, timicheall
   aimsir f. *time*, aimaisir

3. -**s**- before -**mh**- and -**ch**- :
   seasmhach *steadfast*, seas'amhach

In some cases where Svarabhakti is followed by a spirant, the latter disappears, and Svarabhakti attracts and dominates, but does not lengthen, the following vowel :

-**l**-   dh' fhalbhadh—*would go away*, gala'a(g)
          galad f., a ghalad, galghad f., laochan, M.G. galgat
          champion

-**n**-   inbhir m. *confluence of waters*, inir
          gainmheach f. *sand*, gainaich
          inibhe f. *rank condition* ;   adj. inbheach, inich
          inghean f. *daughter*, ni'an, with loss of initial syllable,
              § 68, 1

-**r**-   arbhar m. *standing corn*, arabhar, and ara'ar
          àrach f. *battle field*, àr-mach (àr-mag), àramhach
          aramach m. *arming, rebellion* arm-ach
          dearbhadh m. *proof*, marbhadh m. *killing*
          soirgheas m. *favourable wind*, soiro'is   § 150, 8, § 64

§ 68.

The stress occurring on the Svarabhakti vowel has caused
in some instances—

1. loss of an initial syllable :
      nighean f. *girl*, S. Caithness irinn, O.G. ingen : i-n-i-ghean
      m**ea**rall, air m**ea**rall *amiss, astray* : air iomrall, Munro 153.
      raball m. *tail* : earball, ear-**a**-ball   § 7 iii.

2. the addition of a final syllable :
      ainbi, ainbith *odd, unusual*, O.G. ainb, ainib : n-wid-s
      achmhasan m. *reprimand* :   M.G. ath-chomsán ;   ath-
          com-ness.   § 184, 70
      suairce *pleasant :* O.G. suairc

3. disintegration and rearrangement of medial syllables :
      inich *neat, tidy, lively* : from inbhe, in-i-bhe-ch
      iongantas *wonder*—pronounced igadas (Skye) § 18, 7 for
          ingnathas, ing**an**(a)thas
      moirear m. *a lord*, O.G. mormaer, mor-**o**-mher, M.G.
          morbhair

4. loss of a final vowel :
      calm *brave*, O.G. calma
      éirigh f. *rising*, O.G. éirge
      eitean m. *kernel*, Ir. eitne
      imrich f. *flitting*, O.G. imirce

§ 69. **GENDER.**

There are two genders in Gaelic—mas. and fem.　In O.G. there was a neuter gender also.

1. Nouns signifying males are mas.

　　fear *man*, rìgh *king* ;
　　except sgalag f. *farm-servant, workman*

The diminutive -**ag** is now fem. ; but in O.G. the word was scol-óc m. *scholar*, he who in the monastery performed also the agricultural and menial work.

A pronoun referring to a male denoted by a feminine noun is mas. :

　　Is maith an sgalag **e**—*He is a good workman* :—Munro 179.

2. Nouns signifying females are fem. :

　　màthair f. *mother*, bó f. *cow*

　except :

　　agh m. *heifer*, D. Ban 170, 149
　　boireannach (baineannach) m. *woman*
　　capull m. *horse* or *mare*, commonly *mare*
　　mart m. *cow*

A pronoun referring to a female denoted by a masculine noun is fem. :

　　Is deas am boirionnach **i**—*She is a handsome woman* :—
　　　　Munro 179.

A boat—**bàta, darach, soitheach**—though mas., is thought of and referred to as fem. :

　　Is iomadh gleann ris an cromadh **i** h-earrach—*There's
　　　　many a glen* (trough of the sea) *to which she would
　　　　turn her tail* :—S.O. 47ay.

　Similarly :

　　Fhuair an gobhlan-gaoithe (m) nead **dhi** féin—*The swallow
　　　　hath found a nest for herself* :—Ps. lxxxiv. 3
　　Tha gliocas (m) air a **fireanachadh le a** **c**loinn—*Wisdom
　　　　is justified of her children* :—Math. xi. 19.

3. Mas. nouns denoting a genus or species include the female :

　　cat m. *cat*　　　　　　　leòmhan m. *lion*
　　duine m. *man*　　　　　uan m. *lamb*

　Cha robh duine de theaghlach againn—*We had no family* :—
　　　Arab. i. 18.

§ 70.

The gender is made specific :

1. By using different words for mas. and fem :

Mas.	Fem.	Mas.	Fem.
athair *father*	mathair	each *horse*	làir
amadan *fool*	òinseach	fear *man*	bean
bodach *carl*	cailleach	fleasgach *bachelor*	maideann
boc *buck*	maoiseach	gille *lad*	caile
bràthair *brother*	piuthar	giullan *boy*	caileag
coileach *cock*	cearc	mac *son*	nighean
cù *dog*	gala	oide *stepfather*	muime
damh *ox, stag*	atharla	reatha *ram*	caora
	(agh §69, 2)		
dràchd *drake*	tunnag, lach	tarbh *bull*	bó

2. In the case of human beings (also baniasg f. *spawning fish*) by placing **ban-** before the word denoting the male :

	Mas.	Fem.
as prenoun :	àireach *cow-tender*	banarach, *dairymaid*
as prefix :	coisiche *traveller*	bana-choisiche § 65
	diùc *duke*	ban-diùc
	éisg *satirist*	ban-éisg
	fear-ogha *grandson*	ban-ogha § 102, 6

3. In the case of domestic animals, by affixing the adj. **firionn** *male* to denote the mas. and **boirionn** *female* to denote the fem. :

cat firionn m. *a he cat* : cat boirionn m. *a she cat*

4. In the case of wild animals and birds, by prefixing **boc** and **coilich** respectively to the noun denoting the female, which is then put in the gen. :

earba f. *roe*	boc earba m. *buck*
gobhar f. *goat*	boc goibhre m. *he-goat*
maigheach f. *hare*	boc-maighich m. *buck-hare*
smeòrach f. *thrush*	coileach-smeoraich m. *cock-thrush*

§ 71.

The gender of nouns denoting things inanimate may to some extent be inferred from—1. the termination for mas. and fem. ; 2. the meaning of the noun :

1. **The Termination:**

(a) *Mas.*

	-a	balla *wall* § 81
Inf. in	-adh	bualadh *striking*
Dim. in	-an, -ean	macan *little son*
Concrete in	-as	dànadas *boldness*

Nomina agentis:

	-ach	marcach m. *rider*
	-aiche	searmonaiche m. *preacher*
	-air	brocair m. *fox-hunter*

(b) *Fem.*

Fem.-a-stems	-a	làmh *hand*
Diminutive stems in	-ag	caileag *girl*
Abstract nouns in	-achd, -eachd	beannachd *blessing*
	-ad, -ead	bòidhchead *beauty*
	-e	doille *blindness*
Polysyllables in	-ir	saothair f. *travail*

except those in **-air, -aiche** above.

2. **The meaning of the noun:**

(a) *Mas.* :

The names of the elements, seasons of the year, days of the week, metals, colours, grains, vegetables, liquors, and timber are for the most part mas., e.g.

teine *fire*	earrach *spring*	Di-luain *Monday*
iarunn *iron*	corcur *purple*	cruinneachd *wheat*
càl *kail*	leann *ale*	giubhas *fir*

(b) *Fem.* :

The names of countries, musical instruments, heavenly bodies, diseases, copses are for the most part fem. :

Alba f. *Scotland*	a' phiòb *the bagpipes*
	a' ghrían *the sun*

Eaglais na Roimhe—*the Church of Rome* :—Cuairt. 40, 99
a' bhreac *smallpox*   a' ghiùsach *fir-copse*

§ 72.   **The Neuter Gender.**

The difficulty of determining the gender by classification is increased by the disappearance of the O.G. neuter from Gaelic.

The following old neuter nouns are now distributed between the mas. and fem. :

aodach m. *dress*
gleann m. *glen*
glùn m.f. *knee*
gnè f. *kind, nature*
leann m. *ale.*
leth m. *side*
luach m. *value*
luibh m.f. *herb*

magh m.f. *plain*
muir f. *sea*
neamh m. *heaven*
sliabh m. *mountain*
teach, dat. taig, m. *house*
tìr f.m. *land*
toiseach m. *beginning*

Traces of the O.G. neuter gender survive in :

(a) the nouns teachd-an-tir *income*, tìr mòr *mainland* :—
L.C. 91

(b) Pronominal phrases :
'seadh, O.G. is ed—*It is that ! Yes !*   *or* 'seag'
eadhon, O.G. ed on—*That is it ! even*
An eadh ? O.G. In ed—*Is it that ? Is it so ?*
Ni h-eadh, O.G. ni hed—*It is not that.   No !*
gidheadh, O.G. cid ed—*though it be that, nevertheless*

Is eadh, 'seadh, emerges in answer to a question where **is**, the principal verb, is latent :

Am Muileach e ?—*Is he a Mullman ?* 'Seadh, or Cha n-eadh :—C.R. vi. 299

An Romanach thu ? Is eadh— *Art thou a Roman ?   Yes* :
—Acts xxii. 27

Nach mi-chiatach an gnothach ? Gu dearbh is eadh—*Is it not an unseemly matter ? Indeed it is* :—Arab. i. 67
§ 119, 4

§ 73.   ROOT AND STEM.

A root is the most elementary form to which the word can be reduced :

√gar-*call*

A stem is the root, either simple or infected, with some element of inflection added, and forming a base for further inflection :

gair-m m. *calling, call*, g.s. gairme

Vowel Stems.

I. An-**o**-stem, a class which includes the Latin II. declension in-**us**, ended originally in -**os**, -**o**-**s**. This is known be-

cause of the gen. sing, infection in -i- §6 and from the
form of the word in other languages :

    n.s. each m. *horse*   L. equus   Gk. ʹίππος
    g.s. eich   equi   ʹίππου

II. A fem-ā-stem ended originally in -ā :

    n.s. làmh f. *hand* : *plāmā, L. palma, Gk. παλάμη
    g.s. làimhe   palmae   παλάμης

III. A fem.-i- stem ended originally in -i-s :

    n.s. mil f. *honey*   L. mel   Gk. μέλι
    g.s. meala   mellis   μέλιτος

IV. A -u- stem ended originally in -u-s :

    n.s. loch m. *lake*   L. lacus   Gk. λάκκος
    g.s. locha   lacūs

Consonantal Stems.

V. (a) *guttural stems* :

    n.s. nathair f. *serpent*   L. natrix
    g.s. nathrach   natricis

    (b) *nasal stems* :

    n.s. àra f. *kidney*   L. nefrones   Gr. νεφρός
    g.s. arann
    n.s. cù m. *dog*   L. canis Gr. κύων
    g.s. coin (O.G. con)   canis   κυνός

    (c) *dental stems* :

    n.s. cara m. *friend*   L. carant-ius § 85, 4
    d.s. caraid

    (d) -r- *stems* :

    n.s. athair m. *father*   L. pater Gr. πατήρ
    g.s. athar   patris   πατρός
      For verbal stems, see §184.

§ 74.   **DECLENSION OF NOUNS.**

All nouns have the same form in nom. and acc., the old acc.
being obsolete.

The form of the genitive singular determines the class and
declension to which a noun belongs.

Nouns are of two great classes :

A. Vocalic stems, which show modification of the vowels either by infection, or by a vowel addition to the stem.

B. Consonantal stems, which add, or originally added, consonants.

A.

Vocalic stems have four declensions, distinguished by the following characteristics :

I. A broad vowel with a slender infection : mas.-**o**-stems,
   nom. bàrd *a bard*, gen. bà-i-rd.

II. Any vowel with a slender increase : fem.-**a**-stems,
   n. cluas f. *ear*, g. cluais-e.

III. A slender vowel with a broad increase : -**i**-stems,
   n. sùil f. *eye*, g. sùl-a

IV. A broad vowel with a broad increase : -**u**-stems,
   n. guth m. *voice*, g. guth-a.

B.

V. Consonantal stems are included in one declension, distinguished by the following characteristics :

1 Any vowel with a guttural, nasal, or dental increase in the genitive singular :

   n. cathair f. *chair*, g. cathrach
   n. àra f. *kidney*, g. àrann
   n. bràigh m. *brae*, g. bràghad.

2 In -**r**- stems, a slender vowel with a broad infection in the genitive singular :

   n. athair m. *father*, g. athar

In addition to the regular case endings, the poets used, both for nom. and for oblique cases, an old meaningless termination **-ibh,-aibh** (called in O.G. irisal *humiliation*) which is identical in form with dat. pl., and is still heard in C.S. :

Gur farsuinn do ranntaibh—*Wide are thy domains* :—S.O. 49b17.

Bhi faicinn do chursaibh—*to see thy horses* :—ib. 42b28.

'Se braonaibh faoin, a lìon an cuan—*It is insignificant drops that filled the ocean* :—Clarsach 9.

'S a' Ghàidhlig aosd' ag gleus bhur macaibh—*The old Gaelic moves your sons* :—ib. 42.

Bu tric a bha anamaibh air an dùsgadh—*Often have souls been awakened* :—Cos. xix.

Air son slàinte anamaibh—*for the salvation of souls*:—ib. xxi.

'M b'e sin raghainn nam macaibh—*Were that the choice of boys* ?—S.O. 146ᵇ38.

Bidh an aodnaibh 'gan sgròbadh—*Their faces will be scratched* : —ib. 50.

§ 75.

The vowel changes in the gen. sing. of mas. -o- and fem. -a-stems may for convenience of comparison be placed side by side :

				mas.	fem.
1.	à becomes	ài :		gràdh *love*, gràidh ;	làmh *hand*, làimhe.
	a	,.	ai :	cat *a cat*, cait ;	slat *rod*, slaite.
	a	,,	oi :	dall *blind*, doill ;	clach (O.G. cloch) *stone*, cloiche.
	a	,,	ui :	falt *hair*, fuilt.	
2.	ea	,,	ei :	each *horse*, eich ;	creag *crag*, creige.
	ea	,,	i :	ceann *head*, cinn ;	cearc *hen*, circe.
3.	ia	,,	éi :	fiadh *deer*, féidh ;	grian *sun*, gréine.
4.	ua	,,	uai :	uan *lamb*, uain ;	tuagh *axe*, tuaighe.
5.	ò	,,	òi :	òl *drinking*, òil ;	bròg *shoe*, bròige.
	o	,,	oi :	dos *tuft, tassel*, dois.	
	o	,,	ui :	boc *buck*, buic ;	long *ship*, luinge.
6.	ao	,,	aoi :	laogh *calf*, laoigh ;	gaoth *wind*, gaoithe.
7.	eò	,,	iùi :	ceòl *music*, ciùil.	
8.	ìo	,,	ì :	sìol *seed*, sìl ;	crìoch *end*, crìche.
	io	,,	i ;	airgiod, airgead *silver*, airgid.	
9.	ù	,,	ùi :	cùl *back*, cùil.	
	u	,,	ui :	dorus *door*, doruis ;	muc *pig*, muic.
10.	*eu	,,	eòi :	beul *mouth*, beòil.	

§ 76.   **FIRST DECLENSION.**

A. Vocalic Stems v. § 85.

I.

mas.-**o**-stems.   §73, I.

1.   *sing.*   *plural.*
n. bard *a bard*   bàird *bards*
g. bàird *of a bard*   bhàrd *of bards*
d. bàrd (*to*) *a bard*   bàird, bardaibh (*to*) *bards*
v. a bhàird *O bard*   a bhàrda *O bards*

dual n. dà bhàrd : g. dà bhàird.

ADDITIONAL EXAMPLES :

à into **ài**   àgh *luck*   **a** into **oi**   crann *tree*, croinn
            àl *brood*   (and crainn)
            bàs *death*   dall *blind*, doill
            blàr *a plain*   gad *wythe*, goid
            càl *kale*   Gall *Lowlander*, Goill
            ceàrd *tinker*
            gàradh *garden*   **ao** into **aoi**   caol *a strait*
            gràdh *love*   fraoch *heath*
            ràmh *oar*   laoch *hero*
                                                               laogh *calf*   laoigh
a into **ai**   bad *tuft*   maor *officer*
            cuan *ocean*   saor *carpenter*
            duan *poem*
            feasgar *evening*   **ò** into **òi**   bròn *sorrow*
            garadh (& garaidh)   dreòs *blaze*
                        den   fòd (& fàd) *turf*
            monadh *moor*   gleòs *lamentation*
            òran *song*   lòn *meadow*
            saoghal *world*   nòs *custom*
            sluagh (slògh) *people*
                pl. slòigh   **o** into **oi**   àros *house*, àrois
            sodal *flattery*   dos *tuft, tassel*, dois
            tarbh *bull*   (pl. dois, dosan, & duis)
            polysyllables in -**ach**   pronn *coarsest part of*
            balach *boy*   *oatmeal*, proinn (&
            òglach *youth*   pruinn)
            diminutives in -**an** § 7, II., 3

D

	ù into ùi cùl *back*
a into i mac *son*, mic	dùn *castle*
	rùn *secret*
	sùgh *sap*
	u into ui dorus *door*, doruis,
	pl. dorsan
	lus *herb* – *plant*
	rud *thing*, ruid

2	*Sing.*	*Pl.*	*Dual.*
a into ui	n. càrn *a cairn*	cùirn	n. dà chàrn
	g. cùirn	chàrn	g. dà chùirn
→	d. càrn	cùirn, càrnaib	
	v. a chùirn	a chàrna	

---

a into ui	alt *joint*	calbh *hazel shoot* (and cailbh)
	allt *brook*	calg *prickle*
	balg *wallet*	car *turn*
	ball *member*	clag *bell*, glac (Lewis)
	balt *welt of shoe*	

ò into ui	nòs *beastings*	
	bòrd *plank*	
	còrd *rope*	
	còrn *cup*	
	dòrn *fist*	
	òrd *hammer* (pl.	
	ùird, òrdan)	
	sòrn *flue*	

o into ui	boc *buck*	ploc *round mass* (pl. plocan)
	bonn *foundation*	poll *hole* (puill & pollan)
	broc *badger*	port *harbour* (pl. puirt & portan)
	brod *goad*	pronn (& proinn) *coarsest part of*
	com *chest, breast*	*oatmeal*
	conn *reason*	prop *prop* (pl. pruip & propachan)
	cnoc *knoll*	sgolb *splinetr*
	(pl. cnuic & cnocan)	sgonn *block, lump, crowd*
	cor *condition*	sloc *pit*
	corp *body*	soc *snout*
	crodh *cattle*	sonn *stake, cudgel*
	dos *tuft, tassel*, dois	sop *wisp* (pl. suip & sopan)

droll *tail*, also droill
falt *hair*
fonn *land*
gob *beak*
gorn *ember*
lod *puddle*
lonn *choler* (luinn and lonna)
moll *chaff*
olc *evil*

spong *sponge* pl. spuing & spogan)
stoc *stock*
tolg *hollow*
toll *hole* (pl. tuill & tollan)
tolm *mound*
tom, *round hillock* (pl. tuim & toman)
tonn *wave*, tuinn & tuinne (pl. tuinn, tuinne, tonna, tonnan), gob na (=nan) tuinne the *sea-edge*
torc *boar*

3.	Sing.	Pl.	Dual.
ea into i	n. ceann *head*	cinn	n. dà cheann
	g. cinn	cheann	g. dà chinn
	d. ceann	cinn, ceannaibh	
	v. chinn	a cheanna	

---

biadh *food*, bìdh (also bidhe)
breac *trout*, bric
ceap *block*, cip, pl. cip, ceapa, -an
craiceann *skin*, pl. cracne & craicnean
fear *man*, fir
geall *pledge*, gill
meall *lump*, mill, pl. mill & meallan
meann *kid*, minn
muileann *mill*, muilinn, pl. muileannan & muilnean, muiltean
nead *nest*, nid (f. in Argyll)
preas *bush*, pris
raigeann *obstinacy*, raiginn
sailleann *weavers' paste*, saillinn

Polysyllables in -**each**, unaccented, and of uncertain origin § 124 may be included here :

baisteach *baptist*, baistich
cinneach *heathen*, cinnich
cinneadh *clan*, cinnidh
cléireach *cleric*, cléirich

coigreach *stranger*, coigrich
coileach *cock*, coilich
fitheach (m.f.) *raven*, fithich
gaisgeach *hero*, gaisgich

ea into **ei** breitheamh *judge*, pl. breitheamha, -an, -nan
buideal *cask*
càirdeas *relationship*
caoibhneas *kindness*
ceàrd *tinker*, cèird, cèaird,
    pl. ceàrdan
ceart *right*
cineal *race*, O.O. cinél
cuilean *puppy*

dearg *red colour*
each *horse*
eilean *island*
ministear *minister*
neart *strength*, neirt & nirt
òigear *a youth*, òigeir
searg *puny creature*, seirg,
    & searga, pl. seargan

èa into **èi** nèamh *heaven*, nèimh & nèimhe, pl. nèamhan

eu into **éi** ceum *step*, céim (& ceuma, v. u-stems §84)
eug *death*, éig
sgeun *shyness*, sgéin & sgèin

seun *amulet*, séin & sèin
treun *warrior*, tréin

eò into **iùi** ceòl *music*, ciùil (& ceòil)
seòl *sail*, pl. siùil

seòl *method*, pl. seòlan

eu into **eòi** beul *mouth*, beòil (& béil), § 5, 3
deur *tear*, deòir
eun *bird*, eòin
fairleas (fairleus) *object on skyline*, fairleois
feur *grass*, feòir
gèadh (O.G. géd) *goose*, geòidh
gleus *order*, gleòis (& gleusa)
leud *breadth*, leòid
leus *torch*, leòis
meur *finger*, meòir
neul *cloud*, neòil
seud *jewel*, pl. seòid, seudan
sgeul *story*, sgeòil, sgéil, sgéile, pl. sgeòil, sgeulan

ia into **éi** bian *hide*, béin
cliabh *creel*, cléibh
Dia *God*, Dé, pl. Diathan (Dée, Déith)
fiach *debt*, féich, pl. féich, fiachan
iasg *fish*, éisg
riasg *fen*, réisg

ia into **eoi** cias *fringe*, ceòis pl. ciasan

ia into **ei** lias *hut*, leis

io into **i** lìon *net*, lìn   sìol *seed*, sìl

io into **i** airgiod *silver*, airgid
craicionn *skin*, craicinn

In disyllabic words like the last two examples, the variation of the final vowel or diphthong, apart from such examples as cinél § 76, 3 and diminutives in -**an**, is for the most part a matter of orthography. The only phonetic alternation is between ə and əi.

§ 77.   II.

mas-**io**-stems
(sometimes fem.)
Indeclinable in singular

1 Nouns ending in -**air** (Lat.- **arius** § 135). The singular sometimes retains original -**e**, the pl. ends in -**ean** :

cabhsair *causeway*	forsair *forester*
cabsdair *curb, bit*	gàradair *gardener*
cealgair *hypocrite*	gunnair *gunner*
ceileadair *trustee*	mucair *swineherd*
clàrsair *harper*	òsdair *host*
cùbair *cooper*	pacair *packman*
cungadair *apothecary*	pìobair *piper*
dannsair *dancer*	reachdair *lawgiver*
dealbhadair *painter*	sealgair *hunter*
dorsair *porter*	seòladair *sailor*
feadair *whistler*	seudair *jeweller*
feòladair *butcher*	teachdair *messenger*

2 Nouns ending in -**e** (Lat. -**ius,-iom**). The regular plural adds -**an** :

céile *spouse*	impire *emperor*
ceileiriche *warbler*	maraiche *seaman*
cleasaiche *performer*	pàisde m.f. *child*
cridhe *heart*, pl. cridheachan	ràmhaiche *rower*
cuaille *club* (pl. also -achan)	reithe *ram*, pl. reitheachan
duine *man*, pl. daoine	saduiche m.f. *brush, duster*
guidhe m.f. *prayer*, pl. guidh-	snìomhaiche *spinner*
eachan *curses*	uisge *water* (pl. & uisgeachan)

A few indeclinable monosyllables may be classed with the foregoing :

gnè f. *kind*	ré m.f. *moon*
nì m. *cattle*	tì m. *person*
ni m. *thing*, pl. nithean, nith-	tì m. *earnest intention*
eanna	

§ 78. **SECOND DECLENSION.**

I.

fem.-**ā**-stems

Sing	Plural.	Dual.
n. làmh *hand*	làmhan	n. dà làimh
g. làimhe	làmh	g. dà làmh
d. làimh	làmhan	
v. a làmh	a làmhan	

Thuit a dhà làimh ri a thaobh—*His hands fell to his side*—N.G.P. **369**

Additional examples :

à into **ài** màg *paw*, màige
 tàn (recte tàin) *cattle*, tàine : S.O. 282a16

a into **ai** adharc *horn*, adhairc(e)
 agh *heifer*, aighe m. D. Ban 170, **149**
 clàrsach (also m.) *harp*, clàrsaich(e)
 gealach *moon*, gealaich(e)
 slat *rod*, slaite
 uaigh *grave*, uaighe
 Also diminitives in -**ag** :
 abhag *terrier*, abhaig(e)
 òrdag *thumb*, ordaig(e)
 sgalag *workman*, sgalaig(e) § 69, 1
 tunnag *duck*, tunnaig(e)
 Also those in **ua** :
 bruach *bank*, bruaich(e)
 cluas *ear*, cluaise
 sguab *sheaf*, sguaibe
 tuagh *axe*, tuaighe

ao into **aoi** baobh *a fury, furious woman*, baoibhe
 craobh *tree*, craoibhe
 gaoth *wind*, gaoithe
 But those in -**achd**, having dropped the original -**ao**,
 -**a** of the gen., are now indeclinable :
 beannachd *blessing*
 cleachd *habit*
 feachd *host*
 fuachd *cold*
 naomhachd *holiness*

a into oi bas *palm of hand*, boise (& baise), pl. basan, basa
cas *foot*, coise, pl. casan
clach *stone*, cloiche, pl. clachan
clann *progeny*, cloinne (pl. clainn, clanna, clainne)
fras *shower*, froise, pl. frasan

ò into òi bròg *shoe*, bròige   cròg *claw*, cròige

o into ui dronn *rump*, druinn, droinn
long *ship*, luinge
lorg *staff*, luirge
tromp *Jews' harp*, truimpe

u into ui muc *pig*, muice muic

ea into i breac *smallpox*, brice
cearc *hen*, circe
leac *flagstone*, lice
neas *weasel*, nise

Also those in **-each :**

buidheach *jaundice*, buidhich
cailleach *old woman*, caillich(e)
misneach (& m.) *courage*, misnich

Also the syncopated forms with dat. like nom.; the
regular pl. adds **-an** to gen, sing :

abhainn *river*, aibhne, pl. aibhnichean
aghann *pan*, aighne, pl. aigheannan, aghannan
aisean *rib*, aisne (pl. & aisnichean)
banais *wedding*, bainse
buidheann *troop*, buidhne (pl. & buidhnichean)
dìsinn *die*, dìsne
eilid *hind*, éilde
gualann, gualainn *shoulder*, guailne, guaille § 85, 2
innis *island, holm*, ìnnse (pl. innsean & ìnnseachan)
ionga *nail, claw*, ingne (pl. & ionganan & ìnean)
maduinn *morning*, maidne
nighean *daughter*, ingne, pl. nigheannan, § 68, 1
obair *work*, oibre (obair), pl. obraichean, oibrichean
oisinn *corner*, oisne
sitheann *venison*, sìthne
sliasaid *thigh*, sléisde (sléisne)
uileann, uilinn, *elbow*, uilne, uille

ea into ei beann *peak*, beinne
creag *crag*, creige
creathall *cradle*, créithle (& creathlach)
cuigeal *distaff*, cuigeil
dealg *pin*, deilge
feall *deceit* (indecl. in sing)
fearg *anger*, feirge
sealg *hunt*, seilge

Also the diminutives in -**eag** :
iteag *feather*, iteig(e)
piseag *kitten*, piseig(e)
roineag *hair*, roineig(e)

ia into éi ciall *sense*, céille .   mias *dish*, mèise, méise
cliath *harrow*, cléithe   pian *pain*, péin(e)
dias *ear of corn*, déise   sgiath *wing*, sgéithe
grian *sun*, gréine   sgian *knife*, sgéine, sgìne,
iach *scream*, éiche   d. sgithinn
iall *thong*, éille   srian *bridle*, sréine
liagh *ladle*, léigh

eu into éi breug *lie*, bréige   reul *star*, réil
breun *stench*, bréine   streup *strife*, stréipe
geug *branch*, géige   treubh *tribe*, tréibh

io into ì cloch *pap*, cìche   sìon *storm*, sìne
crìoch *end*, crìche

i into i airneis *furniture*, airneis
cìr *comb*, cìre
cruit *crowd, harp*, cruite : O.G. crot, W. crwth
dris *brier*, drise
éigh *cry*, éighe : O.G. egem
fail, foil, *stye*, faile, foile : old-g-stem, d.p. failgib
féill *festival*, féille : O.G. féil, L. vigilia
foill *deceit*, foille : O.G. foile
fùirneis *furnace*, fùirneis : E.
guit *fan*, guite
igh *tallow*, ighe : M.G. itha, *Laws*
dealbh, deilbh *form*, deilbhe
sealbh, seilbh *possession*, seilbhe

The last **two examples** (with others in this list) show
a leaning to a palatalised dat. sing, as nom.

eo into ì deoch *drink*, dighe (and dibhe)

§ 79.

The following -ā- stem, bean *woman* (a labialised guttural, gᵛean, gᵛeanā, Thess. βανά) is irregular, and is thus declined :

Sing.	*Plural.*
n. bean	mnathan, mnai
g. mnà	bhan, mhnathan
d. mnaoi	mnathaibh
v. a bhean	a mhnathan

§ 80.

The following MAS. nouns of diverse origin, § 72, have the slender increase :

ainm *name*, ainme, pl. ainmean, ainmeannan
bann *belt*, bainne, boinne, pl. bannan, banntan
beur *pinnacle*, béire
calltuinn *hazel*, calltuinne
geinn *wedge*, geinne
gleann *glen*, glinne
glùn *knee*, glùine (& glùin), pl. glùinean, glùintean
im *butter*, ìme
mìr *piece*, mìre, pl. mìrean, mìreannan
nèamh *heaven*, nèimhe (& nèimh), pl. nèamhan
sliabh *hill*, sléibhe, pl. sléibhe, sléibhtean
tigh *house*, tighe, pl. tighean
tìr m.f. *land*, tìre
ugh *egg*, uighe, pl. uighean

§ 81.

The following vowel stems are conveniently classed as :

mas-**a**-stems.
Indeclinable in singular ;
the pl. adds -**chan.**

balla *wall*
bara *barrow*
barra *spike*
cala m.f. *harbour*, (pl. & calaidh, calaichean)
calpa *calf of leg*, pl. calpan, -annan
clobha *pair of tongs*, (pl. & clobhan

bàta *boat*, pl bàtaichean
bogha *bow*

còrsa *coast*, (pl. & corsan)
cupa *cup*
dalta *foster-child*
drola *pot-hook*
rudha *promontory*
sìoda *silk*
tobha *rope*, pl. (& tobhaichean)
tobhta *rower's bench*, (p . & tobhtaichean, tobhtan)

còta *coat*, còtaichean
cùrsa *course*
dannsa *dance*
rola *scroll* (rola and roil)
   pl. rolan
tacsa *support*

§82.

II.

fem.-iă-stems.

Indeclinable in sing.

àithne *command*, pl. àithnte, àitheanta, àitheantan
aithne *knowledge*
boile *rage*
ceirsle *clew*, pl. ceirslean
coille *wood*, pl. coilltean
déile *deal*, pl. déilidh, déileachan
deise *suit*, pl. deiseachan
faire *watch*
fàinne *ring*, pl. fàinnean, fàinneachan
fairge *sea*, pl. fairgeannan, fairgeachan
frìde *tetter*
fuine *a baking*
léine *shirt*, pl. léintean
oidhche *night*, pl. oidhchean, oidhcheannan
seiche *hide*, pl. seichean, seicheannan
slighe *way*, pl. slighean, sligheachan

Also with -e dropped in nom. :

càbhruich *flummery, sowens* fìrinn *truth* tròcair *mercy*

Abstract nouns from adjj., only in sing. :

àirde *height*
bàine *paleness*
bòidhche *beauty*
braise *hastiness*
bréine *rottenness*
buirbe *fierceness*

caise *steepness*
dàine *boldness*
déine *hurry*
doimhne *depth*
duirche *darkness*
foirfe *perfection*

géire *sharpness*	maille *slowness*
làine *fulness*	maoile *baldness*
leisge *laziness*	mìne *smoothness*
luime *bareness*	nàire *shame*
maise *beauty*	sailche *foulness*

§ 83. THIRD DECLENSION

-i- stems, f.m.

sùil f. *eye*

Sing.	Pl.	Dual.
n. sùil	n. sùilean	n. dà shùil
g. sùla	g. shùl	g. da shùla
d. sùil	d. sùilean, sùilibh	
v. a shùil	v. a shùla	

Additional Examples :—

Fem.

bàthaich (and bàthach) *byre*, bàthcha

barail *opinion*, barala

buaidh *victory*, buadha, buadhach, buaidhe

buain *reaping*, buana

coluinn *body*, colna, colla

cuid *portion*, coda (codach)

dàir *pairing of cattle*, dàra

dùthaich *country*, dùthcha

feadhainn *troop, people*, feadhna

feòil *flesh*, feòla

fiacaill *tooth*, fiacla

fuil *blood*, fola

leapaidh *bed*, leaptha, leapa

mil *honey*, meala

mòine (O.G. mòin) *peat*, mòna

muir *sea*, mara

Samhuinn *Hallowtide*, Samhna

sròin *nose*, sròna (& sroine)

tòin (tòn) *bottom*, tòna (& tòine)

tràigh *shore*, tragha

uaimh *cave*, uamha (& uaimhe)

Mas.

braim (and bram) *crepitus ventris*, brama, pl. bramannan

cliamhuinn *son-in-law*, cleamhna

cnàimh *bone*, cnàmha

druim *back*, droma

fàidh *prophet*, indeclinable (O.G. fàdha) g.p. fàdh, fàth, n. pl. fàidhe, fàidhean

gamhuinn *steer*, gamhna

greim *hold*, grama (and greime)

samhuil *likeness*, samhla, samhladh, g.s.m. of foregoing is assumed as a new -o- stem § 85.

Sùil air son sùla, agus fiacail air son fiacla—*An eye for an eye and a tooth for a tooth*:—Math. v. 38

§ 84.   **FOURTH DECLENSION**

-**u**- Stems.

guth m. *voice*, pl. -an, (-annan)

Sing.	*Pl.*	*Dual.*
n. guth	guthan (guthannan)	dà ghuth
g. gutha	ghuth	dà ghutha
d. guth	guthan	
v. a ghuth	a ghutha	

Additional Examples :

1 *Mas.*

àm *time*	dreach *form*
bàrr *top*	driog *drop*
bat (and bata) *stick*	èarr *end*
beach *bee*	feart *quality*
beachd *notice*	feum *need*
beum *stroke*	fiamh *awe*
blog *start*	fiodh *timber*
bior *spit*	fìon *wine*
bùth *shop*	fios *knowledge*
brath *betrayal*	fleadh *feast*
call *loss*	freumh *root*
cath *battle*	gàt *bar of iron*
ceò *mist*	gath *sting*
ceòb *dark nook*	gean *good humour*
ciont *fault*	geòb *wry mouth*
cleòc *cloak*	geum *low*
clòdh *a print*	giall *hostage*
cnead *sigh*	gliong *clink*
cneas *skin*	gnìomh *deed*
corc *fairy, bull*	pl. gniomhtharra,
creadh *clay, body*	-arran
creamh *gentian, garlic*	là *day*, latha, pl. làithean
crios *girdle*	lagh *law*
crobh *hand*	leum *leap*
dag *pistol*	lìomh *polish*
dealbh *picture*	loch *lake*
dog *junk*	lonn *anger*
dram *dram*	meas *fruit*

mìog *smile*
mionn *oath*
mìos *month*
nuall *lamentation*
òb *creek*
peann *pen* (& pinn)
reang *rank*
reann *star*
ròp *rope*
roth *wheel*
seadh *sense*
sèap *long tail*
searg *weakling*
seot *short tail*
seun *charm*
sgread *screech*
sgeamh *disgust*
sgreuch *scream*

sgrios *ruin*
sliochd *seed*
slios *side*
snàth *thread*
sneachd *snow*
snìomh *spinning*
speach *blow*
speal *scythe*
spleadh *romance*
sreath *series*
sruth *stream*
sùgh *sap*
tàrr *belly*
teud *string*
tnùth *envy*
tòrr *hill*
tràth *time*
treud *flock*

The following have (in addition to regular g.s. and n.p.) forms like I. Decl.

dealbh	seun		
feum	sruth		
geum	sùgh		
leum	teud		
lonn	treud		
reann			

The following have also in g.s. forms like II. Decl. :—

beum	sleagh
dealt	srad
giall	srann
lios	treubh
sgeamh	

With syncope : anam m. *soul*, anma, pl. anman, anmanna

---

2 *Fem.*

àth *kiln*
beus *custom*
ceàrn *region*
ciabh *tress*
clob *deer's hair*
corr *heron*

criadh *clay*
dealt *dew* (& m.)
deoch *drink*, (dibhe)
ealt *covey, drove*
eang *foot*
earb *roe*

geàrr *hare*   seàrr f. m. *sickle*
giall *jaw*   sgeamh *polypody*
lach *duck*   sleagh *spear* (pl. sléigh)
lios *garden* (& lise)   smeur *blackberry*
luath *ashes* (&   sneadh *nit*
    luaithe, luathainn)   speach *wasp*
luch *mouse*   srad *spark*
mealg *milt*   srann *snore*
mìol *louse*   steud *race*
modh *manner*   treubh *tribe* (& tréibhe)
pìob *pipe*

The following are indeclinable in sing :

Mas.	*Fem.*
reachd *law*	beatha *life*, pl.
beò *life-time*	beathannan
dream *tribe, people*	cnò *nut*, pl. cnothan
smachd *authority*	deò *breath*
sprochd *gloom*	gleò *fight*, pl.
teachd *arrival*	gleothan
uchd *breast*	màla *bag*

§ 85.   FIFTH DECLENSION

B. Consonantal Stems.

1. *Stems in a guttural.*

Usual Pl. *-ichean.*

Cathair f. *a chair*

Sing.	Pl.	Dual.
n. cathair	cathraichean	n. dà chathair
g. cathrach	chathraichean	g. dà chathrach
d. cathair	cathraichean	
v. a chathair	a chathraiche	

Many guttural stems originated from fem. -à- stems *e.g.* dál *tryst*. The dat. sing. dàil became the nom., and the gen. sing. dàla was augmented by **ch** thus becoming dàlach.

Additional Examples :

Fem.

acair *anchor*, acrach, pl. acraichean

anail *breath*, analach (& anaile), pl. anailean : O.G. anál, W. anadl

caora *sheep*, caorach, pl. caoraich, g. caorach, d. caoraich & caoiribh : cù ri caoiribh :—D, Ban 4, 1, cáirib S.R. **3754**

còir *right*, còrach (& còire), pl. còraichean, còirichean, còirean.

cruaidh *steel*, cruadhach, pl. cruadhaichean

cuid *part*, codach, pl. codaichean

dàil *meeting*, dàlach, pl. dàlaichean : O.G. dál, W. dadl

dinneir *dinner*, dinnearach, pl. dinneireachan, dinneirean

faidhir *fair*, faidhreach, pl. faidhrichean

inneir *dung*, inneireach

iuchair *key*, iuchrach, pl. iuchraichean

làir *mare*, làrach (& làire), pl. làraichean, làiridhean, làiridhnean

lasair *flame*, lasrach (& lasair), pl. lasraichean : O.G. lasair, lassar

litir *letter*, litreach, pl. litrichean

luachair *common rushes*, luachrach

machair *plain*, machrach, macharach, pl. machraichean

mala *eyebrow*, malach, pl. malaichean, mailghean, malaidhean

measair *dish*, measrach, pl. measraichean

muinntir *household*, muinntireach (& muinntire) : O.G. muinter

nathair *snake*, nathrach, pl. nathraichean

peasair *pease*, peasrach, pl. peasraichean

pònair *beans*, pònarach

sàil *heel*, sàlach (& saile) pl. sàilean, sàiltean : O.G. sál, W. sawdl

saothair *toil*, saothrach, pl. saothraichean : O.G. saothar

srathair *pack-saddle*, srathrach (& srathaire), p . srathraichean : O.G. srathar, W. ystrodyr

suipeir *supper*, suipeireach (& suipeire), pl. suipeirean

urchair *a shot*, urchrach (& urchaire), pl. urchraichean : **O.G.** urchur

Mas.

rìgh, indecl., *king*, pl. rìghrean, from rìg-rad *king-folk*

In a few guttural stems, mostly obsolete, the old genitive singular is assumed as a new nominative :

aire m. *chief*, airech   hence   airech m. *watch*

ceò n. *mist*, ciach   ,,   ceathach m. *mist*

dair f. *oak*, darach	hence	darach m. *oak*	
dé *smoke*, diad	,,	deatach f. *smoke*	
eó *salmon*, iach	,,	iach m. *salmon*	
scé *whitethorn*, sciach	,,	sgitheach m. *hawthorn*	

2. *Stems in a Nasal.*

Many of the stems, like ainm, beum, ceum, breitheamh, have passed (except the plural) into other declensions. The following examples show forms more or less true to their origin :

àra f. *kidney*

	Sing.	Pl.
n.	àra	àirnean (& àran)
g.	àrann	àra
d.	àrainn	àirnean, àirnibh
v.	a àra	a àirnean

gobha m. *smith*

	Sing.	Pl.
n.	gobha (& gobhainn)	goibhnean
g.	gobhann	ghobhann
d.	gobhainn	goibhnibh
v.	a ghobha (& ghobhainn)	a ghoibhnean

Alba f. *Scotland*, g. Albann, d. Albainn

bò f. *cow*, g. bà, boin, d. boin, bò, v. a bhò, pl. n. bà, g. bò, d. bà

brà f. *quern*, g. brathann, pl. bràthntan

brù f. *belly*, g. bronn, d. broinn, v. a bhrù, pl. n. brùthan, g. bhronn, d. bronnaibh, v. a bhrùtha

cù m. *dog* (like-o-stem), g. coin, d. cù, v. a choin, pl. n. coin, g. chon, d. coin, v. a. chona

dìle f. *flood*, g. dìleann (& dìlinn), d. dìlinn

(Éire) Éirinn f. *Ireland*, g. Éireann, d. Éirinn ; Srath Éireann, *Strathearn*, *Strath Dearn*

guala, gualainn, f. *shoulder*, g. gualann, gualainn, guailne, guaille, d. gualainn, pl. n. guailnean, guaillean, d. guaillibh

lach f. *wild-duck* (u-stem), pl. lachainn(ean), and lachaidh, lachaichean

leac f. *cheek*, g. leacann ; hence leacann f. *hillside*

lite f. *porridge*, g. litinn

luch f. *mouse*, g. luchann, luchainn, lucha, luchaidh, d. luchainn

lurg f. *shank*, g. lurgann (which becomes nom.), luirg (also nom.) pl. luirgne(an), luirginn

naoidhean m. *infant* : O.G. nóidin, g. nóiden

talamh m. *earth*, g. fem. talmhainn (& talaimh), pl. talmhan, talmhnan, talmhainnean

triath *sea, wave*, g. treathan ; hence treathan n. *wave*

---

3. *Stems in a Dental.*

bràigh m. *neck, brae*, g. bràghad (& bràighe), pl. bràigheachan, bràighde ; hence bràghad m. *neck*

tràigh f. *seashore*, g. tràghad (& tragha, tràighe), pl. tràighean ; hence tràghadh m. *ebbing*

teanga f. *tongue*, g. teangadh, d. teangaidh, pl. teangan, teangannan ; hence teangadh f. *tongue*, teangaidh, pl. teangaidhean

Similarly from O.G. fiche *a score*, g. fichet, comes fichead m. *a score, twenty*

The following datives of dental stems are used as nominatives, and are indeclinable :

O.G. cara m. *friend*, g. carat, d. carait ;   hence G. caraid m.
     drui m. *druid*, g. druad, d. druidh ;   ,,   druidh m.
     fili m. *poet*, g. filed, d. filidh ;   ,,   filidh m.
     luch f. *mouse*, g. luchad, d. luchaidh ;   ,,   luchaidh f.
     nàma m. *enemy*, g. nàmad, d. nàmaid   ,,   nàmhaid m.

Many fem. dental stems in -e- pass into the -ià- declension :
léine *shirt* (§53), seiche *hide*, slighe *way*, troigh *foot*; but teine *fire*, d.s. teinidh

Others like beatha, pass into -u- stems :
ciont *fault*, g. cionta, is from cinta, acc. pl. of cin, cinad § 84

---

4. *Stems of relationship in -r-*

athair m. *father*, d.v. athair, g. athar, pl. aithriche, aithrichean

bràthair m. *brother*, g. bràthar, pl. bràithrean, bràithre

màthair f. *mother*, g. màthar, pl. màthraichean

piuthar f. *sister*, g. peathar, d. piuthair, v.a phiuthair, pl. n.
peathraichean, v. a pheathraiche

seanair m. *grand-father*, pl. seanairean

seanmhair f. *grand-mother*, pl. seanmhairean

§ 86.   EXPRESSIONS USED AS NOUNS.

Familiar expressions—proverbs, verbs, nouns, pronouns,
adjectives, and adverbs—are frequently used substantively,
either loosely as **amorphous** cpds., or crystallised into regularly
declined nouns :

1. *Verbs* :

Cha d'rinn **Theab** (§160, 4) riamh sealg—'*Almost*' *never got
game* :—N.G.P. 99.

Cha deach **Theab** riamh le creig—'*Almost*' *never went over a rock* :—
ib. 92, cf. H.B.

Cha dean **Tiugainn** (§160, 5) ceum, 's cha do chailleadh **Theab**
—'*Come on*' *won't move, and* '*almost*' *was never lost* :—ib. 94

Cha dean **tapadh leis an fhìdhleir** am fìdhleir a phàidheadh
—'*Thank you*' *won't pay the fiddler* :—ib. 94

Bha **beir 's cha bheir** aige—*It was* '*catch and won't catch*' *with
him* :—ib. 56

Fear ri **geallam 's cha tòram** (§5, 2 ; §32, 2)—*A man of* '*I'll
promise and not perform*' :—S.O. 147ᵇ41.

Bu '**shaoil leam**' gu'n tigeadh e—'*Me thought*' *he would come*:—
McKay 17

Mar shaoil leis—*as he thought* :—Am F.C. 275, 187

Ged **shaoil leis** gu'm fàgadh a neo-airidheachd e gun tròcair—
*Though he thought his unworthiness would leave him without
mercy* :—Fois 37

Na bu **tig an la** dhùisgeas tu—*May it not be* '*the day will come*'
when you will waken :—Arab I. 68

Is **feudar** dhomh—*I must*   §160, 1

Gun dealachadh 'sam bith eatorra anns **an dol-a-mach**—*With
no difference whatever between them* '*at the outset*' :—Cos. 166

Gun ach **thig 's cha tig** aige—*With but* '*touch and go*' :—Mac Cor.
107

Feuch, is **nèarachd** (§143) an duine a smachdaidhear le 'Dia—
Behold, happy is the man whom God correcteth :—Job. v. 17

Mur bhiodh **mur b'e** cha bhiodh duine beò—*But for* '*were it not,*'
no man would be alive :—N.G.P. 320

2. *Nouns* :

Canar 'n àm togbhail ris **Bòchdan, mo làmhsa**—*They will say of him at a call to arms, ' A terror, I assure you* :—S.O. 151ʰr.

Bheir thu **car mu thom** do chàch—*You will give the slip to the others*:—Waifs III. 124

Di-beatha f. *welcome*:—Cos. ix. 2: 'Se làn dì do bheatha:—L.C. 38: O.G. Día do bethu—*God is thy life* i.e. *Hail !* :—Str. *Stories*: Bedel, Lk. I. 28

Is e (=E =Día) do bheatha falbh còmhladh rium—*You are welcome to go with me* :—Arab. I. 81

Gu'm b'e mo bheatha fuireach còmhladh ris fhein—*That I was welcome to stay with him* :—ib. II. 4

B'e daonnan **a bheatha**—*He was always welcome* :—Mac Cor. 62

Gu'n cumadh **Ni-maith** bhuam-sa sud—*Providence keep that from me* :—S.O. 284ᵇ14

Bial-sìos air na mnathan, mur faighear 's gach àit iad—*Plague on the women, if they are not found everywhere* :—N.G.P. 63

Car a' mhuiltein m. *somersault*

Eadar-dhà-shian—*time between showers*

A mach as an taigh-fo-thalamh—*out of the underground house*:—Arab. II. 21

Bhur sgrios mu's truagh leam ur càradh—(*Your destruction i.e.*) *May you perish ere I am sorry at your condition* :—S.O. 42ᵃ16

Eadar fheala-dhà 's da-rìreadh—*between jest and earnest* :—Am Fear-Ciùil 283

3. *Pronouns* :

Cha robh **seo** riamh gun mhaoidheadh—' *Here* ' (*Take it*) *was never without grudge* :—N.G.P. 126

Ach gu dé a bha ann gu léir ach **an fhéin, an fhéin, an fhéin**—*But what was in it all but themselves, themselves, themselves*:—Cos. 65

Beireadh air **có 's urrainn**—*Catch him who can* :—Cuairt. 27, 66

4. *Adjectives* :

Cha dìol toileach fiach—' *Willing* ' *pays no debt*:—N.G.P. 97

B'**olc-an-airidh** gu'n deanadh an turadh dolaidh—'*Twere a pity that dry weather should do harm* :—ib. 70

Tha e saor aig **maith-an-airidh**—*It is open to merit* :—D. Ban 334, 79. Bu mhath an airidh :—Arab. I. 39

Dubh-na-h-àmrai—*The Black one of the Almonry* :—S.O. 44ᵇ33

An **Dubh-Chnoideartach**—*The Black* (*galley*) *of Knoydart*:—ib. 47ᵇ33

5. *Adverbs* :

Seamsan m. *hesitation, quibbling* cf. §10 ; san-chan Wi ; san-can
O.R. ; sainchan P.H. ; sán cán—*to and fro* :—O'D Gr. 269

Bhàsaich an **tum-tam** mu phòsadh Iain—*The secret gossip about
John's marriage died down* :—Mac Cormaig 69

§ 87.   **THE ARTICLE 1.**

Sing.

	Mas.	*Fem.*
N.A.	an, am (before p.b.m.f.), an t- (before vowels)	an (before dentals, **f**, and **s** with mutes), a' (before gutturals & p.b.m.), an t- (before **s**)
G.	an, a' (before gutturals & p.b.m.), an t- (before **s**)	na, na h-(before vowels)
D.	an, a' & 'n (before gutturals & p.b.m.f.), an t- (before **s**)	an, a' & 'n (before gutturals and p.b.m.), an t- (before **s**)

Pl.

M. & F.

N.A.D. na, na h- (before vowels)
G.   nan, nam (before p.b.m.f.)

The Dual is the same as the Sing., except in gen. sing. fem. §98, 7.

Initial **a** of the article is always elided after the prepositions
de, do, fo, and generally after other words ending in a vowel.

Sindo, sinda, san are postulated as the original nom. sing.
m., f., and n. of the article.   The slender vowel **i** is weakened to
a in modern Gaelic.   The **d** is hardened into **t** before the aspirated
final **s** of **sindo-s,** which was pronounced **h.**   The initial **s** of
sindo-s is preserved and regularly reappears after the prepositions
a *out of,* **an** *in,* **gu** *unto,* **le** *with,* **ri** *against,* when they govern nouns
having initial **s**, e.g.

as **an t-**saoghal—*out of the world*
anns **an t-**sùil—*in the eye*
gus **an t-**slinnean—*to the shoulder*
leis **an t-**sruth—*down the stream*
ris **an t-**sliabh—*up the hill*

Cha robh iad air an labhairt leis **an t-**Slànuighear—*They had
not been spoken by the Saviour* :—Cos. 158

THE ARTICLE 2.

§88.

Examples of the inflections of the Article before the vowels and the various classes of consonants :

I. MASCULINE NOUNS.

N.		Sing. G.	D.	Plural. N.	G.
Vowels : **a, o, u, e, i.**					
an t-àl	*the brood*	an àil	aig an àl : do'n àl	na h-àil	nan àl
an t-òrd	*the hammer*	an ùird	aig an òrd : do'n òrd	na h-ùird	nan òrd
an t-ùrlar	*the floor*	an ùrlair	aig an ùrlar : do'n urlar	na h-ùrlair	nan ùrlar
an t-each	*the horse*	an eich	aig an each : do'n each	na h-eich	nan each
an t-ionad	*the place*	an ionaid	aig an ionad : do'n ionad	na h-ionaid	nan ionad
Gutturals : **c, g.**					
an cnoc	*the hill*	a' chnuic	aig a' chnoc : do'n chnoc	na cnuic	nan cnoc
an gob	*the beak*	a' ghuib	aig a' ghob : do'n ghob	na guib	nan gob
Dentals and Liquids : **t, d, l, n, r.**					
an toll	*the hole*	an tuill	aig an toll : do'n toll	na tuill	nan toll
an dorn	*the fist*	an duirn	aig an dorn : do'n dorn	na duirn	nan dorn
an laogh	*the calf*	an laoigh	aig an laogh : do'n laogh	na laoigh	nan laogh
an nasg	*the band*	an naisg	aig an nasg : do'n nasg	na naisg	nan nasg
an riasg	*the fen*	an réisg	aig an riasg : do'n riasg	na réisg	nan riasg
Labials : **p, b, m.**					
am preas	*the bush*	a' phris	aig a' phreas : do'n phreas	na pris	nam preas
am bian	*the hide*	a' bhéin	aig a' bhian : do'n bhian	na béin	nam bian
am meann	*the kid*	a' mhinn	aig a' mheann : do'n mheann	na minn	nam meann

N.		G.	D.		N.	G.
am fiadh	*the deer*	an fhéidh	do'n fhiadh	aig an fhiadh :	na féidh	nam fiadh

s *pure and with a liquid* : s, sl, sn, sr.

N.		G.	D.		N.	G.
an searg	*the weakling*	an t-seirg	do'n t-searg	aig an t-searg :	na seargan	nan searg
an sloc	*the pit*	an t-sluic	do'n t-sloc	aig an t-sloc :	na slocan	nan slocan
an snìomh	*the spinning*	an-t-snìomha	do'n t-snìomh	aig an t-snìomh :	na snìomha	nan snìomha
an srath	*the strath*	an t-sratha	do'n t-srath	aig an t-srath :	na srathan	nan srathan

s *with a mute* : sb, sg, sm, sp, st.

N.		G.	D.		N.	G.
an sgadan	*the herring*	an sgadain	do'n sgadan	aig an sgadan :	na sgadain	nan sgadan
an smàl	*the snuff of candle*	an smàil	do'n smàl	aig an smàl :	na smàlan	nan smàlan
an spùt	*the spout*	an spùta	do'n spùt	aig an spùt :	na sputan	nan spùt
an stoc	*the trunk*	an stuic	do'n stoc	aig an stoc :	na stuic	nan stoc

§ 89

THE ARTICLE 3.

II. FEMININE NOUNS.

Vowels : a, o, u, e, i.

Sing.					*Plural.*	
N.		G.	D.		N.	G.
an agh (m.)	*the heifer*	na h-aighe	do'n aigh	aig an aigh :	na h-aighean	nan agh
an oisinn	*the corner*	na h-oisne	do'n oisinn	aig an oisinn :	na h-oisnean	nan oisinn
an ulaidh	*the treasure*	na h-ulaidhe	do'n ulaidh	aig an ulaidh :	na h-ulaidhean	nan ulaidh
an éigh	*the cry*	na h-éighe	do'n éigh	aig an éigh :	na h-éighean	nan éigh(achan)
an iall	*the thong*	na h-éille	do'n éill	aig an éill :	na h-iallan	nan iall

Gutturals : c, g.

a' chearc	*the hen*	**na circe**	do'n chirc	aig a' chirc :	na cearcan	nan cearc
a' ghairm	*the call*	**na gairme**	do'n ghairm	aig a' ghairm :	na gairmean	nan gairm

Dentals *and liquids* : t, d, l, n, r.

an tàir	*the reproach*	**na tàire**	do'n tàir	aig an tàir :	na tàirean	nan tàir
an dias	*the braird*	**na déise**	do'n déis	aig an déis :	na diasan	nan dias
an lach	*the duck*	**na lacha**	do'n lach	aig an lach :	na lachan	nan lach
an nathair	*the snake*	**na nathrach**	do'n nathair	aig an nathair :	na nathraichean	nan nathrach
an roinn	*the portion*	**na roinne**	do'n roinn	aig an roinn :	na roinnean	nan roinn

Labials : p, b, m.

a' phian	*the pain*	**na péine**	do'n phéin	aig a' phéin :	na piantan	nam pian
a' bhreug	*the lie*	**na bréige**	do'n bhréig	aig a' bhréig :	na breugan	nam breug
a' mheidh	*the balance*	**na meidhe**	do'n mheidh	aig a' mheidh :	na meidhean	nan meidh

f.

an fhàilte	*the welcome*	**na fàilte**	do'n fhàilte	aig an fhàilte :	na fàiltean	nam fàilte

s *pure and with a liquid* : s, sl, sn, sr.

an t-sùil	*the eye*	**na sùla**	do'n t-sùil	aig an t-sùil :	na sùilean	nan sùl
an t-slat	*the rod*	**na slaite**	do'n t-slait	aig an t-slait :	na slatan	nan slat
an t-snaois	*the slice*	**na snaoise**	do'n t-snaois	aig an t-snaois :	na snaoisean	nan snaois
an t-sràid	*the street*	**na sràide**	do'n t-sràid	aig an t-sràid :	na sràidean	nan sràid

s *with a mute* : sb, sg, sm, sp, st.

an sguab	*the sheaf*	**na sguaibe**	do'n sguaib	aig an sguaib :	na sguaban	nan sguab
an smid	*the syllable*	**na smide**	do'n smid	aig an smid :	na smidean	nan smid
an spòg	*the claw*	**na spòige**	do'n spòig	aig an spòig :	na spògan	nan spòg
an stéidh	*the basis*	**na stéidhe**	do'n stéidh	aig an stéidh :	na stéidhean	nan stéidh

§ 90.   **THE USE OF THE DEF. ARTICLE.**

The place of the Article is at the beginning of a simple substantive group, §3.

The following are some examples of the use of the Art. :

I. The Art. is not used :

  1. with a governing noun :

    ceòl **nan** teud—*the music of the strings* :—Ross 27
    gu ceann Leitir Blàr **a**' Chaorthainn—*to the head of the
      Slope of the Field of the Rowan* :—S.O. 41ᵇ21

  2. with a proper name :

    Mac Righ Seumas—*The son of King James* :—Ross 26
    an làmhan Chlann-Dòmhnuill—*in the hands of Clan
      Donald* :—S.O. 41ᵇ14

    except occasionally for emphasis :

    Cho làidir ris a' Gharbh Mac Stàirn—*As strong as the
      famous Garv the son of Starn* :—N.G.P. 142
        Leam is aithghearr a' chéilidh
        Rinneas mar ris an t-Seumas—
          *Short methought was the interview
          I had with the famous James* :—S.O. 47ª41
    Sliochd an Alasdair Gharaich—*The seed of the famous
      Alasdair Carrach* :—S.O. 43ᵇr

II. The Article is used :

  1. with a Demonstrative Pronoun accompanying a noun :
    an fhéill so—*this fair* :—Ross 73

  2. with a noun introduced by the Interrogative Pronouns **co,
    cia, ciod e** :

    Cò e **am** fear sin a théid suas ?—*Who is that man that shall
      ascend* ? :—Metr. Ps. xxiv. 3
    Cia **an** rathad a ghabhas mi?—*Which road shall I take* :—
      Forbes 281

  3. with abstract nouns : *? for emphasis ?*

    Ciod i **an** fhìrinn ?   *What is truth* ? :—John xviii. 38, cf.
      § 119, 1
    Agus is i so **a**' bheatha mhaireannach— *And this is eternal
      life* :—ib. xvii. 3

what the road for me ?

(*This is the life eternal*)
There is but the one eternal life, the prophet only
say, so the definite article is appropriate

B'e 'n t-aighear 's an sulas
Bhi sìnte—
It were joy and gladness
To be stretched out :—S.O. 107ᵃt

Ciod i a' ghairm éifeachdach ? *What is effectual calling ?* :—
Catm. 31

4. with common nouns to express a genus or species :

Fhuair iad a mach le cràdh 'us deòir
Gu'n deach **an** duine bhreith gu bròn—
They found out with anguish and tears
That man was born to sorrow :—Clarsach 55
Fhir bu chiùine na **mh**aighdeann
'S bu ghairge na 'n lasair—
O thou who wert milder than maiden,
And fiercer than flame :—S.O. 49ᵇ33

Following **tha** construed with **ann** the article may indicate an individual of a species § 177, 1, (2) :

Cha n'eil annad ach **an** dearg shlaoightire— *You are but an arrant knave* :—Arab. I. 39

5. with adj. patronymics to signify one member of a clan or native of a district :

'S co neònach leams' **am** Frisealach
'S **am** Bàideanach bhi deanamh réit—
It is as amazing to me that Fraser
And the Badenoch man are reconciled:—S.O. 150ᵃt
Gè beag orts' **an** Caimbeulach dubh— *Though you despise black Campbell* :—ib. 133a3
'S ged bu ghuineach **na** Duibhnich— *And though the Campbells were keen* :—S.O. 43ᵃ32

but cf.

'S fad' bhios Duibhnich gun urram— *Long will Campbells be dishonoured* :—ib. 44ᵃ24
Na Camshronaich mheanmnach bu gharg air **an** tòir—
The spirited Camerons who were rough in pursuit:—D. Ban 208, 26

6. with names of (a) cities, (b) countries, (c) districts, (d) continents :

(a) Coltas Hector Mòr **na** Tròidhe,

'S nan gaisgeach bha 'm feachd **na** Ròimhe—
Like great Hector of Troy,
And the heroes that were in the army of Rome :—S.O. 156^b13

Tha suaicheantas **na** h-Alb' agaibh— *Ye have the badge of Scotland* :—D. Ban 270, 65

But exceptions are frequent :

Tha '**n** Albainn gu léir, '**s an** Lunnainn—*That are in all Scotland and in London* :—ib. 332, 58

Dun-éideann still preserves a sense of the founder's name, and hence does not take the art.

(b) Air astar do'**n** Ghearmailt—*On the way to Germany*:— D. Ban 260, 106

Ag òl air fìon **na** Spàinnt'—*Quaffing the wine of Spain*:—ib. 376, 96

Rìgh **na** Fràinge—*The King of France* :—Ross 83

Gliocas eagnuidh **na** Gréige—*A fine knowledge of Greece:*—L.C. 135

(c) Thachair so '**san** Ros ri linn Bhonaparte—*This happened in Ross (of Mull) in the time of Buonaparte* :— MacCor. 39

(d) Stòras **na** h-Eòrpa—*the wealth of Europe* :—Ross 87 ainnir **na** Roinn-Eòrpa—*the maiden of Europe*:—ib. 62

7. with names of languages :

Tha **L**aideann . . . thràilleil
Do'**n** Ghàidhlig chòir,
'**San** Athen mhòir
Bha **Gh**reugais còrr na tìm—
   Latin is subservient
   To honest Gaelic ;
   In great Athens
   Was Greek sometime :—S.O. 106^a17-22
Am faigh **a**' Ghàidhlig bàs—*Will Gaelic die ?* :—Clar. 18
Anns **a**' Bheurla chruaidh—*in hard English* :—L.C. 135

8. with divisions of time :

Am fear nach cuir '**sa**' Mhart cha bhuain e **a's**' t-Fhoghar—
He that does not sow in March will not reap in Autumn :
—N.G.P. 20

'N uair thig **a**' Bhealltainn,
'S **an** Samhradh lusanach—
When Beltane comes,
And luxuriant Summer :—Ross 45

O bheul **na** h-oidhche
Gu soills' **na** maidne—
From the mouth of night
To the light of morning :—ib. 44

seach bruthainn **a**' Mhaigh—
past the sultriness of May :—ib. 75

aon uair '**sa**' bhliadhna—*once a year* :—C.S.

9. with names of tools and articles in common use :

Cho geur ris **an** ealtainn—*as sharp as a razor* :—S.O.
152^{b}14

'S tric a dh' fhaobhaich **na** sporain
Fhir nach d' fhòghlum **an** onoir—
Thou who hast often despoiled purses,
And has learnt no honour :—ib. 147b34

Bu maith **na h**-airm na bodchrannan—
Cruppers were good weapons :—ib. 150^{b}33

Oran do'**n** Mhusg—*Song to a Musket* :—D. Ban 16
Oran do'**n** Bhriogais—*Song to Trowsers* :—ib. 142
Oran **a**' Bhotail—*Song to a Bottle* :—ib. 296
Comasach air **an** uisge bheatha a dhìteadh—*able to destroy*
whisky :—Ross 41

mac **na** bracha—*the son of malt* :—ib.

10. with names denoting rank or office :

Aon duine a bhiodh am freasdal ris **an** léigh—*Whoever*
would be attending a doctor :—D. Ban 376, 85

an t-ollamh MacIain—*Dr. Johnson* :—Ross 43

11. with names of diseases and vices :

a' chaitheamh—*consumption*
a' bhreac—*smallpox*
iadsan air an robh an tuiteamach—*those who had epilepsy* :—
Math. iv. 24

neach air an robh am pairilis—*one who had paralysis* :—
Mk. ii. 3

Nach fan thu as an eucoir—*Will you not stay from
wrong* ? :—Ross 76

trom air an òl—*heavy on drink* :—C.S.

12. with names expressing customs :
Ag gearradh nan sùrdag—*Cutting capers* :—Clar. 92

§ 91.   **THE ADJECTIVE.**

Adjectives are of two genders, mas. and fem. The plural
is without distinction of gender or case. Mas. -o- and -u- stems
are declined in the singular like nouns of the I. Decl. ; fem. -ā-
stems like nouns of II. Decl. The plural is formed by adding -a
or -e to the nom. sing., e.g. **beag** *small*, pl. beaga; **còir** *just*, pl. còire.
-io-, -iā- stems are indeclinable except that in some, e.g. **fiadhaich**
wild, **inich** *neat*, the g.s.f. may have the slender increase, which
appears also in the first comparative. -i- stems, e.g. **còir** *just*,
are indeclinable in the sing. mas. ; and in the gen. sing. fem.
they have the slender increase, as in the comparative. -u- stems,
e.g. **dubh** *black*, being declined like -o- stems, have in the comparative the slender increase of the gen. sing. fem.

Briefly : in the pl. broad monosyllabic stems have the broad
increase :

Slender monosyllabic stems have the slender (or g.s.f.) increase.

The pl. of polysyllables is the same as the sing.

§ 92.

1. The following are examples of (1) -o- stems ; (2) -i- stems :
   (1) mòr *great*.

	Sing.		Pl.
	Mas.	Fem.	Mas. and Fem.
n.	mòr	mhòr	mòra
g.	mhòir	mòire	mòra
d.	mòr	mhòir	mòra
v.	mhòir	mhòr	mòra

(2) còir *just.*

	Sing.		Pl.
	Mas.	Fem.	Mas. and Fem.
n.	còir	chòir	còire
g.	chòir	còire	còire
d.	còir	chòir	còire
v.	chòir	chòir	còire

2. A noun and an adjective are thus declined together, without the article :

fear m. *man,* an -**o**- stem : beag *small,* an -**o**- stem :

	Sing.	Pl.
n.	fear beag	fir bheaga (feara beaga, old acc.)
g.	(*neart*) fir bhig	fhear beaga
d.	(*aig*) fear beag	fearaibh beaga (fir bheaga, nom.)
v.	a fhir bhig	a fheara beaga

caileag f. *girl* : bheag *small,* both -**a**- stems :

	Sing.	Pl.
n.	caileag bheag	caileagan beaga
g.	(*dealbh*) caileige bige	chaileagan beaga
d.	(*aig*) caileig bhig	caileagaibh beaga
v.	a chaileag bheag	a chaileagan beaga

gille m. *lad,* an-**io**-stem : dubh *black, black-haired,* a -**u**- stem

	Sing.	Pl.
n.	gille dubh	gillean dubha
g.	(*neart*) gille dhuibh	ghillean dubha
d.	(*aig*) gille dubh	gillean dubha
v.	a ghille dhuibh	a ghillean dubha

caile f. *girl,* an -**iā**- stem : mìn *delicate,* an -**i**- stem :

	Sing.	Pl.
n.	caile mhìn	cailean mìne
g.	(*dreach*) caile mìne	chailean mìne
d.	(*aig*) caile mhìn	cailean mìne
v.	a chaile mhìn	a chailean mìne

An adj. qualifying two nouns agrees with the nearest

Eòrna agus peasair mhath—*good barley and pease*
Peasair agus eòrna math—*good pease and barley* :—Munro 176

A collective noun sometimes takes a plural adj.

Clann bheaga—*little children* :—Munro 177
Chuireadh e sunnt air muinntir òga—*It would put gladness in young people* :—D. Ban 240, 42.

An adj. used as a noun is declined like a noun :

mar na doill—*like the blind* : Is. lix. 10
mar dhaoine dalla—*like blind men* :—Lam. iv. 14

3.

When a noun and an adj. are declined together, *with the article*, the adj. is declined in the same way as it is declined with the noun alone, but the aspiration of the adj. is extended in masculine -o-stems to the *dat. sing.* also.

duine m. *man,* an -io- stem ; pl. daoine, and maith *good,* -i-stems ; breac *trout,* mòr *big,* -o- stems.

Without the Article.

	Sing.	*Pl.*
n.	duine maith	daoine maithe
g.	(*neart*) duine mhaith	dhaoine maithe
d.	(*aig*) duine maith	daoinibh maithe

---

n.	breac mòr	bric mhòra
g.	(*neart*) bric mhòir	bhreac mòra
d.	(*aig*) breac mòr	breacaibh mòra

With the Article.

n.	an duine maith	na daoine maithe
g.	(*neart*) an duine mhaith	nan daoine maithe
d.	(*aig*) an duine mhaith	na daoinibh maithe

---

n.	am breac mòr	na bric mhòra
g.	(*neart*) a' bhric mhòir	nam breac mòra
d.	(*aig*) a' bhreac mhòr	na breacaibh mòra

§ 93. COMPARISON OF ADJECTIVES.

1. When the subject is introduced by **is** and a personal pronoun (both of which may be omitted), the relative form of **is** precedes an adjective predicate, the complement of which may be (1) a noun, (2) a relative clause, or (3) a prepositional phrase.

(1) The noun complement is in the nom. without inflection or aspiration.

The adjective may be in the Positive Degree :

Do'n Fìr-eun is **pailte ciall**—*To the Eagle who abounds in sense* :—An t-Òran. 450

Sin am morair bu **mhath feum** dhuinn—*That is the Lord who was good at need to us* :—D. Ban 338, 52

When an adjective is in the First Comparative, and qualified by a word or phrase, the comparison is with a class and is equivalent in force to a superlative :

A' phìob-mhòr as **bòidhche guileag**—*The great pipe which is bonniest in warbling* :—D. Ban 334, 66

Leannan an fhir léith As **farumaiche ceum**—*The grey one's darling, Which is noisiest in step* :—D. Ban 188, 423, § 27

'S tu 's **glaine** 's **cannaiche banaile snuadh**—*Thou art the purest and most sweetly feminine in appearance* :—ib. 206, 5

Am fear as **luaithe làmh**, 's e as **fheàrr cuid**—*Quickest hand gets biggest share* :—N.G.P. 16

(2) Is i bhó fhéin as **luaithe a mhothaicheas** d'a laogh—*The cow is the first to notice her own calf* :—N.G.P. 257

'S i as binne 's as **àirde a sheinneas**—*It is she that plays sweetest and loudest* :—D. Ban 326, 39

Is·e Dia as *cumhachdaiche a tha ann*—*God is the mightiest in existence* :—Munro 65

Thòisich e aig an fhear bu **shine,** agus sguir e aig an fhear a b'**òige**—*He began at the eldest and left off at the youngest* :—Gen. 44, 12

(3) 'S i beinn Nibheis as **àirde an Albainn**—*Ben Nevis is the highest mountain in Scotland* :—Munro 65

So a' chaora as **fheàrr 'nam measg**—*This is the best sheep among them* :—ib.

Is i Màiri as **sine do'n teaghlach**—*Mary is the eldest of the family* :—McB. XIX.

2. When **na** (O.G. indas *than is*) follows the first comparative and introduces a new subject (cf. the above examples) ; or when **is** introduces the first comparative to be followed by **na**, the result is a comparison of superiority between individuals :

Is mise as luaithe na thusa—'*Tis* **I** *that am swifter than* **you** —Munro 63

An truime a' chlach sin na i so ?—*Is that stone heavier than this ?*—ib.

Is binne na gach beus Anail mhic an fhéidh—*Sweeter than any bass viol is the stag's breath* :—D. Ban 170, 141

Gur deirge na'n t-subhag an rudha tha 'd ghruaidh—*Redder than the strawberry is the flush on thy cheek* :—ib. 206, 6

3. But when the principal verb is **tha** (or any verb save **is**), the relative form of **is** is preceded by **na,** and is written **na's** (what is), pres. ; **na bu** (what was), past.

Tha Màiri na's sine na Seònaid—**Mary** *is older than* **Jessie** :— McB. xix.

Che robh riamh sluagh ann na bu ghaisgeile no na bu dìlse na iadsan—*Never was there a people more heroic or faithful than they.*

4. In Modern Irish instead of **na's** the usual form is **ni's,** for **ni is, ni as**—*a thing which is.* **Ni's** is also the usual form in the Gaelic Bible (derived doubtless from Bedel's version) which has spread in common speech, and has come to be regarded as the classical form in Gaelic, e.g.

ainm **ni's** feàrr na ainm mhac agus nighean—*A better name than of sons and daughters* :—Is. lvi. 5.

Agus **ni's** ro phailte gu mòr—*And much more abundant* :— ib. 12, cf. Job iv. 17.

§ 94.

In the following adjective stems is shown the development of the genitive singular feminine, which is, in many instances, identical in form with the abstract noun, and with the First Comparative. The Second Comparative, formed by the addition of **-de** *thereby*, to the First Comparative, changes the final **-e** into **-ide, -id.** An abstract noun, often called the Third Comparative, adds **-ad**, or less frequently **-as,** to the First Comparative.

The Second and Third Comparatives are of rare occurrence, and are lacking in many adjectives ; but where one occurs, both are found.

à into **ài**	bàn	*white,*	g.s.f.	bàine
	làn	*full,*	,,	làine
	slàn	*healthy,*	,,	slàine
a into **ai**	cam	*crooked,*	,,	caime
	cas	*steep*	,,	caise
	fada	*long,*	,,	faide
	fiar	*awry*	,,	(fiaire)
	glan	*clean*	,,	glaine
	glas	*grey*	,,	glaise
	lag	*weak*	,,	laige
	tana	*thin*	,,	taine
ao into **aoi**	caol	*slender*	,,	caoile
	daor	*enslaved*	,,	daoire
	maol	*bald*	,,	maoile
	naomh	*holy*	,,	naoimhe
	saor	*free,*	,,	saoire
a into **oi**	dall	*blind*	,,	doille
	mall	*slow*	,,	moille
ò into **òi**	òg	*young*	,,	òige
o into **oi**	grod	*putrid*	,,	groide
o into **ui**	bog	*soft*	,,	buige
	borb	*fierce*	,,	buirbe
	crom	*crooked*	,,	cruime
	donn	*brown*	,,	duinne
	dorch	*dark*	,,	duirche
	gorm	*blue*	,,	guirme
	lom	*bare*	,,	luime
	moch	*early,*	,,	muiche (& moich
	pronn	*pounded,*	,,	pruinne
	trom	*heavy,*	,,	truime
ù and **ùi**	dùr	*dull*	,,	dùire
	ùr	*fresh,*	,,	ùire
u into **ui**	dubh	*black*	,,	duibhe
ua into **uai**	luath	*swift*	,,	luaithe
ea into **i**	beag	*small,*	,,	bige
	breac	*speckled*	,,	brice
	cinnteach	*certain*	,,	cinntich(e)

E

	dìreach	*straight*	g.s.f.	dìriche
	geal	*white*	,,	gile
	maiseach	*beautiful*	,,	maisich(e)
	ceart	*right*	,,	ceirte
ea into ei	dearg	*red*	,,	deirge
	deas	*ready*	,,	deise
	searbh	*bitter*	,,	seirbhe (& searbha)
	teann	*tense*	,,	teinne
	tearc	*rare*	,,	teirce
eu into éi	beur	*shrill*	,,	béire
	geur	*sharp*	,,	géire
	treun	*strong*	,,	tréine
ia into éi	cian	*distant*	,,	céine
	ciar	*dusky*	,,	céire
	dian	*keen*	,,	déine
	fial	*liberal*	,,	féile
	liath	*hoary*	,,	léithe

					abstract noun.
i into i	binn	*melodious*	g.s.f.	binne	binneas
	còir	*just*	,,	còire	
	glic	*wise*	,,	glice	gliocas
	mìn	*delicate*	,,	mìne	
	tinn	*sick*	,,	tinne	tinneas
io into ì	crìon	*withered*	,,	crìne	
	fìor	*true*	,,	fìre	
io into i	coitchionn	*catholic*	,,	coitchinn(e)	coitcheannas
	fionn	*white*	,,	finne	

§ 95. EXAMPLES OF REGULAR COMPARATIVES.

1. *First—*

Is glice an saoghal a thuigsinn na dhìteadh—*It is wiser to understand the world than to condemn it* :—N.G.P. 254

Is i an dias as truime as ìsle chromas a ceann—*It is the heaviest ear of corn that bends its head lowest* :—ib. 256

Is luaithe gnìomh na tuarasdal—*Work is before (quicker than) wages* :—ib. 264

'S i bu mholaiche na'n lìon—*It was she that was shaggier than flax* :—D. Ban 224, 21

2. *Second*—

Is giorraid an t-slighe cuideachd—*The way is the shorter for company.*

Is tiughaid am brat a dhùbladh—*The mantle is the thicker of being doubled* :—N.G.P. 288

Is giorraid an Gall an ceann a chur dheth—*The Lowlander is the shorter of losing his head* :—ib. 254

Is gloinid am baile an cartadh ud—*The town is the cleaner of that clearing out* :—ib. 254

3. *Third*—

Cha n' eil làmh an Tighearna air dol an giorrad—*The Lord's hand is not shortened* :—Is. lix. 1.

Tha mhin a' dol an daoiread—*Meal is getting dearer* :—Munro 63

Théid gach craobh an ciataichead—*Every tree grows more excellent* :—D. Ban 90, 107

A'dol an suaraichead uime—*Getting more indifferent about it* :—H.B.

Na cuir an suarachas an ni so—*Do not slight this* :—H.B.

A' dol am feabhas, no an olcas—*Getting better, or worse* :—ib.

4. *Fourth*—

Equative comparison is formed by the correlatives **cho . . . agus, cho . . . ri** : the correlatives **cho . . . agus**, imply a verb following ; in **cho . . . ri, ri** governs a noun or pronoun : § 217, 4, § 203, 7

(Air) Cho caillte 's gu'm bheil an duine, cha n-ionann sin 's an diabhul—*However lost man is, that is not the same as the Devil* :—Cos. 123.

Cho caillte ris an diabhul féin—*As lost as the Devil himself* :—ib. 123

Tha ise cho glic riutsa, cho glic agus [a tha] thusa—*She is as wise as thou* :—Munro 63

Saighdear dìleas, agus co làidir ri triùir—*A faithful soldier and as strong as three* :—Cuairt. 27, 68

5. *A few adjectives, when inflected and compared, suffer:*

(a) *Syncope,* § 5 :

bòidheach	*pretty*	g.s.f.	bòidhche
daingeann	*firm*	,,	daingne (& daingeinn)
reamhar	*fat*	,,	reamhra
sleamhuinn	*slippery*		sleamhna

An talamh as roimhre—*the fattest land* :—Cos. 7
'S iad an fheadhainn as roimhre nàdur—*They are the people of richest nature* :—ib. 9.

(b) *Syncope and metathesis,* § 11 :

dìleas	*faithful*	g.s.f.	dìlse, dìsle
ìosal	*low*	,,	ìlse, ìsle
milis	*sweet*	,,	mìlse, mìsle
uasal	*noble*	,,	uaisle, uailse

(c) *Syncope and infection of first syllable,* § 6 :

bodhar	*deaf*	g.s.f.	buidhre (& bodhaire)
cumhang	*narrow*	,,	cuinge
leathan(n)	*broad*	,,	léithne
odhar	*dun*	,,	uidhre, idhre
salach	*foul*	,,	sailche
uasal	*noble*	,,	uaisle, uailse

also the monosyllables:

fliuch	*wet*	,,	fliche
tiugh	*thick*	,,	tighe

6. Examples of **-io, -iā** stems (indeclinable) are :

   eile *other*
   uile *all*

and the past participles :

briste *broken*		sàbhailte *saved*
buailte *struck*		sgaoilte *scattered*

7. Some adjectives suffer no inflection either in declension or comparison, e.g.

   biadhta *fatted* (p.p. pass.)
   blasda *palatable*
   gasda *handsome*
   meata *feeble*
   sona *happy*

8. Some indeclinable adjectives in **-idh, -ail (-eil)** are compared regularly :

> beadaidh *impudent*, beadaidhe
> clìth *left*, clithe
> faoilidh *hospitable*, faoilidhe
> fialaidh *bountiful*, fialaidhe
> foillidh *latent*
> iomchuidh *fit*
> nèamhaidh *heavenly*
> réidh *plain*
> banail *womanly*, banaile, banala
> duineil *manly*, duineala
> fearail *heroic*, fearala
> foilleil *deceitful*, foilleala

9. The following adjectives are indeclinable in the sing. but form the pl. and the First Comparative by adding **a** :

> aithghearr *short*, aithghearra (& aithghiorra)
> beò *alive*, beòtha
> bochd *poor*
> ceàrr *wrong*
> dorch *dark* (dorcha & duirche)
> leamh *importunate* (& leimhe)
> mear *merry* (& meire)
> nochd *naked*
> seamh *mild* (& séimhe)

To these may be added : lugha, dorra, giorra, miosa, §96,1

§ 96.

1. The following are irregularly compared :

	1st Comp.	2nd.	Abstract noun. 3rd.
beag *small*	(lugha	lughaide	lughad)
	bige	bigide	bigead
duilich *difficult*	duilghe	duilghide	duilghead
	(dorra	dorraide	dorrad)
geàrr *short* goirid	giorra	giorraide	giorrad

	1st Comp.	2nd.	Abstract noun. 3rd.
làidir *strong*	(treasa làidire	treasaide làidiride	treasad) làidiread
maith, *good* math	(feàrr	feàirrde fèirde)	feabhas
mòr *great*	mò	mòide	mòid, meud
olc *bad*	(miosa	misde)	olcas
teth *hot*	teoithe	teoithide	teothad

2. The following make the first comparative in **-a**, but want the second and third :

> brèagh *fine*, brèagha, brèaghaiche
> càr *friendly*, càra
> còir *just*, còire, còra (& càra)
> dòigh *likely*, dòcha (& dàcha)
> dùth (dùthoig) *hereditary*, dùcha (dùthcha)
> fagus *near*, faisge
> furas, furasda *easy*, fusa (fasaide, fasad)
> ion *fit*, iona
> ionmhuinn *beloved* (annsa is used as Compar.)
> leathann *broad*, leatha, léithne
> toigh *agreeable*, tocha

§ 97.   EXAMPLES OF IRREGULAR COMPARATIVES.

First—

> Is mò am fuaim na bhuil—*The noise is greater than the effect* :—N.G.P. 280
> Is teotha fuil na bùrn—*Blood is hotter than (fresh) water* :— N.G.P. 288
> Is treasa Tuath na Tighearna—*Tenantry are stronger than Laird* :—N.G.P. 289

Second—

> Is feàirrde cù cù a chrochadh— *A dog is the better of another dog being hanged* :—N.G.P. 238.
> Is mòid rud a roinn— *A thing is the bigger of being shared* :— N.G.P. 281

'S misde mi gu'n d'rinn i m' fhàgail ;
'S b' fheàirrde mi 'm fad 's a dh' fhan i—
  I am the worse that she has left me ;
  I was the better while she stayed :—D. Ban 234, 143

Third—

The so-called Third Comparative is an abstract noun :

  Le bòidhchead a sliosa—*From the beauty of its side* :—
  D. Ban 174, 222.

Idiomatic usages :

  (1) with *cuir* :
    Na cuir an lughad a cliù—*Do not diminish her praise* :—
    Munro 63
    A prìs a chur am mòid—*To put up her price* :—ib.
    Cur anabarra dhreach bòidhcheid air—*Adding a surpassing
    appearance of beauty* :—D. Ban 92, 128
    Am fuaradh chuir ar gluasad an trumad—*The weather that
    made our going heavy* :—S.O. 153^b 34

  (2) with *dol* :
    Tha an duine tinn a' dol am feabhas—*The sick man is
    getting better* :—H.B.

  (3) with *air* : § 188.
    Air fhuairid 's gu'm biodh an t-earrach—*However cold the
    spring might be* :—D. Ban 224, 28
    Air cho fuar 's gu'm biodh an oidhche—*However cold the
    night might be* :—A' Choisir 15
    Air chaisead na leacainn—*However steep the slope* :—D.
    Ban 178, 281
    Air fheabhas gu'm faighear thu—*No matter how you exert
    yourself* :—H.B.
    'S ann air a theothad—*It is rather hot* :—Munro 64
    Air faidead bhur saoghal—*No matter how long you may
    live* :—H.B.

  (4) with *an* :
    An sinead 's an donad mar a bha cuilean a' mhadaidh-
    ruaidh—*The older the worse like the fox's whelp* :—
    N.G.P. 36

§ 98. **NUMERALS.**

Numeral adjectives are either cardinal or ordinal.

1. Cardinal numbers, when unaccompanied by a noun, are preceded by **a**, which aspirates **dà**, but no other numeral.

Before vowels **a** becomes **a h-**, e.g. **a h-aon** *one*, **a h-ochd** *eight*.

Cha téid **a h-aon** dhinn as—*Not one of us will escape* :—Arab. II., 38.
Aon mhìle 's **a h-aon-**, Mìle 's **a h-aon**—1001.
Ni mò a rinn mi cron air **a h-aon** diubh—
Neither have I hurt one of them :—Num. xvi. 15.
Gu **h-aon** de na bailtibh sin— *Unto one of those cities* :—Deut.
iv. 42; xix. 5

2. **Aon** (and **fear**) may be used as pronouns. § 118, 4

Fear de na coin so—*One of these dogs* :—Arab. I. 26, § 98, 5
'S i a **dhà-'s-an-da-fhichead**—'*Tis the " Forty-twa "* (the 42nd Regiment) :—D. Ban 264, 146
Aon bhó a bhristeas an gàradh, 's a dhà dhiag a leumas—
One cow breaks the dyke, and a dozen leap it :—N.G.P. 45.
Foidhidinn nam ban—**a trì**—*Women's patience—till you count three* :—ib. 186.

3. **Aon,** used not strictly as one of a series, but as a pronoun, drops **a h-**, and is declined like an **-o-** stem, m. or f., **an t-aon**, **an aon**, e.g.

Cia **an aon** de threubhan Israeil—*What one is there of the tribes of Israel* ? :—Judg. xxi. 8.
Aon agus **aon**—*one by one* :—Is. xxvii. 12.

4. **Aon** has also an idiomatic distributive use :

Tha mac **an t-aon** aca—*They have each a son* :—Gillies 71.
Tha fear **an t-aon** againn—*We have one* (m) *each* :—ib.
Tha té **an t-aon** againn—*We have one* (f) *each* :—ib.
Rug iad air fear **an t-aon**—*They seized a man each* :—Arab.
I. 105.
Bha damh agus aiseal aige ann an cùil **an t-aon,** taobh ri taobh—*He had an ox and an ass in a stall each, side by side* :—Arab. I. 1.

A réir an t-seana chleachdainn bha bean-an-tighe an geall
air Bonnach-Caluinn **an t-aon** a thoirt do na balachain—
*According to the old custom the housewife was bound to
give the boys a New Year's bannock a-piece* :—MacCor. 13.
Le each meanmnach **an t-aon**, e féin 's a ghille—*With a
spirited horse each, himself and his servant* :—Cuairt. 27, 66.
Dh' fhàg e mìle bonn airgid **an t-aon** againn—*He left us
1000 pieces of silver each* :—Arab. I. 25.

5. A similar distributive use is expressed by the def. art. :

Thug mi dhaibh mìle bonn **am fear**—*I gave them 1000 pieces
each* (or per man) :—ib. 27.
Sheinn na mnathan òran **an té**—*The ladies sang a song each* :
—ib. 90.
Cha d' fhuair mi ach tri ùbhlan agus thug mi bonn òir **an té**
orra—*I got only three apples and gave a gold piece for each
of them* :—ib. III. 53.

6. Cardinal numbers when accompanied by nouns, are adjj.
preceding their nouns. Except **aon** they are indeclinable ; and
except **aon** and **dà** they do not aspirate a following consonant ;
but besides **aon** and **dà**, **trì** *three*, and **ceithir** *four*, aspirate **ceud**
a hundred. § 22, § 23.

7. **Dà** is said to govern the dat. sing., and also sometimes to take
the gen. after it. This statement, which may be retained as a
useful mnemonic, is based on the fact that in O.G. **dà** (fem. **dí**)
is followed by the DUAL, and is still used for pairs of things, e.g. :

dà chìch, **dà** chluais, **dà** chois, **dà** ghruaidh, **dà** làimh, **dà**
mhala—*two breasts, ears, feet, cheeks, hands, eye-brows.*

(1) Gu maol an **dà** shùl . . . (2) gu maol na **dà** ghualainn . . .
thar an **dà** achlais . . .   gu caol na **dà** choise—

(1) *To the two eye-brows* . . . (2) *to the top of the two shoulders* . .
over the two armpits . . .   *to the smalls (ankles) of his
two feet* :—Waifs III. 13.

Of these examples, (1) represents the old dual ; (2) represents
the modern tendency which is towards the gen. sing. fem.

(1) Clann an dà mhnà—*the children of the two women.*
cathair an dà làimhe—*the double-handed chair* :—C.R. vii. 7.

8. Dà is used as an adj. preceding its noun.   The noun is always
singular or dual, and always aspirated.   An adj. accompanying
the noun is in older Gaelic plural, as if the noun were plural.
Now the adj. is sing., aspirated, and declined like the noun.   If
the noun be masculine, with or without the article, the inflections
are regular ; but if the noun be feminine, it retains the old nom.
dual (identical in form with the dative singular) and the old
gen. dual (identical in form with the gen. sing., except in -à-
and -io- stems where it is identical in form with the gen. plural).

    Mas.   **Examples** :

Nom. Tha **dà** chinneach ad bholg—*Two nations are within thee* :
        —Gen. xxv. 23.

        Dà bhonnach bheag—*Two small cakes* :—Forbes 297.

        B' eòlach ur **dà** athair air a chéile— *Your two fathers knew
        one another* :—L.C. 8.

        Leugh mi an **dà** sgrìobhadh so—*I have read these two
        records* :—Cuairt. 27, 61.

        A' saothrachadh a **dhà** uiread 's a rinn iad—*Labouring
        twice as much as they have done* :—Cuairt. 40, 101.

        Agus **dà** chù dhubh aige— *And two black dogs with him* :—
        Arab. I. 17.

        An **dà** chù dhubh so—*Those two black dogs* :—ib. I. 24, 25.

        Dà iasg bheag—*Two little fishes* :—John vi. 9 (bheaga,
        Ed. 1807 ; Forbes, 2 ed., 199).

Gen. B' fhada bho chéile crodh laoigh an **dà** sheanar—*Far
        apart were the milch-cows of their grandfathers* :—
        N.G.P. 54.

        Prìs an **dà** osain—*The price of a pair of hose* :—Forbes 297.

        Buaidh an **dà** chatha sin—*The victory of these two battles* :—
        Red Bk. 178, 30.

        A' slugadh suas an **dà** uile-bheist mhi-nàdurra so—*Swallow-
        ing up these two unnatural monsters* :—Arab. I. 73.

        Sealladh an **dà** shaoghail—*The vision of the two worlds* :—
        F.T. 182.

        An carbad an **dà** eich—*in a carriage and pair* :—L.C. 308.

        Amadan an **dà** fhichead bliadhna cha bhi e ciallach ri
        beò—*The fool of forty will never be wise* :—N.G.P. 25.

Dat. air **dà** phunnd Shasunnach—*for two pounds sterling* :—
        Forbes 297.

Fem.

Nom. Ma bhios aig duine **dà** mhnaoi—*If a man have two wives* :
—Deut. xxi. 15.

Phaisg ise a **dà** làimh air a h-uchd—*She folded her hands upon her breast* :—L.C. 7.

Is feàrr dhuit sin na **dà** làimh no **dà** chois a bhi agad— *That is better for thee than having two hands or two feet* : —Matt. xviii. 8.

Gus am bi mo **dhà làimh** as mo ghuailnibh—*till my two arms come from my shoulders* :—Waifs, III. 10.

cf. W. Trefna waith ein **dwylaw**—*Stablish the work of our hands* :—Ps. xc. 17.

Ghabh Lamech **dà** mhnaoi—*Lamech took two wives* :— Gen. iv. 19.

Agus **dà** ghalladh dhubh aige air lomhainn—*And he holding two black bitches in a leash* :—Arab. I. 99.

Gen. Tha clann na **dà** mhnà so beò—*The children of these two women are alive* :—Munro 189.

Air son mo **dhà** shùl—*For my two eyes* :—Judges xvi. 28.

Mu chaol a **dà** làimhe— *About the wrist of her two arms* :— Arab. I. 57. § 98, 7.

Buinn mo **dhà** choise—*The soles of both my feet*:—Forbes 297.

Clann na **dà** pheathar—*The children of two sisters* (i.e. cousins) :—ib.

Dat. Do **dhà** thréibh agus do leth-thréibh—*Of two tribes and of an half tribe* :—Josh. xiv. 3.

Le **dà** chirc bhric—*With two speckled hens* :—McB. xxi.

Do **dhà** mhnaoi òig— *For two young wives* :—Forbes 297.

Bha e cluiche air **dà** thruimb mhòr Abrach—*He was playing on two big Lochaber trumps* :—L.C. 81.

'Nuair a bha mi air an **dà** chois—*When I stood upon (was on) the two feet* :—S.O. 19ᵇ29.

Ghabhadh air an **dà** ghallaidh—*The two bitches were beaten* : —Arab. I. 102.

Anns an **dà** chuaich bhig—*In the two small cups* :— Forbes 297.

9. The cardinal numbers, when used absolutely, are nouns feminine, e.g.

Fàsaidh an aon bheag 'na mìle agus an aon shuarach 'na cinneach làidir— *A little one shall become* 1000 *and a small one a strong nation* :—Is. lx. 22.

An **trì** bheag so—*These three* ; A' **cheithir** mhòr sin—*Those four* :—Munro 69.

10. But **fichead, ceud, mìle, mullean** are mas. A noun following these (or any multiple of these) is in the nom. sing. and unaspirated :

Ceud **conspunn** gun ghiorrag—100 *heroes without panic* :—Turner 83, 12.

Còrr is trì fichead **fear**—*More than* 300 *men* :—Cuairt. 27, 68.

Mìle **fàilte** dhuit le d' bhréid— *A thousand welcomes to thee with thy kerchief* :—L.C. 295.

Ghluais e le ceithir-cheud-deug **fear** fo'n armaibh — *He advanced with* 1400 *men under arms* :—C.G. 411.

Mìle, mìle **taing**—1000, 1000 *thanks* :—L.C. 7.

Air cheann mìle **fear** a thuilleadh air trì fichead **fear**-sleagha — *At the head of* 1000 *men besides* 60 *spearmen* :—Cuairt. 27, 68.

Thog iad fichead **punnd** Sasunnach, ceithir fichead mìle **punnd** Sasunnach—*They raised* £20, £80,000 :—Cuairt. 40, 101.

But if the noun following **ceud** be fem., the adj. accompanying the noun is fem. :

Coig ceud asal bhoirionn—500 *she-asses* :—Job. i. 3.

These numerals take the article :

an ceud fear, **am** mìle fear—*the* 100, *the* 1000 *men*.

'S gu'n tugainn féin di **na** ceudan pòg— *And I would give her hundreds of kisses* :—A' Choisir 14.

They are used also regularly as common nouns :

Am fichead mòr so—*This great score.*

Brùchdaidh iad 'nan **ceudan**—*They will burst forth in their hundreds* :—Munro, 69.

11. Multiplicatives are formed :

(1) by annexing to the cardinals the words—

(a) **uair**, e.g. **aon uair**—*once* ; **dà uair**—*twice* ; **trì** uairean—thrice ; Thuirt e so **a dhà** no **trì dh' uairean**—*He said this twice or thrice* :—Arab. I. 63, cf. § 193, (2).

(b) **fillte**—*folded*, e.g. **aon fhillte**—*single* ; **dà fhillte**—*double* ; **trì fillte**—triple :

(2) by an idiomatic use of :

(a) **uiread** f. *as much* (in time or space) :

Thu labhairt **na h-uiread**—*That you should say so much* :—S.O. 148aS.

Tha **uiread** agus **uiread** eile—*There is as much and as much again* :—H.S. Report 38.

Oir rinn mi air a' bhathar a dheich uiread's a chuir mi ann —*For I made by the goods ten times what I had advanced* : —Arab. I. 28.

An **uiread** so de bhliadhnaibh—*These many years* :—Lk. xv. 29.

Tha cheart **uiread** a dh' ioghnadh ormsa—*I am quite as much astonished* :—Arab. I. 103.

Thugadh **uiread** is **uiread** do gach aon—*Share and share alike was given to each* :—ib. II. 72.

Bha **na h-uiread** de choinnlean ann—*There were so many candles there* :—ib. I. 115.

Urad slachdain buntata—*The size of a potato-masher* :—Clarsach 16.

(b) **uibhir** f. *as much, quantity, even* ; L. numerus § 18.

Aig an robh **uibhir** dhe inntinn—*Who had so much of his mind* :—Cos. 17.

Cha rachadh e **uibhir** agus a stigh—*He would not even go in* :—ib. 136.

Theagamh gu'n dean sinne **uibhir** ri sin air do shon-sa—*Perhaps we may do as much for thee* :—F.T. 90.

(c) **liutha, luithad**, *many, so many*.

An déidh **a liuthad** pian a dh' fhuiling mi—*After I have suffered so much pain* :—Arab. I. 64.

(d) **mar** before ceud :

B' fheàrr leam uam e **mar cheud**—*I had rather be without it* 100 *times* :—S.O. 37a26.

'S binn' an tathaich sud **mar cheud**—*Sweeter is that resort* 100 *times* :—S.O. 281a1.

12. The partitives are—leth m. *half*, trian m. *a third*, ceathramh m. *a fourth*, etc.

Leth expresses one of a pair of things, e.g. leth-chas f. *one foot*, leth-shùil f. *one eye* : gu leth expresses *and a half*, mìle gu leth—1500.

Cha n-fhaca mi riamh seòmar anns an robh innsreadh a leith cho briagha ris—*I have never seen a room in which was furniture half so beautiful as that* :—Arab. II. 76.

Is e leth-pheathraichean a tha anns an dithis—*The two are half-sisters* :—ib. II. 71.

Mu thrì troidhean air gach rathad— *About three feet square* :—ib. II. 43.

§ 99. ## NUMBERS.

Cardinal.	Ordinal.
1 aon fhear, chraobh, duine	1st an ceud (a' cheud) fhear, a' cheud chraobh
2 dà fhear, chraoibh, dhuine	2nd an dara (an darna) fear, craobh
3 trì fir, craobhan, daoine	3rd an treas fear, an tritheamh fear
4 ceithir fir, &c.	4th an ceathramh fear, craobh
5 cóig	5th an cóigeamh fear
6 sè, sia	6th an sèathamh fear, an t-seathamh craobh
7 seachd	7th an seachdamh fear, an t-seachdamh craobh
8 ochd	8th an t-ochdamh fear, an ochdamh craobh
9 naoi	9th an naothamh fear, craobh
10 deich	10th an deicheamh fear
11 aon fhear deug, aon chraobh dheug	11th an t-aon(a) fear deug, an aona chraobh dheug
12 dà fhear dheug, dà chraoibh dheug	12th an dara fear deug, an dara craobh dheug
13 trì fir dheug, tri craobhan deug	13th an treas fear deug, an treas craobh dheug
20 fichead fear, fichead craobh	20th am ficheadamh fear, an fhicheadamh craobh

Cardinal.	Ordinal.
21 fear ar fhichead, craobh ar fh.	21st an t-aona fear fichead, an aona chraobh f.
22 dà fhear (ar) fhichead	22nd an dara fear fichead, an dara craobh f.
23 trì fir fhichead	23rd an treas fear fichead, an treas craobh f.
30 deich fir (ar) fhichead	30th an deicheamh fear fichead
31 aon fhear deug ar fh.	31st an t-aon(a) fear deug ar fh., an aona craobh dheug ar fh.
32 dà fhear deug ar fh.	32nd an dara fear deug ar fh.
33 trì fir dheug ar fh.	33rd an treas fear deug ar fh.
40 dà fhichead fear, craobh	40th an dà fhicheadamh fear, craobh
41 fear is dà fhichead	41st an aon 's an dà fhicheadamh fear
42 dà fhear is da fhichead	42nd an dà 's an dà fhicheadamh fear
50 deich is dà fhichead fear, da fhichead fear 's a deich, leth-cheud fear	50th an deich 's an dà fhicheadamh fear ; an leth-cheudamh fear, craobh
60 trì fichead fear, craobh	60th an trì ficheadamh fear, craobh
70 trì fichead fear 's a deich	70th an deich 's an trì ficheadamh fear
100 ceud fear, cóig fichead fear	100th an cóig ficheadamh fear, craobh ; an ceudamh fear, craobh
101 ceud fear 's a h-aon	101st an aon 's an ceudamh fear
120 sè fichead fear, craobh	120th an sè ficheadamh fear
130 sè fichead fear 's a deich	130th an deich 's an sè fichead-. amh fear
140 seachd fichead fear	140th an seachd ficheadamh fear, craobh
150 seachd fichead fear 's a deich, ceud gu leth de fhearaibh	150th an deich 's an seachd f.f.

Cardinal.	Ordinal.
160 ochd fichead fear, craobh	160th an ochd ficheadamh fear, craobh
170 ochd fichead fear 's a deich	170th an deich 's an ochd ficheadamh fear
180 naoi fichead fear, craobh	180th an naoi ficheadamh fear
190 naoi fichead fear 's a deich	190th an deich 's an naoi f.f.
200 dà cheud fear, craobh	200th an dà cheudamh fear, craobh
300 trì cheud fear, craobh	300th an trì cheudamh fear
400 ceithir cheud fear, craobh	400th an ceithir cheudamh fear
1000 mìle fear, craobh	1000th am mìle(-amh) fear, craobh
50,000 leth-cheud mìle fear, craobh	50,000th an leth-cheud mìle(-amh) fear
100,000 ceud mìle fear, craobh	100,000th an ceud mìle(-amh) fear
1,000,000 muillean fear, craobh	1,000,000th am muilleanamh fear, a' mhuilleanamh craobh

1. **Aonar** m. *one person* is used chiefly with the prep. *an* and possessive pronouns : **am aonar**—*by myself*, **at aonar**—*by thyself*, **'na aonar**—*he alone*.

Tha mise 'm aonar, tha sibh-se 'nur mòran—
I am one, ye are many :—Waifs III. 120.

2. The following collective nouns, denoting groups of persons from two to ten, are fem., are used only in the singular, all (except **dithis**) are indeclinable, and take an accompanying adj. in the plural :

dithis, old g.s. déise	
triùir	seachdnar
ceathrar	ochdnar
cúignear	naoinear
sèanar	deichnear

Bha **dithis** bhan aige—*He had two wives* :—1 Sam. i. 2.
Sinn féin 'nar **dithis**—*Ourselves twain* :—1 K. iii. 18.
Thug e a **thriùir** chaomh chompanaich g'a faicinn—*He took his three bosom friends to see it* :—L.C. 50.
Rugadh a' cheathrar sin do'n fhamhair—*These four were born to the giant* :—2 Sam. xxi. 22.

Chunnaic e **seachdnar** dhaoine tighinn—*He saw a company of seven men coming* :—Waifs III. 10.

Bha **an t-seachdnar** fear 'nan suidhe—*The seven men were seated* :—Arab. I. 108.

Ochdnar chloinne—*eight children* :—J. W. 90.

3. Of the ordinals, **an ceud, a' cheud**—*the first*, alone aspirates a following noun, e.g. haleluia a cheud fhàilte—*Halelujah his first welcome* :—L.C. 48.

4. The order of the Kings in a dynasty is expressed by

    (a) Ordinal Numbers, and less properly by

    (b) Cardinal Numbers.

      (a) Oran le Iain Lom air dha a chluinntinn an **dara** Rìgh Tearlach bhi air a chrùnadh—*Song by Iain Lom on hearing that Charles* II. *had been crowned* :—Turner 56.

      'San àm 'san robh an **Ceathramh** Deòrsa ann an Albainn — *At the time when George* IV. *was in Scotland* :— Cuairt. No. 40, 87.

      Mu thobar Theàrlaich an IV.—*about the well of Charles* IV. :—C.G. 135.

      (b) Ri linn fògradh Rìgh Tearlach **a dhà**—*During the banishment of Charles* II. :—Turner 53.

§ 100.   **COMPOUND WORDS.**

Nominal and Adjectival Compounds.

1. A Perfect Compound combines its elements into one word, has the stress on the first syllable, and is declined regularly, e.g.

àigeach, òigeach m. *colt, horse*, g. oigeich : òg *young* +each *horse*.

aimhfheoil f. *proud flesh*, g. aimhfheola, an-**i**-stem : amh *raw* +feòil *flesh*.

banais f. *wedding*, an-**a**-stem : ban *women* +féis *feast*

bantrach f. *widow* : ban-treb-thach *female farmer*

caorunn, caorthann m. *rowan-tree, berry-tree*, g. caoruinn, an-**o**-stem : caor +tann § 122, 7.

déirc f. *alms* : Dé +sheirc *God's-love*

fadal m. *delay, weariness* : fad +dáil f. *long meeting*

gealbhonn m. *sparrow*, g. gealbhuinn, an-**o**-stem : geal +bonn

iodhlann f. *cornyard*, g. iodhlainn(e), an-**a**-stem : iodh +lann

oilbheum m. *offence*, g. oilbheim, an-**o**-stem : ail *rock* +beum *striking*

óisg f. *yearling ewe*, g. óisge, an-**a**-stem : ovi-s *sheep* +seasg *barren*

Samhuinn f. *Hallowtide*, g. Samhna, an-**i**-stem : Sam *summer* +fuin *end*

seanair m. *grandfather*, g. seanar, an-**r**-stem : sean +athair

trocair(e) f. *mercy*, an-**ia**-stem : L. trux, truc[s] *doomed person* +car *loving*

uamhas m. *terrible death, horror, mortal terror* an-**o**-stem : uath *dread* +bàs *death*

2. In a pf. cpd. the first element is a monosyllable. When the genitive stem differs from the nominative, the genitive stem is used for pf. cpds., and the nominative for ipf. cpds. (but cf. § 29, 4) e.g.

bó f. *cow*, gen. bà, bàthaich m. *byre* ; bò-choinneil f. *Mullein*

cù m. *dog*, gen. coin, O.G. con, conablach m. *mangled corpse* ; cù-uisge m. *spaniel*

muir m.f. *sea*, gen. mara, O.G. mora, morfhaich f. *sea plain* ; muir-làn m. *full-tide*

§ 101.

1. An Imperfect Compound combines its elements loosely. The article or a possessive pronoun, when present, is always attached to the first element ; the second element is aspirated, § 29, as stated below, § 102, 1 ; and the stress falls upon the last word of the compound, or upon both elements, e.g.

Mar chù gu cat, mar chat gu luch,
Tha bean mic gu **màthair-chéile**—
  Like dog to cat, like cat to mouse,
  A son's wife is to her mother-in-law :—N.G.P. 312.

2. A cpd. generally expresses a complex idea not suggested by the separate words. Simple phrases formed of genitives used as adjj. are not cpds., e.g.

Mar mhart caol a' tighinn gu baile tha cabhanach na **maidne Earraich**—

> *Like a lean cow coming to a farm is the dawn of a spring morning* :—N.G.P. 313.

Na **dorsa praise** brisidh tu—

> *Thou wilt break the gates of brass* :—Laoidh xxiii. 8.

An triùir dhaoine treuna—*The three strong men*:—2 Sam xxiii. 16, 17

§ 102.

Imperfect Compounds are of five classes :—I. Dependent ; II. Adjectival ; III. Descriptive ; IV. Copulative ; V. Possessive.

I. 1. In **Dependent Compounds** the first word modifies the second ; all adjectives, and all nouns occurring as first words in a compound are initially aspirated in the same way as a single word ; but they preserve their stems uninflected either in the nom. sing., or in the gen. sing. without increase ; the second word is always aspirated, § 29, is declined regularly, and determines the gender of the compound.

2. Declension of Dependent Compounds (a) when the **first word** is **an adjective** :

An gorm-phreas m. *The green bush.*

	Sing.	*Pl.*
n.	an gorm-phreas	na gorm-phris (-phreasan)
g.	(barr) a' ghorm-phris	nan gorm-phreas
d.	do'n ghorm-phreas	do na gorm-phreasaibh
v.	a ghorm-phris	a ghorm-phreasa

A' ghlas-bheinn   f. *The grey mountain.*

	Sing.	*Pl.*
n.	a' ghlas-bheinn	na glas-bheanntan
g.	(mullach) na glas-bheinne	nan glas-bheann(-tan)
d.	do'n ghlas-bheinn	do na glas-bheanntan
v.	a ghlas-bheann	a ghlas-bheannta

3. Additional Examples :

Mas.

bàn-chu m. *a white dog*

dearbh-bhràthair m. O.G. *a brother by birth*, L. frater carnalis
(cf. *Collect. Reb. Alb.* 83 n.), bràthair *a member of a
religious community.*

A bha aig Iùdas do dhearbh-bhràthair—*Which Judas, your
brother, had* :—D. Ban 430, 38 ; 348, 64.

Bha mise Eòin bhur dearbh-bhràthair . . . anns an eilean
—*I, John, who am your brother, . . . was in the isle*:—
Rev. i. 9.

glas-bhreac *a smolt*

mion-dhuine *manikin*

trom-chadal *heavy sleep*

Fem.

bras-bhuinne *torrent*

glas-fhairge *a green sea*

mìn-chlach *smooth stone*

mór-thir *mainland*

Two adjectives compounded are declined as above, e.g.

minbhreac *delicately spotted*

lomlan *brimfull*

Sometimes when the first element seems to be inflected, it
is an instance of Svarabhkti :

Shaoil leis gu'n robh iad luma-lan éisg—
He thought that they were quite full of fish :—Arab. I. 32.

Cho luma-luath :—ib. 68.   cf. § 65.

4. (b) when the **first word** is **a noun** :

An cis-mhaor   m. *the tax-gatherer*

	Sing.	*Pl.*
n.	an cis-mhaor	na cis-mhaoir
g.	(sporran) a' chis-mhaoir	nan cis-mhaor
d.	do'n chis-mhaor	do na cis-mhaoraibh
v.	a chis-mhaoir	a chis-mhaora

A' mhuilt-fheoil f. *the mutton*, also muiltfheoil, a pf. cpd.

Sing.

n. a' **mhuilt-fheoil**
g. (fàileadh) na muilt-fheola
d. do'n mhuilt-fheoil
v. a mhuilt-fheoil

5. Additional Examples :

Mas		*Fem.*	
arm-chrios	*sword-belt*	fraoch-bheinn	*heathy hill*
cas-cheum	*foot-step*	leth-shùil	*one eye*
ceud-chathach	*hundred fighter*	mairt-fheoil	*beef*
crith-cheòl	*warbling*	muic-fheoil	*pork*
leine-chrios	*body-guard, valet*	rìgh-chathair	*throne*
lùth-chleas	*feat of agility*	sealbh-chòir	*propriety*
muir-làn	*full tide*		
oil-thigh	*school of learning*		
sul-radharc	*eyesight*		
tamh-neul	*death-cloud*, Metr. Ps. cxxi. 2.		

6. Except compounds in **ban**-, which are fem, and **ban** itself determines the gender, e.g.

ban-dia	*goddess*
ban-diùc	*duchess*
ban-léigh	*female physician*
ban-òglach (and banoglach)	*handmaid*
ban-rìgh	*queen*
ban-seirbhiseach	*maid servant*
ban-stiùbhart	*housekeeper*

§ 103.

II. In **Adjectival Compounds** the second word depends upon the first.

1. When the **second word** is **an adjective**, the compound is inflected in the same way as a noun with an accompanying adjective, § 92, e.g.

An coileach-dubh m. *the blackcock.*

	Sing.	Pl.
n.	an coileach-dubh	na coilich-dhubha
g.	(ceann) a' choilich-dhuibh	nan coileach-dubha
d.	do'n choileach-dhubh	na coilich(ibh)-dhubha
v.	a choilich-dhuibh	a choileacha-dubha

Additional Examples :

brù-dhearg m. *robin red-breast,* n.s.m. of Poss. cpd., § 106
coileach-ruadh m. *a red grouse cock*
gobhlan-dubh m. *black marten*
luch-mhòr f. *a seal*
sgoil-dubh f. *black-art*

2. When an adjectival compound consists of **two nouns**, the first is declined regularly, except that the genitive sing. increase is usually dropped ; the second is always in the genitive. If it be (a) in the gen. pl. it is always aspirated ex. § 20, 2. If it be (b) in the gen. sing., it is aspirated like an adjective accompanying a noun, e.g.

(a) am plocan-bhuntàta m. *the potato masher.*

	Sing.	Pl.
n.	am plocan-bhuntàta	na plocain-bhuntàta
g.	(ceann) a' phlocain-bhuntàta	nam plocan-bhuntàta
d.	do'n phlocan-bhuntàta	do na plocanaibh-bhuntàta
v.	a phlocain-bhuntàta	a phlocana-bhuntàta

Additional Examples :

ball-dobhrain	m.	*mole on the skin* :—Waifs III. 15.
coille-chnò	f.	*a nuttery*
tigh-chaorach	m.	*sheep-cot,* g.s. tigh-chaorach
tigh-chearc	m.	*hen-house,* g.s. tigh-chearc

(b) anart-bàis m. *shroud.*

	Sing.	Pl.
n.	an t-anart-bàis	na h-anartan-bàis
g.	(ceann) an anairt-bhàis	nan anartan-bàis
d.	do'n anart-bhàis	do na h-anartaibh-bàis
v.	a anairt-bhàis	a anarta-bàis

slat-mhara f. *sea-tangle.*

	Sing.	*Pl.*
n.	an t-slat-mhara	na slatan-mara
g.	na slait(e)-mara	nan slat(an)-mara
d.	do'n t-slait-mhara	do na slaitibh-mara
v.	a shlat-mhara	a shlata-mara

Additional Examples:

Mas.

ait-àraich	*rearing place*
baile-margaidh	*market town*
bothan-àirigh	*sheiling*
cù-uisge	*spaniel*
cuman-bainne	*milk cogue*
each-fuinn	*heriot, death-duty*
fear-ciùil	*musician*
fraoch-faloisg	*stumps of burnt heather*
gàradh-droma	*march dyke*
leac-ùrlair	*floor-flag*
mac-samhuil	*likeness, like* (O.G. mac-samhla) § 83.
maide-droma	*ridge-board*
maoim-sléibhe	*mountain torrent*
marsanta-paca	*packman*
muileann-gaoithe	*windmill*
seol-mara	*tide*

Fem.

adharc-fhùdair	*powderhorn*
bean-shìth(e)	*brownie*
bó-ghamhna	*farrow cow*
clach-lìobhaidh	*grindstone*
crith-thalmhainn	*earthquake*
cuinneag-bhainne	*milk pail*
deoch-slàinte	*a toast*
glas-ghuib	*a gag*
leabaidh-mhuill	*chaff-bed*
marcachd-shìne	*driving storm*
muir-shàile	*salt-sea*
slat-thomhais	*ellwand*
slige-chreachainn	*scallop-shell*

Some Compounds combine I. and II., having both Dependent and Adjectival elements, e.g.

Crùnair gasda nan rìgh-bhrat-sròil—*The gallant crowner of the kingly banners of silk* :—S.O. 48ᵇ28

Chaidh a ghlacadh droch spioraid—*His being possessed of an evil spirit took place*, i.e. *He was possessed of an evil spirit* :—S.O. 36ᵇ32

> *droch-spioraid* is a Dependent cpd.
> *ghlacadh-droch-spioraid* is an Adjectival cpd.

§ 104.

III. In **Descriptive Compounds** the first word describes the second, which is in the gen. without the art, e.g.

Rug i **leanabh mic,** an **leanabh mic**—*She brought forth a manchild, the manchild* :—Rev. xii. 5, 13

Rug i a **ceud-ghin mic**—*She brought forth her first born son* :—Matt. i. 25

Thug e **aon-ghin Mhic féin**—*He gave His only begotten son* :—John iii. 16

cf. is tu rofhóid do **mac oen-geni**—*Thou didst send Thine only begotten son* :—P.H. 2086

Ach 's e 's truaighe do **chéile mna** dheth—*But saddest of all is thy wife* :—Stewarts 302, 9

maise mna—*a beauty of a woman* :—S.O. 98ᵃ44

Ciod e **ghnè dhuine** so—*What manner of man is this* :—Matt. viii. 27

Mo **rogha céile**—*My choice of a companion* :—A' Choisir 14, 7

Is éigin duinn a ràdh gur **úmpaidh balaich** e—*We must say that he is a blockhead of a fellow* :—C.G. 135.

cf. An triùir bhràithrean—*the three brothers* :—S.O. 49ᵇS

On bu droch **dhuine cloinn'** e—*Since he was a bad son* :—ib. 46ᵃ30

t'aon **duine cloinne**—*thine only child* :—L.C. 6

Air son aon **phàiste** beag (leanaibh) **leinibh**—*For one little chit of a child* :—Cos. 130

Cha robh annta ach creithleagan dhaoine—*They were but gadflies of men* :—Cos. 119

Broc liath-chorrach **éilde**— *A grey-snouted badger of a hind* :—
D. Ban 521 (sic corr.) ; 168, 133

Bha Domhnull an Dùin innt, Do **mhac oighre**—*Donald of
the Dun was aboard her, thy son and heir* :—S.O. 47[b]t ;
50[a]30

§ 105.

IV. In **Copulative Compounds** the parts are of equal emphasis,
the noun cpds. are connected in sense by ' and ' and declined like
adj. cpds. § 103; and adj. cpds. are declined like Dependent
cpds. § 102, 3, e.g.

dubhghlas—*black and grey* ; caoingheal—*soft and white*
Ioc-shlainte f. *a remedy and cure.*
' Sa ' mhaduinn **chiùin-ghil** an àm dhomh dùsgadh—*In the
calm and bright morning when I awoke* :—D. Ban 48, 89
Chuala mi na brataichean **ban-dearg** a' plabraich 'sa '
ghaoidh—*I heard the red and white banners fluttering in
the wind* :—Còmhraidhean 47

§ 106.

V. In **Possessive Compounds**, consisting of noun and adj.,
both elements are declined and aspirated as already explained
(§ 102), e.g.

1. Craobh bhàrr-bhuidhe   f.   *A tree having a yellow top*
2. Duine starr-shuileach   m.   *A man having distorted eyes*
3. Fairge thonn-gheal   f.   *A sea having white waves*
4. Gille cas-fhliuch   m.   *A servant having wet-feet*

Bean ruadh dhubh-shuileach, cù lachdunn las-shuileach— *A
red-haired, black-eyed woman, a dun fiery-eyed dog* :—
N.G.P. 52

Gur h-iom' oganach Lub bhachlach sgiath chrom—*There's
many a youth with bended bow and hollow shield:*—S.O. 36[b]y

Bidh luinneag aig rìbhinn chùl-duinn daib—*A brown-haired
maid will have a lay for them* :—D. Ban 94, 159

Gu còs sgora dhìonach craige—*to a cliff-sheltered crevice of a
rock :*—L.C. 37

sgorr-dhìona § 103, sgorr-dhìonach § 106

§ 107. PROPER NAMES AND THEIR COMPOUNDS.

1. The grammatical basis of a proper name is the personal or baptismal name, e.g. Domhnull *Donald*, Seumas *James*, Màiri *Mary*, Seònaid *Janet*. The clan or family name is added in the form (a) of an adj., e.g. Alasdair Domhnullach — *Alexander Macdonald*; Màiri Dhomhnullach—*Mary Macdonald*, or (b) of a patronymic cpd., e.g. Alasdair MacDhomhnuill, Màiri Nic Dhomhnuill.

Proper names are definite and indefinite.

In the genitive singular a proper name, masculine, if definite, is aspirated ; and a proper name, feminine, is unaspirated :

Contrast :

> Mac dé—*a son of a god* (common noun).
>
> Mac Dhé—*the Son of God* (proper noun).
>
> Mac Dòmhnuill—*a son of a Donald*.
>
> Mac Dhòmhnuill—*the son of Donald*.
>
> Ceit nic Phàdruig—*Catherine Paterson*,
> where nic = nighean — (contracted to ni) + mhic.

2. A single noun in apposition to a single proper name does not require the def. art. :

> Eobhan cìobair—*Ewen the shepherd* ;
>
> Ioseph saor—*Joseph the carpenter* :—Munro 177
>
> Beannachd Chaluim ghobha—'mo thogair ged nach (*read* gar an, § 218) till'—
>
> *Smith Malcolm's blessing—I care not if he come not back* :— N.G.P.52.

3. When a single proper name is accompanied by an adjectival cpd., § 103, the latter requires the article : (*as in* E.)

> Alasdair, an ceard-umha— *Alexander the coppersmith* ;
>
> Ailean, am muillear-luaidh— *Allan the fulling-miller*.

4. When a name and surname are accompanied by a common noun in apposition, the latter requires the article : (*as in* E.)

> Alasdair Tàillear, an clachair— *Alexander Taylor the mason* ;
>
> Iain Caimbeul, am maor— *Alexander Campbell the Officer.*
>
> *John*

5. When a proper noun is accompanied—   *unlike E*

   (1) by a single adj., a noun in apposition is without the article :

    Domhnull ruadh tàillear—*Red Donald the tailor*

   (2) by two or more adjj., the noun in apposition requires the article :

    Eachainn glas òg, an tuathanach—

    Young wan Hector, the farmer ;

    Mòrag bheag chiar, a' bhanarach—

    Little swarthy Sally the Dairymaid :—Munro 178

6. When a proper name preceded by a title is governed in the gen., only the title is inflected :

   Mac Rìgh Seumas, Tearlach Stiubhart—

   Charles Stewart, son of King James :—S.O. 115^{a}13

   Do theaghlach rìgh Fionghall—

   To the family of King Fingal :—S.O. 38^{a}19

   Sin as onoir Shir Seumas—

   That is the honour of Sir James :—Turner 86, 5, 7

   Ri linn ban-righ Màiri—*In Queen Mary's reign* :—Munro 178.

7. When a proper noun in an oblique case (gen. or dat.) is followed by a noun in apposition, the latter if definite is in the nom. case :

   (1) *gen.* Each Iain Chaimbeil, am maor—

       The horse of John Campbell the Officer :—ib.

       Tigh Sheumais, a mhac—*The house of James his son* : —ib.

   but if indefinite, in the genitive case :

       Bean fhada chaol dhìreach, miann Dhomhnuill amadain—*Fool Donald's fancy, a tall, slender, straight wife* :—N.G.P. 51 ; cf. § 107, 2

       Le suidhe air deas làimh Dhé an athar—*By sitting on the right hand of God, the Father* :—Catm. 28

In this example for 'an athar,' the spoken form 'an t-athair' is more correct.

   (2) *dat.* Thug e cuireadh da bhràithribh uile, mic an rìgh—

       He sent an invitation to all his brothers, the King's sons :—1 Kings i. 9

       Thubhairt e ri Sarai, a bhean—

       He said to Sarai his wife :—Gen. xii. 11

8. (1) Proper names forming adjectival compounds, § 103, are inflected regularly : Calum Cille—*S. Columba.*

Aig I Chaluim Chille—*at Iona* :—S.O. 55ᵇs.

'S i caismeachd Chloinn Chamrain a th' ann—

'*Tis the march of the Cameron men* :—A'Choisir 21, cf. §107, 10

This and similar examples are sometimes treated as dependent compounds, §102 : Curaidhnean Chlann Chamshroin—

The heroes of the Clan Cameron :—S.O. 114ᵃ25

(2) **Mac** *son* is used in forming proper names of adjectival compounds. There are two classes of such cpds. :

    1. Patronymic, which include the names of clans and septs. §107, 9

    2. Hagiological or Ecclesiastical, which include the followers of Saints. §108-§110, §112

Mac was assumed by Norse and some Lowland peoples, e.g., MacLeod, MacRerick and dropped again in some instances, e.g. Cloud, Rerick

    For the -**c**- of Mac projected, which is the rule in Manx, e.g. Quilliam, Crobbin, v. §12 i. 3 ; and for the -**c**- retracted, v. §12 ii.

The **c** is softened to **g** in Galloway and N. Ireland

(3) **O, ua** m. *grandson*, prevalent in Ireland since XI. century, also occurs :

    O Duibhne, O Gille bhuidhe, O hÆdha § 111

(4) Prefixed also to Saints' names is **maol** (O.G. máel) *tonsured one*, which in tenth and eleventh centuries gave place to **gille** *lad, servant*. In cpds. gille is confused with maol ; and maol is often difficult to distinguish from mo *my*, e.g. Adamnanus *Kilmaveonaig.* §112, 9 ; § 7 iv. 2, 3, 5 ; cf. W. **gwas,** O.W. **guas** *servant*, e.g. O Muirgheasain, Déibhiosdan, MacPetrus § 108, Mac Niallgus § 111, Duffus § 112

9. Only chiefs bear the simple patronymic, or territorial designation, an adjectival compound :

    Do goiredh Iarla Rois agus Mac Domnaill agus Ardfhlath Innsigall dhe— *He was styled Earl of Ross, and Macdonald, and High Chief of the Isles* :—Red Bk. 160

In a proper name like Mac Dhomhnuill *Macdonald*, the second part of the adjectival compound is definite §107, 1, and therefore in English the definite article is not regularly placed before the compound. The chief of the Clan Donald was spoken of simply as Mac Dhomhnuill *Macdonald*:

Ach ma mhol thu ar daoin' uaisle,
C'uim nach do luaidh thu Mac Dhòmhnuill ?—
But if you praised our nobles,
Why did you not mention Macdonald ? :—S.O. 155^b21 ; cf. Dr. Johnson's Journey, pp. 114, 224

Similarly before compound proper names that already contain the definite article, the definite article is not placed in English. The chief of the MacKintoshes is simply Mac-an-tòisich *MacKintosh*, and his clan Tòisichean *MacKintoshes* :—S.O. 114^a42

But later, for the sake of greater clearness even in Gaelic, the genitive plural of the clan name was introduced into the compound :

Ach, a Dhonuill nan Donall—
But O ! Macdonald of Macdonald :—Maclagan MSS. No. 14

The territorial designation is frequently added to the patronymic of the chief :

Mac Mhoirich á Atholl—*Murray from Atholl* :—Turner 85, 9
Mac Coinnich mòr Chinn-Tàile—*Great MacKenzie of Kintail* : —S.O. 114^a34
Bìrlinn Mhic Nèill Bhara—
The galley of MacNeill of Barra :—C.G. 140

Minor distinctions and pet names are expressed by the same or similar grammatical means :

Coileach Strath-bhalgaidh—
The cock of Strathbogie (Lord Huntly) :—S.O. 41^b32
Fear Mhurlagain—
The proprietor, or *the tenant farmer of Murlagan* :—Munro 185
A Iain Mhuideartaich nan seòl soilleir—
O John of Moydart of the bright sails :—S.O. 41^b25
Thighearna Lathair—*O Laird of Lawers* :—ib. 41^a21
Fear Shrath-mhaisidh—
The goodman of Strathmasie :—S.O. 260
Chlisg Raonull Shrath-Mhathaisidh—
Ronald of Strathmashie started :—Poetry of Badenoch 187
Fuil uasal Chuinn Cheud-chathaich—*The noble blood of Conn of the hundred battles* :—Turner 85, 22

10. A proper name fem. remains unaspirated in the gen., cf. common nouns preceded by the article :

Mac Muire dhìon t' anma—*The Son of Mary to* (i.e., *May the Son of Mary*) *defend thy soul* :—Turner 84, 19

Mhic Muire na h-Òighe—

O Son of Mary, the virgin :—Turner 74, 13

but in some districts and instances the gen. is aspirated :

Fear-pòsda Mhuire—*The husband of Mary* :—Math. i. 16

Bràthair Cheit— *Kate's brother.*

An accompanying adj. is in the nom. :

Bràthair Cheit mhòr—*big Kate's brother* ; banais Sheonaid bhàn—*Fair Janet's wedding* :—Munro 186

This variety is probably connected with the common blunder of aspirating the gen. sing. fem. :

Ré ùine **bh**ig (*for* ré ùine **b**ige)—*For a little time* :—Rev. xx. 3, so ed. 1902 ; re h-uair bhig—Metr. Ps. xxxvii. 10

Chum na beatha **mh**aireannaich = chum na beatha **m**aireannaich

Air uachdar lice uaine **bh**réagha—

On the top of a fine green stone :—Cos. 96

11. When unstressed words aspirating a following proper noun are dropped (1) the initial consonant of the proper noun is deaspirated, the gen. being retained, e.g. MacDhughail *Doyle* ; (2) soft initial consonants are hardened by analogy, e.g. Gilfoyle *Boyle*, § 108, 3

12. The unstressed first elements of a compound (§7 iv.) are stressed if the second element is dropped, *v.* mac, maolan

§ 108.   PROPER NAMES DERIVED FROM SCRIPTURES.

1. Dia, Mac Dhé *son of God* ; Céile Dé *Culdee* ; Mac Gille Dé *Kildea, Gildea, Gilday, Day, Dey* ; cf. Dàidh §108, 3

Iosa, Gille Iosa *Gillies* ; Mac Gille Iosa *MacLeish* ; Maol Iosa *Malise, Lees*

Crìosd, Gilla Crist, later Mac Gille Chriosda *MacGilchrist* (Anglicised *Christie* ; also *Christopher*).

2. Apostles :

Aindreas, Gille Anndrais *Gillanders, MacAndrew, Anderson*

Bartholomeu, G. Parlan, O.G. Partholon ; Mac Pharlain *MacFarlane, Bartley,* a pet name for Bartolomeu-s ; Anglicised *Barclay* (Ulster)

Eòin, Mac Iain *MacIan, Mackean* ; later Seathan, Mac Gille
Sheathain *MacLean, MacLaine, MacClean, Clean, Lean.*
Eòin, Heb. Gk. L. Iohannes *Ewan, Ewing, MacEwen,
Kewin* (Man) was confused with eòin *birds,* hence En was
a common form of Eòin (still spoken in Sutherl.) Iain is
regarded as the diphthongised form of En §40. Sean,
dim. Seinícin *Jenkin,* MacGillwham *Gillon* (Galloway).
W. Iefan, Ifan *Evan.*

Iudas g.s. Judais S.O. 44b21

Tadeus, MacCaog *MacCaig, MacHaig, Haig* §111 ; from
Tadhg, O.G. Tadc, Gall. Moritasgus, Tasgius. In Munster
Tahig, N. of Ireland Taeg. Latinised to Tadeus (Thady),
and to Timotheus. Mac Thaidhgin *Keigeen* (Man).

Mata, Mac Matha *Mathewson,* and (non-Gaelic) *Matheson.*

Peadar *Peter,* Mac Pheadair *MacPhater, Peters* ; Peter +
gus *MacPetrus, MacFetridge, MacFedries, Ferries,
MacPhedran, Macfeat, Peat.*

Philip, L. Philippus, Mac Fhilip *Mackillop, MacGilp.*

Seumas, Heb. Jacob, *James* ; voc. a Sheumais *Hamish !*
MacSheumais, translated *Jamieson* (Islay) ; *Cammaish*
(Man).

Tómas, Tomas, Tomhus ; Mac Thaimhs, Mac Thamhais
MacTavish, Tawse ; *Cause* ; *MacCosh, Cosh, Cash* ; Mac-a-
Chombaich, Mac Thomai(dh) *MacCombie* for which is
substituted *Colquhoun,* i.e. G. Mac-Thomh-án, Comhán,
McCoun (Galloway) ; *Thompson, Holmes* ; Mac gille
Thomhas *Maclehose* ; *Comish* (Man).

Simon, Simidh, Mac Shimidh, personal name of Lord Lovat ;
Sim, Syme, Mackim, Mackimmie.

3. Adhamh *Adam,* Mac Adaimh *MacAdam, MacCaw, Mac-
Cadie, MacGaw* ; probably often from Adamnan §110

Daibhidh, Dàidh ; Clann Dàidh *the Davidsons* ; Déibhiosdan
Davidson ; *Day, Dey,* cf. §108, 1

Isaac, Mac Isaac *MacIsaac, MacKessack, MacKissock,
Kessack.*

Lucas, Mac Lucais *MacLucas* ; Anglicised to *Douglas,
Macdougall* ; Clucas (Man).

Marcus *Mark,* Mac Marcuis *Marquis* ; *Quark* (Man).

Michael, Mac Gille Mhìcheil *Carmichael* (W. caer, G. cathair,
+ Mhìcheil) ; later Mac Mhìcheil *MacMichael, Mitchel,*
Maol Mhichil *Melville.*

Moire, Muire, L. Maria *Mary* ; Maol-moire *Myles* (L. Miles,
Milo) Moireasdan, Ir. O Muirgheasain *Morrison* (i e.
Muir *Mary* + W. gwas, pl. gweision *youth, servant*) ; Gilla
Muire, MacGillivour (1781) *servant of Mary*, W. Gilla-mwri ;

Pòl, Pàl, L. Paulus, Mac Phàil *MacPhail, Polson* ; *Quale*
(Man), Clan Quhele ; Sen Pol (the hermit) *Semple* ;
Gilfoyle, Boyle (Galloway). § 29, 7 ; § 107, 11

§ 109. PROPER NAMES DERIVED FROM CHURCH OFFICIALS.

Ab, L. abbas *abbot* ; Mac an Aba *MacNab*

Biocair, L. vicarius *vicar* ; Mac Bhiocair *MacVicar*

Bràthair, Mac brathair *MacBrair* (Bute) ; Mac Briar, Mac
Brayer (Galloway)

Canan, L. canon ; Cananaich (with **buth**, later **both** for original
mo § 107, 8 (3) § 7 iv. 2)—*Buchanans*

Ceallair, L. cellarius *cellerer* ; Mac Cellair *Mackellar, Ellar*

Cléireach, L. clericus *clerk, Clark* ; Mac a' Chléirich *MacChlery,*

Deòir, Deòireach, G. deòrad (*exile, pilgrim) Dewar, Macindeor,
Macjore, MacGeorge* ; Mac Gille Dheóraidh *MacLeora*

Easbuig, L. episcopus *bishop* ; Gilleasbuig *Gillespie* (Angl. to
Archibald)—Mac-an-espie

Maighistir, L. Magister ; Mac a' Mhaighistir *MacMaster,
Masterton*

Osdair, L. ostiarius, *Porter* F.T. 42,322 ; *MacCosker*

Pàp, L. papa *Pope*

Pearsa, L. Persona *parson* ; Mac a' Phearsain *MacPherson,
Carson, Corson.*

Sagart, L. sacerdos *priest* ; Mac an t-sagairt *MacTaggart,
Haggart, Haggarty.*

§ 110. PROPER NAMES DERIVED FROM NAMES OF SAINTS.

Adhmhnan, L. Adammanus, Mac Adhaimh *MacGaw* §108, 3,
Mac Gille Adhamhnagain *MacLagan*

Aonghas, O.G. oen-gus—*only choice* (Balquhidder, where was
Oirinn .i. Oiffrend Aonghais) *Angus, MacAinsh, T-ainsh*

MacInnes, Macginnes, MacNish, Angl. *Æneas* ; *Kinnish, Kennish* (Man) ; *Hennessy*

Brandan, Brendan, Mac gille Bhrā, Mac gille Bhrāi, Mac gille Bhrē § 112, 9, *MacGillivray*

Briget f., Gillebrigde, Maelbrigde *MacBryde, Brydon, Brydeson, Bryson* ; also Gilleabart *Gilbert* (A. S. Gislebert), *Gibson, Gibb, MacGibbon* ; Mac gille Brigte—*Kilbride*

Catan, Gillacatain *Cattanach, Chattan*

Ciaran *Kiaran,* Maol Ciaran (S.O. 154^bt) *MacKerron* ; Mac Gille Chiarnain (Angl. *Sharp*)

Colum, L. columba, Mac Gille Calum *MacCallum, Callum* ; Maol Calum *Malcolm, Malcolmson* ; dim. *Calman*

Comgán, Mac gille Comgan *MacCowan, Cowan*

Constantine *Chousland, MacAuslan, Ausland* ; *Costain, Costean* (Man)

Diarmait, Mo-dimmóc, Do-dimmóc *Dymmock*

Dominic, Maoldònuich *Ludovic, Lewis* (Fr. Louis from Chlovis Chlodwig, whence Hludvig)—*Ludwig*

Donnan, Donn-i §112, 2 ; Mac gille Donn-i *MacGillonie* ; maol Donnan *Millony,* v. Ninian p. 161

Earnan, Mac Gille Earnain *MacLearnan*

Faol-an (*little wolf*), Gille Faolain *Gilfillan* ; Mac Gille Fhaolain *MacLellan, Clelland* ; Mac Gille Fhaolagain *MacKilligan*

Fail-chu (*wolf dog*), Volucus §112-7 ; W. gweil-gi f. *torrent, ocean,* with initial -g- mutated i.e. dropped, g-weil-ci *Wilkie* ; Faelfi, Faelbi (*wolf-slayer*) *MacKelvie*

Find-barr, from the first part of the cpd. is (Mo-fhionn-i) *Minn* ; (Mo-fhionn-u) *Munn* ; Mac Mhunnu *MacPhunn, Phyn, Mac Gill Munn* ; and from the second *Barr*

Finnen (fionn-shen *white and old*) ; Mac Gille Fhionnain, Mac Gille Fhinneain *MacLennan, MacLinnin* : with Sv. §65

Finntan (find-shean) *MacGinty* ; Mac Gille Fhinntog *MacLintock* ; Mac gille Fhinntan *MacClinton, Clinton, Linton*

Fìngon (fíon-gon *wine-born* cf. S.O. 37^b12), MacFhinguine *MacKinnon*

Gildas *Geddes* : *Gēltas

Gregoir, L. Gregorius, Mac Griogair *MacGregor, Gregory*

Labhran, L. Laurentius, MacLabhrainn *MacLaren*

Maolan, maol-án (*little tonsured one*) Mac Mhaolain, Mac Gille Mhaoil *MacMillan,* Angl. *Bell* (Islay) : § 107, 12

Martin, L. Martinus *Martin* ; Mac Gille Mhartain *MacMartin*

Odhràn *Oran, MacCorran, Corren*

Padruig, Paruig, L. Patricius (O. Ir. Cothraige)—*Patrick*;
Mac Gille Phadruig *MacPhatrick, Kilpatrick, Kirkpatrick*
dim. *Para* with a defining term taking the accent e.g. Para
Mór ; Pad *Pat*; Mac Phaidein *MacFadyen, MacFadzean,
Paton*

P. Mac Calphuirn has been suggested by Zimmer as the
origin of Mac Alpine §111, §12 ii.

§ 111. PROPER NAMES DERIVED FROM KINGS AND NOTABLES.

1. Ailean, L. Alumnus *Allan, MacAllan, Callan, Callen*

Ailpein, W. Elphin, Elffin ; MacAilpein *MacAlpine* §110

Alasdair, L. Alexander, Mac Alasdair *Macalister*, Callister
(Man), MacAndie, from Sandy

Artair, L. Arturius, MacArtair *MacArthur, MacArt, Hart*(e)
MacWhirter (Galloway)

Bàn *Whyte*; Mac Gille Bhàin *MacGilivane, McIlvane* v. Mac
Gille

Bàrd, Mac a' Bhàird *Baird, Ward*

Brùn, Briùin *Broon, Brown*; Mac-a Briuthainn, Ériu 4, 68 ;
Waifs v. 12

Breathamh (*judge*) *MacBrayne*   ⌊ *b ret v e* ⌋

Cailean, MacCailein *Chief of the Campbells* : *Colin*, perhaps
from Ailean

Caimbeul (*wry mouth* cf. cerrbél)—*Campbell* p. 151

Camshron, Camaran (*wry nose*)—*Cameron*

Cathal, W. Catgaul (catu-val-os *war powerful*)—*Kathel,
MacAll, Call, MacKail*

Ceallach (ceall *cell*, cf. N. Kjallakr) *Kelly, MacKelly, Mac-
killaig, Kellock*

Ceanaidech *Kennedy*, ceann-aodach *head-protector* H.S.D.,
MacCennétig *id*. (Bk. of Deer); alternatively, MacUaraig,
Mac Ualraig (Mull and Lagan) from Irish Ualgharg
proud and fierce ; Ulgric (Galloway), *Greig* cf. Cyricus :
v. Ulrick

Cinaed (cináed *fire-sprung*) *Kenny, MacKenna, MacKinnie*

Coinneach, Ir. L. Cainnechus *Kenneth, MacKenzie, Mac-
Whinnie* (Galloway)

Colla, MacColla *MacColl*

Conchobhar *(dog-help)*, *MacConcher* (Lorne), *Connacher* (Atholl), *Crohore* (Ulster)

Conn *Conn*, Mac Cuinn *MacQueen*, *MacCunn*, *MacGuinn*, *Quinn*, S.O. 150ᵇv ; *MacWhan* (Galloway)

Criathra(i)r *(sievwright) Crerar*, Angl. *Caesar*

Diarmad (di-format *un-envy*, L. Diormitius) *Dermid*, *Mac-Dermid*, *Kermode* (Man)

Domhnall (dubno-valdo-s *world-ruler*), MacDomhnuill *Macdonald*, *MacCainil* (Tiree), *MacWhannell* (Galloway)

Donnchadh (donno-catu-s *lord and warrior*) *Duncan* ; Mac Dhonnchad *MacConachie*

Dubh *(black one) Duff* ; Mac Duibh *Macduff* ; and Mac-in-duibh, Mac-an-duibh *MacIndoe*, *MacAdoo*

Dubhgall *(a Black Gaul)*, MacDhughaill *MacDougall*, *Mac-Dowel*, *Doyle*

Eachunn (eqo-donno-s *horse lord*), *Hector* (Gk. holder), *MacEchan*

Eanruig (Ger. Heim-ric *home ruler)—MacKendrick*, *Henry*, *Henderson*, *Henryson*, *Harrison*

Eideard E. *Edward*, *MacEdward* ; also N. Imhear, Iomhar v. MacIamhair. Anglicised *Edward* for *Ivor*

Eireamhon *Irvine*, *Irwin*

Eòghann, Gall. Esu-gen(us), L. Eugenius, Gk. ἐυ-γενής, M.W. Ywein, Ewein, later Owein, *well-born*, Angl. *Hugh* (Argyll)

Fearchar *(man-loving)*, Mac Fearchair *MacKerracher*, *Farquharson*, *MacFarquhar*

Fearghas *(man-choice*, W. gwr-gwst) *Fergus*, *MacKerras*, *Fergusson*, *Ferguson*, *Corkish* (Man)

Fionnghall *(a white Gaul)—Fingal*

Fionnla, Fionnlagh (fionn-laoch *white hero)—Finlay* ; Mac-Fhionnlaigh *MacKinlay*, *Finlayson*, *Kinley*

Gall, L. gallus, (1) *a Gaul*, (2) *a Viking*, Innse Gall *the Hebrides*, (3) *a Lowlander* ; hence *Gallie*, Gall chobhair *Gallagher*, Mac an Ghoill *MacGill*, Mac Gall Breath—*Galbraith*, G. Mac a' Bhreathnaich, Mac a' Bhreatunn-aich ; hence *Coubruch*, *Coubrough*, *Brough*, cf. Tannahill poems p. 19 where W. Galbraith is called Willie Cobreath i.e. Cuimbreach *Welshman*

Goraidh, N. god-fridr *(God's peace)—Godfrey*, *MacGorry*, *Gorrie*, *Corrie*

Guinne, Gunnach, N. Gunn- *war* + (-bjorn *bear*, or -olfr *wolf*)
—*Gunn*, Ir. MacGiolladhuinn (*son of the brown lad*),
Gunson, § 107, 12

Harailt (N. Haraldr, E. *Herald*)—*Harold, MacRaild* ; by
metathesis *Walter*, Mac Bhaltair whence *Watt, MacWattie,
Watson, MacQuat, Howat, Hewitt, Huie, Balaire, Qualter*,
(Man), Gwatkin (Wales), *MacQuoid* (Gall.), *Boyd*

Lachlan, Lachunn, Mac (Maol, or) Gille Sheachlainn
MacLachlan, Lachlan ; Mac Mhaol-sheachlainn (Mart.
Donegal)

Ladman, Mac Laomuinn (*law-man*)—*Lamond, MacClymond*

Mac *son*, as a surname, *Mack*, began the name of some
Saint, §107, 12 ; similarly Mac Gille *MacGill* : v. Gall

Mac-a-Phì, Mac Dub shíthe (*son of the Black one of peace* or
Faëry)—*Macduffie, MacPhee, MacGuffie, MacHaffie,
MacCràbhaidh, MacVey*

Mac Amhlaidh (Mac Óláfr, Anláf)—*MacAulay, Cawley,
Collie, Cowley*

Mac Dhuinn shléibhe—*son of the Brown one of the hill*—Ir.
Dunlevy (*Dunlop*). Anglicised *Livingstone*

Mac an Léigh (*son of the physician*, liaig, g. lega)—*MacLeay*

Mac an Tòisich (TOVISACI)—*MacIntosh*

Mac an t-Saoir (*son of the artificer*)—*MacIntyre, MacTear,
MacTeer*

Mac Aidh (O.G. éd *fire*, Gk. $\hat{a}\iota\theta$os, L. aestus)—*MacKay,
MacGhie, Mackie*; Mac hÆdha *MacHeth, Heth, Head,
Hugh*, Angl. *Hugh* (Hugo), hence *MacCue, Cue,
Kew, Keugh* (Man) ; dim. Maedoc *Maddock* (Wales),
Aed-uc-an, Aoidhean *MacKeegan, Egan, Macquien* ;
O hÆdha *Hay*

Mac Asgaill (N. Askell, Asketill *sacrificial kettle*)—*Mac
Askill, Caskell, Castell*

Mac Beatha (*son of life*) later aspirated Mac Bheatha
MacBeth

Mac Beathain (id. with suff. -án, -agno-s §123, 2)—*MacBean*
(*MacBain*), *Mac Vean, Beaton*

Mac Calmain (*son of a little dove*)—*MacCalman* ; Anglicised
also *Murchison, Dove, Dubh*

MacCaog (Tadg, Tasg-os *Teague*)—MacCaig, Ir. *Thady,
Timothy*, v. Tadeus

Mac Cardaidh *MacHardy*, Mac na Ceàrd dubha *or* umha *son of the blacksmiths* or *copper-smiths*

Mac Codrum (N. Got-ormr *good serpent, holy serpent*)—*Mac-Codrum*

Mac Cormaig, Cormac (corb mac *charioteer*)—*Cormack, MacCormic*

Mac Corcadail (Mac Thorketill *son of Thor's kettle*)—*Mac-Corquodale, MacCorkindale, McCorkle*

Mac Cruimein (N. Ruman, Hromundr, but cf. as more likely Crimthan *fox* § 112, 2) — *Mac Crimmon, MacCriomthainn*

Mac Cuaig *MacCuaig* : Anglicised *Cook*

Mac Cuimrid (W. Cymro *Welshman*, *com-brogo-s)—*Montgomery, McGommery*

Mac Cuinn v. *Conn*

Mac Cullach (Mac-Cu-Uladh *son of the Dog of Ulster*, A.U. 1072)—*MacCulloch, Culloch* ; Mac gille Ulaidh *Mac-Lulaich*

Maceachuinn, Mac-Each-dhuinn (*son of the horse-lord*)—*Maceachan*

Mac-Each-ri (*son of the horse-king*, A.U. 1102)—*Mac Kechnie*

Mac-Each-thighearn (*son of the horse-lord*)—*MacKechern*

Mac Fhitheachain (*son of the little raven*)—*Mackichan*

Mac Fhraing, Mac Fhraingein (*son of S. Francis*)—*Rankein, MacCracken* (Galloway)

Mac Gille *MacGill* (*a curtailment of a name*, e.g.) Mac-gille-maol *MacMillan* : v. Mac, § 107, 12

Mac gille—some adjj., notably names for colours following a personal name, are translated into surnames, and compounded with mac and mac gille :

fear (e.g. Iain) bàn *Whyte*, Mac báin *Macbain, Bain* ;
    Mac gille bhàin *MacElvaine*

    buidhe *Yellow*(lees), Macbuidhe *Bowie* ;
    Mac gille bhuidhe *MacElvee, Gilbey* ;
    O gille bhuidhe *O'Gilvie, Ogilvie*

    dubh *Black, Dow*, transliterated *Dove*,
    whence *MacCalmain* ; Mac duibh
    MacDuff, Duff ; Mac gille dhuibh
    MacGillewie

glas *Glass, Grey, Green* ; Mac gille ghlais, dim. Mac gille ghlaisein *MacGlashan*

gorm, Mac gille ghuirm *Blue*, dim. Macguirmein *MacGorman*

mòr *More, Moore* ; gille mor *Gilmour*, W. Gillamor

naomh, gille naomh-an *Niven* ; Mac gille naoimh *MacNiven, Macgilnew* (Bute)

odhar *Orr, Brown* ; Mac an uidhir *Maguire, Weir* ; Mac gille uidhir *MacClure*

riabhach *Rioch* ; Mac gille riabhach *MacIlwrath, MacIlraith, MacIlraick* (Galloway), *Darroch* (Jura)

ruadh, Mac ruaidh *Roy*, Sc. *Reid* ; MacIain-ruaidh *MacInroy* ; gille ruadh *Gilroy* (Sc. *Reid*) ; O maol ruadh *Milroy* ; Mac gille ruaidh *MacIlroy*

MacGuaire (Ir. guaire *noble*, Gk. γαῦρος *proud*, L. gaudeo *rejoice*) *MacQuarrie, MacHarry, Quarrie*

Mac Iain v. Eòin

Mac Iamhair (N. Ivarr) *MacIver, MacEur, Ure, MacCure* (Galloway) ; Mac gille Ivair *MacLiver, Cleaver*

Mac Labhartaigh *MacLarty*, Ir. *MacLaverty, MacLardie* ; O Flaithbheartaigh (*resourceful prince*)—*Flaherty*

Mac Lachlan v. Lachlann

Mac Leòid (ljòtr *ugly* sc. ulf *wolf*, cf. Thor-ljòtr) *Macleod, Cloud*

Mac Mathan, Mathanach, Mac a' mhathain (mathgaman *bear*)—*Matheson, MacMahon*

MacNair, 1. Mac an uidhir—*son of the dun one* (Gareloch, Lennox) ; Mac-in-uidhir *Kinnear* ; Mac Iain Uidhir (Glengarry)

2. Mac an oighre (*son of the heir*) Perthshire

3. Mac an fhuibhir (*son of the artificer*) Argyll

4. Mac an fhuidhir (*son of the stranger*) McB.

5. Mac an mhaoir (*son of the officer*) Ir. cf. Waifs v. 18, also *Weir*

Mac Neacail, L. Nicolas *Nicholson, MacNicol* ; Mac Creacail, *Knickell* (Man)

Mac Neachduinn (necht *pure*, nigh *wash*)—*MacNaughton, MacNaught, MacCracken*

Mac Nèill (G. dub, L. niger, dim. nigellus, N. Njall, Niall
champion)—*MacNeil, Neil, Nigel, Nelson, Neilson* ;
MacRèill *MacReul,* Mac Niall-gus — *Mac Nelis* whence
Mac Neilage ; *Kneal(e)* (Man)

Mac Neis, Naois, dial. *son of Aonghus*, perhaps Naoise

Mac Niadh (*son of a champion*, nia)—*Mac Nee*

Mac Rath (*son of grace*)—*Mac Rae, Macraw, Craw, Crow*

Mac Raonuill (N. Rögn-valdr *gods' ruler*)—*Ranald, Randal,
Mac Ranald, Mc Crindle, Clanranald* ; Mac Ic Raonuill,
Macdonald of Keppoch, Reynold

Mac Suibhne (an t-Suain *Sweden,* N. Svænskr *Swedish*)
Sweeney, MacSweyne, MacSween, MacSwan ; *Sweden*

Manus, Mànus (N. & L. magnus) *Magnus, MacManus, Mac-
Venish, MacVanish, MacVarrais*

Méinn, Méinnear, Méinnearach *Menzies*

Moirreach (Moravia, Mor-apia) *Murray, Morra, Morrow*

Muireach (Muiredhaich, Muiredach) *Murdoch,* Mac Muireach,
MacMurich, MacVurich, Currie, Corie (Galloway)

Murchadh (mori-catu-s *sea warrior*)—*Murchie, MacMurchy,
Murphy, Murcheson* ; *Curphy* (Man)

Muir-cheartach (*sea-director*)—*Mac Ururdaigh, Mac Kirdy,
Mac Kurdy, MacMurtrie,* Ir. *Moriarity, Mac Curdie,
Curdie*

Muriel f. (mori-gela *sea-white*)—*Muriel*

O Duibhne (*grandson of* Duben f., gen. duibhne, Ogham
DOVVINIAS) Duimhneach, better Duibhneach, the
Campbell surname *O'Dwine, O'Duinn*

Raibert, Robart, Rob (A.S. hrôdr *fame* + berht, bjartr *bright*)
—*Robert, Robertson, MacRobin, MacRobbie* ; MagRobhar-
taigh *Magrourty, Rafferty*

Rothach, Mac an Rothaich (bun-roe mouth of R. Roe in
Derry) *Munro*

Ruadh (*red*) *Roy* ; v. Mac gille

Ruairidh (ruadh-rí *red king*)—*Rory, Mac Rory, Mac Ryrie,
Mac Creery, Rorison*

Seaghdh (segda *stately*)—*Shaw* ; Mac Gille Sheathanaich,
Angl. *Seth*

Sigfrid, Sigurd *MacSiridh, Sherry*

Sigtrygg, Sitrig *Mac Kittrick, MacKettrick*

Somhairle (N. sumar-lidi *summer sailor*)—*Somerled, Sorley,
   MacSorley, MacGourlay, Gourlay*;   Angl. *Samuel,
   Samuelson*

Torcul, Torcall (N. Thorkell, Thorketill, v. Mac Thor Ketill)
   —*Torquil*; *MacCorkell, Corkill, Corkhill*

Tormoid, Tòrmod, dial. Tormailt ;   earlier Tormund (Thór-
   módr *Thor's wrath*, Thormundr *Thor's protection*)—
   Norman

Uilleam (Ger. Will-helm *helmet of resolution*)—*William,
   MacWilliam, Williamson, Willison*

Uisdean (N. Hug-steinn, poet. *heart-stone*) — *Uisdean,
   MacQuiston, MacCutcheon, Hutcheson, Hugh* (Uist)

Ul-rick (*patrimonially rich*) confused with O.G. Ualgarg
   (*high tempered*) hence *Ulgrig, Mac Ualraig, Mac Uaraig,
   Gouldrick* ; v. Ceanaidech

§ 112.   PLACE NAMES DERIVED FROM THE NAMES OF SAINTS.

1. Place-names are formed by the aid of prefixes and suffixes,
usually from the stem of the Saints' baptismal name, the first
syllable of which is stressed, § 112, 4

2. Pet names are formed by using part of the baptismal name,
or by using a pet name from another source, and adding a suffix
or suffixes expressing endearment, eg. **-oc**, **-och**, **-ac**, **-ach**, **-an**
(**-can**), **-en**, **-ene**, **-in** ;   and the vowels **-a**, **-o**, **-u**, **-e**, **-i**, to a part of
the original baptismal name, or to the pet name.

The following are instances of two or more names for the same
person :

Baptismal.	Popular.	Alternative.
Cadoc	Cathmael	
Cathach	Mochuda	
Centigern	Mungo	Glaschu
Crimthan *fox*	Columba	St. Colm, Malcolm, O.G. Mo Chumma
Cronan	Mochua	
Darerca	Monenna	
(St. Patrick's sister)		
Fintan	Berach	Mobhí

Baptismal.	*Popular.*	*Alternative.*
Succat	Patricius	Cothraige
		MacCalphuirn
		Magonius
		Molemnach

Examples of honorific vowel suffixes :

-a- Barr-a (Island of)
-o- Moli-o (Blackwaterfoot)
-u- Munn-u (St. Munn)
-e- Barr-e, Dolais-e
-i- Brig-i (Brigit, mo Brigi:—Hy. v. 99), Mo-ninn-i (Ninian), Kinglas-i

3. Along with these suffixes, prefixes of endearment are used, i.e. the 1st and 2nd sing. possessive pronouns **mo** (also **ma, mi**) *my*, **do** (also **da, de**) *thy* (**to, t'**, before vowels or under the accent, §121, 2) following a locative case of baile, ceall, ceann, dùn, eaglais, teampul etc., §7 iv., such prefixes one or more are generally used with the suffix of endearment §7 iv.

St. Earn is styled Mo-Earn-oc—*Marnock*
T'Earn, Bennchar-t-Earn-an—*Banchory Ternan*

The pet name may be an entirely different word, recalling some incident of the Saint's history, e.g. Calumcille—*the dove of the church.*

4. The stress seldom rests (except by elision) on the possessive or other prefix, but almost always on the first syllable of the stem of the baptismal name or of the pet name. Occasionally it rests upon the affix—e.g. Kill-mo-Aed-oc—*Kilmadock* (Doune) §7 ii. 3

5. Unstressed pretonic syllables are sometimes dropped :

(Ecc)Lesmahago *Lesmahago*, v. Cutus § 112, 9
(Ei)Lean-mo-Lais *Lamlash*
(I)renaeus *Rinnieshill, Kilrenny* (Fife)
(Mur)Dockie's Chapel (Monifieth)

Many instances occur of

(1) Assimilation : Maelrubha *Maree*
(2) Nasalisation : *Moness* (Aberfeldy) : Bun-ess §16, 4
(3) Denasalisation : *Poll-ma-dì* (Ninian), §112, 9

(4) Metathesis : St. Pensandus   *Kilspindie*
                   Nathalan   *Bothelney*

(5) Syncope : Brigit g.s. Brigde   *Bryde*
              Llan Ethernascus   *Lathrisk*
              Sanct Rowan   *Strowan*

6. In either the baptismal name or the pet name of a Saint, part of the name may be used for the whole.

(1) In dissyllabic cpds. either syllable may be taken :
    Findbarr *white-poll*
       Mo + find + u—(Eilean) *Mund* ; *Barr* (Dornock, Ayr)

(2) In polysyllabic names not cpds., the part taken is the first syllable, close or open ; or the first letter only :

    (a) close—
          Mo-Lais-e   :   Lassar
          Mo-Bhrìgh :   Brigit

    (b) open—
          Kilma-lu-og :   Lu- Lugaid
          Poll-ma-dí   :   Ni- Ninian

(3) The first letter only :
        (Mo) **Bhí** stands for the aspirated -**b**- of Bega, Berchan, Brenaind ; **Kildavie**, *Kil-da-bhi* (Kintyre), **St. Mauvie**, *Mo-bhi* (Kirkhill)

7. In place and proper names compounded of two elements when the first element is a monosyllable ending in a liquid, e.g. barr m. *top* ; beinn f. *peak* ; cam *crooked* ; ceann m. *head* ; cill *at the cell* ; druim m. *ridge* ; gèarr *short* ; gleann m. *glen* ; poll m. *pool* ; toll m. *hole* ; torr m. *hill*, a **Svarabhakti vowel**, § 65, occurs between the first element and the second :—

    am Barr-a-Calltuinn *Barcaldine*
    am Barr-a-glas, *near Oban*
    am Barr-a-mór, *in Appin*
    am Beinn-e-ghlas, *in Glenfalloch*
    Camshron, Camaran *Cameron*
    an Ceann-a-garbh, *on Loch Sheil*
    Cill-i-Mhàilidh *Kilmallie*
    Cill-i-Mhóire *Kilmore*

Druim-i-liath *Drumalea* in Kintyre
Gleann-a-Comhann *Glencoe*
an Torr-a-donn, *in Glengarry*
an Tom-a-bàn *Tombane*

8. The language of Scotland and of the Highlands before the advent of Gaidhelic, modern Gaelic, from Ireland was Old British, now called Welsh. Gaelic almost completely displaced British surnames. An exception is found in :

Morgan, M.G. clann Mhorghuinn : *mori-canto-s
sea-white, G. MacAoidh *MacKay*

Clans of Norse origin are situated within the Highland Line, and speak Gaelic.

The names of some clans originate from place names or territorial designations outwith the Highland Line, and the members of some of these clans are chiefly Lowland :

Chisholm, G. *Siosal, Siosalaich,* Chisholm in Roxburghshire
Cumming, G. *Cuimein, Cuimeanach,* De Comines
Forbes, G. *Foirbeis, Foirbiseach,* Forbes in Aberdeenshire
Fraser, G. *Friseal, Frisealach,* De Fresel a family of Touraine
Gordon, G. *Gòrdan, Gòrdon, Gòrdonach,* Gordon in Berwickshire
Logan, G. *Logain, Loganach,* Logan in Ayrshire

The names of some clans are English :

Durward (doorward), G. *Mac in Dorsair* ; earlier clan-an -oister, L. ostiarius *Porter* §109
Grant (grand, E. and French), G. *grannd* : but cf., as more likely, grant .i. liath O'Cl.
Stewart, from (Robert II.) High Steward of Scotland, G. *Stiubhartach*
Sutherland, from the name of the County, G. *Suthurlanach*

9. EXAMPLES OF PLACE NAMES FROM SAINTS' NAMES, from which old Scottish Place Names have to a large extent originated :

Adamnanus, Abdomnan L.C. 46
with **mo**- (repeated and aspirated) and -**oc**, Kill-mo-mo-Eon-aig *Kilmaveonaig* (Atholl)
with **do**- *T-eunan Kirk* (Forglen), S. *Tennent's Well* (Angus), S. *Tennent's Fair* (Beith)

with **ard-** and **-oc** *Ard-Eon-aig* (Lochtay), *Tunnie, Theunan, Kill-Eunan* (Kintyre)

Aed, with **mo-** and **-an**, Kill-mo-Aed-an *Kilmodan* (Glendaruel), *Balmhaodan* (Ardchattan), *Balmaghie* (Mag Aodha, Ir. form in Galloway, §107, 8, (2))

with **mo-** and **-oc,** *Kilmadock* (Doune)

with **mo-** and **-ocus**, Mo-Aed-oc-us *St. Madoes* (perhaps Madianus), *Balmadies* (Forfar)

with **mo-** and **-an-us**, Mo-Aed-anus, Middanus—*St. Maidies* Well (Airlie), *St. Maddan* (Freswick)

with **mo-** repeated and aspirated, the Saint's name appears as mo-mo-Aed-oc *Momhaedoc*

Be-an, Ir. mophiog = mo-Bhí-og *Kirkbean* (Kirkcudbright), Bail-Beni-mor *Balvanie* (Mortlach),
Begha f. *Kilbagie, St. Bees*

Berach *Kilberry, Barryhill* (Alyth), with **-án** Berchan *Kilbarchan*

Blane *Dunblane* (Dun Blathnan)

Boisil *St. Boswell's, Basil*

Brandan *Kilbrandon* Sound, *Kilbrennan, Kilvrannyn* (Mull), *Kilbrengan* (Kilbar, Banff, St. Kilda) ; Kilbirinn-i *Kilbirnie, Dunbarney* ; Birin-i *Birney* (Moray) ; Brend-i *well* (Abernethy)

The clan name MacGillivray is hence derived. Three forms of it are in common use, corresponding to three forms of the Saints' name :

Brannan hence Mac gille Bhrá
Brannain ,, Mac gille Bhrái
Brennen ,, Mac gille Bhré

Briget, g.s. Brígde f.—*Kilbride* (Glasgow, Arran), *Brydehill* (Dumfries), *Cladh mo Bhrìgh* (Dingwall), *Kirkmabreck* (i.e. Brigheag (dedicated to St. Brigit), *Lhanbryd* (Elgin), *Panbride* (Carnoustie)

L. Canicus, G. Cainnech, E. Kenneth, *Kennaway, Inch Chenzie* (R. Islay), *Kilchenzie* (Maybole), *Cambuskenneth*

Cathan *Kilchattan, Ardchatan*

Colm-an, L. columbanus, Colman-eala *Calmonel, Kilcalmonel* with **mo-, -oc**, *Kilmochalmaig* (Rothesay), *Portmahomac* (Tarbert) a dim. from

Columba, I Cholum Chille *Iona, Kilcholmkill, Kilmalcolm* ; Comman *Kilchoman* (Islay) i.e. Kilchomm-an, Kil-cholumb-an ; Conan *Kilconan* (Fortingal), *St. Conan* (Glenorchy) i.e. Kilconn-an, Kilcolman-an ; with **mo-, -oc**, Mochonog

Conchobhar (*dog-help, powerful-help*), Connor—*Kilconquhar*

Congal, Congall *Cowall, Dercongal (Daughter of Congal)* or *Holywood*

Congan, Comgan *Kilchoan, Kilchowan* (Kiltearn), *St. Congan* (Skye), *Kirkcowan*

Connell *Kirkconnel*

Constantine *Chousland* Chapel (nr. Cranston), *Kilchouslan* (Campbeltown), *Kil-d-uslan, Kilduskland* (Loch Gilp), *Kircostintyn* (Calmonell), *St. Causnan's Well* (Dunnichen)

Cormac *Coirechormaic* (Killin), *Kirkcormac* (Kelton)

Cumine *Suidh-chuiman* (Boleskine), *Kilchuimen* (Fort Augustus)

Cutus, Machutus, Machud, Killmochuda *Kilmacuddy* (King's Co.), Eccles-ma-Chuda *Lesmahago*, and perhaps *Kilmahoe* (Kintyre) and *Kilmahew* (Cardross)

Cyricus, Ciric, Giric *Ecclesgreg, Ceres*, n. pr. Malgirg

Dalta, Eoin na bruinne Dalta Dei — *John of the breast, fosterling of God*, hence *Kildalton* (Islay)

Davius, Dabius, Dabiu (mobiu, mo-phi-og, Mo-ve-an, Movean derived from **-b-** or **-bi-**, the first letter or syllable of some saint's baptismal name §112, 6, and used ex-hagiogenesi for *David* ; hence *Kildavie* (Kilninian, Mull) ; with **mo**, *Mauvie's* well (Kirkhill) ; with dim., Dun-dyv-an

Devi is the Welsh Saint c. at Bennchar Devi-nic *Banchory Devenic, St. Denick's* fair (Methlick), *Teavneck* (Criech)

Diarmid *Chapel Dermid* (Ross)

Donan *Kildonan* (Arran, Egg, Colmonel, Kintail, Lochbroom, Uig, Uist) ; v. Ninian p. 161

Dronach *Glen-dronach*

Drostan (corrupted from Drusus) *St. Drostan* (Caithness, Cannisby, Edzell, Lochlee) *Newdosk, Skirdurstan (parish of Drostan, now joined to Aberlour), St. Trostan* (Halkirk,

Duffus (from Dubh *black*) *Duffus,* cf. W. Duffws, N. Dufgus

Duthach, Dubtach *Kilduich* (head of Loch Duich), *Kilduthie* (nr. Loch of Leys), *Arduthie* (nr. Stonehaven), *S. Duthus' Well* (Cromarty)

Ebba *St. Abbs's Head*

Englatius *T'anglan* (well, and ford, at Tarves)

Ernadil *Kilernadil* (Jura)

Ernan *Killernan*, G. Cill-iùrnain, dedications uncertain, **v.** Laisren

with **mo**-, and **-oc**, **-och**—*Marnoch* (Strathbogie), *Marnock* (Arbroath), *Dalmarnock* (Little Dunkeld), *Inchmarnock* (Aboyne), *Kilmarnock* (Ayr) ; with **to**- Bennchar T' ernan—*Banchory Ternan* (confused with Torannan), *Baldernock* (older Buthirnok cf. F.M. 714)

Etaoin f.—*Ethan's Well* (Burghead) ; with **mo**-, Moduena, Moedoena, Mandoena, Modwenna (or Monynne) ; perhaps also M'Edana *St. Medan's* (Luce), *Kirkmaiden* (Wigton-shire)

Ethernanus, Iphernan *St. Eddran's Slack* ;

with **to**-, *Tu-Etheren's Fair* (Brechin),

Eglish Taran (Island of Taransay)

Ethernascus, with **Llan**- *Lathrisk* (Fife)

Fechin *St. Vigean's* : with **mo**- Mo(fh)écu, called Corvulus in Latin (from fíach m. *raven*),

with **eclais**- *Ecclesfechan*

Fergus *S. Fergus* (Buchan)

Fiachra, Fiacre *S. Fithoc's* (graveyard), *S. Ficker's* Bay, *S. Fiacer's* Church (Nigg, nr. Aberdeen) ; with **mo**-Mofutack now locally *Fittie*. The church is later *S. Muffett's*, *S. Musset's*. Further corrupted to Mill of *Pottie* (Dron), *Kirkpottie* (Dunbarney). §107, 11

Fillan (faol-an *little wolf*), two saints :—1. *S. Fillan's* (Loch-earn), 2. *Strathfillan* (Killin), whence *Killellan* (Renfrew), *Killellan* (Lochlash), *S. Phillan's* (Forgan)

Fincana f.—*S. Phinks* Chapel (Bendochy, Coupar-Angus)

Findbarr, Finnbarr, Finbarr—

Barr (Ayrshire), *Inchbarr* (Forfar), Isle of *Barr-a* where is *Kilbarr* ; with **mo**- *Kilmorack* (Inverness), *Maworrock* (Lecropt), *Kilmorick* (Dowally) ; *S. Barr's Island* (Kilkerran) has now **do**-, *Davar*, *Devar*

Findchan *Kilfinnichen* (Mull)

Finlagan *Lochfinlagan* (Islay)

Finnianus, Finian—*Finzean* (Brise), *St. Finzean's Fair* (Migvie, Perth)

Fintan—*Kilintag* (Morvern), *Glenfintaig* (Lochaber) § 110

Fintan (Munnu, Mun, i.e. mo-Find-u)—
Kilmunn (Holy Loch), *Eleanmande* (Appin).
S. Munde's Island (Invercoe) ; with Llann-, and -án
Lumphanan (Mar), *Lumphinnan* (Dunfermline) ; with
Inis-, and -án *Inchinnan*

Flannan (red), *Flannan Islands* (Lewis)

Fotinus, Pothinus (of Torry, Aberdeen) hence perhaps
Kirkpottie v. sub Fiachra

Francis, Teampull Frangach (Strath, Skye)

Fyndoca f.—*Findo-Gask* (Dunblane)

Glascianus (i.e. Mungo)—*Kinglassie* (i.e. cill-mo-glass-i, near
Kirkcaldy), *Kilmaglas* or *Kilmalosh* (Strachur) i.e. kill-
ma-ghlais

Gorman *Suidhe-Ghuirmein* (Glen Urquhart)

Herald *Killespickerrel* (Muckairn)

Hilary, with **to**-, *Teller's Well* (Drumblade)

Inan (=Adamnan)
with **to**- *Tenant's Day* (Beith), and *S. Inan's Well*,
Southenan (Capella Sti. Annandi)

Kennere f. *Kirkinner* (Galloway)

Kentigern v. Mungo

Kessog (MacIsaac), *Kessock Ferry* (Inverness) : with **do**,
Kin-t-essack (Forres) : with **mo**, *Feil-ma-Chessaig* (Callander, Cumbrae), *Tom-ma-Chessaig* (Callander) Eccles-
Malesoch, or Eglis-Malescok (Mael-Isaac-oc) i.e. *Carluke* ;
also Kil-mal-isaig

Kevoca f., later m. (Caemh-og, mo-chaemhoc)—
S. Quivox, S. Evox (Ayr), *Kevockburn* (Eaglesham)

Laisren (lassar, lassair f. *flame* ; éd, Aed *fire*, and for the
idea cf. the Heb. Seraphim *burning ones*). The name
is perhaps divided into two (1) Lais- (2) -ren, with the
Svarabhakti vowel, -iren -eren whence Ern, Ernan, etc.
   (a) with **mo**-, Mo-lais-i *Kilmalash, Lamlash* (Eilean-mo-
      Laisi), Mo Li-o
   (b) with **do**-, Do-lass-e, Da-lais-e : F.M. 638

Laurentius *Lawrencekirk*

Lugaid (**Lu**-, or **L**- only, is used in S. Moloc's name) with **mo**- and **-oc,**

>   Kil-mo-lu-ag (Lismore, Skye, Mull, Tiree), Luoch Fair (Tarland), Molouach, Malachi, Malogue (Alyth), Balmoloch (Kilsyth), Kilmoloig (Killean), Kilmolowaig (Kilberry)

Mac-Eòghan, Kil-vic-euen (Mull, Ulva) and probably S. Skeoch (Dunninald, Rothesay, S. Ninians), Skay

Machalus, Machella, Manchold Kilmaichlie (Inveravon)

Machan, Manchan Ecclesmachan, Chapel S. Machan (Clyne), S. Machan's Altar (Glasgow Cathedral)

Machua, Kirkmahoe (Dumfries) called also Cronan §112, 2. There is, however, S. Coe, Mochoe of Oendruim, June 23

Maelrubha Loch Maree, Kilmolray (Arasaig), Kilarrow (Islay), Kethmalruf i.e. Keith : Poll Mhàilidh (Glen Urquhart), Cill Mhàilidh Kilmallie, and Dail Mhàilidh Dalmally ; Maol-ag-an Stron Milliken (Dalmally)

Magnus S. Magnus' Cathedral (Kirkwall), S. Magnus Bay (Shetland)

Malduff, for Mailduff, founder of Malmesbury, Kylmalduff i.e. Inverary, Kilmaliew (Argyll) ; Cross Malduff Crossmyloof (Glasgow)

Malie (**Le**-, or **Li**-, the first letter of the name of some saint unidentified) Kilmalie i.e. Golspie, Kilmalie (Morvern), Egsmalee (Kinghorn), Killmalenoch and Kmilmalemnoc (Elgin) may be Lemnach Lennoxman, i.e. Patrick.

Mauritius, Machar, Mocumma.

>   His baptismal name was Mo-cumma or Mo-chonna v. Columba ; with **do**-, Do-chonna and To-channu ; Mauritius —Moorish, whence Maurice, Morris, Meyrick (Wales) was given him by Pope Gregory. Machar (my loving one) Old and New Machar (Aberdeen), Macker's Haugh (Kildrummie)

Mungo whose baptismal name was W. Cen-tigern Dog-Lord (protecting house-master). The pet name cen-, which is its form as first part of a cpd., resumes its nom. sing. form, W. ci., G. cù. In a Welsh population with an Irish Church, G. glas + cù becomes and remains Glaschu §100, 2 ; W. glas + cù, with soft mutation, becomes Glasgu ; and later the -**u**- was weakened to -o- thus becoming *Glasgow*. In earlier and pure W. glas + ci was infected to Glesci §6 ; and later the -i- was weakened to -a- thus becoming *Glesca*.

By substituting for glas, the ecclesiastical word finn *white, blessed* (W. gwyn eu byd *blessed are*), prefixing honorific mo *my*, and mutating cu, is obtained mo-fhinn-gu which by infection becomes Mungu ; and by the weakening of final unstressed -u- to -o- *Mungo* §7, 2

Similarly by substituting G. liath *grey* (W. llwyd) for glas is obtained Linn-liath-go (*grey dog's pool*)—*Linlithgow*

Murdoch—*S. Murdoch's* Chapel (InverKeillor), *Chapel Dockie* (Monifieth)

Muriel, *Rath-Muriel,* and *Muriel's Well* (Garioch)

Nathalan, Nachlan, Nauchlan (Nechtán nár—*noble Nechtan*) *Bothelney* (Meldrum) corrupted from Bothnethalen ; also *Naughlan's Well, Kilnaughtan* (Kildalton)

Neamhan—Kil-mo-neamh-aig *Kilmonivaig* (Lochaber)

Nethan—*Cambus-nethan.*

Neveth, Neuyeth i.e. *Nevay* (Meigle)

Ninian, *S. Ninian's Bay,* and *Chapel* (Bute), and at least 70 dedications ; in Gaelic -**cn**- is pronounced -**cr**- §59, e.g. MacNicol, MacNaughton ; hence Sanc' Ninian, is often S. Ringan, Rynnan, e.g. *Ringan's Well* (Arbirlot), *S. Rynnanis Chapel* (Stirling), *Kilintringen* or Kilsanctninian (Calmonel), Slios an Trinnein (=Slios Sanct Rinnein) *the hillside of S. Ninian* (Glenmoriston) ; with **mo**-, Mo-nenn (=mo-nēn =mo-nī-ān §40) Moi-nend, Monan *S. Monans* (Fife) ; with accent on first syllable Ní-, *Polmadi* (Pollmadí, for Poll-ma-ni-i, near Glasgow, a leper Hospital dedicated to S. Ninian) ; with **do**-, Kel-du-nin-ach, Kyldonach, Kildonan q.v.

Ninnidius *Kil Saint Ninian* (Mull)

Odhran, Oran *Relig-Oran* (Iona), *Killoran* (Colonsay), *Cladh Odhrain* (Tiree), Oran's-ey i.e. *Oronsay*

Olave *S. Ollow's* Parish, *S. Olla's Isle* (Kirkwall), *S. Ole's Fair* (Cruden), *S. Olla's Chair* (Shetland)

Palladius—*Paldy, Paddy* or *Padie Fair* and *Well* and *Pade Kirk* (Fordoun), *Caisteal Pheallaidh* (nr. Falls of Moness), and *Aberfeldy*

Patricius §112 (Patrician) ; Magonius (well-born) ; Succat, Suthat (Warrior), the last was his Welsh baptismal name. In slavery in Ireland he was called Cothraige, Codrige, a transliteration of Patrici-us ; Gaels having no P, used C for P.

Kilpatrick (Clydeside), *Temple-Patrick* (Tiree), *Kirkpatrick* (Closeburn), *Kilpeter* (Houston), *Kilfether* (Wigtown)

Pensandus *Kilspindie.*

Queranus, Kieran *Kilkerran* (Kintyre), *Kilcheran* (Lismore), *Dalkerran* (Dailly)

Regulus, Rule, Rieul, with **t-**, *Trewell Fair* (Kennethmont). *Crossraguel*

Renny *Kilrenny* (older Kylrethyny, Rothney, popularly *S. Irnie*) corrupted from S. Itharnan

Ronald *Chapel Ronald* (Glenkindie)

Ronan *Kilmaronock*, older Kilmaronen (Lennox, Muckairn), *Tempul Ronain* (Iona), Isle of *Ronay* off Raasay, *Rona* off Lewes, *S. Ronan's* Isle off Zetland

Rowan, S. Rowan *Strowan* (Monzievaird)

Rochus *S. Roque, S. Rook's Chapel, S. Rollach's, S. Rollox* (Glasgow) ; with **suidhe maol**, *Seemi Rookie* (Dundee), Simon Rollock's Kirk (Boroughmuir) § 7, 5

Senan *Killenach* (Mull), *Kilynaig* (Coll), *Killeneck* (Ewes) with **mo-**, Moshenoc, *Kilmahunach, Kilmashenaghan* (Kintyre) with **do-**, *Achdashenaig* (Mull)

Servanus *Serf* (Culross), *S. Sair* in Aberdeen, *S. Serwe* (Dunnottar), *S. Sare's bank* (Culsamond). *Sheer's Well* (Cardross) preserves Gaelic pronunciation of -e-

Talaricanus, Tallorcen, Tallorc (tal-org *Silver Cross*) *Kiltarlity* (Inverness), *Tarkin's Well* (Fordyce), *Céilltarlagan* (Portree)

Thenew, Thanes f., San Theneuke's Kirk *St. Enoch's* (Glasgow)

Tighernach, *Buthtighernach* (Glenlivet), *Killtearn*

Triduana *S. Tredwell* (Restalrig), *Kintradwell* (Loth)

Volucus (Faélchu), Makwoloch, *Wala fair* (Mar), *Wallach's Baths, Kirk* and *Well* (Glass)

Wynnin *Kilwinning, Caer-winning hill* (Dalry)
gwyn-en (gwyn-hen) is the Welsh for Finn-en (finn-shen)
white and old, a pet name for S. Findbarr. Unlenited
gwyn-en appears in Kirk*gunzeon* (Kirkcudbright).
Lenited, i.e. having lost initial -g-, gwyn-en appears
as *Winnin, Winning,* e.g. *Kilwinning.*

§113. **THE PRONOUNS.**

I. PERSONAL PRONOUNS.

Simple.	*Emphatic.*	*Reflexive* with féin *self* added.
	Singular.	
1. mi *I, me*	mise	mi féin, mi fhéin
2. tu, thu *thou* ; thu *thee*	tusa, thusa	thu féin, thu fhéin
3. e *he, him* ; se *he* ; i *she, her* ; si *she*	esan, ese ise	e féin, e fhéin
	Plural.	
1. sinn *we, us*	sinne	sinn féin
2. sibh *ye, you*	sibhse	sibh féin
3. iad, siad *they, them.*	iadsan	iad féin

Gender is distinguished only in 3rd sing. ; case only in 2nd sing.,
3rd sing., and 3rd plural. **mi** may be aspirated. Cha **mhi**—*It is
not I* :—John i. 21 ; Bu **mhi**—*It was I* §24. se *he,* si *she,* siad *they,*
are used only in the nom. and when followed immediately by e,
i, iad ; and only in scriptural language :

Phòg se e—*He kissed him* :—Lk. xv. 20

mi, mise ; thu, thusa ; e, esan ; i, ise, are the forms used in the
acc. or predicate, e.g. :

Cò e a bhrathas thu ?—
Who is he that betrayeth thee ? John xxi. 20

Sts. a preceding final **s** prevents the aspiration of tu :
Is fearr an cù a ni miodal na an cù a ghearras tu—
Better the dog that fawns than the dog that bites :—N.G.P. 240
B'e an gille thu—*What a fine fellow you are* :—Z.C.P. v.474
Féin is used with the 2nd and 3rd persons, N. & S. In the N.
they say : Thu fhéin 's **mi fhin**—*Thyself and myself.*

A form **péin** is in use after 2 pl. **sib péin, sip péin** :—Munro 70;
§20, 5, (4)

Tu is used in addressing the Deity, equals, children, and dependents. **Sibh** is used by children in addressing their parents, by inferiors in addressing their superiors or their elders, and generally as a mark of courtesy whenever appropriate. Hence a plural verb is used of a singular subject :

O ! athair, na bristibh mo chridhe—
O ! father, do not break my heart :—L.C. 63

§ 114.   II. Possessive Pronouns.

1. Possessive pronouns precede their nouns, and the possessive pronouns of the 1st and 2nd sing., and 3rd sing. m. cause aspiration.

    Sing.
1. **mo, m'** (before a vowel)   *my*
2. **do, t'** (before a vowel)   *thy, your*
3. **a** *his*, **a, a h-** (before a vowel)   *her*

    Plural.
1. **ar** (also **nar**), **ar n-** (before a vowel)   *our*
2. **bhur, ur** ; **bhur n-, ur n-** (before a vowel) *your*
3. **an, am** (before labials)   *their*

The emphatic particles—Sing. 1 **-sa**, 2 **-sa**, 3 **-san**, fem. **-sa, -se**,
           Pl.   1 **-ne**, 2 **-se**, 3 **-san**.

and féin in all cases, sing. and pl., are appended to the last word of the expression. Examples of possessives (a) before a consonant, (b) before a vowel, with emphatic particle appended :

(a)   cù m. *dog*
    Sing.   *Plural.*
1. mo chù-**sa**—*my dog*   ar cù-**ne**—*our dog*
2. do chù-**sa**—*thy dog*   bhur cù-**se**—*your dog*
3. a chù-**san**—*his dog*   an cù-**san**—*their dog*
   a cù-**sa**—*her dog*

(b)   athair m. *father*
1. m'athair-**sa**—*my father*   ar n-athair-**ne**—*our father*
2. t'athair-**sa**—*thy father*   bhur n-athair-**se**—*your father*
3. a athair-**san**—*his father*   an athair-**san**—*their father*
   a h-athair-**se**—*her father*

When an adj. qualifies and follows the noun, the emphatic particles are appended to the adj. and conclude the phrase :

mo chù dubh-**sa**	*my black dog*
a each bàn **féin**	*his own white horse*
an diugh **fhein**	*this very day* :—Arab. II. 83

2. The Possessive Pronouns combine in a syncopated form with the prepositions **an**, and **ag** §187, §189 :

an : **am** *in my*, **ad** *in thy*, '**na** *in his* ; e.g. **ad** cheann—*in thy head*, later '**nam**, '**nad** : '**nar** *in our*, '**nur** *in your*, e.g. '**nur** n-àite—*in your place* ; '**na** chridhe—*in his heart* ; or with the preposition doubled—**ann ad** chridhe—*in thy heart* ; **ann am aire**—*in my thoughts*.

'S mi '**m** shuidh' aig an uaigh— *As I sit at the grave* :— S.O. 175ᵃ37

ag : '**gam**, '**gad**, '**ga** :

Ach c'fhada bhios mi 'n so '**gam** chràdh ?—*But how long shall I remain here being tormented* ? :—S.O. 174ᵇ11

'S a gaol **am** mhealladh o m' chéill—

And her love wiling me out of my wits :—D.Ban 204, 114

'Na mhac samhla '**ga** ghoid sud—

In his likeness to steal that :—S.O. 46ᵇ23

3. The possessive pronouns of 3rd person are often used proleptically, anticipating a subject or clause not yet expressed :

A leith cho mhath rium—*half so well as I* :—Arab. II. 2

Thachair **a** leithid de nithean—

Such things have happened :—J. Wesley 9

Cha n'eil **fhios** agam ciod a ni e—

I have no knowledge—of it—what he will do :—L. & W.

'S math **an** cuideachadh sluaigh dhuit—

Good is their help, viz., *of a host—for thee* :—Turner 55, 10

Gun toirt suas **a bh**eag no **mh**òr d'ar saorsa spioradail—

Without giving up (its) *much or little of our spiritual freedom* :— Cuairt. 40, 96

Far an robh **a ch**oilion duine naomh—

Where lived so many good men :—L.C. 58

'Ga cur fhéin '**na** leithid de staid air son ni nach mòr a b' fhiach—*Putting herself in such a state about a thing of little importance* :—Arab. I. 7

Occasionally the 2nd person is so used :—

Cha diùlt sinne fabhar 'sam bith a dh' iarras **bhur** leithid-sa
de mhnathan-uaisle oirnn—*We shall not refuse any favour
that ladies like you will ask of us* :—Arab. I. 97

4. A Possessive Pronoun preceding a verbal noun has the
force of a genitive following the verbal noun :

Oich ! ma ni iad **mo** mharbhadh—
Oh dear ! If they will (make my killing i.e.) *kill me* :—S.O. 55ᵃx
Cha n-e **do** chogadh a shaoil mi theachd orm—
It is not fighting with thee I thought would befall me :—S.O. 38ᵇ6

5. A Possessive Pronoun accompanying a verbal noun, and
following a word that governs the genitive, prevents the verbal
noun from being thrown into the genitive :

Bha h-aon no dhà ag iarraidh **mo** phòs**adh**—
One or two were seeking to marry me :—L.C. 12
Is beò duine an déidh **a** shàrach**adh**, ach cha bheò e an déidh
a nàrach**adh** — *A man may survive distress but not disgrace* :—N.G.P. 218

This usage is sometimes extended to common nouns :

Measg **ar** cinne mòr féin—
Among our own great kin :—S.O. 36ᵃ17
Thar **an** ceann—*Over their head* :—S.O. 174ᵃ20
Thar a ghualainn—*Over his shoulder* :—Cuairt. 27, 61z. §206

6. The presence of a possessive pronoun, though not written,
is inferred in examples like the following—

(1) when a verbal noun stands in the nom. instead of in the gen.:
Ach fuil Dhuibhneach an déidh reòth**adh**—*But the blood
of the Campbells after its coagulation* :—S.O. 42ᵃ14

(2) when (a) **a** *his* causes, and (b) **a** *her*, prevents, aspiration :
(a) mas. Cha tiomaich e le **ph**éin—
He will not soften owing to its pain :—McD. 107
Bu mhaith leam **fh**aicinn—
I should like to see him :—J.W. 85
O sin ta **sh**liochd 'nan deòraibh truagh—*Since then his
descendants are wretched exiles* :—S.O. 178ᵃ23
Grad-thréigidh fhàileadh e 's a shnuadh—
Its fragrance and beauty at once forsake it :—S.O. 178ᵇ4

(b) fem. Fo **d**osraich ùrair (i.e. craobh na beatha) suidhibh
sìos— *Under its fresh foliage sit ye down* :—S.O. 173ᵇ5
O **d**uilleach chùbhraidh òlaibh slàint'—
From its fragrant leafage drink ye salvation :—S.O. 173ᵇ11
'N uair a chairte (also thairte *l.* chu rte) fo **s**eòl i—
When she was put under sail :—S.O. 37ᵇ26

a *his*, being assimilated between vowels, is understood :

Do thilg m**i à**itheanta air mo chùl—
I cast his commandments behind me :—Là Bhr. 449

The following line contains an ex. of a possessive m. and a
possessive f. both omitted in writing :

Cha leagh i **r**ùn le **m**iannaibh laist'—*She will not melt his resolution with her inflamed desires* :—An Gaisgeach 48
The -**r**- of **r**ùn is aspirated.

§ 115. III.—Relative Pronouns.

The rel. forms are :

1. **a** *who, whom, which, that.*
2. **an, am** (before labials).
3. **na** *what, all that.*
4. The negative form is **nach** *that . . . not.*

a is either nom. or acc., sing. or pl.

1. nom. Esan **a** bha agus **a** ta 'na Dhia—
He who was and who is God :—Catm. 21
nom. or acc. Esan a mharbh e—
He who killed him. He whom he killed.
An ti **a** thig am dhéidh—
He that cometh after me :—Math. iii. 11.
acc. Leabhar **a** bheir iad do neach aig am bheil fòghlum—
A book which men deliver to one that is learned :—Is. xxix. 11
Ge b'e taobh **a** théid e—*Whithersoever* (that) *he go* :—L.C. 53
Parataxis with rel. omitted. §116, 1.

2. **An, am** are used in the oblique cases with prepositions :
Tre **an** d' fhuair sinne gràs—
By whom we have obtained grace :—Rom. i. 5

An duine mu'**m** bheil sinn a' labhairt—
The man of whom we speak :—L.C. 44
Thill anam chum an Dé o'**n** tàinig e—
His soul returned to the God whence it came :—L.C. 52

The prepositions **a, an, gu, le, ri**, are followed by an **s** before the relative :

Magdalen **as an** deachaidh seachd deamhain—
Magdalen out of whom went seven devils :—Lk. viii. 2
An dòigh '**san** do chum e suas uachdaranachd—
The way in which he upheld his authority :—L.C. 46
Bha e 'na thosd gu**s an** do bhuail an clag air mheadhon oidhche—
He remained silent till the bell rang at midnight :—L.C. 52
A làn do airgiod agus do òr lei**s an** togainn eaglaisean agus lei**s am** fuasglainn air uireasbhuidh nam bochd—
The full thereof of silver and gold wherewith I might build churches and relieve the want of the poor :—ib. 50
Bha mise ann**s an** eilean ri**s an** abrar Patmos—
I was in the island which is called Patmos :—Rev. i. 9

Whose is expressed
(a) usually by the rel. **a, nach**, with a possessive pronoun and a preposition.
(b) sometimes by an oblique case of the rel. with the article, or
(c) by **agus** with the possessive pronoun, e.g.

(a) So an té **a** fhuair sinn an t-uan o **a** bràthair—*This is the woman from whose brother we got the lamb* :—Munro 180
Sud a' bhean **a** bha sinn a's tigh **aice**—
Yon is the woman in whose house we were :—ib.
Is lìonmhor ròs nach fhaca sùil an glòir—
Many are the roses whose glory eye hath not seen :—Clarsach 21
An rìoghachd **nach** faic **a** sonas crìoch gu bràth—*The kingdom whose happiness shall never see an end* :—S.O. 173ª40
Fo dosraich nach searg 's **nach** crìon am feasd **a** blàth—
Under foliage whose bloom will never wither, never fade :—173ᵇ6
Caisteal mòr nach fhac' Alasdair riamh a leithid—
A great castle the like of which A. had never seen :—Waifs iii.121
Laoch a bha mheud thar gach fear—
A hero whose size exceeded every one :—S.O. 98ᵇ34
Ar ceannard nach robh shamhla measg Ghàidheal—
Our chief whose like was not among Gaels :—151ª34

(b) A' bhean le 'm bu **leis** am mac beò—
   The woman whose the living child was :—1 Kings iii. 26

(c) Is fada cobhair o mhnaoi **'s a** muinntir an Éirinn—
   Aid is far from her whose folk are in Ireland :—N.G.P. 235

Sometimes with **cia** :
   An cual' thu cia 'n t-urram
   An taobh-sa do Lunnuinn ?—
   Have you heard whose is the precedence
   On this side of London ? :—S.O. 148ªw.

3. **Na** *what, all that* : with no antecedent.

nom. Ghabh thu ann an càirdeas **na** thairgeadh gu fialaidh—
   Thou didst take in friendship what was freely offered :—
   L.C. 42
   Thuig gach aon **na** bha 'na bheachd—
   Every one understood what was in his aim :—L.C. 68
   Na thuigeas cha tuig, na ni cha dean—
   They that can understand and act, will not.

acc. Taisg ann ad chridhe **na** chunnaic 's **na** chuala (thu)—
   Lay up in thy heart all that thou hast seen and heard :—
   L.C. 42
   A dh' aindeoin 's **na** their càch—
   In spite of all that others will say :—S.O. 284ª20

gen. Cha n'eil mi a' faotainn **na** tha mi ag iarraidh—
   I do not get what I ask :—Cos. 127

dat. Chuimhnich e air **na** labhair gruagach an fhuilt òir—
   He remembered all that the golden-haired maiden had
   said :—L.C. 39

4. **nach** *that . . . not* : L. ne-que.

nom. Ni **nach** robh, **nach** 'eil, 's **nach** bì—
   What was not, is not, and will not be :—L.C. 42

acc. Nàire **nach** taisicheadh fuathas—
   Self-possession that fear would not sap :—McD. 117

dat. Air neamh air **nach** gluais ceò no neul—*In heaven over*
   which mist or cloud will not pass :—A 'Choisir 9
   Air **nach** cualas mi-chliù—
   Of whom has been heard no ill-report :—S.O. 49ª10
   An àit **nach** robh duine riamh—
   In a place where man never was before :—A'Choisir 16

§ 116.

1. The Rel. **a** is of late origin. It does not occur in the Red Book of Clanranald circ. 1700 A.D., and it is but sparsely met with in the MacRae collection, but it appears regularly in the Turner collection 50 years later.

In the Red Book the rel. **a** still coincides with the past preverb **do-** from which it is chiefly evolved :

> Ag brosnughadh an tshluaigh **do** bhí an ait éisdechta dó—
> *Inciting the host that was within hearing distance of him* :— Red Bk. 190
>
> Do shéol a shoighed ar Raghnall **do** bhuail san pheirceall—
> *He aimed his arrow at Ronald which struck him in the jaw* :— ib. 188
>
> Do chonnaic an seiser as mo . . .**da** faca se . . . roimhe—
> *He saw the greatest six that he had ever seen* :—ib. 192

The verb in these examples is paratactic, i.e. connected with the foregoing part of the sentence only by position.

As its rel. force increased and its preverb force weakened, **a** spread to tenses other than the past. In present-day Gaelic **a** with **dh'**, a relic of the preverb **do-**, is used even before a pres. rel. :

> Fhir **a dh**' imicheas thar chuantan—
> *O man who dost voyage over oceans* :—A' Choisir 15

The development of **do** into rel. **a** was facilitated by forms like **dobheir** *brings*, which became **a bheir** *who brings* ; **do chuaidh** *went*, **a chuaidh** *who went*, **a théid** *who goes*.

> Mach a ghabh na fir—*out went the men* :—Cuairt. 27, 68

Other preverbs like -**ad**-, **as**-, helped to evolve **a** :

> (O.G. adchí) chì *sees*, a chì—*who sees* ;
> (O.G. abair) adeir *says*, a deir, a their—*who says* ;
> (O.G. atá) tha *is*, a tha—*who is*

2. **an, am** in the oblique cases are forms of the true rel.

In origin the rel. is the same as the neuter sing. of the article. The proof is that the original **s** of the article, which is preserved after the prepositions **a, an, gu, le, ri** §115, 2, is preserved also between these propositions and the rel.

A simple preposition, **an** *in*, *in which* is in use :

> Monadh fada réidh,

Cuile 'm faighte féidh—*a long smooth hill, nooks where deer used to be found* :—D. Ban 160, 5

An ro mhaith 'n cinn an stuth—
  in which the crop grows very well :—ib. 80, 18

3. **Na** *what, that which* is in construction and meaning derived from **aní** (neut. sing. of article + **i**) *that which*. As to the form, **ní, na-ní**, neut. sing. of **nech** *anyone*, followed by the relative of the verb ; and **no**- the relative preverb, sometimes written **na**- in M.G., contributed to evolve the modern **na**.

4. **Nach** *that . . . not*, is a development of the O.G. dependent negative **na, nach**. In M.G. it became the nom. of the negative relative pronoun. In O.G. **nach** was the negative particle almost invariably used with an infixed pronoun, or with an infixed relative particle -**n**- e.g.

Con**nach** (-**n**-) rancatar—*so that they reached him not.*

Hence in Modern Irish it causes eclipsis, and in G. except in N. Inverness, it reduces -t- to -d- :

Ciod e nach d' thig (=tig) a Glaschu !—
  What will not come from Glasgow !—Teacht. i. 5
Nach **t**ugadh càch an sgiath chùil deth—
  Whose back wing others would not take off him :—S.O. 50ᵃ8
Bu neònach leis nach **t**àinig iad—
  He was astonished that they had not come :—ib. 150ᵇu
So agaibh brìgh na ceisde dh'a nach d' thugadh (=tugadh)
  freagradh—*Here you have the gist of a question that has not been answered* :—Cos. 28
O nach d'thig (=tig) thu chaoidh nan cian—
  Since thou wilt never never come :—Ross 19
Nach d' thug (=tug) mi dhut do shaorsa ?—
  Have I not given you your freedom ? :—Arab. i. 34

but it does not affect other consonants :

Is fuar an càirdeas nach caoidh bàs caraid—*Cold is the friendship that weeps not the death of a friend* :—L.C. 254
Is ainneamh iad nach feud an gearan bochd so a dheanamh—
  Few are they that cannot make this poor complaint :—ib.

5. **Na** (negative Ipv.) eclipses a following initial -t- :
Na tog mi gus an tuit mi—
  Do not lift me till I fall :—N.G.P. 331. §14

§ 117.   IV. Demonstrative Pronouns.

Indeclinable.

sin—(pronounced slender except in parts of Inverness where it is pronounced broad) *that.*   §57

so—(sometimes written and always pronounced **seo**) *this*

sud—(sometimes written and always pronounced **siud**, or **siod**). *yon, yonder.*

Demonstartive pronouns are sing. or pl.

They are neither declined nor aspirated.

They are used without or with the art. :

so e—*this is he* ; sin iad—*those are they* ; sud i—*yonder is she.*

am fear **so**—*this man.*

am fear **sin**—*that man.*

am fear **ud**—*yon man.*

also along with and qualifying pronouns :

e **so**—*he here* ; iad **sin**—*those there.*

§ 118.   V. Indefinite Pronouns.

1. Có air bith, có 'sam bith, cia 'sam bith, cia b'e air bith—
   Who in the world, whoever, whoso, whosoever.
   Ciod air bith, ciod 'sam bith—*Whatever, whatsoever.*
   Ce b'e 'sam bith—*Whoever, whichever, whichsoever* :—Cos. 45
   Ce b'e có thu—*Whoever you are* :—MacCor. 89

2. Aon—*one*, gach—*each*, a h-uile—*every*, aon eile—*any other one*, aon 'sam bith—*any one*, cuid-eigin—*some one, somebody*, cuid eile—*some others, another part*, feadhainn eile—*others, other people*, a leithid eile—*such another.*

A pronoun referring to càch, gach, feadhainn, sluagh, etc., is in the pl. :
   Chaidh gach duine gu'n àite—
   Each man went to their place :—Munro 179

3. Càch—*others, the rest* ; Càch a chéile—*each other.*
   Is éiginn daibh giùlan le càch a chéile—
   They must bear with one another :—Cos. 45
   Ge h-olc ' sud ' cha n-e ' siad ' as fhearr—
   Tho' ' sud ' be bad, ' siad ' is no better :—N.G.P. 196
   Cia air bith co dòmhail 's a bha e—
   However bulky he was :—Cuairt. 27, 61

4. A common noun fear m. *man, one.*   té f. *woman, one.*
   Fear de na coin so—*One of these dogs* :—Arab. i. 26. §98, 1, 2.
   Té ùr an diugh is té ùr eile am màireach—
   A fresh report to-day and another one to-morrow :—MacCor. 41

§ 119.　　VI. Interrogative Pronouns.

1. Có—*who* ?　Có e—*Who is he* ?　Co í—*Who is she* ?　Co iad—*Who are they* ?

Co dhiùbh—*Which of them* ?　*Whether, indeed.*

Co leis thu—*Whose art thou* ?　*To whom dost thou belong* ?

Co uaidh—*From whom* ?　Cha n'eil fhios agam co iad— *I do not know who they are.*

Co do'n innis mi e—*To whom shall I tell it* ?

Co is i fhéin (*Who and herself* ? i.e.) *Whom will she marry* ?

Cia—*which* ?　Cia lìon—*How many* ?　Cia minig—*How often* ?

Cia meud—*How many* ?　Cia as a thàinig thu—*Where have you come from* ?

Cia mòr do shaoibhreas—*How great is thy richness* :—Là Bhr. 159

Ciamar a tha thu—*How are you* ?

Cionnas (cia-indas)—*how* ?　Cionnas a mhealas sibh gu bràth—*How will you ever enjoy* ? :—Là Bhr. 269

Ceana (cia ionadh)—*whither* ?

Cia fhad', a Thighearna—*How long, O Lord* ? :—Ps. 79, 5

C'ainm a tha ort—*What is thy name* ?

C'àit an robh thu—*Where were you* ? :—C.G. 153

C'uime—*Wherefore, why* ?

C'eadh tha eadar fhlaitheamhnas agus iutharn— *How far is it between heaven and hell* ? :—Z.C.P. V. 462

Ciod—*What is it* ?　O.G. cote ? pl. coteet ?　Ciod uime ? *Why, wherefore* ?

O ! ciod e Dia, no ciod e ainm ?— *O what is God, or what is his name* ? :—Mòrachd Dhé 1.

Ciod e, often spelt Gu dé, Dé—*What is it* ?

The colloquial expressions **Dé** do bheachd ?　**Dé** do bharail ? *What is your opinion* ? throw doubt upon the form ciod e, and especially ciod i. The gender (always mas.) and the pronunciation generally, point to a connection with O.G. cote, catte, cate—*What is* ? pl. cateet cateat—*What are* ?

Ciod e cosmhalachd ?　*What is a parable* ? :—Cos. 1.

2. Dependent Interrogative :

Ag carnadh suas gun fhios **co dhà**— *Heaping up (money) without knowing for whom* :—Clasrach 7

Co ac' a b' eadh no nach b'eadh— *Whether he was or not* :—Cuairt. 27, 68

3. As an alternative :

Cha bhitheadh fios agadsa **co dhiùbh** 's e do cheann no
do chasan a bhitheadh fodhad—*You would not know
whether your head or your feet were under you* :—Cos. 170
cf. **Co dhiùbh** tha thu 'n ad sheasamh air do cheann no air
do chasan :—Am F.C. 240

4. The **answer** to a question contains (or assumes) a repetition
of the verb :

Co as a **thàinig** thu—*Where have you come from* ?
Thàinig mi as an Uachdar—*I have come from Uachdar* :—
Uist Bards, p. xxv.
Am **bheil** Mr. Eachann a stigh ?   Cha n'**eil**—
Is Mr. Hector at home ?   *No.*
Am **bi** e stigh am màireach ?   Cha **bhi**—
Will he be at home to-morrow ?   *No* :—J. W. 85.

While the corresponding form of **is** always appears in the
reply (§72, §144, 1) **is** often brings forward and emphasises
(§180, 1) the real answer, which is a different word :

An **tusa** a rinn Beinn-dòrain—*Did you make Ben Dorain* ?
'Se **Dia** a rinn Beinn-dòrain, ach is **mise** a mhol e—
God made Ben Dorain but I praised it :—D. Ban p. xxxvi.

When the question is complex, the verb may be omitted, and
the answer given to the gist of the question :

Am feud mi Mr. Seumas, no Mr. Iain fhaicinn, ma ta ?—
May I see Mr. James, or Mr. John, then ?
Tha Mr. Iain a stigh.   Ach tha e 'n sàs, agus cha tric leis
mnathan fhaicinn—*Mr. John is at home, but he is engaged, and he seldom sees ladies* :—J. W. 85.

Similarly when the answer requires brevity :

An ann o thuath thàinig sibh—
Have you come from the North ?
Pairt o thuath 's pairt o Thighearnan—
Partly from tenantry and partly from Lairds :—Uist Bards,
p. xxv.

The verb repeated in answer to a question is in the 3rd sing.
as above, §155, 1 (2).   But if emphasis is desired, or if the verb
have an object, the 1st person is used :

An cuireadh tu geall ?   Chuirinn, Chuirinn sin.—
Would you bet ?   *Certainly I would.   That I would.*
An cuireadh sibh geall ?   Chuireamaid.   Dheanamaid sin—
Would ye bet ?   *Certainly we would.   We would do that* :—
Munro 109.

§ 120. THE PERSONAL PRONOUNS COMBINED WITH PREPOSITIONS.

	Sing. 1. *mi me*	Sing. 2. *tu thou*	Sing. 3 Mas. *e him*	Sing. 3 Fem. *i her*	Pl. 1. *sinn us*	Pl. 2. *sibh you*	Pl. 3. *iad them*
ag *at*	agam	agad	aige	aice	againn	agaibh	aca
air *on*	orm	ort	air	oirre	oirnn	orbh	orra
ann *in*	annam	annad	ann	innte	annainn	annaibh	annta
as *out of*	asam	asad	as	aiste	asainn	asaibh	asta
de *of*	diom	diot	deth	dith	dinn	dibh	diubh
do *to*	domh	dut, duit	dà	di	duinn	duibh	doibh
eadar *between*					eadarainn	eadaraibh	eatorra
fo *under*	fodham	fodhad	fodha	foipe	fodhaim	fodhaibh	fopa
gu *towards*	chugam	chugad	chuige	chuice	chugainn	chugaibh	chuca
le *with*	leam	leat	leis	leithe	leinn	leibh	leò, leotha
mu *about*	umam	umad	uime	uimpe	umainn	umaibh	umpa
ua *from*	uam	uat	uaidh	uaithe	uainn	uaibh	uapa
ri *to*	rium	riut	ris	rithe	rinn	ribh	riù, riutha
roimh *before*	romham	romhad	roimhe	roimpe	romhainn	romhaibh	rompa
thar *over*	tharam	tharad	thairis air	thairis oirre	tharainn	tharaibh	tharta
troimh *through*	tromham	tromhad	troimhe	troimpe	tromhainn	tromhaibh	trompa

In 3 pl. only **de, do** have dat. forms, all other prepositions may be used adverbially.

The 3 s.m. of the prepositional pronouns use the acc. forms of the pronouns.

A petrified 2 s. of a prepositional compound is used as—

1. verb, 2 sing. Ipv. Chugad, thugad *away! say away! look out!*
siuthad *here thou! say away!* **siu** dat. sing of **so** *this.*
thallad, thalla, thaillabh *over there, come along,* from **thall** §215, 1, 5
tiugainn *let us come! come along!* is probably founded on **chugainn** with leaning upon **tiug**—*come.*
tromhad, trobhad *here! come hither!* derived from romhad

2. adv.—seachad *past* (lit. *past thee*).

§ 121.   *Remarks on the Cpd. Personal Pronouns.*
cf. Ped. II. 167.

1. 1 sing. **mi** *I.*

The Indoeuropean 1st pers. pronoun (e.g. L. ego, Gk. ἐγω,
Sk. ahám) does not appear in the nom. in the Celtic languages.
me is an acc. like Gk. με, and the dat. *moi is assumed. The
gen. mene, inferred from O. Sl. mene was assumed as reduplicated
meme (Sk. máma *of me*), and goes back to *mewe, *mowe (Corn.
ow), G. **mo** *my.*

2. 2 sing. **tu, thu** *thou.*

The old Indoeur. nom., L. tu, Gk. (doric) τυ. is retained in G.
tu. The W. ti *thou*, rests on acc. te < *twe, Gk. σε.

The gen. *towe, *tewe, Sk. táva *of me*, gives G. **to** *thy* : under
the stress, **t'** athair—*thy father* ; as proclitic it becomes **do, do**
mhàthair—*thy mother.*

3. 1 and 2 pl. **sinn** *we* : **sibh** *ye, you.*

The Indoeuropean nominatives (e.g. Sk. vayám *we*, yûyám *you*)
are lost in Celtic, and are replaced by oblique cases as in Sk.
nas *us*, L. nōs ; and Sk. vas *you*, L. vōs. **sinn** *we* (O.G. snisni), and
sibh *you* (O.G. sini, sib) are reduplicated, but the intensive particles **-ni** (sinn-**ne**) and **-si** (sibh-**se**) are simple. Hence the original
forms were probably *snēs, *swes ; or regard being had to the -u-
timbre of -**nn** in **sinn** *we*, the forms *snōs, *swēs ; or *snos, *swes,
L. nōster, vester, may be postulated.

4. **ar n-** *our* ; **bhur n-, ur n-** (O.G. bar, far) *your.*

The old independent genitives athar, ár *our*, sethar, sár *your*,
have comparitive endings like L. nostrum, vestrum, Goth. unsara,
izwara, but they do not directly represent ancient forms.
*nserōm, sweserōm < ésar (unstressed asar), sear, may be assumed
as the origin of the G. **ar n-** *our*, **ur n-** *your.*

5. In 1 and 2 sing. the suffixed -**m** and -**t** are broad except in
the case of **do** + **tu** which is now often written **duit** ; and of 1 sing.
only **domh** is aspirated.   In 1 and 2 pl. -**nn** and -**bh** are slender,
and -**b -bh** is aspirated throughout.

6. 3 sing.   Nom. sing. mas. G. **e, se**, *he*, O.G. hé (lengthened),
L. is, Goth is. Gk. εἷς *one*, *sem-s, ἅμα *together.*
nom. sing. fem., G. **i, si** *she*, Ir. sí, W. hi.
nom. sing. neut, G. **eadh** *it*, *id, earlier idā, O.G.
ed, L. id, Goth. ita.

7. 3 pl. M. *joi, W. **wy**
f. *ijas, O.G. **hé**
n. ***i** Corn., M. Br. y, Br. hi

8. The fem. nom. pl. **hé** has occupied the field in Gaelic, e.g. O.G. é-side *they* ; but -**ē**- is changed into later -**ia**-, contamination with the neuter Br. **hi** has originated a prothetic -**s**-; and analogy to 3 pl. of verbs (and cpd. pronouns in W.) has added -**nt**-, -**d**, giving **s-ia-d, ia-d** *they*. The pronunciation in Islay is still **ēad**, in other (Northern) parts chiefly **iad**. **è** as 3 pl. is still met with occasionally :

> Is **e** na smuaintean a bhuail ann an ceann mo bhràthar bu shine—*These are the thoughts that occurred to my elder brother* :—Arab. i. 25

9. acc. sing. mas *im, O.G. -**a n**-, W. **e** : suffixed to prepositions, sometimes -**i**, e.g. **chuige, uime**, sometimes nothing but infection of previous syllable e.g. **air** *on him*.

acc. sing. fem. *sijäm, O.G. -**s n**- : after prepositions -**e** : influenced by a foregoing -**h**- it becomes -**he** e.g. chuice (**cuic-he, co-co-he**), **impe** (im-he), **innte** (inn-he), **roimpe** (roim-he) **troimpe** ; and **foipe** by analogy.

acc. pl. mas. *sōns : after verbal forms -**s**- with **u**-timbre : after prepositions -**u**, influenced by a foreeging **h**- : O.G. impu, G. **umpa** : **uapa** by analogy : and -**su**, O.G. tairsiu, G. **tharta** through depalatisation.

acc. pl. neut. *ijā appears only with a singular function : after the prepositions
O.G. cen (G. gun) *without*, **cheana** (without it) *already*. seach *past*, O.G. sechae—*past it*, G. **seach**.

dat. sing mas. neut. *jō (instr.) *jōi (Indoeur. dat.) *jōd (abl.), e.g. **aige** (O.G. occo), **da** (O.G. dau), **fodha** (O.G. fou).
It has phps. disappeared in **riamh**.
It appears by analogy in **uaidh** (O.G. huad).

dat. sing. fem. *jāi or *ijāi, after prepositions -**i** : **aice, di, dith, uaithe**.

pl. mas. neut. *jobhis, fem. *jābhis : O.G. after prepositions -ib, -aib, G. -**ibh**, -**aibh**.

G

§ 122.   **SUFFIXES.**

The following are derived from words known or in use :

1. **-ail** : samail *likeness*,   L. similis   §129, 2
          banail *womanly*
          fearail *manly*

2. **-car, -char** *loving* : caraim *I love*
          beul-chair (having a loving mouth) *fair-spoken*
          trocair(e) f. *mercy* : truagh + car

3. **-lach** m. : sluagh m. *host, people*
          eachlach m. *groom* : each m. *horse*
          fiallach, fianlach m. *hero* : fian m. *champion*
          òglach m. *soldier, lad* : òg *young*
          teaghlach, teg-lach m. *household*

4. **-mhor** : mòr *great*
          àghmhor *glorious*
          neartmhor *powerful*

5. **-rad** f. : ríadaim *ride*, réidh *plain*
          eachraidh f. *cavalry*
          laochraidh f. *warriors*
          macraidh f. *youths*
          madraidh f. *dogs*, O.G. madrad m. *dog*
          òigridh f. *children*
          righre pl. *kings;* O.G. rig-rad

6. **-rad** n., hardly distinguishable from above :
          eadradh m. *lust*   O.G. étrad n.
          gnìomharra pl. *deeds*   O.G. gnímrad
          geamhradh m. *winter*   O.G. gem-rad
          luaithre f. *ashes*   O.G. luaith-red
          oighre f. *ice*   O.G. aig-red, oig-red
          samhradh m. *summer*   O.G. sam-rad
          sònrach *distinguished*   O.G. sàin-red-ach

7. **-tan** *tree, copse*
          calltuinn m. *hazel-tree*   O.G. coll *hazel*, L. corylus
          caorthunn m. *rowan-tree*   O.G. cáer *berry*
          uinnseann m. *ash-tree*   O.G. uinnius *ash* but cf.
                                          § 85, 2

§ 123. **DIMINUTIVES.**

1. -**ag** f., in O.G. m. (sts. f.), is not from **òg**, *young*, or Ir. -**ach**, but a loan -**k**- suffix developed from Brythonic sources: Ped. Gr. 29, 31

  in collectives:
  feus-ag f. *beard*, cf. find *hair*, Gk. ἴονθος *first-beard*
  deannt-ag f. *nettle* ; *nenati : O.H.G. nezzila
  in diminutives:
  cuile-ag f. *fly*, L. culex
  duille-ag f. *leaflet*
  in pet names:
  Kil-mo-earn-oc *Kilmarnock* §112, 3
  Kil-mo-æd-oc *Kilmadock* 112, 4
But this dim. has nothing to do with:
  uinne-ag f. *window*, N. wind-auga *windeye*

2. -**an**, -**in**, from -a-gno-, -i-gno-, (-u-gno-) ; √ gen-   § 184

  g.s.   Broccagni, later Borccán
      Ulcagni, later Olcán
      beag-an m. *a little*
      cail-in f. *girl*, caile *quean*
      cnoc-an m. *hillock*
      cuile-an m. *young dog, whelp*
      fear-an m. *mannikin*
      truag-an m. *poor wretch*
      meadhon m. *midst*, C.S. meadhan, O.G. med-ón

3. -**ag** + -**an**
  àilleagan m. *little beauty, jewel* : àille

§ 124.   -**k**- Suffixes.

  -**ach** -**ko**- and -**kā**- stems :
      -**o**- curach f. *boat, coracle*, W. corwc, cwrwgl *coracle*
          cf. Gk. κώρυκος *leathern sack*
      -**ā**- aodach m. *dress*
          aonach m. *hill, fair*
          cumhachdach *powerful*
          deudach m. *the teeth, set of teeth*,
            cf. O. Corn. denshoc **dour**

fàsach m. *desert* : fàs *void*
gealach m. *moon* : geal *white*
marcach m. *rider*, M.W. marchawc, W. marchog
§ 125

-each **-jā-** buidheach *thankful* : buidhe
cailleach f. *hag*, nun : caille *vail*, L. pallium, E. *pall*
coileach m. *cock*, M.W. keil-yawc, W. ceil-iog
raineach f. fern : raith-n-each
-āko-
changed to
-jāko tòiseach, m. *chief*, but W. tywysog ;
Ogam gs. TOVISACI
after -ĭ- stem : buadhach *victorious*,
M.W. bud-ic : buaidh
with -st- addition :
seanchas m. *history*, O.W. hen-c-ass-ou
(monimenta) : sen *old*

§ 125. **-actā** (cf. L. sen-ecta), and **-jaktā**

1. **-achd**, **-eachd** f. §176

daoineachd f. *population*
flaitheachd f. *supremacy*
marc-achd f. *riding*, G. marc—*horse*, W. march, O.E.
mearh, E. mare, mar-shall
mòrachd f. *greatness*

with fore-suffixes :
-air-, breug-air-eachd f. *practice of lying*
-al-, duine-al-achd f. *manliness*
-idh-, fil-idh-eachd f. *versification*

with post-suffixes :
-ach, dàs-achd-ach *furious* : *dhwost, dhwast, O.E.
dwáes *foolish*
-i- klo-

2. **-eal** muineal m. *neck* : muin f. *neck*, W. mwn, mwnwgl, L.
monīle

3. suffixes with consonant + **-k-**

-ag, -eag,

-aig   (1) **-nk-**

        imleag f. *navel*, O.G. imbliu, L. umbilīcus, Gk. ὀμφαλός *mbhllin-k.

        leug f. *precious stone*, O.G. lie, lia, g.s. liac, d.s. liic, Gk. λέπας *bare-rock*, L. lapis

        lùda-g f. *the little finger*, O.G. lùta, leaning to lùd-ag

        òg *young*, O.G. o-ac, W. ieu-anc, L. iuuenis, iuuencus

-air (2) **-rk-**

        casair m. *sea-drift*

-easg,-isg (3) **-sg-**

        brisg *brisk, friable* : bris *break*

        duileasg m. *dulse*, W. delysc : duille f. *leaf, sheath*

        easga f. *moon* : *ms- skijo-m, Sk. mās *moon, month*, G. mìos : or from eid-skijo- L. īdūs (Ides *full light*)

        fleasg f. *wand*, a contamination of W. gwrysg-en *boughs*, and llysg *wand* (Ped.)

        uisge m. *water* : * ud-skijo, Sk. ud-ā (Instrumental), L. u-n-da, Goth. watō

4.   **-kᵘo-, -kᵘa-**

        cá-ch *every*, W. paw-b

        crì-ch f. *end*, Gk. κρί-νω, L. dis-crī-men

§ 126.   **-st-**

-as, -is, -us

    -st- (-stu-, -sto-, -stā, -sti-) L. tempus, tempestas

        1. *Monosyllables* :

            -stu- aois f. *age*, W. oes, cf. L. aeuum, Gk. αἰών

                    dorus m. *door*, W. drws, L. foris, Gk. θύρᾱ : * dhru-st-

                    lus m. *herb* : luibh m. f. : *luibh + stu-

                    teas m. *heat* : *tep-stu-, L. tepeo, Sk. tapas

-sto- blas m. *taste*, O.G. mlas

-stā- fras f. *shower*, L. rōs

-sti- gnùis f. *face*, Gk. γνά'θος *jaw*

dris f. *thorn*, Gk. δρίος

after the adj. suffix **-to-** :

baois f. *levity*	baoth *foolish*
bàs m. *death*	bath *dead*
drùis f. *lust*	drùth *unchaste*
gaos m. *wisdom*	gaoth *prudent*
gnàths m. *custom*	gnàth *usual*
luathas m. *speed*	luath *swift*
sgìos f. *fatigue*	sgìth *weary*

Similarly after the noun suffix **-to-** :

leis f. *thigh*   leth *side*, cf. L. lat-us

2. *Polysyllables* :

-sto- old **-u**-stems :

geanas m. *chastity*, O.G. gein *child*, hence G. gin
f. *anyone*
muinntearas m. *service* : muinntir f. *people*
seanchas m. *story* : sean *old*, § 124

-o- stems : caoimhneas m. *kindness*, O.G. coibnes
L. cognatio
g.s. in choibnis, cf. coibnes-ta, L. affinis
* con- fine- sto- *relationship*

old **-ā-** stems : loingeas m. (f. in O.G.) *shipping*
sanas m. (f. in O.G.) *whisper*, W. hanes
f. *history*

old **-i-** stems : binneas m. *melodiousness*,
O.G. bindius : binn *sweet*
comharbas m. *succession*, O.G. com-arbe
m. *co-heir*
ionracas m. *righteousness*, ionraic *just*

In. G. all these are declined as **-o-** stems without regard to
their origin.

§ 127.   **-d- SUFFIXES.**

-d   (1) **-d** bunadh m. *origin*, W. bonedd, cf. bun
-de, -ide   (2) **-de, -ide**
                     céilidh f. *visiting, gossiping* : céile
                     diadha (and diadhaidh) *godly* : dia
                     neamhaidh, *heavenly*   : neamh
-nd, -nn   **-nd, -nn**, a loan from Latin :
                     aiffrionn m. *mass, chapel* : L. offerenda
                     léighean m. *instruction, erudition*: L. legendum
                     sgrìobhainn f. *bill*, W. ysgrifen: L. scrībendum

§ 128.   **-g- SUFFIXES.**

-g, -ch laogh m. *calf*, W. llo, Br. leue : phps. from *lapego-,
            Alb. lopa (*lāpā) *cow*
            luach m. *value*, O.G. log *reward*, lo- g, Gk. ἀπολαύω
            muing f. *mane*, O.G. mong, mon-g : muin f. *neck*
            -ich, (-g-)

            Verbs in **-ich**, like sàraich *oppress*, O.G. sáraigim :
            Nouns **-aiche** (-aige-, -*agjo-, cf. L. agō)
                buanaiche m. *reaper*
                ceannaiche m. *buyer*
                gadaiche m. *thief*
                mearaiche m. *merry-Andrew*
                searmonaiche m. *preacher*
                sgeulaiche m. *narrator of tales*

-gl-   **-g-** + consonant (1) **-g-l-, -gl-**

            bao-ghal m. *danger*, Lit. bái-mê *fear*, Sk. bhīmá-s
                fearful,
            inna baise L. hebetudinis, ml. 33ᶜ2

-gal-   with the infinitives :

                          (a) **-gal, -gail**

            brad-ghail *thieving*, hence bradalach *thievish*
            crann-ghail f. *mast-rigging, pulpit*
            fead-ghail, feadail f. *whistling*
            sian-ghail, sianail f. *screaming*

(b) -glā-

-glā (=ail) gabhail f. *taking*, O.G. gabál, d.s. gabail.
   Similarly :
      carnal f. *mole, small heap of stones* : carn
      fuaigheal f. *seam* : O.G. uaimm, fuaim
      teagmhail f. *occurrence* : tecmang, to-in-com-nc
      teasdail f. *want, defect* : do-ess-tá

-gn-   -g-n-, -gn-
         bairghean, bairghin m. *bread, cake* : L. farrāgo
         -gn- to -gg-
            frag f. *woman, wife*, O.G. fracc, W. gwrach : L.
               virgō, virāgō

   also dearc f. *berry*, O.G. deru-cc glans, g.s. dercon : daur *oak*

§ 129.   -l- Suffixes :

-l   1. after a monosyllable :
         àl m. *brood*, W. ael, Gk. ἀγέλη *herd*
         gobhal, gabhal m. *fork*, W. gabl f., Br. gaol f., O.G.H.
            gibil, L. habeo
         màl m. *prince*, W. Maelgwn, Goth. mikils, Sc. *muckle*
         neul m. *cloud*, W. niwl, nifwl : *nebhlo ;
            L. nebula, Gk. νεφέλη ; but cf. Thur. Gr. p. 74
         seòl m. *sail*, O.W. huil, W. hwyl, N. segl
         sìol m. *seed*, L. se-vi *I have sown*, se-men *seed*

-(a)l   2. after polysyllables :
         with fore-suffix -a- :
            samhail, samhuil m. *likeness*, a-li-stem,
               W. hafal, O.W. amal, L. similis, * s‚m‚l,
               Gk. ὁμαλός : √ sem *one*, εἶς < *sems

-(e)l   with fore-suffix -e- :
         ìse-l, ìosa-l *low, lowly* : G. ìos *under* :
            W. is, isel : *ped-su *footwards, under feet*
            formed like
         uasa-l *noble*, W. uchel,
         Gaul. Uxello-dunum : *upsel, Gk. ὑψηλός, ὑψι, ὑψίων.

§ 130.

-lach, -leach

> brisleach f. *overthrow of an army, breach* : bris *break*
> broclach f. *badger's den* : broc m. *badger*
> brollach, broilleach m. *breast* : bruinne f. *breast*, brù f.,
>> g.s. bronn *belly*   cf. Loth R.C. xiv., xv.
> cabhlach m. *fleet*, O.G. coblach : L. cybaea *transport*,
>> cymba *boat*
> connlach f. *straw, stubble* : L. canna *reed*
> crannlach f. *brushwood, jetsom* : crann m. *tree*
> cuallach f. *corporation, family*, M.G. cuan-lacht f. *litter*
> mèirleach m. *thief*, phps. from mairnim *betray*, Inf. brath
> mullach m. *top, summit* : mul m. *conical heap, mound*
> òirleach, f. *inch*, O.G. ordlach *inch* : ord *thumb*
> teallach m. *hearth*, O.G. tenlach : teine *fire*

> also probably
>> mach-lag, f. *matrix* : mac *son*
>> tromlach m. *weight, bulk* : trom

§ 131.   **-m- SUFFIXES.**

1. with monosyllables

-m   freumh m. *root, stem*, O.G. fré-m,
>> W. gwraidd, sing. gwreiddyn, L. rādix, rāmus *bough*,
>> O.H.G. wurz, N. rót
> gnìomh m. *deed*, O.G. gní-m, Inf. of gní *does*
> seinn, f. *singing* : O.G. seinm
> snìomh m. *twist, sadness*, O.G. sní-m, Inf. of sní
> tairm, toirm f. *noise*, W. twrf *tumult*, L. turba,
>> O.G. tor-ann *thunder*, W. taran

2. with polysyllables :—

>   **-o-** stems (1) old -ā- stems :
>> agallamh m. *conferring, conversation*, O.G. accaldam,
>>> acallam, Inf. of ad-glád-ur
>> caitheamh m. *spending*, O.G. caith-em, Inf. of caithim
>> creideamh m. *faith*, O.G. cret-em
>> feitheamh m. *waiting*, O.G. feth-em, Inf. of fethim
>> seachamh-inntinn, f. *satisfaction, gratification*,
>>> O.G. sech-em, *following*

(2) old **-u-** stems :

aineamh m. *flaw*, W. anaf, Gk. ὄνομαι

aitheamh m.f. *fathom*, O.W. etem, pl. adaued,
 W. edaf, edeu, N. faþemr, Gk. πετάννῡμι

altrum m. *rearing* § 184

anam m. *soul* ; O.G. animm, O. Corn. enef, M. Corn.
 enef, ene, Corn. ena, Br. anaoun, L. anima *soul*, animus
 mind

deanamh m. doing, O.G. denum, denam, Inf. of do-gníu

seasamh m. *standing*, O.G. sessom, sessam, Inf. of siss-iur,
 L. sisto, sto.

with dropped post suffix **ad** :

The ordinals from ceathramh, O.G. cethram-ad, *fourth*
 to deachamh, O.G. dechm-ad *tenth* and multiples of
 of ten § 99

3. -mm-

braim m. crepitus ventris, Ir. braidm, from M. Corn.
 brúim : an **-n-** stem :
 W. Corn. bram, Br. bramm, Ir. braigim *pēdo*

gairm f. *call*, W. Cor. Br. garm : Inf. of gair-

gorm *blue*, W. gwrm *dusky*, cf. L. formus

gleam m. *loud noise, echo* : Inf. of glenn-

fòghlum m. *learning* : Inf. of fo-glenn-

greim m. *authority, hold, morsel* : Inf. of grenn-

inghreim m. *clutching, persecution* : Inf. of ingrenn-

nàim f. *bargain, covenant* : O.G. naidm, Inf. of nasc-

snaim m. *knot* : O.G. snaidm : * snad-mm

teum m. *bite, sudden snatch, wound*, with broad -t : taom
 m. *fit of rage*, W. tam *morsel, bit*, Corn. tam, Br.
 tamm : *tnsmu, tnsmn : Gk. τένδω

4. -mm- from -sm-

beum *stroke, cut, taunt* ; *bhei-smn, O.G. béim, Inf. of
 benim, Cor. bom, Br. boem (beum, ceum are miswritten
 in G., the **m** is slender as proved by the absence of
 diphthongisation : sgeul, sgial but not biam, ciam)
 with **-sm-**, **-ms-** :

ceum m. *step* O.G. céimm, Inf. of cingim *keng-(s)men

dréim m. *endeavour*, dreimm, Inf. of dringim *dring-(s)men

leum m. *leap* O.G. léimm   Inf. of lingim *leng-men
feamainn f. *sea-weed*, W. gwymon, Sk. vapati, *strews*,
Ir. feam *stump* ; hence feaman m. *tail, rump*

-nsm-

réim *course*, O.G. réimm, W. rhamu,
*rndsmn : riadaim, *I ride*
tailm *sling*, Br. talm, W. telm, Gk. τελαμών *strap, belt*
tiom *soft, timid* ; time *fear*, O.G. timme *heat*, W. twym,
*tepesmn.

§ 132.   -n SUFFIXES.

1. Monosyllables :—

-n   aoin f. *rush*, O.G. áin *play*, L. ag-o *drive*
bàn *white*, Sk. bhā *shine*, bhā-nu *glance, light, sun*.
Lit. bá-l-ta-s, N. bá-l *bale, pyre*
dàn m. *fate*, L. donum *gift*, do *I give*,
Gk. δίδωμι, δώρον, Lit. duomi *I give*
domhan m. *world, Universe*, domhain *deep*
W. dwfn m., dofn f., Gaul. Dubno-reix *world king*
eun m. *bird*, W. edn. L. penna *feather*,
Gk. πτερόν *wing*, πέτομαι *fly*, L. peto *seek*
feun m. *waggon*, W. gwain, N. uagn,
Sk. vāhana-m, L. veho *I carry*
gràin f. *abhorrence*, W. graen *asperity, grief, grievous*,
G. garg *fierce*, Gk. γοργός *frightful*
làn *full*, W. llawn, Goth. fulls, Lit. pìlnas : *pelē-
lìnn m. *age, country, generation*, L. plēnus
slàn *healthy, whole*, L. saluus, sollus (for solnus) =totus,
Gk. ὅλος
sleamhuinn *slippery, smooth*, W. llyfn, L. līma
file, limax *snail*, Gk. λείμαξ, N. slìm *slime*
treun *strong*, compar. treise, W. trech,
Br. treac'h (-gs-), N. þrek *strength, courage*

2. Polysyllables :

-n   with -no-, -nā- -nī-,
with fore-suffix -a- :
-no- leathann *broad*, W. llydan, Gaul.   Litano-briga
Broad-burg, Gk. πλάτανος *plane tree*, πλατύς *broad*

-**nā**- clann f. *wool, lock of hair*, W. gwlan, Goth. vulla,
L. lāna, Gk. λῆνος, λᾶνος, Sk. ūrnā : *ulanā

with fore-suffix -**o**- :

(o)-**n**   -**na** abhainn f. *river*, W. afon f., Gallo-Brit. Abona,
Br. Pont-aven, L. amnis (=abnis)
bleoghann f. *milking*
gamhainn, gamhinn m. *year-old-calf*, -**i**- stem, from gam
winter
orcain, orgain f. *slaughter*
samhuinn f. *Hallowtide* : or sam-fuin *Summer-end* §100

(e)- **n** with fore-suffix -**e**- :
-**no**- craiceann m. *hide*, W. croen, Br. croc'hen ; *krokn,
qroq, qereq, √ qer. cf. L. corium, cortex
-**na**- éiginn f. *necessity*, O.G. écen, W. angen, Gk. ἀνάγκη :
*nk-en-

with fore-suffix -**i**- :

-**no**-   -**no**- daingean *strong*, W. dengyn *strong, inflexible*

-**ni**-   -**nī**- -**n(i)jio**-, -**n(i)ja**-
bliadhna f. *year*, Ir. bliadin, W. blwyddyn :* blidnni.
colann f. *body* (g.s. colainn, colna and colla), O.G. colinn
flesh, W. celain *corpse*
léine f. *shirt*, O.W. liein, W. lliain *linen*, Br. lien
rìbhinn f. *quean*, O.G. rigain *queen*, W. rhiain *dame*, Gk.
πότ-νια, θέ-αινα, an-**i**-stem which becomes an-**ā**- stem,
rìoghann, O.G. régan : rí *king*, L. rēx, Sk. rāgan-

§ 133. -**n**- SUFFIX.

-**n**-   1. with polysyllables :
maic-n-e pl. *children, relations*

with fore-suffix -**i**- :

-(ī)**n**   buidheann f. *company*, O.G. buiden, W. byddin f.,
O. Br. bodin
foireann m. *crowd*, O.G. foirenn f., W. gwerin
ionga f. *nail*, O.G. ingen f., W. ewin, Br. ivin : *engīnā
uileann f. *elbow*, O.G. uilen f., W. Cor. elin, Br. ilin,
L. ulna, Gk. ὠλένη.

-(i)-nja **īnjā-**, àirne f. *sloe*, W. aeron (only in pl.) *fruits of trees*,
eirin, (new s.g. eirinen) *plums*, Br. irin, hirin *sloe*,
Goth. akran *fruit*, N. akarn *acorn*
aoibhinn *pleasant, joyful*, O.G. áim-in,
M.G. óeb-ind : óiph *beautiful appearance*
tarsuinn *transverse, across*, O.G. tarsnu, tarsna : tar
across
and the abstract formations like :
bochdainn(e) f. *poverty*
faistine f. *prophecy*, fait-s-ine : fàith *prophet*, L. vātes
fìrinn(e) f. *truth*, G. fìor *true*, L. ver-us

-n- Stems.

2. with fore-suffix **-a-**, or **-ja-** :
ainm m. *name*, pl. anmannan, p.p.p. ainmnichte *named*,
O.W. anu, pl. enuin, W. enw, Gk. ὄνομα, L. nōmen,
Sk. nāma

-a-or-ja + -m-
breitheamh m. *judge*, g.s. O.G. brethemon ; hence breith-
eamh-**n**-as f. *judgment*
dùileamh, m. *creator*, g.s. O.G. dúleman : dùil *element*
O.G. flaitheam m. *lord*, hence flaith-eamh-**n**-as m. *heaven*
meamna, meanmna m. *spirit, will*, W. menw, Sk. manma
thought
oll-amh m., g.s. ollamhan *doctor, chief-bard* : oll *great*
suaineadh, suaineamh m. *twisting, rope*, O.G. suanem,
g.s. suaneman, *rope*, sén *bird-net*, W. hoenyn *springe*
talamh m. *earth*, g.s. talmhainn, O.G. talman, Sk.
talima-m *floor*, Gk. τηλία *dice-board*
-mnnā
fal-bhan, falbh m. *going*, M.G. fo-lua-main *flying* : O.G.
lú-ur
gin-eamhuinn m. *begetting, birth*, geanmna-idh *chaste* : gein
làn-amhain, lànain m. *a couple* : làn
lean-mhuinn m. *following* : lean
oilean m. *nurture, training*, M.G. oileamain : O.G. al-im
I rear
seachduin f. *week* : O.G. seachd-man
adj. dil-main *meet, proper*

§ 134   **-ro-, -ra-,** (-ru-)

-r-   àr m. *battle, slaughter,* W. aer f., Gk. ἄγρα

     clàr m. *table, board,* W. clawr, Gk. κλῆρος, κλᾶρος *lot,*
         κλῆ-μα *vine-twig,* κλάω *break*

     dobhar-(chù) m. *water-(dog),* otter, W. dwfr, Gaul. Verno-
         dubrum (river name) : dub *deep*

     lobhar m. *a leper,* O.G. lobur (infirmus), W. llwfr *feeble,*
         G. lobh *rot,* Gk. λώβη *outrage*

     mìr m. *piece* (originally *piece of flesh*) : *mems, mēs *flesh* ;
         L. membrum (=memsrum), Gk. μηρός *ham*

     mò-r, mà-r *great,* compar. mò,
         Gk. ἐγχεσί-μωρος *great with spears*

     reamhar *fat,* O.G. remor, W. rhef *thick* : *remro, premro

     sì-or *long, continual,* W. hir, L. sē-ru-s

§ 135.   **-ro-, -rā-**

-st- + **-ra-** aimsir f. *time :* am m. *time*

    with adj. suffix **-ail, -ta :** -aimsireil, aimsiorrtha *temporal*
    after polysyllables with-a- :

     conair f. *way :* cù *dog* (?)

     galar m. *disease,* W. Cor. galar, Br. gl-ach-ar, Gk. χολέρα

     iar n- *after,* G. air, Goth *afar,* Sk. apara *later,* Gk.
         ἀπο, ἐπι : *epero-n § 148, §188

     lasair f. *flame,* W. llachar : *lapsar, Gk. λάμπω

     uabhar m. *pride,* W. ofer *waste, vain,* Goth. abrs *strong.*

-ar   The origin of **-ar** is doubtful, failing British examples :

     aon-ar m. *one person,* tri-ur *three persons,* etc. §99, 2

     bru-an m. *fragment,* O.G. bru-ar

     bu-ar m. *kine*

     cloch-ar m. *wheezing*

     glomh-ar m. *muzzle, gag*

     iasg-air m. *fisher,* O.G. iasc-ar

     iol-ar m. *variety :* G. il, iol *many*

     lombar, lompair *bare :* G. lom

     oirer f. (wrongly oirthir) *coast, haven,*
         O.G. for-ar *finis,* W. gor-or, from O.G. or *bank, border*

     salch-ar m. *filth :* G. salach

     beurla f. *speech, English,* O.G. bél-r-e, from bél *lip* + -a-
         r(i)jo-, Gaillbherla *English :*—Carswell, Titlepage

§ 136.   -rno-

-rno- aobhrann m. *ankle*, W. uffarn, ucharn,
         Ir. odb, G. faob,   Gk. ὀσφύς
       cilleorn m. *urn*, W. celeorn, L. calpar *wine-cask*
       iarunn m. *iron*, W. hayarn, haiarn, haearn ;
         Gall. Isarnus, L. aes *copper*, Goth. aiz, Sk. ajas
       lòchran m. *light*, O.G. lócharn f., W. llygorn,
         L. lūx *light*, L. lucerna *lamp*, Gk. λευκός
       mugharn m. *ankle*, W. migwrn, mughraile f. (Islay)
       tighearn m. *house-master*, *lord*, W. teyrn *king*

§ 137.   -st(i)jo-

-sa, -se fiadhnais f. *witness*, fiadh-n-ais(-e),
           O.G. fiadu, acc. fiadain
         folmhaise f. *advantage*   § 184
         saorsa f. *freedom*, O.G. saoirse : saor
         tànaiste m. next in *succession*, *tanist*, *second* (probably
           related to im-thánad *change*)

-sach, -sech   -stikā-

           bunnsach f. *rod* : bun m. *base*
           ràidseach *querulous* : ràdh m. *saying*

-sir   -stero-, -sterā-

           aimsir f. *time* : àm m. *time*,
             Gall. Epostero-vidus, Epotsoro-vidus n. pr.   §135

-sin   -stīn(i)ja-, or -stun(i)jā-

           faistinn f. *prophecy*, fait-sinn-e : fàith m. *prophet* §133

§ 138.   -t- Suffixes.

-t, -th   With monosyllables :
    1. -t- bi-th m. *being*, O.G. buith, Gk. φύσις
            bi-th m. *world*, W. byd, Gall. Bitu-riges : *g^{n}ei
            blei-th f. *grinding*, O.G. melim
            bra-th m. *judgment*, W. brawd, Ir. barn *judge*
              Gk. βρατουδε ex iudicio
            breac *speckled*, O.G. mrecht
            brei-th f. *birth* : beir

clei-th, *concealing* :   ceil

clo-th f.m. *fame*, L. in-**clu**-tus *famous*

cru-th m. *form*, W. pryd, Sk. krtv-as *time*

flath, flai-th m. *prince* : *wla-ti-s, L. val-ēre

ìobair-t f. *offering* : aith-od + *beir*

ra-th m. *grace*, Sk. rātá *given*

sru-th m. *stream* : *srutus, Gk. ῥέω, Sk. sravati *flows*

su-th m. *anything*, O.G. *birth*, *fruit*, Sk. sutu, *pregnancy*

teachd, teach-t f. *going*, O.G. tiagu *I go*, Gk. στείχω, W. taith *journey*

After -**s**-, (-tst-) fras f. *shower*, L. rōs :* ros-ts, ros-tst

After -**d**-, fios m. *knowledge* : *vissus *vid-tu-s

meas m. *esteem* :   O.G. mid-iur

amus m. *hit* : ad-mid-iur

tomhas m. *measure* : to-mid-iur

seas *stand*, O.G. suide, G. suidhe *seat*

2. -**tjo**-   clais(e) f. *burrow* : claidh *dig*

comh-dhal-ta m. *foster brother* : alim *I rear*

teach-d *lawful*, O.G. techte

tuigse f. *understanding* : tuig

3. Suffixes with a consonant + -**t**-

-**t** -**rt**-   adha-r-t m. *pillow*, O. Sl. odru *bed*

anar-t m. *linen*, O.G. inar *tunic*

conar-t *pack of dogs*, hence conartaich *bait with dogs*

-**nto**-, -**ntā**-, -**ntī**-

-**nto**-   airgiod m. *silver* : L. argent-um

carbad m. *chariot*, Gaul. Carbant-ia

drochaid f. *bridge* : *druk-anto : dru *wood* + -k- + anto-

reult f. *star*, O.G. retglu : ret from *rijanto : ré *moon*

-**ntā**-   fiodhag f. (fiodhadh) *wild cherry*, *wild fig* : *widu-ntā

sliasaid f. *thigh*, g.s. sléisde : *spleigh-stu-ntā, cf. slios

snathad f. *needle*, W. nodwydd, cf. snìomh, L. neo, G. νέω

-**ntī**-   eilid f. *hind*, Gk. ἐλα-φος, Lit. élnis

frìde f. *a tetter*, *ringworm*, O.G. frigit, W. gwraint

Brigid f. *Briget*, W. braint f. *prerogative*

-anti- cf. L. con-sta-ntia

   goirid *short*, O.G. garaid, originally a subst.
   leithid f. *like, compeer*, from leithead *breadth*
   lugh-ad f. *littleness* (from lugu, laigiu *less*),
     W. llai, O. Br. nahu-lei gl. nihilo-minus, Gk.
     ἐλάσσων, ἐλαχύς
   meud m. *size*, W. maint, O.W. pa-mint, Cor. myns,
     Br. ment.
   tugaid f. *cause, reason*, pl. tugaidean *witticisms* :
     to-ucc *understand*

-(t)-al, -(t)eal   **-tlo-, -tlā**, (-tli-) with (rare) instrumental
   meaning :

   anail f. *breath*, W. anadl
   ceòl m. *music*, O.G. cétal, G. ceadal m. *story*, from
     can *sing*, O.W. centhiliat, centhliat : *-ntl-
   cineal m. *offspring, clan*, O.G. cenél, W. cenetl, cenedl
   dàil f. *meeting*, W. datl, dadl
   giall f. *hostage*, W. gwystl
   sàil f. *heel*, W. sawdl, L. ta-lus : *sta-tlā
   slios m. *side*, W. ystlys : L. latus : *stlat-os

-tinn, -tuinn   **-ti- + en**

   eiridinn m. *nursing* : *air-em-ti-nn
   faotainn f. *getting* : fo-em-ti-nn   § 176

-sinn, -suinn   **-s- + en**

   f-aic-s-inn f. *seeing*

   Similar in form but of native origin are :
   deàrnadh f. *palm of hand*, Ir. dearnóid, W.
     dyrn-awt, dyrn-od f. *slap, cuff*
   liathroid f. *ball*, W. llithr-ed *a glide, slip*
   neasgaid f. *boil*
   om-oid-each *obedient*, Ir. ómós
   smearoid f. *coal, burning coal*

-tann, -teann

   -tijen- + adj. formation
     car-thann-ach *loving*
     oirbhidneach *honoured*, O.G. ermitneach
     toill-teann-ach *deserving*

§ 139.   *Suffixes of comparison or contrast* :

-dar, -tar

  -t-r, -tr-, -tro-

uach-dar m. *top, surface*, W. uthr, ar-uthr—
  wonderful, Goth. iup *upwards* : *oup-tro,
  oup-tero

ioch-dar, m. *bottom* (by analogy)

  -tero-, -is-tero-

sinn-sear m. *ancestors*, a gen. pl. (?)
eachdraidh f. *history*, O.G. echtra
  adventures, expedition : *eks-tero, hence
eachdranach m. *foreigner*

  -tri-   eilthir m. *sequestered region, coast*, hence
eilthireach m. *pilgrim*, cf. L. camp-es-ter, Ped.
  otherwise, but cf. § 62

-thar -tro, -trā, as name of agent, instrument, place, or action :

bria-thar f. *word* : *bhrei-tro *word-conflict* : L.
  ferio *strike*
cria-thar m. *sieve* : *krei-tro, cf. L. cribrum
eathar m. *boat, vessel* : *pi-tro, Sk. pā-tra-m
làthair f. *place, site, presence*, là-r *floor*
leastar m. *small boat* : L. linter
saothair f. *labour*, O.G. sai-th, G. saoth f. *labour*,
  Sc. sai-r, E. *sore*

  Verbs :

altru-m m. *fostering* : L. al-tor
riastradh m. *confusion*, W. rhwystro *to hinder,
  obstruct*

§ 140.   **-to-, -tā-, -tu-, -ti-**

-adh, -eadh   the old **-u-** stems, verbal nouns in **-ad** :

ceusadh m. *crucifying*
moladh m. *praising*, a -w- suffix : W. mol-ud,
  Br. meul-eud-i *energy*
sileadh m. *dropping*

noun and adj. stems in **-e-to-** :

dligh-eadh m. *law, right* : W. dylyu, Goth. dulgs
  debt

-ta, -te	**-t-** suffixes augmented by **-w-** or **-j-** :
	molta *praised*, mol-ta
	leigte *permitted*, leig-te
-teach	**-tiko-**, (**-t-** + **-k-**, **-ku-** suffixes), L. surrep-ticius
	caoin-teach *weeping*
	e-cinn-teach *uncertain*
	lon-ach *voracious*, loing-theach
	-tū-t-, L. iuuen-tūs
	aon-ta f. *lease*, O.G. oin-tu *unity*
-ta, -tha	beatha f. *life* O.G. be-thu, *guiwo-tūt-s
	-tu-, -atu-, -etu-,
	beathadh g.s. *guiwo-tūt-os
	uaislead f. *state of nobility*, O.G. huasle-tu
	-t- + **as**
	dàna-d-as m. *audacity*
	dorcha-d-as m. *darkness*
-(t)-aid	L. **-tāt-**
	Trianaid (?) f. *Trinity*, O.G. Trin-dóit
-tar,-atar	L. **-tor, -tōr-em**
	ùghdar m. *author*, L. auctor
	brath-adair m. *betrayer*
	breab-adair m. *weaver*
	reachd-adair m. *lawgiver*
	L. **-tūra**
	srathair f. *pack saddle*, L. stratura
	creutair m. f. *creature*, L. creatura

§ 141. PREVERBS.

Prefixed to verbs are certain words or particles named preverbs which may change, or may assume, the stress, and strongly influence the form and the meaning of verbs.

Preverbs are of three classes—Prepositional, Adverbial, and Conjunctional—according to their origin.

I.—PREPOSITIONAL PREVERBS.

In the first class—**ad-**, **aith-**, **for-**, **iar n-**, **od-** are now obsolete as prepositions. **ad-** and **aith-** are confused with one another and with **ess-** and **in-**. **for-** and **iar n-** are still used as **air-**. In this form the three coalesce in Gaelic, but **air** representing O.G. **ar** always aspirates; **air**, representing O.G. **for-** and **iar n-**, does not aspirate.

Prepositional preverbs usually form perfect compounds with one another and with the verb which they modify. The stress then falls on the first syllable of the compound. But the preverb **do-** merely marking the tenses is not perfectly compounded, e.g. do rìnn mi— *I have done*, § 155, 4.

§ 142.

ad-, L. ad

1. *movement towards* :
   glaodh *call*, O.G. ad-glád-ur, cf. L. loquor, alloquor, ad-loquor; inf. agallamh (ad-glad-am, ac-cald-am) m. *address, conversation*
   iom-ad-, iomagail f. *dialogue*
   tadhal m. *visit*, to- ad- √ell

2. *at a place* :
   fàgail f. *leaving*, fo-ad-gabail, L. ad-hibere *to employ*
   The agent allows the action to remain at the place, but he himself does not remain.

ath-, aith-, W. ad-, Gk. ἔτι, Gaul. ate-, Sk. áti *over*, Sl. otu, oti.

1. *back*
   athadh m. *going backward* or *away, flinching*
   aithreachas m. *repentance*, aith-air- √reg

2. *again*
   aithne f. *recognition*, gni-n- *know*

air, ar *on, upon, for*, W. ar-, Gaul. are-, Gk. παρά, L. prae, E. *for, fore* : causes aspiration.
   air-leag *lend*, O.G. air-léicim
   oir-feid m. *music*, O.G. air-sétim *I play*
   ur-chair m. *shot*, O.G. air-chuirim

   air, ar may be followed by one or more preverbs :
   air-com-, urchoid f. *hurt*, air-com- √fed
   air-fo-, eiridinn f. *attendance on sick*, air-fo- √em
   air-ro-, ullamh *ready*, air-ro- + làmh *hand*
   ear-ghabh *arrest*, L. pro-hibere *to hinder*

air-od-,   artach m. *quarry,* air-ud- √ ding
to-air-com-, tairngire f. *promise,* to-air-com- √gair

com- *with,* W. cyf-, L. com, cum ;   * kom § 143.
    cadal m. *sleep,* O.G. co-tlud, L. com-dormire, cf. Gk.
       κατα-δαρθάνω, καθ-εύδω
    cum *hold thou,* O.G. con-gbail, cf. Gk. κατα-λαμβάνω
    caisg *check thou,* com- √sech
    teagaisg *teach thou,* to-in-com- √sech
   Often perfective in sense :
    chunnaic *has seen,* ad-con-darc, L. con-spicio, cf. Gk.
       καθ-οράω

di- *from,* L. dē
    dìmeas *despise,* dí- √mid
    dìobair *forsake,* di-od- √beir
    achuinge f. *prayer,* aith-com-di- √saig

do- proclitic of **di-, to-**

es(s)- *out of,* L. ex, abair *say thou,* ess- √beir, L. effero *I utter*
    aiseirigh f. *resurrection,* ess-ess- √reg
    teasairg *save,* to-ess-√orc

eadar- *between, among,* L. inter, Sk. antar, O.W. ithr
    eadradh m. *division of time,* eadar-thràth
    eadar-sgaradh m. *separation,* eadar- √sgar

fo- *under,* L. s-ub, Gk. ὑπό, Goth. uf, Sk. úpa *upon, next, below*

   1. *under.*
    foidhidinn f. *patience,* fo-daim-im, fo- dam-aim *I suffer*
    fulang m. *suffering,* fo-√long, fo-loing *he puts himself under*

   2. *secrecy.*
    fochaid f. *ridicule,* O.G. fo-chuitbuid : fo-con-√tib-im,
      I laugh at secretly
    fanaid f. *mockery,* O.G. fo-nomat *secret enmity*

   3. *assistance.*
    fòir *help thou,* fo- √reth, L. suc-currere
    foghain *suffice thou :* fo- √gní-m, L. suf-ficere

for- *for, over,* L. s-uper, Gk. ὑπέρ, Goth. ufar, Sk. upári
    for-bairt f. *increase, profit,* for- √beir
    furtachd f. *help, comfort,* for- √tiag
    tàrmachadh m. *increasing, producing,* do-for- √mach

frith- most frequent and oldest of new preverbs, cf. prep. fri
to, against, W. gwrth, gwryth. But **wry** became **-ur-, g** disappears through lenition, leaving W. wrth, Cor. worth, Br. ouz.
The Cor. and Br. forms are used for **ag**, a mere sign of Inf., like
ri in Uist : *vrtos, L. versus, Ger. -wärts, E. *-wards.* Originally
a noun, nom. fres, loc. fris, under the stress, frith.

<blockquote>
freasgabhail f. <i>ascension to heaven,</i> fris-in (com. ?)
- √gab
</blockquote>

ipf. cpd. frith-bhac m. *barb*
pf. cpd. friochnadh m. *care,* fris- √gní
freagair *answer,* fris- √gar, W. gwrth-air
freiteach m. *vow,* fris- √tong
freacair m. *use,* fris- √cuir
freapadh m. *medicine,* fris- √ben

iar- *after,* O.G. iar n-, comparative of epi, Gk. ἐπί : *eperon
With suffixed pronoun iarmi *after him* or *it* :
feòraich *enquire,* iarmi-fo- √saig, iarmi-foig, f-ia-fraig

im-, iom- *about,* L. amb-, amb-igo, O.G. im-aig-im, Inf.
iom-ain f. *driving*

in- *in,* G. **an,** L. in, Gk. ἐν. In G. in an accented syllable **-n-**
is assimilated to a following consonant, and the resulting vowel
is **e** :

eallach f.m. *burden, being put in,* in -√lo-n-g *puts in*
cuideachd f. *company,* com-in- √ teachd, O.G. com-etacht
aodach m. *dress,* O.G. étach : in- √tuig *clothe*
eugas(g), aogas m. *appearance,* in-com- √ sech
teagasg m. *teaching,* to-in-com- √ sech

Contaminated with **inn, ind** below, **in, an** becomes **ean** : § 148, 5
eanghnath m. *prudence,* cf. L. ignosco, *inwardly know*

inn-, ind *over, to,* O.G. ind, inn, Gaul. ande-, Sk. adhi *over,* ndhi.
In G. always with vowel **i** : aspirates a following consonant.

tiodhlac, O.G. t-ind-nac-ul *handing over,* L. nac-tus
tionndadh, O.G. tintud, to-ind-soud *turning over,* to-ind-
√so
t-ionnail f. *likeness,* to-ind-samail
ionnd-ruinn m. *wandering* : ind- √reth *overrun*
tionnsgainn f. *tossing over, beginning* : to-ind- √scann

le- *with,* a weakened form of le-th m. *side,* used as a rel. preverb.

od- *out*, Sk. úd- *out, up*, O.N. út *out*, Sl. ud : **d** is assimílated,
becoming **-m-** before **-b-**, and is retained only before vowels.

 dìobair *forsake*, di-od- √beir, O.G. diùbair *bear away out*
 diomas m. *pride*, di-od- √mes *away out of measure*
 diombuan *transitory*, di-od- √buan *away out from lasting*
 togail *take away up, lift*, to-od- √gab
 diomb m. *anger*: diumaidm, di-od-maidm *eruption* Ml.
  85ᶜ6, √mad *burst*
 dùisg, *awake*, to-di-od- √sech *call out* or *up*
 od-ess may become -ess- or -oss- (from -odss-)
 osnadh m. *sigh*, od-ess- √an, W. uchenaid f.
 fosgladh m. *letting out*, f-os-lucud, √leic

rem- *before*, cf. the prep. **re** n- √pr, L. prius, Gk. πρῶτος
 ream-ain f. *beginning* (lit. *at first drive*)
 reamh-ain f. *foretelling*
later roimhe *before it*, or *him*,
 in ipf. cpd.
 roimh-ràdh m. *prologue*

ro-, L. pro, Gk. πρό, Sk. prá, Sl. pro-.

 (a) *before*,
  rabhadh m. *warning*, O.G. ro-bud, W. rhy-budd,
   Gk. προ-πυνθάνομαι
  ro-gha *act of preferring one before another, choice*
  taircheadal m. *prophecy*, to-air-ro- √can, W. aroganu,
   d-aroganu *portend*

 (b) *through*, Sl. pro-
  ru-ig, *reach*, O.G. ro-icc *go to goal, go through*
  rochduin f. *reaching*, ro- √saigim *I make for through*
  teàruinn *save, escape*, to-ess-ro- √sní
  deàrrsg *polish*, di-ro-od- √scuich

 (c) *in an untoward sense*, Goth. fra, Ir. ro, Eng. *forg*et,
*for*lorn, Ger. *ver*spielen *waste, lose*
  dearmad *forgetfulness*, di-ro- √moin
  iomrall m. *error, wandering, false throw, miss*, imb-ro-
   √là, i.e. imb-ro *about in a false way* + √lá *throw* ;
  earghabhail f. *miserable captivity*, air-ro- √gabh ;
  eur *refuse*, ess-ro- √ so-

sech- *past*, O.W. hep, heb *without*, L. secus *otherwise, ill, badly*; as preverb **sechm-, sechmi-** *beyond him* or *it*.

seachmh-al m. *passing by, forgetfulness*, √al
seach-labhradh m. *allegory*

to- *from*, Sl. otu, oti, with the first vowel dropped.
1. *from*, t-àin f. *driving from, drove*, √ag-im
2. *back, again*, teachd f. *going*, tidheachd, tiochd, f. *going back, coming*, ti-theachd, √tiag

tre- *through*, W. trwy ; as preverb **tremi** *through it*.
treamh-laigh f. *lingering illness*
treamh-(gh)nadh m. *conduct*

Without infixed pronoun,
trea-chail *dig through* or *deeply*; Inf. trea-chladh m. *fatigue*
trea-ghaid f. *piercing* or *darting pain*, O.G. tris-gataim (analogy of fris) *I steal through*, also tre-catim, L. pre-hendo, √gat *steal*

§ 143. II.—ADVERBIAL PREVERBS.

mad, ma, mo *well*, W. mad, is proclitic of maith, an autonymous adverb which was later felt to be a preverb. In the following examples it is confused with **ma** *if* and **mo** *my* :

Chunnaic iad, ma b' fhìor dhaibh fhéin, cogul—*They saw, as they probably thought, tares* :—Cos. 23

ma b' fhìor e féin :—Am Fear-Ciùil 334

ma tá—*well !* ma dh' fhaoidte (math dhaoite)—*it might well be, perhaps* :—Munro 126

The meaning survives also in

maith a dh'fhaoidhte :—Am Fear-Ciùil 175

mo nèarachd (O.G. mad-génatar, Ir. moigheanar—*Well were they born* i.e. *blessed* is, are) nèarachd *happy, happiness*, dial. meurachd, miarachd:

Is nèarachd an duine a smachdaichear le Dia—*Happy is the man whom God correcteth* :—Job v. 17

'S bu néarachd fear 'gam bi dhiubh sud
A ghlac 's a dhorlach làn—
> *Happy is the man who has of those*
> *His quiver and his grasp full :*
>   —Metr. Ps. cxxvii. 5 (1783).   § 184, 37

mo thogair ged nach till—*I care not if he comes not back* :
—N.G.P. 52

ma thogair !—Am Fear-Ciùil 111, 329

mo chion (lit. *well has he grown*) later used as a noun.

gur mòr mo chion féin ort—*great is my affection for thee* :
—S.O. 48a5, MacCor. 36

mo chion ort féin, a Dhia, mo threis—*My blessing on thee, O God, my strength* :—Metr. Ps. xviii. 1.

Is mo chion-gràidh da-rìreadh thu—*Thou art indeed my darling* :
—A' Choisir. 12

Horó ! agus mo chion oirbh féin, a bhean a' chìobair—*Horo and my blessing on yourself, the shepherd's wife* :—Mac Cor. 36

mi- *ill*, E. *mis-* is not an autonymous adverb. It is used chiefly as a noun prefix :

mi-ghnìomh m. *bad action* ;

but also as a late preverb :

mi-chòrd *disagree*, mi-ghnàthaich *misuse* § 150, 6

mo-, mos- *soon*, L. mox., mos-sgail *awake*, § 184 s. scann

caoin *kind* is an old adj. preverb still in use :

caoin-chonaich *admonish*

caoin-mhol *flatter*

Many monosyllabic adjj. are used as preverbs, e.g.

beò-ghlac *take alive, apprehend*

bith-dheanamh m. *constant work*

deann-ruith *run at full speed*

dlùth-ghabh *accept, embrace*

dlùth-lean *cleave to*

geur-lean *persecute*

grad-las *suddenly flame*

sìor-ruith *ever flowing*

also the adjectives :

ceud *first*, W. cynt, Gaul. Cintu-, cf. E. *hind*-most, *hind*-er, be-*hind* : * cent *point* (?)

Identical in form is the preverb :

ceud *with*, O.W. cant, W can, gan, Gk. κατά, *km-ta, a derivative of * kom- § 142

ceud-fadh m. *sense*, O.G. cét-buid, W. can-fod *to perceive*

hence
  ceutach *elegant, becoming,* Ir. ceudfadhach § 184, 114
  ceud-bhean f. *wife (with-woman),* e.g.

  B'i coimeas mo cheud-mhna Reul na maidne—*The morning
    star was the likeness of my wife* :—D.Ban 200, 55
  'S oil leam càradh do cheud-mhna—*I am grieved at the
    plight of thy wife* :—ib. 140, 149

cf. M.G. cét-munter f., L. conjux m.f. *husband* or *wife*

§ 144. III.—CONJUNCTIONAL PREVERBS OR PROCLITICS.

Proclitic particles precede certain tenses of the verb § 7, III.
Proclitic particles are not themselves stressed, but they cause
the stress of the verb to be raised to the syllable immediately
following the proclitic particle, e.g. in the irregular verbs which
drop the preverb in the 3 s. pres. -chì (for atchí), -gheibh (for
fogheibh) § 155, 8, under the influence of the proclitic particles,
the preverb is restored :

  gu'm (O.G. atchí) f-aic, gu'm (O.G. fogheibh) faigh.

Proclitics are used in independent and dependent narration, but
  in the latter they become conjunctions : § 155, 8

  I. Independent Proclitics.
      1. Interrogative **an**, (**am**) : neg. **nach**
      2. Negative   **na, cha, ni** *not*
  II. Dependent Proclitics.
      1. Unconditional, **gu'n** *that* : neg. **nach** *that—not*
      2. Conditional, **ge** *though,* **ma** *if* (§ 145, 3), **mur** *if not,*
          na'n *if,* **o'n** *since*

I.—Independent Proclitics.

1. **An, am** (before gutturals and labials), **ni, ní** *not,* old I.G. form
-**ne**, is appended to **an** (O.G. **in**) the interrogative particle,
W. **a** (non-leniting). **an** fused with -**ne** (of which the **e**
was lost early) is the origin of the present interrogative,
which eclipses the tenues, puts the question without bias,
and has itself an interrogative meaning :

  An téid (pronounced **d**éid) thu leam—
      Wilt thou go with me ?—An t-Òran. 29

Am mò thusa na ar n-athair Jacob—
 Art thou greater than our father Jacob ?—John iv. 12
A dhuine ! **An** c**ual'** (pronounced gual') thu no '**m** fac' thu—
 Man ! hast thou heard or seen ?—S.O. 146ᵇ4

An do is often contracted to **na** followed by aspiration :
 Na smuainich thu riamh air cridhe agus ionndrainn Dé ?—
  Have you ever thought of the love and yearning of God ?
  —Cos. 110
 O **na** chaidil thu gu sìor—
  Since thou hast fallen asleep for ever :—Ross 19

In dependent use **an** becomes a conjunction, and may be translated ' whether ' :
 Cha n-aithne dhomh **an** téid thu—
  I do not know whether you will go.
 Cha n'eil fhios agam an robh neo nach robh—
  I do not know whether he was or not :—Munro 162 n.

Nach in independent use expects the answer ' yes ' :
 Chailin òg, **nach** stiùir thu mi—*O young girl, wilt thou not
  guide me* ?—An t-Òran. **21**
Also—
 Chailin òg, an stiùir thu mi ?—Ir. Song quoted by Shakes-
 peare :—Henry V., Act iv., Sc. iv.

 Nach boidheach an spors—*Is not the sport fine* ?—S.O. 147ᵃ1

Since the effect of the question is to emphasise the copula verb (though omitted), the answer must correspond :
 Seadh—*It is that.* Nach brèagh an là e ? Seadh—*Is it not
  a fine day* ? Yes.
 Nach till thu nall ? Tillidh—*Wilt thou not come over* ? *Yes* :—
  An t-Òran. 263

But if **e**, or another pronoun, is emphasised, it appears in the answer :
 An **e** là brèagh a tha ann ? 'S **e**—*Is it a fine day* ? *It is.*
 An e **mise**, athair ? 'S **tu**,—*Is it I, father* ? *Yes* :—L.C. 182 ;
  § 119, 4

In dependent use **nach** means ' *that . . . not*,' and is a con-junction :
 Is truagh nach robh mi an riochd na faoilinn—'*Tis a pity
  that I were not in the form of a seagull* :—An t-Òran. 263

A similar use of **nach** is :

Ged nach—*though it be that . . . not,* e.g.

Ged nach d' fhuair me e dhomh fhìn—*Though (it be that) I have not got him for myself* :—ib. 167

2. **Na** is used with the Ipv. only :

Na sir is na seachain an cath—*Nor seek nor shun the fight*: —N.G.P. 330

Na h-abair facal—*Speak not a word* :—Munro 107

3. **Cha**, **cha n**- (O.G. nícon', ní co n': M.G. no co n-é:—P.H. 1290 ; Ir. no cha n-) is the independent negative. It aspirates gutturals and labials, eclipses **-t-**, but does not affect **-d-** ; before vowels it projects a nasal ; and before **-f-** pure it projects a nasal and causes aspiration :

Cha **gh**ille mur h-ùmhailt e—*He is no servant unless he obeys* : —N.G.P. 102

Cha **mh**ol duine sheud is e aige—*A man does not praise his jewel while he has it* :—ib. 105

Cha **t**oir duine chall d'a charaid—*No man gives his friend his loss* :—ib. 133

Cha **d**uine duine 'na aonar—*A man alone is no man* :—ib. 101

Cha **n**-e an ro chabhag as fheàrr—*Great speed is not best* —ib. 107

Cha **n**'eil ach a leth-taobh ris—*He has but a half side to it*: —ib. 109

Cha **n**-fhaighear an dè air ais an diugh—*You cannot to-day recall yesterday* :—ib. 117

4. **Ni** is the O.G. form of the negative in independent narration. The 3 sing. of the negative form of the copula is also **ní** which includes both the negative and the copula § 48, 2. A trace of this double origin is still seen in the projected **h-** which follows **ní** when the predicate begins with a vowel :

Ni **h**-eagal leam 's ni 'n càs—*I am in no fear or distress* :— Metr. Ps. xxiii., 4.

Ni'n, **ni'm**, stands for **ni co n**- (with Fut.) ; **nior** aspirating tenues, for **ni-ro** (with Perf.)

Is lochd **ni'n** caidir thu — *And evil thou wilt not cherish* : —ib. V. 4

'S **ni** '**n** coinnich sibh aon ni gu bràth— *And ye shall never meet anything* :—Là Bhr. 343

ni + **ro** becomes **nior**, **nir**, and is used along with a pf.

Nir facas creutair dhiùbh— *Not one of them appeared* :— S.O. 107ª15

'S **nior** ghabh mi d'a fhuil phrìseil suim— *And I gave no heed to his precious blood* :—Là Bhr. 444

Nior cheil mi m' aingidheachd— *I have not concealed my wickedness* :—Metr. Ps. xxxii. 5

'S **nior** ghabh mi tàmh no fois— *I have taken no ease or rest* : —ib. cxix. 60

Nior dhearmad mi do reachd— *I have not neglected thy law* : —ib. 61

Nior thréig mi d' iarrtus naomh— *I have not forsaken thy holy command* :—ib. 87

Nior chlaon mi fos od' bhreitheanais— *Moreover I have not turned aside from thy judgments* :—ib. 102, 110

Nior, causing aspiration, is also 3 s. ipf. of **is** and in Ir. is written **níor bh**, and **níor** + asp. as in the examples above.

By contamination with **air neo**, § 221, **nior** becomes petrified into **neo-air-**, in the phrase **neo-air-**thaing— *it is (was) no thanks*

Fhad 's a bha sporan làn aige, **neo-air-**thaing mur an robh companaich gu leòir aige— *As long as he had a full purse, no fear but he had companions enough* :—Cos. 119

Tha thu fhathast 'sna brògan

Anns am bì thu ri d' beò 's **neo-ar-**thaing—
   You are still in the shoes
   In which you will stand while you live, no fear :—L. nan Gleann 83, 20

Neo'r thaing do rìgh na Fraing, cha n'eil mi 'n taing a shiùcair— *No thanks to the king of France, I don't need his sugar* :—N.G.P. 332

neo-air-thaing cho trom, cho breugach— *quite as heavy, as untruthful* :—Am F.C. 206, 290

neo-air-thaing mur an robh e deas leis na duirn— *No doubt but he was ready with his fists* :—ib. 236

cf. neo-air-chàs m. *indifference*, neo-air-thoirt m. *carelessness*

Nì causes eclipsis in beil, fìl : § 13, 2
Ni bheil sibh iomchuidh air mo rìoghachd—
    Ye are not fit for my kingdom :—Là Bhr. 249
Is **ni** bheil eucoir buntainn rium—
    And injustice is not touching me :—ib. 442

§ 145.   II.—Dependent Proclitics.

1. **Gu'n, gu'm** (before labials), O.G. co n- *that*, is used with all
tenses of indicative and subjunctive.

In the pres. subj. of **is** the nasal is assimilated to -**r**- :
    Chum **gur** léir dhuit—*That* (it may be clear to thee, *i.e.*
    that) *thou mayest see* :—Rev. iii. 18
    Agus **gur** creutairean an là an diugh iad— *And that they*
    are creatures of to-day :—Cos. 57

Gur is used independently as an indicative :
    Theagamh **gur** e so an t-aobhar—*Perhaps this is the reason* :
    —Am Fear-Ciùil 210
    Gur tric an t-eug gu geur 'g ur sealg-se—
    Death is often keenly hunting you :—S.O. 59ª31
    Gur beag tha ghliocas 'na do ghlòir—
    Little wisdom is in thy voice :—Clarsach 6

Gu'n is often so used with other tenses, and especially in
(a) wishes and (b) imprecations :
(a) Gu'm b' òg bha sinn còmhladh— *Young were we together* :
    —Clarsach 38
    Gu'n tug i spéis do'n Armunn—*She loved the soldier* :—
    MacCor. Title
(b) Ach an là a dh'éirinn leibhse, **gu'n** robh mi gun fhasgadh
    na h-oidhche—*But on the day I'd go with you, may I*
    be without shelter at night :—L.C. 183
    Gu'n tugadh crodh Chailean Dhomh bainn' air an raon—
    Colin's cattle used to give me milk on the field :—A'Choisir 7

2. **Ge** (O.G. ciaᶜ, ceᶜ, ciᶜ) *though, although* (with O.G. ed, **ged**—
though it be). In present tense, with pronouns and adjj.,
is being assimilated : Ge h-e—*Tho' it is he* :—Munro 161
    Ge glas am fiar, fàsaidh e—*Though grey the grass it will grow* :
    —N.G.P. 196
In past, ge b'e air bith—*whoever*

3. **Ma** *if*, (O.G. má, ma) aspirates a following consonant, is used with pres. and past of subst. verb (ma tha, ma bha), with the rel. form, the fut. uncompounded, and the perf. § 21, cf. § 155, 6

> **Mas** rìgh no **mas** diùc thu féin—*If thyself be a king or a duke* :—An Claig. 33
>
> **Ma** tharras mise thu, is tu gheibh e—*If I get hold of you, you will catch it* :—Munro 123
>
> Is beannaichte sibh **ma** ni sibh iad—*Happy are ye if ye do them* :—John xiii. 17
>
> **Ma** rinn mi so—*If I have done this* :—Ps. vii. 3
>
> **Ma** chaidh tu 'nan sealbhaidh—
> *If you took to do with them* :—S.O. 155ᵇ37

4. **Mur, mura** *if not, unless* (neg. of ma, O.G. ma-ni, main ; with pres. subj. of **is**, ma-ni-p : M.G. ma-ni, manip, mi-na, mi-ne, mo-na ; man, men, mun).

In G. the -n- is pronounced -r- § 18, and the final -nì- still projects h- before vowels § 48, 2 :

> **Mur** h-e Bran, is e bhràthair—*If it be not Bran, it is his brother* :—N.G.P. 321
>
> **Mur** robh thusa fìor—*If thou wert not true* :—An Claig. 67
>
> **Mur** bhuin e dh' an bhuidhinn no dh'an bheachd acasan, cha n-fhiach e fhéin no obair—*Unless he belongs to their party or way of thinking, neither he nor his work matters* :—Cos. 139
>
> **Mur** tig an rìgh nach fhuirich e ?—*If the king will not come, let him stay* :—N.G.P. 321

Occasionally rel. **an** follows **mur** :

> **Muna** ndiongantaoi an móireachd—*If the great deed were not done* :—Reliq. Celt. ii. 452

Compare this sentence with the following, where **mur** introduces direct interrogative sentences :

> Neo-air-thaing **mur an** robh companaich gu leòir aige—*No fear, but he had plenty of companions* :—Cos. 119
>
> **Mur an** e an rìgh a tha ann, 's e a ghille a th'ann—*If it be not the king, it is his lad* :—MacCor. 43

5. **Na 'n** (O.G. dia n-, § 13, influenced by **muna n-**, v. above).

Only with ipf. or plpf. subj : § 173, 2

> **Na'm** b' ionann do chàch 's do Ghoill—*If it were the same with the rest as with Lowlanders* :—S.O. 59ᵇ27

> **Na'm** faigheadh e an cothrom—*If he got the opportunity* :— Cos. xix.

6. **O, o'n (bho'n, bho na)** *since, seeing that* :

> **O** 's e so deireadh an t-saoghail bhrionnaich—*Since this is the end of the pretty world* :—S.O. 59ᵃv.

> Nise **bho na** dh' fhalbh na bràithrean— *Now since the brethren have gone* :—S.O. 59ᵃ34.

§ 146. **COMPOSITION OF NOUNS.**

Nouns are compounded with preceding prepositions and particles.

An account has been given, §100, showing how nouns are compounded with nouns and with adjectives.

Nouns are also compounded with prepositions, and with negative and intensive particles. These prepositions and particles regularly precede the noun. When the result is a Perfect Compound, §100, the preposition or particle may be called—(1) a prenoun. When the result is an Imperfect Compound, the particle is called (2) a prefix.

The **prepositions** compounded with nouns are of four classes— I., Obsolete ; II., Inseparable ; III., Separable ; and IV., Prepositions used in a negative sense.

I.—Obsolete.

1 **ad-, inn-, od-** §142 are prenouns. They always carry the stress, and they are dead in the sense that they are inseparable from their nouns, and do not enter into new formations, e.g.

> **ad-,** aigne f. *mind, disposition,* ad-√gen-it-on, § 184, 44
> oitir f. *sea-bank under water* : ad-√tir
> adharc f. *horn* : ad-(ess)-√arc (?) ad(ess)-√arc (?)

2.   **inn-**, ànart m. *pride*
      annlann m. *kitchen, condiment*, cf. leann, W. llyn
      innean m. *anvil*, Ir. inneóin : ndhe (= ind) -√poni
      innear f. *dung* : ind-ebar
      innlinn f. *provender* : inn-√el
      innsgin f. *mind*

3.   **od-**, v. diomas, diomb, diombuan §142, osnad §184, √an

§ 147.   II. Inseparable.

ath- (aith-), **com- (con-)**, and **ro** are used as (1) prenouns.
                                   (2) prefixes.

1. **ath- (aith-)**
   (1) aimheal m. *vexation*, O.G. aith-méla *repentance*
      (Ir. T. II. 131), Gk. μέμφομαι, μεμφωλή *blame*
      aithinne f. *embers*, ath-teine
      aithlis f. *disgrace*, aith-les (*abandoned fort*)
      athailt f. *mark, scar*, ath-meil
      athais f. *leisure*, ath-fois
      eathlamh *expert, dexterous*, ath-lamh
   (2) ath-bheachd m. *retrospect*
      ath-là m. *next day*
      ath-sgeul m. *tale at second hand, second telling*
      ath-theine m. *second volley*

2. **com- (con-)**
   (1) coingheall m. *loan*, Ir. coingheall *covenant, condition*,
                       O.G. con-geallaim *I pledge*
      coimhearsnach m. *neighbour*, O.G. com-arse
      comain f. *obligation*, com-máin, cf. L. communio
      comharradh m. *mark*, O.G. airde *sign*, W. ar-wydd,
         L. vid-eo   § 60, 5
      cothrom m. *equipoise*, com-trom
   (2) comh-aigne f. *similar turn of mind*
      comh-aimsireil *contemporary, coeval*
      comh-aois m. *a contemporary*
      comh-charaid m. *mutual friend*

3. **ro-**
   (1) radharc m. *sight*, O.G. ro-√darc   § 184, 19
      roille f. *fawning welcome*, ro-thoil

H

ròisgeul m. *romance*, ro-sgeul
rosg m. *eyelid, eye*, ro-√sech § 184, 94
    cf. W. rhy-wynt *hurricane*
Am fear a chuir an rò- sgeul r'a chéile— *He who composed
the romance* :—Am Fear-Ciùil 330

(2) ro-sheòl m. *top gallant sails*
    With adjj. in the sense of *very, too* :
ro mhor *very great*, ro throm *too heavy*
Seall air mo chàs-sa, cha n'eil mi ro ghlic— *Look on my
case, I am not over wise* :—Am Fear-Ciùil 210

§ 148.   III.—Separable.

**air (for, iar), eadar, fo, iom (im), in (*en), ri (frith), roimh
(re n-), seach, troimh (tre),** are in use as prepositions and also
as (1) prenouns ; (2) prefixes.

1. **air-** (a) air- arabhaig f. *strife,*   ar + bág
                    arabhalach m. *traitor,*   ar + balach
                    earrann f. *portion,*   ar + rann
                    iriosal *humble,*   ar + iosal
                    oirthir f. *coast,*   ar + tìr § 135
                    uiread m. *as much* (of
                        space or time),   ar + ed
                    ùirlios m. *walled garden,* ar + lios
                    uirsgeul m. *fable,*   ar + sgeul
                    urlar m. *floor,*   ar-làr

        Also with prothetic **f,** § 33 :
             farbhalach m. *stranger*
             farcluais f. *secret listening*
             fariasg, farasg m. *spent fish*

  (b) for- (1) fairleus m. *smoke hole,* for + lés
                farrusg m. *inner rind,* for + rusg
                fóirneart m. *oppression,* for + neart
                fairsing *wide,*   for + seang, cf. W.
                         e-ang *wide,* * *eks-* ang

        (2) for-dhorus m. *porch*
                foir-iomall m. *limit*
                foir-sheòmar m. *lobby*

  (c) iar- (1) iarbhail f. *consequence,* iar + buil
      iargail f. *the West,* iar + cùl
      iarmad m. *offspring,* iarmart
    (2) iar-bhuille m. *second stroke*
      iar-cheann m. *hindhead*
      iar-chuan m. *western sea*
      iar-ogha m. f. *great-grandchild*

2. eadar-   (1) eadradh m. *division of time,* eadar-thràth
       (between canonical hours)
    (2) eadar-sholus m. *twilight*
      eadar-thuinn f. *hollow between waves*

3. fo- (1) famhair m. *giant* (fo + muir *along-sea,* Ir. fo-mhor, old Bulg. po-morije *coast-land,* Pruss. po-morze *Pommeranian,* Lith. pa-marionis *strand-dweller)*
      fasgadh m. *shelter,* O.G. fo + scad *shadow,* W. gwa-sgod, Gr. σκότος *darkness*
      foghail f. *hostile incursion,* fo + gal
    (2) fo-bhuille f. *gentle blow*
      fo-dhuine m. *dwarf*

4. iom- (im--) with Svarabhakti, ioma- : aspirates :
    (1) imcheist f. *anxiety,* im + ceist, L. quaestio
      iomall m. *border,* im + pel, Gk. πέλομαι
      iomlan *complete,* im + slàn
      iomshruth m. *eddy,* im + sruth
    (2) iom-throm *very heavy*
      ioma-ghaoth f. *whirlwind*
      iom-ghlòir f. *noise of a multitude*

5. in- (*en) eanchainn, eanchaill f. *brains,* W. ymennydd, M. Corn. empynnyon, M. W. penn, G. ceann *head*
      inghean, nighean f. *daughter,* Ogam INGENA, Gk. ἐγγόνη *grand-daughter,* L. indigena *the inborn,* *eni-gena
      inilt f. *bondmaid,* O.G. inailt, g.s. inalta : * en-alti *brought up in the house,* § 142

6. ri- (O.G., and cpds., **frith-**)
    (1) friobhag, frithbhac f. *barb,* frith + bac
      friochd m. *second dram,* fri + teachd
      frisgis f. *hope, expectation,* frescissiu, fri-ad-cì,

§ 184, 19

   (2)   frith-ainm m. *nickname*
         frith-iasg m. *small fry*
         frith-sheirc, f. *return of affection*

7. roimh- (O.G. rem-)
   (1)   roimheach *relative*
         roimhear m. *antecedent*
   (2)   roimh-chùis f. *prelude*
         roimh-eòlas m. *foreknowledge*

8. seach-
   (1)   seachbho,   f. *barren cow,* seach + bó
         seachlach   *heifer,*   seach + laogh
         seachlaimh f. *savings,*   seach + làmh
   (2)   seach-briathar m. *allegory*
         seach-labhradh m. id.
         seach-rathad m. *by-way*

do- *to,* **thar** *over,* **tre** and **troimh** *through,* are not used as prenouns and prefixes.

§ 149.   IV.—NEGATIVE.

a- (**as-**), and **de** (**do**) are used as Prepositions and as (1) prenouns, (2) negative prefixes :

as-   (1)   ablach m. *mangled carcase,*   ess + ball
             eagal m. *fear,*   ess + gal
             éirig f. *ransom,*   ess + recc
             éislean m. *grief,*   ess + slán

        Later forms are :
             asbhuain f. *without being reaped,* ess + bong- §184, 6
                        stubble
             ascaoin *unkind,*   ess + caoin
             easbhuidh f. *want, defect,*   ess + buith
             eascaraid m. *enemy*   ess + cara
   (2)   eas-ionracas m. *dishonesty*
         eas-ùmhail *disobedient*
         eas-urram m. *disrespect*

de-   O.G. de, di, L. dē, di(s) ; therewith **di-** and **do-**, proclitics of the preverb **to-**, are confused. According to Pedersen

Gr. § 532, 2, the -**m**- of **dim**- is developed from **ml**-, **mr**-
as they passed from **mbl**- **mbr**- to **bl**- **br**- : the -**m**- was
retracted and adhered to **di**- spreading by analogy to other
combinations :

(1) dibhearg f. *vengeance, wrath,*   dí + berg f. *brigandage*
dìbrigh, dimbrigh f. *contempt,*   di-m-brìgh
dìnimh f. *weakness,*   di + snìomh
dìogan m. *revenge,*   di + gon
dìthreamh f. *desert,*   di + treb
dìleas *faithful, own, proper,*   di + leas, leas as in
leas-ainm,
leas-athair, leas-mhac,
from leth, *side, half.*

(2) dì-neart m. *imbecility*
diom-buaidh f. *unsuccessfulness*
diom-buil f. *prodigality*

The so-called intensive particles may be explained :

dimor (away from great) *very great*
diardan m. (away from pride) *anger*

The O.G. dé- *two, twice,* for which **dà** (e.g. dà-chrannach
two-masted) is now used may have had an influence.

§ 150.

1. **an**-, E. *un*- ; I.E., N, Br. and Celt. an- ; Sk. a-, an- ; Gk. ά, άν- ;
L. in- :

an- is (1) a prenoun in older cpds. with stress, and modification to **ain**-, **amh**-, **aimh**-, corresponding to the vowel
of the following word, e.g.

aineol m. *stranger*
ainfhios m. *ignorance*
amharus m. *suspicion* (am- (p)ires *un-faith*)

(2) a prefix, in later cpds. unstressed, and generally
unmodified, e.g.

an-diadhaidh *ungodly*
an-earbsa f. *distrust*
an-dìleas, ain-dìleas *unfaithful.*

2. before vowels, **an-**, **ain-** :

    (2) an-abaich *unripe*
         an-diùid f. *boldness*
         an-dùthchas m. *degeneracy*
         an-duine m. *wicked man*
         an-eagal m. *fearlessness*
         an-obair f. *trifle*
         an-uair f. *bad weather*

3. before labials and liquids, **am-**, **aim-**, **amh-**, **aimh** :

    (1) aimbeart f. *poverty*
         aimhleas m. *hurt* : W. af-les, am + leas *non-profit*
         aimrid *barren* (with -b- eclipsed,) am-brit, O.G.
            birit *sow*
         amhlair *fool, boor*, O.G. am-labar *mute*, W. af-
            lafar, L. labrum *lip*
         amhnarach *shameless*

4. before -**f**-, **an-** aspirates :

         an-fhuras m. *impatience*

  but when -**f**- represents -**u**- ; **an-**, **ain-**, become **anbh-**,
        ainbh-, e.g.

    (1) ainbhfeile f. *impudence*
         ainbhfheoil f. *proud flesh*
         ainbhfhiach m. *debt*
         ainbhfhios m. *ignorance*
         ainbhtheach *stormy* (feth, fèath *breeze*)
         ainbi, ainbith *odd, unusual*, O.G. ainb, ainib
            ignorant : * n-wid-s

5. **an-** before -**c**-, -**t**-, and -**s**- :

  (a) adjj. **eu-**, **ao-** (after which -**c**- and -**t**- are in pronunciation
     reduced to -**g**- and -**d**-) :

    (1) eu-ceart *unjust*,   an-ceart
         eucoir *unjust*,   an-còir, W. anghywir,
                              anwir

         aotrom *light*,   an-trom, cf. aodraman
                              m. *bladder*

         eugsamhuil *various*, an-con-samuil
         easgaidh *nimble*,   an-sgìth
         easlan *infirm*,   an-slàn

(2) eu-céillidh *mad*
eu-cosmhail *dissimilar*
eu-tròcair f. *want of mercy*

(b) nouns : **an-**, **ain-**, with Svarabhakti vowel, **ana-** which may aspirate a following -**c**-, -**g**- :

(1) ainsearc f. *hatred*
antlachd m. *dislike*
antruas m. *want of pity*

(2) ana-cleachdadh m. *inexperience*, ana-chleachdadh
ana-cothrom f. *injustice*
ana-creideamh m. *infidelity*, an-chreideamh
ana-measarra *immoderate*

(c) **an-**, **ain-** before -**d**-, -**g**- :

(1) aingidh, *wicked*, O.G. andach, andgaid : an + deg
àmhghar m. *disadvantage* (*pronounced* amhn-gar, Din.) from am-gar *un-nearness*

(d)   (2) an-ghnàth, ana-ghnàth m. *bad custom*
but eu-dìon m. *leak*
eu-dòchas m. *despair*

With doubled negative, an- : an-easguidh *lazy*
an + an + sgìth

6. **mì-** *un-*, **mis-** *ill-* : aspirates : O.G. mi- from miss-, e.g. misiomairt,

missimbert *foul-play*, an old comparative, cf. L. nimis *not too little*.

miosguinn f. *malice*, O.G. mis-cen *hatred* (from miscinn, *ill has he grown*), cf. § 143

(1) **as** prenoun, rare :
miabhail *harsh*, also mi-bhàidheil
mìorun m. *ill-will*, also mi-rùn

(2) **as** prefix, frequent, e.g.
mi-dhùrachd f. *negligence*
mi-thlusar *hard-hearted*

7. **neo-** *un-* ; Ir. neamh-, neimh- ; O.G. neb, neph ; from **ne** *not* (later ni, ní,) and -**b**-, some part of the verb ' to be ': aspirates by analogy :

(1) as prenoun, rare :

neoghlan *impure*
neònach *curious,*   neo + ghnàthach
neoni f. *nothing,*   neo + ni

(2) as prefix, frequent, e.g.

neo-ascaoin *friendly*
neo-eagnaidh *unlearned*
neo-fhallan *unsound*

8. **so-**, **su-**, *well* : **do-**, **du-**, *ill*, W. hy-, dy-, Gk. δυσ-

(1) as prenouns, e.g.

saoibhir *rich*

daibhir *poor* : O.G. saidber, cf. aobhar
material, substance

saoi, saoidh m. *sage*

daoi m. *wicked man* : *su-wid-s

saor *free*

daor *bound* : *sapero, L. sapio

socair f. *ease*

docair f. *trouble* : càr *loving,* W.achar
ad + car

sochair f. *benefit*

dochair f. *hurt* : car *state*

soicheal m. *mirth*

doicheall m. *churlishness* : ciall *sense*

soilgheas m. *fair-wind*

doilgheas m. *sorrow* : longas, §64

soilleir *clear*

doilleir *dark* : léir

soinnionn, soineann f.
fair weather

doinionn f. *storm* : (do)-sín-enn

soirbh *easy*

doirbh *hard* : reabh *feat, sport.* .i.
cleas O'Cl. :

soisgeul m. *evangel*

sgeul m. *story*

soitheamh *gentle*

doitheamh *bluff* : tiom *timid*

solar m. *providing* Ir. so-láthar m.

sòlas m. L. solatium

dòlas m. *grief* : do-sòlas

solod O.G. *profit*

dolaidh f. *harm* : folad *substance*

solus m. *light*

L. lux

sona *happy*

dona *bad* : gnàth *usual*

soraidh f. *farewell*

doraidh f. *strife* ; réidh *plain*

sorcha *bright*

dorch *dark*

subhach *merry*

dubhach *sad*

subhailc f. *virtue*

dubhailc f. *vice*

suaicheantas *ensign*

duaichnidh *gloomy, ugly* : aithne
knowledge

suaigh *prosperous*　　　duagh m. *hardship* : àgh *prosperity*
suaimhneach *genial, secure* (O.G. so-menmnach *cheerful*)
sùmhail *closely-packed*　dòmhail *bulky* : L. humilis

(2) as prefixes, frequent :
so-ghiùlan *portable*　　do-ghiùlan *insupportable*

§ 151.　　　　　**Gun** as a Negative.

A clause closely connected in meaning with the principal
sentence, and containing a nominative and a verbal noun, may
be negatived by the preposition **gun** :

Fhuair iad rabhadh iad a philltinn—*They got warning to
return*

Fhuair iad robhadh **gun** iad a philltinn—*They got a warning
not to return* :—Stewart 130

A' spleuchdadh air a bhrògan, dìreach mar gu'm biodh
iongantas air—iad a bhi air a chasan—*Gazing at his
shoes, just as if he were astonished that they were on his
feet* :—Am F.C. 234

—**gun** iad a bhi air a chasan—*that they were not on his feet.*

With bhi omitted :

Is truagh **gun** thu agam— *Alas ! that I am without thee* :—
H.B. v. gun.

'S truagh **gun** agam féin

Sgiath calmain gu dol as—'*Tis sad that I myself have not a
dove's wing to go away* :—Metr. Ps. lv., 6

§ 152.　　　　　INTENSIVE PREFIXES.

1. **an-**, I.E. ndhi, Ir. án-, W. en-, Gaul, Ande-(Combogius) :
with Svarabhakti, ana- ;　often aspirates :

(1) anabarr, anbharr m. *excess*
onfhadh m. *storm,* O.G. anboth, anfud m. Related
is M.G. an-féth *storm,* whence ainbthine *storm,*
G. ainbhtheach *stormy,* according to Ped. féth (in
G. *gentle breeze*) = spì-t-, cf. L. spī-r-āre, W. ffun,
ffyned

(2) ana-bhiorach m. *centipede*
ana-ghràdhach, ana-gràdhach *doting*
an-amharus m. *extreme distrust*
an-bhàs m. *sudden death*

With a slender vowel, **ain-** :

(1) aineas f. *passion, joy* : ain + theas
ainneart m. *violence*
ainriochd m. *pitiful plight*
(2) ain-teas m. *excessive heat*
ain-treun *ungovernable*

2. ion-, in- *worthy of, fit for*, O.G. in : *eni, confused with *ndhi above ; aspirates ; in O.G. it preceded -i- stems and p.p. pass. in-**te**, **-the** ; hence in G. it is said to precede a gen. and a p.p. pass.

(1) inleighis *curable*, also ion-leighis
ionmhuin *beloved*, in + mòin, -màin, L. mūnus
(2) in-mheadhonach *mean, moderate*
ion-dhèanta *feasible*
ion-phòsda *marriageable*

3. fo- *under*. This prep. is used as a prefix with diminutive force in a few instances :

(1) faoighe f. *thigging* : fo-guide
(2) fo-bhaile m. *suburb*
fo-dhuine m. *dwarf*
fo-neul m. *cloudlet*
fo-rann m. *versicle*

4. il-, iol- *many* : O.G. hil-, Ger. viel, Got filu, Gk. πολύς, Sk. puru-s

(1) ileach *variegated*
ilbhinn f. *craggy mountain*
(2) iol-àireamh m. *ennumeration*
iol-bhéist m. *serpent*

5. ioma-, iomadh- *many*, O.G. imbed, immad : does not regularly aspirate : often confused with iom-, which, with Svarabhakti, becomes ioma- :

(1) iomadach *numerous*
iomadan m. *a concurrence of disasters*, iomadh + dàn

(2) ioma-cheannach *many-headed*
iomad-labhrach *multiloquous*
iom-àlach *multiparous*

6. deagh- *good,* **droch-** *bad,* **bith-, cath-, sìor-** *continually,* are inseparable adj. prefixes ; and nearly all monosyllabic adjj. may be used as prefixes, aspirating the second member of the cpd. § 29, 5 ; § 143

§ 153.   **THE VERB.**

Verbs are of four classes :

I. Regular, with the past preverb **do** (in O.G. **ro**), **do bhuail** —*he struck.* Being pretonic and unaccented **do** disappears in the Indic. absolute, leaving its influence in the aspirated initial, **bhuail.** But **do** is resumed after a proclitic particle, e.g. **gu'n do bhuail**—*that he struck* § 7 iii.

II. Irregular, which show (1) different roots in the pres. and past : **rach** *will go* ; **tèid** *goes, will go* ; **chaidh** *went.* (2) different inflections : **cluinn** *hear,* **cuala** *heard* ; **chì** *see,* **chunnaic** *saw.* (3) different preverbs : **rinn** *has done* (**ro-gnì**) ; **gu'm faigh**—*that he will get* (**fo-gabh**) ; **ad-chì** *sees* ; **ad-** (earlier **ro**)-**chluinn**—*hears* ; **to-icc** *comes* ; **ro-icc** *reaches* ; **ad-** (earlier **as-**) -**beir** *says*

III. Auxiliary, **is, tha** *is,* **gabh** *can,* **dean** *make,* **tèid** *will go* ; **chaidh,** gu'n **deachaidh** *went*

IV. Defective, consisting of surviving parts of O.G. verbs, or of new formations.

§ 154.

The Gaelic verb is transitive or intransitive. The latter, the intransitive verb, has no passive voice ; but one or two intransitive verbs of motion govern a **cognate accusative,** § 213, 3 :

Sin dìreach far an deach mi dochair :—*That is just where I came to grief* :—Cos. 129

Faodaidh a' chaora dol bàs, a' feitheamh ris an fhiar ùr— *The sheep may die waiting for the new grass* :—N.G.P. 176 : Am Fear-Ciùil 232, 320

Tha shnuadh dol a mugha—*Its beauty is going to waste* :—
Ross 75

The transitive verb has two Voices—Active and Passive ;
five Tenses—Present, Future, Imperfect, Perfect, and Pluperfect.

Present and Future, Perfect and Pluperfect are distinguishable only by the context.

Four Moods—Indicative, Subjunctive, Imperative, and
Infinitive, the last being both Active and Passive :—

Tha e cur suas ùrnuigh—*He is offering up prayer.*
Fhad 's a bha an ùrnuigh 'ga cur suas—*Whilst the prayer
was being offered* :—L.C. 69, § 187, 2 (c)

Two Numbers—Singular and Plural

Three Persons—First, Second, and Third

§ 155.

1. The parts of the old Gaelic verb now in use are
    (1) the third sing. of the Present (including the Relative form)
        and 3 s. of the Perfect, for all persons in all moods.
    M.G. Pres. 3 s. **buailid** *he strikes.*   G. **buailidh** *strikes* or
    will strike, Rel. **bhuaileas** *who strikes* or *will strike.*
    M.G. Pf. 3 s. **ro buail** *he has struck,* G. **(do-)bhuail** *has* or
    had struck

The Pres. and Pf. not being inflected, the 1 and 2 persons are
distinguished by the 1 and 2 personal pronouns, and the 3 person
by the 3 personal pronoun (or a noun or other pronoun) as
nominatives immediately following the verb, except in the case
of the Rel. form when the noun may precede the verb.

	Present.		*Perfect*
Sing. :		Sing. :	
1.	buailidh mi	1.	bhuail mi
2.	buailidh tu, thu	2.	bhuail **thu**
3.	buailidh e	3.	bhuail e
Pl. :		Pl. :	
1.	buailidh sinn	1.	bhuail sinn
2.	buailidh sibh	2.	bhuail sibh
3.	buailidh iad	3.	bhuail iad

Relative.

Sing. :	Pl. :
1. mi a bhuaileas	1. sinn a bhuaileas
2. tu a bhuaileas	2. sibh a bhuaileas
3. e a bhuaileas	3. iad a bhuaileas

(2) The Ipv. mood and

(3) The Ipf. (Ind. and Subj.) which retain some of the old inflections.

The Ipv. 2 s. is the stem of the verb. The first sing. Ipv. is of recent origin and is used chiefly in poetry ; but it is still heard—notably in the correction of children :

Na cluinneam sin bhuat a rìs—*Do not let me hear that from you again* :—C.S., cf. § 166

Ipv.

Sing.	*Plural.*
1. (buaileam *let me strike*)	buaileamaid *let us strike*
2. buail *strike thou*	buailibh, bualadh sibh *strike ye*
3. buaileadh *let him strike*	buaileadh iad *let them strike*

Ipf.

1. bhuailinn *I used to*, or *would, strike*	bhuaileamaid *we used to*, or *would, strike*
2. bhuaileadh tu *thou usedst to*, or *wouldest, strike*	bhuaileadh sibh *ye used to*, or *would, strike*
3. bhuaileadh e *he used to*, or *would, strike*	bhuaileadh iad *they used to*, or *would, strike*

The 3 sing. is often used as rel. even when other forms peculiar, e.g. to 1 sing. exist, as above, cf. §119, 4 :

Gur mi dheanadh sòlas—*I would rejoice* :—Clarsach **38.**

Bha 'n droch bhoirionnach coma co dhiubh bhithinnsa toilichte no nach **bitheadh**—*The evil woman was indifferent whether I would be pleased or not* :—Arab. I. 21

2. **ro-** was the preverb of the Pf. in O.G. : **ro buail**—*he struck* :

    ro in later Gaelic caused aspiration. In G. **do-** took the place of **ro-** as preverb of Pf. causing aspiration, and it spread to the Ipf. and even to the (Fut.) Rel. ; hence these tenses are aspirated in G.

    bhuaileadh *he would strike,* **bhuaileas** *who strike, strikes,* or *will strike,* in verbs with initial consonants. Before vowel initials and **f-** pure, the **-o-** of **do** is elided in these tenses, and the **-d-** aspirated.

dh' òl e *he drank*	dh' fhàg e *he left*
dh' òladh e *he would drink*	dh' fhàgadh e *he would leave*
a dh' òlas *who will drink*	dh' fhanas *who will stay*

3. After proclitics ending in a nasal the **-d-** of **do** is not aspirated § 20, 4

    gu'n d' òl e—*that he drank*

4. Proclitics preceding compound verbs raise the stress to the first preverb :

    gu'n d'rinn—*that he did*
    cha n-fhaigh e—*he will not get*

5. Proclitics preceding a Perfect with initial consonant restore **do** to its place between the proclitic and the verb :

    mu'n do mharbh—*before he slew*
    An do ghlacadh e—*Was he caught ?*

6. The following are the verbal proclitics : § 144.

Interrogative.	Negative.	Conditional.
an ? am ?	cha	gu'n *that*
	na	mu'n *before*
negative, nach ?	nach	mur *unless*
		na'n *if*
		o'n *since*

    But **ma,** having been originally accented, does not act as proclitic so as to restore the preverb to stressed position,. § 145, 3, 4

am faigh e—*will he get ?*   ma gheibh e—*if he will get*
nach dean e—*will he not do ?*   ma ni e—*if he will do*

I.

§ 156.   **The regular verb.**

1.   M.G. glacaim—*I grasp*, 3 s. **glacaidh**

	Indicative.		*Subjunctive.*
	ABSOLUTE.	CONJUNCT.	
		Active.	
Pres. &	glacaidh—*he grasps*	gu'n glac—*that he*	gu'n glac—*that he*
Fut.	or *will grasp*	*will grasp*	*may grasp*
	rel. ghlacas		
Ipv.	glac—*grasp thou*		
Ipf.	ghlacainn *I used to*	gu'n glacainn—*that I*	gu'n glacainn—*that*
	grasp	*used to grasp*	*I should grasp*
Perf. &	ghlac mi—*I grasped*	gu'n do ghlac mi—	na'n do ghlac mi—
Plup.	or *have grasped*	*that I grasped*	*had I grasped*
		Passive	
Pres. &	glacar—*it is* or *will*	gu'n glacar—*that it*	gu'n glacar—*that it*
Fut.	*be grasped*	*will be grasped*	*may be grasped*
Ipv.	glacar, glactar—*let it*		
	be grasped		
Ipf.	ghlacte(adh)—*it used*	gu'n glacte(adh)—	gu'n glacte(adh)—
	to be grasped	*that it used to be*	*that it might be*
		grasped	*grasped*
Perf. &	ghlacadh—*it was* or	gu'n do ghlacadh	na'n do ghlacadh—
Plup.	*has been grasped*	*that it was grasped*	*had it been grasped*
Verbal	glacadh m.—		
Noun	*grasping*		
Perf.	glacte		
Part.			

2.   M.G. òlaim—*I drink*, 3 s. **òlaidh**

	Indicative.		*Subjunctive.*
	ABSOLUTE.	CONJUNCT.	
		Active.	
Pres. &	òlaidh	gu'n òl	gu'n òl
Fut.	rel. dh' òlas		
Ipv.	òl		
Ipf.	dh' òlainn	gu'n òlainn	gu'n òlainn
Perf. &	dh' òl	gu'n do dh' òl	na'n do dh' òl
Plup.		d' òl	
		Passive.	
Pres. &	òlar	gu'n òlar	gu'n òlar
Fut.			
Ipv.	òlar, òlthar		
Ipf.	òlte(adh)	gu'n òlte(adh)	gu'n òlte(adh)
Perf. &	dh' òltadh	gu'n do dh' òltadh	na'n do dh' òltadh
Plup.	dh' òladh		
Verbal	òl m.		
Noun			
Perf.	òlte		
Part.			

II.

§ 157.   **The Irregular Verbs.**

1. M.G. at-chím—*I see*, 3 s. at-chí, **chí** ; perf. 3 s. at-chon dairc, at-**chonnaic** ; conjunct con-**aca**

	Indicative.		*Subjunctive.*
	ABSOLUTE.	CONJUNCT.	
		Active.	
Pres. &	chì	gu'm faic	gu'm faic
Fut.			
Ipv.	faic		
Ipf.	chìthinn	gu'm faicinn	gu'm faicinn
Perf. &	chunnaic	gu'm faca	na'm faca
Plup.			
		Passive.	
Pres. &	chìthear	gu'm faictear	gu'm faicear, faictear
Fut.			
Ipv.	faicear		
Ipf.	chìtheadh	gu'm faicteadh	gu'm faicteadh
Perf. &	chunncadh	gu'm facadh	na'm facadh
Plup.	rel. chunncas	rel. nach facas (Skye)	
Verbal Noun	faicinn f.		
Perf. Part.	faicte		

2. Fo-gabim—*I get*, 3 s. fo-gheibh, **gheibh** ; perf. 3 s. **fuair**

	Indicative.		*Subjunctive.*
	ABSOLUTE.	CONJUNCT.	
		Active.	
Pres. &	gheibh	gu'm faigh	gu'm faigh
Fut.	gheabh		
Ipv.	faigh		
Ipf.	gheibhinn	gu'm faighinn	gu'm faighinn
Perf. &	fhuair	gu'n d'fhuair	na'n d'fhuair
Plup.			
		Passive.	
Pres. &	gheibhear	gu'm faightear	gu'm faightear
Fut.			
Ipv.	faigheadh		
Ipf.	gheibheadh	gu'm faighte(adh)	gu'm faighte(adh)
Pf. &	fhuaradh	gu'n d'fuaradh	na'n d'fhuaradh
Plup.	rel. fhuaras		
Verbal Noun	faighinn, faghail (faotainn) f.		
Perf. Part.	faighte		

3. At-chluinim—*I hear*, **3** s. at-chluinid, **cluinidh**

	Indicative.		*Subjunctive.*
	ABSOLUTE.	CONJUNCT.	
		Active.	
Pres. &	cluinnidh	gu'n cluinn	gu'n cluinn
Fut.	rel. chluinneas		
Ipv.	cluinn		
Ipf.	chluinninn	gu'n cluinninn	gu'n cluinninn
Perf. &	chuala	gu'n cuala	na'n cuala
Plup.			
		Passive.	
Pres. &	cluinnear, cluinntear	gu'n cluinnear,	gu'n cluinnear,
Fut.		cluinntear	cluinntear
Ipv.	cluinntear		
Ipf.	chluinnte(adh)	gu'n cluinnte(adh)	gu'n cluinnte(adh)
Perf. &	chualadh	gu'n cualadh	na'n cualadh
Plup.	(rel.) chualas		
Verbal	cluinntinn f.		
Noun			

4. Dogníu—*I do*, **3** s. act. do-gní, do-ní, **ni**

	Indicative.		*Subjunctive.*
	ABSOLUTE.	CONJUNCT.	
		Active.	
Pres. &	ni	gu'n dean	gu'n dean
Fut.			
Ipv.	dean		
Ipf.	dheanainn	gu'n deanainn	gu'n deanainn
Perf. &	rinn	gu'n d'rinn	na'n d'rinn
Plup.			
		Passive.	
Pres. &	nithear	gu'n deanar	gu'n deanar
Fut.			deantar
Ipv.	deantar		
Ipf.	dheanadh, dheantadh	gu'n deanadh,	gu'n deanadh,
		deantadh	deantadh
Perf. &	rinneadh	gu'n d'rinneadh	na'n d'rinneadh
Plup.	dearnadh		
Verbal	deanamh m.		
Noun.			
Perf.	deante, deanta		
Part.			

5. T-iccim—*I come*, 3 s. **tic**

	Indicative.		*Subjunctive.*
	ABSOLUTE.	CONJUNCT.	

Active.

Pres. & Fut.	thig	gu'n tig	gu'n tig
Ipv.	thig		
Ipf.	thiginn	gu'n tiginn	gu'n tiginn
Perf. & Plup.	thàinig	gu'n tàinig	na'n tàinig

Passive.

Pres. & Fut.	thigear, thigtear	gu'n tigear, tigtear	gu'n tigear, tigtear
Ipv.	thigtear		
Perf.	thàinigear rel. thàineas (Skye)		
Verbal Noun	tighinn m.		

6. R-iccim—*I reach*, 3 s. **ric**

	Indicative.		*Subjunctive.*
	ABSOLUTE.	CONJUNCT.	

Active.

Pres. & Fut.	ruigidh rel. ruigeas	gu'n ruig	gu'n ruig
Ipv.	ruig		
Ipf.	ruiginn	gu'n ruiginn	gu'n ruiginn
Perf. & Plup.	ràinig	gu'n do ràinig an do rùig ?	na'n do ràinig

Passive.

Pres. & Fut.	ruigear		
Ipv.	ruigear, ruigtear		
Ipf.	ruigte(adh)	gu'n ruigte(adh)	
Perf.	ràinigear rel. ràineas	gu'n d' ràinigear (Skye)	
Verbal Nouns	ruigsinn, ruigheachd f.		

7. Tiagu—*I go*, 3 s. **téid** : fut. rega—*I shall go* : perf. do
chuaidh—*he went*

Verbal noun techd **f.** ; dul, **dol** m.

	Indicative.		*Subjunctive.*
	ABSOLUTE.	CONJUNCT.	
		Active.	
Pres. &	théid	gu'n téid	gu'n téid
Fut.	rel. rachas, théid		
Ipv.	rach, na téid		
Ipf.	rachainn	gu'n rachainn	gu'n rachainn
		nach téideadh,	
Perf. &	chaidh	gu'n deachaidh, deach, na'n deach	
Plup.	rel. chaitheas	rel. an deachas	
		Passive.	
Ipv.	rachtar	na téidear	
Ipf.	nach d' rachadh	rachta	
		rachte	
Verbal	dol. m.		
Noun	teachd m.		

8. Berim––*I bear, take*, 3 s. **beridh** ; perf. **r-uc**

	Indicative.		*Subjunctive.*
	ABSOLUTE.	CONJUNCT.	
		Active.	
Pres. &	beiridh	gu'm beir	gu'm beir
Fut.	rel. bheireas		
Ipv.	beir		
Ipf.	bheirinn	gu'm beirinn	gu'm beirinn
Perf. &	rug	gu'n do rug	(na'n d'rugainn) do
Plup.			rug
		Passive.	
Pres. &	beirear, beirtear		
Fut.			
Ipv.	beirear, beirtear		
Ipf.	bheirte(adh)	gu'm beirte(adh)	gu'm beirte(adh)
Perf. &	rugadh	gu'n do rugadh	gu'n do rugadh
Plup.			
Verbal	breith, beirsinn f.		
Noun			
Perf. Pt.	beirte		
Pass.			

9. Do-berim—*I give*, 3 s. do-**beir** ; Perf, **t-uc**

	Indicative.		Subjunctive.
	Absolute.	Conjunct.	
		Active.	
Pres. & Fut.	bheir	gu'n tobhair, tabhair, toir	gu'n tobhair, tabhair toir
Ipv.	thugam, thoir (tobhair, tabhair)		
Ipf.	bheirinn	gu'n toirinn	gu'n toirinn
Perf. & Plup.	thug	gu'n tug	na'n tugainn, tug
		Passive.	
Pres. & Fut.	bheirear	gu'n toirear, tabhairear	gu'n tugar, tugthar ; thugthar
Ipv.	thoirear, bheirear		
Ipf.	bheirte(adh),bheireadh	gu'n tugtadh	
Perf. & Plup.	thugadh	gu'n tugadh	gu'n tugadh
Verbal Noun	tobhairt, tabhairt, toirt f.		

10. At-berim—*I say*, 3 s. atbeir, **adeir, deir**

	Indicative.		Subjunctive.
	Absolute.	Conjunct.	
		Active.	
Pres. & Fut.	their	gu'n abair	gu'n abair
Ipv.	abair		
Ipf.	theirinn	gu'n abrainn	gu'n abrainn
Perf. & Plup.	thubhairt	gu'n dubhairt	na'n dubhairt
		Passive.	
Pres. & Fut.	theirear	gu'n abrar	gu'n abrar
Ipv.	abairear, abrar		
Ipf.	theirte(adh)	gu'n abairte(adh)	gu'n abairte(adh)
Perf. & Plup.	thubhairteadh	gu'n dùbhradh	gu'n dubhairteadh
Verbal Nouns	ràdh, ràdhainn, ràitinnn, ràite m.		

§ 158. *The Auxiliary Verbs.*

1. The Substantive verb. : táim—*I am, I exist* 3 s. **-tá** :
fuilim, 3 s. gu **bhfhuil** . 3 s. consuetudinal pres. **bi**

	Indicative.		*Subjunctive.*
	Absolute.	Conjunct.	
		Active.	
Pres.	thà, tà	gu'm bheil,	gu'm bheil,
		(a) gu bheil (b) nach ⎫	gu bheil
		mur ⎬ 'eil	
		cha n ⎭	
Fut.	bithidh, rel.	gu'm bi	gu'm bi
	bhitheas, bhios		
Ipv.	(bitheam), bi,	bitheadh e,	(bithibh), bitheadh
		pl. bitheamaid	iad
Ipf.	bhithinn	gu'm bithinn	gu'm bithinn
Perf.	bha	gu'n robh	na'n robh
Verbal Noun	bith, bi m.		
		Passive.	
Pres.	thatar	gu'm beilear	gu'm beilear
	rel. thathas	rel. am beileas,	
		nach 'eileas	
Fut.	bitear, bithear		
Ipv.	bithear, bitear		
Ipf.	bhiteadh	gu'm biteadh	gu'm biteadh
Perf.	bhatar, bhathar,	gu'n robhar,	gu'n robhar,
	rel. bhathas	rel. nach robhas	rel. nach robhas

thar leam, dar leam, ar leam—*it appears to me, methinks* :

> O.G. ata, da, inda lim
> M.G. atar, dar, indar lim

II.

2. The copula verb. : O.G. **am**—*I am,* O.G. and G. 3 s. **is**—
it is, 'tis

	Indicative.		*Subjunctive.*
	Absolute.	Conjunct.	
Pres.	is, rel. as, is	gur	gur, masa, mur, and ged
			(followed by rel.)
Ipf.	bu	gu'm bu	bu, gu'm bu, guma (O.G.
			co mbad, co mad)

3. **Is** accompanied by a noun or adjective and a prepositional pronoun (or phrase with **air**, **do**, **le**) forms a composite verb, the subject of which immediately follows the prepositional pronoun or phrase :

Is mór ort sin a dheanamh—

> (*It is much upon you to do that* i.e.) *You would not condescend to do that*
> Is toigh leam Anna—*I love Anna*
> Bu bheag orm Màiri—*I disliked Mary* :—Munro 133
> B' fhearr do Mhac Dhomhnuill còmhdach a bhi aige dha fhéin—*Better were it for MacDonald to have as much as would cover himself* :—N.G.P. 55

Additional examples :

1. Nouns.	2. Adjectives
Is aithne dhomh—*I know*	Is còir dhomh—*I ought*
Is éiginn domh—*I am under the necessity*	Is dual dhomh—*It is natural to me*
Is eudar dhomh—*I must*	Is ion domh—*It becomes me*
Is urrainn domh—*I can*	Is nàrach dhomh—*I am ashamed*
Is eagal leam—*I fear*	
Is nàir leam—*I think it a shame*	Is àrd leam—*I think it high*
Is tràth leam—*I think it early*	Is docha leam—*I prefer*
	Is fiach leam—*I value, condescend*

Is gann orm—*I can hardly*
Is lugh' orm—*I hate more*

urrainn, a noun, is used as a verb :

> Seadh tuilleadh fòs, mas urrainn tuilleadh a bhi ann—*Yea still more, if more can be* :—Fois 9

mas urrainn thu—*if you can* :—ib.

and the barbarous passive form :

> Nach b' urrainnear agus nach fhaodar a labhairt—*that cannot and may not be spoken* :—ib. 6

> Cha b' urrainnear a bàthadh—*She could not be drowned* : Arab. I. 28

III.

§ 159.   **Regular Verbs as Auxiliaries.**

Certain regular (and irregular) verbs governing an Infinitive are used as auxiliaries to express in any tense or mood the meaning of the infinitive :

1. **dean** *make, cause* :

Caismeachd bhinn, 's i bras, dian,
Ni tais' a's fiamh fhògradh—
A melodious, quick, and vigorous march
Banishes softness and fear :—S.O. 148ᵇ6

G'e b'e céile a ni do bhuannachd—*Whatever partner will win thee* :—Clarsach 25

Rinn ar n-anail a mhùchadh 's ar dàna—*It choked our breath and our songs* : S.O. 153ᵇy

O gu'n **deanadh** an Spiorad Naomh gach amharus agus teagamh fhuadach :—*Oh that the Holy Spirit would banish all suspicion and doubt* :—L.C. 10

2. **cuir** *put* :

Cha mhòr nach **do chuir** an sealladh **a ghul** mi—*The sight almost made me weep* :—Cos. 8

3. **gabh** *can* :

Is gann a **ghabhas** creidsinn—*It is scarcely credible* :—C.S.

Na nithean sin a **ghabhas** crathadh—*Those things which can be shaken* :—Heb. xii. 27

Rinn mi gach ni **ghabhadh** deanamh—*I did everything that could be done* :—Arab. I. 116

Fhuair a cursadh'n sgàth gàraidh—*She got her reprimand in the shade of a garden* :—S.O. 46ª2.

4. **téid** *go* : is used passively. The grammatical nom. to this auxiliary is the Inf. ; the logical nom. is the person of the poss. pronoun accompanying the Inf. :

Théid do chur gu bàs—*You will be put to death* :—Arab. I. 53

Mur **téid** do thoirt air bòrd ann am bocsa cleas nan damh — *Unless you are brought on board in a box like the oxen* :—Cos. 127

Na'n tigeadh iad chum na cuirme, cha **rachadh** an cur air falbh—*Had they come to the feast, they would not have been sent away* :—ib. 150

Chaidh a ghlacadh droch spioraid—
He became possessed of an evil spirit :—S.O. 36ᵇ31

If the nom. to the auxiliary is not the Inf., the Inf. with *do* follows :

Gun deach an duine **bh**reith gu bròn—
That man was made to mourn :—Clar. 55.

IV.

§ 160. **Defective Verbs.**

1. faod *may*

Active.

		Indicative.		Subjunctive.
	Absolute.	Conjunct.		
Pass. &	faodaidh	gu'm faod		gu'm faod
Fut.	rel. (ma) dh' fhaodas			
Ipf.	dh' fhaodainn	gu'm faodainn		gu'm faodainn
Pf.	dh' fhaod	gu'n d' fhaod		gu'n d' fhaod

Passive.

Pres. &	faodar	gu'm faodar		gu'm faodar
Fut.	rel. (ma) dh' fhaodar			
Ipf.	dh' fhaoidte	gu'm faoidte		gu'm faoidte
Pf.	dh' fhaodadh	gu'n d' fhaodadh		gu'n d' fhaodadh

2. feum, *must, need*

Active.

Pres. &	feumaidh	gu'm feum		gu'm feum
Fut.	rel. (ma) dh' fheumas			
Ipf.	dh' fheumainn	gu'm feumainn		gu'm feumainn
Pf.	dh' fheum	gu'n d' fheum		gu'n d' fheum

Passive.

Pres. &	feumar	gu'm feumar		gu'm feumar
Fut.	rel. (ma) dh' fheumas			
Ipf.	dh' fheumtadh	gu'n d' fheumtadh		gu'n d' fheumtadh
Pf.	dh' fheumadh	gu'n d' fheumadh		gu'n d' fheumadh

3. fimir *must*

Active.

Pres. &	fimridh	gu'm fimir		gu'm fimir
Fut.				
Ipf.	dh' fhimirinn	gu'm fimirinn		gu'm fimirinn
Pf.	dh' fhimir	gu'n d' fhimir		gu'n d' fhimir
Pres. &	fimirear	gu'm fimirear		gu'm fimirear
Rel.	(ma) dh' fhimreas			
Ipf.	dh' fhimirte	gu'n d' fhimirte		gu'n d' fhimirte
Pf.	dh' fhimireadh	gu'n d' fhimireadh		gu'n d' fhimireadh

4. Theab—*came within a little of*

Perf. 3. s. Theab, Pass. theabadh, rel. theabas

 Theab nach rachadh againn air fhosgladh—*We almost failed in opening it* :—Arab. I. 115

 Theab i 'n deò a chall leis an eagal—*She almost expired with fear* :—Am F.C. 316

5.

Ipv. **2.** s. feuch *behold* ! 2 pl. feuchaibh

 siuthad *proceed*, siuthadaibh

 thallad, thalla *come along*, thallaibh *away over there*

 tiugainn *come along*, tiugainnibh

 tromhad *come hither*, tromhadaibh. § 120

6.

Pres. **3.** s. arsa, ol *says*, *quoth he* from O.G. ar se, ol se *says he*

7.

caithear **3.** s. pres. pass. of caithim—*I must* (an adj. according to McB.)

Am fear nach cathair da bhuaireadh—*He whom one must not tempt* :—Turner 77

§ 161.   **THE TENSES OF THE VERB.**

The Present Tense.

Indicative.

1. The synthetic 1st sing. Present in **-am** is obsolete save as a rare surviving literary form, probably dependent on the writer's familiarity with Bible language :

 Comhairlicheam dhuit òr a cheannach—

 I counsel thee to buy gold :—Rev. iii. 18

 A chompanaich, innis dhomh, **guidheam** ort—

 My companion, tell me, I beseech thee :—Arab. I. 5 ; F.C. 139

 Cluinneam sin ach **fuaghaim** so—

 Chì mi (also **chitheam**) sin agus **fuaghaim** so—

 I hear (or *see*) *that but I sew this* :—Folk Tales 322

2. The 2 and 3 sing., and the Relative, though generally used as Future, may be used also as Present.

The Present Absolute is rare, but the following are examples :

Saoilidh mi gu bheil cuid de'n mhodh-labhairt so—
I think there are some of this way of speaking :—

Saoilidh mi gur e bha 'm beachd a' bhàird—
I think it was the bard's opinion :—Am Fear-Ciùil 220, cf. 270, 275, 290, 291

Saoilidh mi fhéin nach urrainn e bhi . . .
I myself think that it cannot be :—Cos. 24

Chì mi sin, 's fuaighaidh mi so—
I see that, but I sew this :—Am Fear-Ciùil, 328

Chì mi Iain air uilinn—
I see John embarrassed :—MacCor. 47

Cha n' eil anns a' chulaidh-bhròin a **chì** sibh orm ach comhar-radh—*In this sorrow in which you see me is but a symptom* :—Arab. I. 70

3. Hovering between Present and Future, and resembling the old Consuetudinal Present, are proverbial sayings like :

Thig an donas ri iomradh—
Evil comes by talking of it :—N.G.P. 365

Their gach fear, Ochóin mi fhéin—
Every one says, ' alas for me ' :—ib.

Théid seòltachd thar spionnadh—
Cunning beats strength :—ib.

4. The Pres. Pass. is also established :

Thug mi sùil le leathad 's **faicear** mo bhrigis comdaichte le seangain—*I gave a glance down, and my trews are seen covered with ants* :—Am Fear-Ciùil 152

5. The Consuetudinal Pass. :

Beus an tuath far am **bitear**, is e a **nitear**—*The manners of the folk one lives among will be followed* :—N.G.P. 53

§ 162.

1. The Conjunct Present is frequent :

Nach **cluinn** thu bith-fhuaim suathain seamh ?
Do you not hear an unceasing gentle sound ?—S.O. 280ᵃs.

Bha mi smaointean nach do ghabh i amhrus **gur** mi a mharbh a leannan—*I kept thinking she did not doubt but 'twas I that had killed her lover* :—Arab. I. 70

Feumaidh mi innseadh dhut **gur** mac righ mi—
I must tell you that I am a king's son :—ib. 109

Bha mi an dùil **gur** e bruadar a chunnaic mi—*I was under the
impression that it was a dream I had seen* :—ib. 111

2. The Conjunct is frequently used as Absolute :
Gu'n dh' fhalbh mo bhean-chomuinn—
My wife is gone :—F.T. 112

3. The Conjunct Relative, and the Synthetic Relative is **-as,**
are also frequently used in a Present sense :

O's ionmhuinn leam na **chì** mi thall—
O ! dear to me is all I see over there :—Ross 1

Guth an tì a **ghlaodhas** anns an fhàsach—
The voice of one crying in the wilderness :—Math. iii. 3

3. Verging on the Consuetudinal use are the following :
Is iomad rud a **chì** am fear a **bhios** am muigh anmoch—
Many a thing the man sees who is out late :—MacCormaig 45

The Periphrastic Present :
Tha sìol nan sonn 'gan cur air chùl—
The scions of heroes are being set back :—Clarsach 18

For Continuous Present see §178, 2, and for the Perf. with tha
§170, 4, (2), §188, 3

§ 163.   **Subjunctive.**

1. Ung do shùilean le sàbh-shùl chum **gur** léir dhuit—
Anoint thine eyes with eye-salve that thou mayest see :—
Rev. iii. 18

Gu'n tugadh an Tighearn dhuibh gu'm **faigh** sibh fois—
The Lord grant you that ye may find peace :—Ruth i. 9

Tog do shùil 'S gu **faic** thu nis am mùthadh mòr—*Lift thine
eye that thou mayest now see the great change*:—Là Bhr. 197

Ma bheir sibh dàil thri latha dhomh, gheibh mi an t-iasg
dhuibh—*If you give me three days' grace, I shall get the
fish for you* :—Arab. I. 59

2. A wish may be expressed by the Pres. Subj. with **gu'n** :
Gu'n **gabh** a' bhochdainn thu !—
Poverty take thee ! :—N.G.P. 207

3. In wishes the verb (Pres. Subj.) is often omitted :

Dia na stiùir air an darach—
The God of the helm be aboard :—S.O. 47ª29
Saoghal sona sàmhach dhuit,
Do chridhe seirmeach slàn—
A happy peaceful life to you,
Your heart tuneful and whole :—MacCor. 52
Slàinte mhòr agadsa—*Great health to you* :—ib.

4. The place of the Pres. Subj. is taken sometimes by the Inf. preceded by **do**, which may be reduced to **a** or omitted :

Dia **a chuideachadh** leam !—*God help me* :—L.C. 64
Am Freasdal **a thoirt** maitheanais dhomh !—
Providence forgive me !—Am Fear-Ciùil 223
Am Freasdal **bhi** stiùradh nan gaothan le ciùine—
Providence guide the winds with tranquility !—Clarsach 38
Mac Muire **dhìon** t-anma—
May the Son of Mary guard thy soul :—Turner 84

5. The Pres. Subj. Passive :

Na tugaibh breth chum nach **toirear** breth oirbh—
Judge not that ye be not judged :—Matt. vii. 1

§ 164.   **Future.**

1. Absolute :

Gabhaidh sinn an rathad mòr—
We shall take the high road :—N.G.P. 189
Tachraidh d' fhiadh féin riut—
Your own deer will come in your way :—ib. 352
Ach co dhiùbh **gabhaidh** sinn beachd—*But, at all events, we*
shall take note :—MacCor. 73
" 'S mi **ni** sin," ars' athair, " **chì** mise dh' an sin nach fhalbh
thu tuilleadh—" *I'll do that," said his father, " I'll see*
to it that you will not go away again " :—Cos. 135

2. Conjunct :

Ach c'àit am **faigh** iad e ?—
But where will they find it ? :—Teachd. I. 5
Air fheobhas gu'n **coisich** e—
However well he walk :—Waifs III. 45

O nach gabh sin a bhi, mo làmh dheas duit nach **téid** currac
orm gus an **till** thu—
*Since that cannot be, I assure you that mutch will not be worn
by me till you shall return* :—MacCor. 20

3. The old 3 s. Pres. Rel. form in **-eas**, **-as** in Fut. Rel. clauses
is very frequent and distinctive :

Och ! mo thruaighe ! Ciod a dh éireas dhomh ?—
Oh ! woes me ! What will happen to me ?—Arab. I. 58
Tha againn na **dh' fhòghnas** an nochd, agus na **chuireas**
seachad an t-sàbaid—*We have what will suffice to-night,
and tide over the Sunday* :—L.C. 182
Le còmhradh, òrain, agus duain A **chuireas** fuadach air gach
gruaim—*With talk, songs and poems that will put to
flight all gloom* :—Clar. 50
Gu ma h-ann mar sin a **dhealraicheas** bhur solus—
Let your light so shine :—Matt. v. 16

4. The old **Pres.** Rel. form is also used occasionally for the
Fut. Perf. :

Cho luath 's a **chluinneas** e gu'n d'ràinig tu Bagdad, bheir e
dhuit gach ni a bhios a dhìth ort—*As soon as he
hears* (shall have heard) *that you have reached Baghdad,
he will give you everything you want* :—Arab. II. 80
Mu'n **ruig** mise, théid mo mhathair a stigh—
Before I arrive (shall have arrived) *my mother will go
in* :—Waifs III. 114

cf. the Periphrastic Fut. Perf. :

Ma **théid** agad air mise a leigheas, ni mi thu féin agus do
shliochd saoibhir—
If you succeed (shall have succeeded) *in healing me, I shall
make yourself and your posterity rich* :—Arab. I. 40

A Jussive Future is often used as an Ipv. :

Bheir thu leat am bocsa so ionnsaidh na faidhreach—
You will take this box with you to the fair :—F. Tales 22
Gabhaidh tu aoidheachd o bheathach no bho dhuine—
Thou shalt accept hospitality from animal or man :—Waifs
III. 138
Glèidhidh tu so gu cùramach—
Thou shalt keep this carefully :—ib. 129

5. From the old Fut. 2 s. **reg-a**, 3 s. **regaid**, Gk. $\check{\epsilon}$-$\rho\chi$-$o\mu\alpha\iota$, used as a Jussive, is developed the Ipv. **rach** :

Rach agus feòraich dheth—
Go thou and ask him :—Waifs III. 136
Rachaibh-se air 'ur n-aghaidh gu furachail—
Go ye forward cautiously :—C.G. 779

faigh *get*, has two Conjunct forms in use as future :

(1) **gheibh**, 3 s. Pres. Indic. as in Irish, pronounced iev in Morvern and parts of Skye and Inverness.

(2) **gheabh**, **gheobh**, 3 s. Fut. Indic, as in Irish, pronounced ioh in most other parts of the Highlands :

Gheobh mi fhathast òigear grinn—
I shall yet get a handsome young man :—An t-Oran. 167

§ 165. The Future Passive.

1. An tìr do'n **tigear** is i **ghabhar**—
The land that is come to will be taken :—N.G.P. 37

2. Prephrastic Fut. Pass. :
Théid do chur gu bàs—*You will be put to death* :—Arab. I. 53
An t-iasg a chriomas gach boiteag, **théid** a **ghlacadh** uair-
eigin—*The fish that bites every bait will be caught some
time* :—N.G.P. 37

§ 166. The Imperative.

The 1st sing. Ipv. is rare in literature, and has almost ceased
to be spoken ; but the other forms are in use—the 1st pl. occasionally, and the 2nd pl. less frequently :

1 sing :
Cluinneam do sgeul—*Let me hear your story* :—MacCor. 63
Cluinneam i, mata—*Well, let me hear it* :—Waifs III. 119
Na cluinneam a leithid so do chainnt—
Do not let me hear this sort of talk :—L.C. 66
Ach na faiceam-sa leithid sud a rithist—*But do not let me
see the like of that again* :—Am Fear-Ciùil.
Cuiream tuath e, cuiream deas e,
Cuiream siar e, cuiream sear e—
Let me send him, N.S.W.E. :—S.O. 134a33

1 pl. :

Fanamaid r'a dheireadh—
Let us wait for the end of it :—MacCor. 74
'N uair a bhios sinn ri maorach, biomaid ri maorach—
When we are at shell-fish, let us be so :—Am Fear-Ciùil 194

2 pl. :

Cuiribh thugam e gun dàil—
Send it me without delay :—Am Fear-Ciùil 327
Gabhaibh mo leisgeul—*Excuse me* :—ib. 321
Stadaibh ! *Stop you !*—O.M. 58
O càraibh mi ri taobh nan allt—
O ! place me near the brooks :—S.O. 14ª2

The 2 sing. is of most frequent occurrence :

Thoir dhomh mathanas—*Pardon me* :—Arab. I. 36
Na abair ach beag 's abair gu math e—
Say but little, and say it well :—N.G.P. 322

The 3 sing. :

Deanadh do bhean féin brochan dut—
Let your own wife make gruel for you :—N.G.P. 163

§ 167.   **The Imperfect Indicative.**

1. The Ipf. expresses continued or habitual incompleted action.
Liable to be confused with the Preterite, the true Ipf. is recognised
when the Periphrastic Ipf. to which it corresponds can be substituted for it :

Chunnaic e gach beathach a **bhuineadh** (= a bha buntainn)
    dha ag ionaltradh far am fac' e mu dheireadh iad—
*He saw every beast that belonged to him pasturing where he
    had last seen them* :—Folk Tales 4
Sgeul a b'aite 'n uair a **thigeadh**—
The pleasantest tale when it was coming :—S.O. 41ª w.
H-uile dream dhiubh mar a **thigeadh**—
Every company of them as it came :—ib. 41ªy.
Na'm **falbhadh** am faoileach
Bheirinn sgrìob thar a' mhonaidh—
*When the winter was going,
I used to take a turn over the moor* :—An t-Oran. 193.

Agus na leisgeulan a **gheibhinn !**—
And the excuses I used to get ! :—Cos. 148
Chuireadh foirm fo na macaibh
'N uair a **thachradh** iad ris—
Who put liveliness in the boys
When they foregathered with him :—S.O. 146ª7

Similarly in the passive :

Gheibhte rainn agus òrain—
Verses and songs were being sung :—ib. 10
Chluinnte cuach ann do choille—
The cuckoo would be heard in thy wood :—Stewarts 91
Na daimh gu sònraichte, cha n-obadh iad a' chùis a leigeil
gu ràdh nan cabar, 'n uair **chuirteadh** a bheag 'nan
aghaidh—*The stags in particular would not refuse to put*
the matter to the arbitrament of the horns when they were
a little provoked :—Am Fear-Ciùil 293

2. Compare the Periphrastic Ipf. Pass. :

Fhad 's a **bha** an ùrnuigh **'ga cur** suas—
Whilst the prayer was being offered :—L.C. 69
Bha an crodh **'gan leigeadh**—
The cows were a-milking :—Stewart, Gr. 90

§ 168. **The Ipf. Subjunctive.**

This mood, which is occasionally confused with the Ipf. Indic.,
is used chiefly as a Past-Future to express :

1. A Conditional, with both Protasis and Apodosis in Ipf.
Subj. :

Na'n **innseadh** e gu'n robh an t-eòlas so aige, cha **bhiodh** an
tuilleadh saoghail aige—
But were he to say that he possessed this knowledge, his days
would not be prolonged :—Arab. I. 1
Tha aon leabhar agam a **bhithinn** deònach fhàgail agaibh
fhéin, na'n **gabhadh** sibh e—
I have one book that I should be willing to leave with yourself,
if you would take it :—ib. 52
Ged a dh' **innsinn** dhuit a h-uile car, cha **deanadh** e dh'fheum
dhutsa—*Though I should tell you every detail, it would*
be of no use to you :—ib. 26

cf. The use of **rach**, itself an old Future, and always used in a future sense :

Cha b'urrainn duine air bith dol a dh' ionnsaidh a' Chaisteil, mur **rachadh** e siòs leis a' chreig—

No one could go to the Castle unless he should go (have gone) *down the rock* :—Folk Tales 42

2. A Potential expressing possibility, or supposition, thus :

Bha toil agam deuchainn a chur ort feuch am **faighinn** am mach an robh mathas agus caoimhneas agad—

I wished to apply to you a test to see whether I could discover whether you were good and kind :—Arab. I. 29

Cha robh rathad agam air a bhi sàbhailte, mur **cuirinn** mi fhéin gu buileach as aithne—

I had no way of being saved, unless I could render myself quite unrecognisable :—Arab. I. 118

Leabhraichean a **gheibheadh** mòran do dhaoinibh fòghlumta r'an leughadh—*Books which would find many learned men to read them* :—L.C. 50, cf. §115, 1

An **cuireadh** tu geall ? **Chuireadh**—

Would you bet ? Yes :—Munro 109

Cò nach **tugadh** gaol dhi ?—

Who would not love her :—An t-Oran. 75

Far am **faiceadh** iad gach aon 'us nach **faiceadh** aon idir iad—

Where they could see everyone, and no one at all could see them :—Waifs III. 9

Ach ged bha, cha **toireadh** Màiri a gaol do shean fhear—

But though it was so, Mary would not fall in love with an old man :—MacCor. 67

cf. The Periphrastic Passive :

Rinn mi gach ni a **ghabhadh deanamh**—

I did everything that could be done :—Arab. I. 116

3. An Optative, expressing a wish :

(1) with **gu'm** :

Gu sealladh Ni Math ort—

Goodness watch over you :—Arab. I. 12

Gu ma h-ann leis a chìs-mhaor a gheibhear sibhse ag gul agus ni h-ann mar am Phairiseach uaibhreach—

May it be with the publican that ye will be found weeping, and not as the proud Pharisee :—L.C. 122

(2) with **ro** : A few examples survive :

Thigeadh **nara tigeadh** e—
Let him come or not :—Munro 162
Nar leigeadh Dia—*God forbid !*—Rom. iii. 4, 6, 31

Ro is used also with a Pres. Sub. Pass :

Nar fhaicear laogh càraid
Nuas gu làr as a pòca—*May no twin calves be seen dropping
from her bag* :—S.O. 46ᵇ1.

§ 169   Uses of the Infinitive.

The Inf. is often used with the force of a Present Subjunctive :
§ 163, 4

Dia bhi maille ribh—*God be with you* :—L.C. 65
Dia g'ur beannachadh—*God bless you* :—ib. 68

Occasionally the Ipv. is expressed Periphrastically by an
Inf. :

O Bhreithimh cheirt na talmhainn, dean Thu féin a thogail
suas—*O righteous Judge of the earth, Lift up thyself* :—
Ps. xciv. 2

2. The Inf. is often used with the force of an Ipf. Subjunctive :

The Nom. before the Inf. may express

(1) purpose :

Iad a chàradh 'na m' dhòrn-se
Na bha 'm phòca de chùineadh—
*That they should put into my hand
All the coin that had been in my pocket* :—Clar. 15
Thuirt e rium **mi dhol** dachaidh—
He said that I should go home :—ib.
Thuirt i rium **mi dheanamh** tàmh—
She told me that I should rest :—ib. 21
Ghuidh mi air gu dùrachdach le deuraibh **e leigeadh** mo
bheatha leam—*I besought him earnestly with tears that
he would grant me my life* :—Arab. I. 113
Dh' iarr thu air **e thighinn** an so an diugh— *You asked of
him that he should come here to-day* :—Cos. 134

Luchd dheiseachan màdair
Bhi cràidht' air droch dhìol !—
That the folk of the madder dyed garments
Should be anguished by a bad requital !—S.O. 148ᵇ24

Some examples are not strictly grammatical, the Inf. clause being unconnected with the sentence :

Thuirt mi ris **e dh' itheadh** a leòir ach gun e phòcachadh
mìr—*I told him to eat enough but not to pocket a piece* :—
Am Fear-Ciùil 244

Thuirt e ris an ard-chomhairleach **e dhùnadh** a bheòil—
He said to the Prime Minister that he should shut his
mouth :—Arab. I. 104

(2) condition,

(a) often introduced by **ach** *but, provided only, only* :

Nach ruig iad a leas feitheamh air son ullachaidh 'sam
bith **ach** iad **a thighinn** air ball—
That they need not wait for any preparation, but that they
should come at once :—Cos. 133

Bha fiughair ri réisimid Iain . . . **ach** a' ghaoth **a bhi**
fàbharach—*John's regiment was expected, provided*
only the wind were favourable :—MacCor. 60

Co b' urainn d'ar smàladh-**Ach** do làmhans' **bhi** leinn—
Who could extinguish us—Provided only thy hands were
with us ?—S.O. 45ᵃq.

(b) sometimes expressed by simple Inf. clause :

Shaoil leam **thusa bhi** cho fada 'sa' bhaile-mhor gu'm b'i
Bheurla bu deise leat—
I thought you had been so long in the city that English
would come more readily to you :—Am Fear-Ciùil 187

Dìreach mar gu'm biodh iongantas air **iad a bhi** air a chasan
—*Just as if he were astonished that they* (his shoes)
were (should be) *on his feet* :—ib. 234

§ 170. **The Past Tense.**

The same verbal form may in Gaelic express :

1. The Preterite, or narrative tense.
2. The Perfect, indicating a state attained by completed
action.

3. The Pluperfect, pointing to a time anterior to the time of the other principal verb in the sentence.

All three are exemplified in the following Perfects whether they be old compounds or formed with the moveable preverb **do** :

An uair a **chunnaic** (3) mi gu'n **robh** (2) iad cho fada air falbh 's nach tugadh iad an aire dhomh, **thàinig** (1) mi 'nuas as a chraoibh, agus **chaidh** (1) mi far am **faca** (3) mi iad ag cladhach na talmhainn—*When I had seen that they were gone away so long that they could not observe me, I came down out of the tree, and I went to the place where I had seen them digging the earth* :—Arab. II. 43

Dh' ith (1) e 'm biadh mu'n·**d' rinn** (3) e altachadh—
He ate the food before he had said grace :—N.G.P. 167

Dh' fhalbh (2) na **thàinig** (1) romhainn—
All that came before us have gone :—L.C. 246

Thàinig (2) ialtag a steach, bidh frasan a mach air ball—
A bat has come in, it is going to rain :—N.G.P. 364

Thàinig (2) gille gu Mac-a-leisg—
Mac-Lazy has got a servant :—ib. 363

Dh'amais (2) thu air do thapadh—
You have lighted on your luck :—ib. 165

4.   **The Periphrastic Past.**

(1) Preterite :

Lagh cho chearr 's a bha 'm Breatunn
Rinn am meirleach **a sheasamh**—*As bad law as was in Britain upheld the thief* :—S.O. 38ᵇ13

(2) Perfect :

Tha lionn-dubh **air** mo **bhualadh**—
Melancholy has struck me :—Turner, 45
A dhaoine uaisle, a **tha air ùr-thighinn** do'n bhaile—
Gentlemen, who have newly come to town :—Arab. II. 69
Saoilidh ar maighstir gu'm **bheil** thu **air a dhol** am feobhas—
Our master will think that you have improved :—ib. I. 6

5.   **The Periphrastic Past Passive.**

Chaidh innseadh dhomh—*I have been told* :—Waifs III. 12
Fad agus leud do dhroma de'n fhearann sin a **chaidh a ghealltainn** duit—

*The length and breadth of thy back of that land which has
   been promised thee* :—Am Fear-Ciùil 139.
Bha sud là agus **chaidh** am fear a b'òige **air chall**—
One day the youngest one was lost :—Cos. 130
Is iomadh deoch-slàint mhath a **chaidh** òl—
Many is the good-health that was drunk :—Mac-Cor. 51

6. A synthetic Past Passive in-**as** (rarely-**adh**) is formed from
the Perf. Act. of irregular verbs. This formation follows the
analogy of O.G. Perf. Passives, e.g. **rocloss**—*it has been heard* ;
adcess—*it has been seen.*

(a) It is chiefly used relatively :

Mar **fhuaras** Bran—*How Bran was found* :—Waifs III. 16
Is maith a **fhuaras** agad e—*Well done !*—Mac Cor. 48
Ceutaidh Nach **fhacas** leam féin fa m' chòir—
Gracefulness That had not been seen by me at close quarters :—
   S.O. 285[b]37.
'S e 'n ceòl bu bhinne **chualas**—
It is the sweetest music that has been heard :—D. Ban 406, 15
O dhealradh glòir nan aingeal sin a **chunnacas** air uairibh
   'san t-saoghal so—
*From the glorious brightness of those angels that have been
   seen sometimes in this world* :—L.C. 166
Air gach làrach lom
Am **facas** uair mo chàirdean treun—
On every desolate site where once were seen my sturdy kin :—
   ib. 71

But it is also used :

(b) absolutely :

Chualas an guth so bliadhna an déidh bliadhna o'n uair sin—
This voice has been heard year after year since then :—
   Arab. II. 79
Leughas litir naigheachd leinn—
A news letter was read by us :—S.O. 282[b]s
Chunnacas a' seòladh o'n lear
Curach ceò agus bean ann—
*One saw sailing from the expanse
A misty coracle with a lady on board* :—ib. 98[a]38

(c) autonymously :

Dhearcas fa leath air na h-òighean—
One looked at the maidens individually :—S.O. 285ᵇ14

(d) In a few cases -**adh** occurs suffixed to Perf. Act. :

Chunnacadh comharradh na h-anuair a' tighinn—*The sign of bad weather was seen approaching* :—Am Fear-Ciùil 265

§ 171. **The Pluperfect.** *✗ Mark, p²²(c) says airdo*

In the sequence of tenses,

1. a Plup. correlated with an Ipf. is expressed by an Ipf., and
2. a Plup. correlated with a Perf. is expressed by a Perf. :

1 B' fhearr nach **beirte** gu aois e—*It were better that he had not been brought to mature age* :—S.O. 148ᵃ19
Na'm bitheadh, chuireadh e car eile 'san ràdh sin—
If he had been, he would have given another turn to that expression :—Am F.C. 334

2 Dh' fheòraich an rìgh de cheannardan am **faca** iad idir an lochan gus a sid—*The king asked of his captains whether they had hitherto seen the lochan* :—Arab. I. 61

§ 172. **The Periphrastic Pluperfect.**

1. with **air** (= iar n-) :

'S maith dh' an struidhear bhochd gu'm b'e athair agus nach b'e a bhràthair a thachair ris an toiseach air neo cha **robh air dol** leis mar a chaidh—
Well for the poor prodigal that his father met him first and not his brother, otherwise it would not have gone with him as it did :—Cos. 138

Is maith a bha fios aige na'n **robh** E **air** sin a **dheanamh**, nach **bitheadh** fios agadsa co dhiùbh 's e do cheann no do chasan a bhitheadh fothad :—*He well knew that had He done that, you would not have known whether it was your head or your feet that were under you* :—ib. 170

Na'n **robh** a' cheud mhuinntir **air tighinn**, **bhatas air gabhail** riu—*Had the first people come, they would have been accepted* :—ib. 150

✗ **Bha** B. **air teicheadh** as a' phrìosun—
B. had escaped out of prison :—MacCor. 39

The Periphrastic Plup. may with this construction be used in expressing a wish :

O ! nach **robh** mi riamh **air** t' **fhàgail !**—
Oh ! that I had never left thee !—L.C. 20

2. with Possessive Pronoun and Verbal Noun :

Na'n tigeadh iad chum na cuirme, cha **rachadh an cur** air falbh—*If they had come to the feast, they would not have been sent away* :—Cos. 150

3. with Inf. Passive :

Cha robh duine nach robh air a chorra-biod a chluinntinn an **deach** blàr **a thoirt**—*There was not a man but was on tip-toe to hear whether a battle had been fought* :—Mac-C. 62

§ 173.   **Perf. and Plup. Subjunctive.**

The Conditional, expressing a Perfective sense, may affirm or deny—(1) a fact, or (2) a supposition :

(1) Protasis, Ipf. Subj. ; Apodosis, Perf. Indic.   §145, 5.
Mur **deanamaid** feum le'r casan,
Cha **tug** sinne srad le'r musgan—
Had we not made use of our feet,
We had never fired our guns :—D. Ban 2, 7
Na'm **biodh** agad armuinn Mhuile,
Thug thu air na dh' fhalbh dhiubh fuireach—
If you had had the heroes of Mull with you,
You had compelled those that fled to stay :—S.O. 42ª2
Mur **biomaid** treun, cha **robh** sinn beò—
Were we not brave, we had not been alive :—C.S.
Ged **chuirinn** mìle bliadhna seach . . .
Cha d' **imich** seach de'n t-siorruidheachd mhòir
Ach mar gu'n **tòisicheadh** i 'n dé—
Though I had put past a thousand years,
There had not gone by of the great eternity
Save as much as if it had begun yesterday :—Là Bhr. 409, 11, 12
Gus am **b'** fhearr leat na ni nach abair thu gu'n **do ghabh** e seachad air an taobh eile—
Till you would prefer to anything you can say that he had passed by on the other side :—Am Fear-Ciùil 226

Cha **b'** e leum a mach as a' bhàta agus beannachd a leigeil
leatha a **rinn** iad—*It would not be leaping out of the boat
and taking leave of it that they had done* :—Cos. 21

Ged do **cheilinn** sud air àm,

Bhruchd e mach 's cha mhiste leam—

Though I should have concealed that for a time,
It would have broken forth, and methinks I am none the
worse :—S.O. 283ᵃ8.

(2) Protasis, Perf. Indic. ; Apodosis, Ipf. Subj. :

Cha **robh** an Tighearna air an dà chosmhalachd a liubhairt
dhuinn, mur a **biodh** atharrachadh teagaisg air chor-
eigin 'na bheachd—*The Lord would not have delivered
the two parables to us, had there not been, in his opinion,
some difference of doctrine* :—Cos. 35

Na'n **tug** (*misspelt* d'thug) thusa dhomhsa am fàbhar a bha
mi 'g iarraidh ort, **bhiodh** truas agam riut—
*Had you shown me the favour I asked of you, I would have
had pity upon you* :—Arab. I. 54

Na'n **do leig** an rìgh Greugach leis an lighiche a bhi beò,
leigeadh Dia dha fhéin a bhi beò—
*Had the Greek king suffered the physician to live, God would
have allowed himself to live* :—ib.

Na'n **d' fhan** iad aig an taighean a' toirt an aire air an gnothach mar a rinn mise, gu'n **robh** iad mòran na b' fhearr
dheth na bha iad—*If they had remained at their houses,
attending to their business as I did, that they would have
been much better off than they were* :—ib. 27

Na'n **d' fhosgail** e shùilean mu'n do labhair e, **chitheadh** e
gu soilleir gu bheil an saoghal de dh' atharrach barail—
*Had he opened his eyes before he spoke he would have seen
clearly that the world is of a different opinion* :—Am
F.C. 221

§ 174. **The Infinitive.**

The Inf., being a Verbal Noun, has all the constructions of a
noun §3, 1, §74

The Inf. is formed regularly by adding **-adh** to a broad stem,
-eadh to a slender stem :

Ipv. aom *incline*   Inf. aomadh

     ith   *eat*   itheadh

The first syllable of the Inf. is always stressed.

In polysyllabic cpds., when the Inf. termination is added, the post tonic syllable is sometimes syncopated:

Ipv.	caomhain	*spare*	Inf.	caomhnadh m.
	coisin	*win*		coisneadh, cosnadh m.

§ 175.

Denominative verbs formed from O.G. Infinitives show the following variations:

(1) The Ipv. is like the Inf.

Ipv.	Inf.	O.G. Inf.
àireamh *number*	f.	áram
aithris *relate*	f.	aithris, aithrus
anacail *protect*	f.	anacul
		gen. anacuil
at *swell*	m.	att
bleith *grind*	f.	mlith, bleth
bruich *boil*	f.	bruith
buain *reap*	f.	buain
caoidh *lament*	f.	cái, M.G. cói
casaid *accuse*	f.	(L. accusatio)
dearmad *neglect*	m.	dermat
dìon *protect*	m.	dín
fàs *grow*	m.	ás
gairm *call*	f.	gairm
iomain *drive*	f.	immáin
ionndrainn *miss*	m.	
meas *estimate*	m.	mess
òl *drink*	m.	ól
reic *sell*	m.	reicc (dat.)
ruith *run*	f.	rith, riuth
seinn *sing*	f.	senim
snàmh *swim*	m.	snám
snìomh *twist, spin*	m.	sním
tarraing *pull*	f.	tarraing d.s.
triall *depart*	m.	triall
trod *scold*	m.	trod

(2) The Ipv. is palatalised, but the Inf. is formed regularly by adding -**adh** to the O.G. Inf.:

Ipv.	Inf. m.	O.G. Inf.
blais *taste*	blasadh	blas
ceannaich *buy*	ceannachadh	cennach
coisg *check*	cosgadh	cosg
naisg *bind*	nasgadh	nasc
smuainich *think*	smuaineachadh	smuain
paisg *wrap*	pasgadh	Ir. faisg, fasg *bundle*, W. ffasg, L. fasces

The following are formed by analogy to the above :

buail *strike*	bualadh	bualad
fàisg *wring*	fàsgadh	fàsgad
loisg *burn*	losgadh	loscud
luaisg *rock*	luasgadh	luascad

(3) The Ipv. is palatalised, but the Inf. remains broad as in O.G. :

Ipv.	Inf. m.	O.G. Inf.
amhairc *see*	amharc	amarc
amais *hit*	amas	amus
bleoghainn *milk*	bleoghann f.	blegon
caidil *sleep*	cadal	cotlud
caill *lose*	call	coll
coimhid *watch*	coimhead	comét
cuir *put*	cur	cor
dochainn *hurt*	dochann	(dochonach)
falaich *hide*	falach	folach
fuirich *stay*	fuireach	furech
fulaing *suffer*	fulang	fulang
gearain *complain*	gearan	(gerán)
guil *weep*	gul	gol
iasgaich *fish*	iasgach	(iascach *batch of fish*)
leighis *cure*	leigheas	leges
marcaich *ride*	marcachd	(marc *horse*)
sguir *cease*	sgur	scor, scar
siubhail *walk*	siubhal	siubal
tachrais *wind up*	tachras	tochrus
tadhail *visit*	tadhal	tadall
tionail *gather*	tional	tinól
tiondaidh *turn*	tionndadh	tintuúth

Ipv.	Inf. m.	O.G. Inf.
tionnsgail *contrive*	tionnsgal	tinscetal
toirmisg *forbid*	toirmeasg	tairmeac
similarly :		
ceangail *bind*	ceangal	L. cingulum

§ 176.   THE INF. SUFFIXES.

The Inf. in a few instances ends in a vowel :

Ipv.	Inf.
guidh *pray*	guidhe m.
luigh *lie down*	luighe f.
rogh *choose*	rogha m., roghainn m.
suidh *sit*	suidhe m.
tuig *understand*	tuigse f., tuigsinn f.

The following are the chief consonantal Inf. Suffixes :

-achd, -eachd (-kt-)   § 125.

caisd *listen*	caisdeachd f.
coisich *walk*	coiseachd f.
éisd *hearken*	éisdeachd f.
faighnich *enquire*	faighneachd f.
fan *stay*	fanachd f.
gluais *move*	gluasachd f.
imich *depart*	imeachd f.
lean *follow*	leanachd f.

-achd, -aich marcaich, *ride*   marcachd f.

-achd -ainn fairich *feel*   faireachdainn f., faireachadh m.

gàir *laugh*   gàireachdaich f., gàireachduinn f.

-ad   gluais *move*   gluasad m.

old Inf. cumsanad m. *rest*

-adh   The regular form of the Inf. Suffix is -adh, -eadh   § 140

-aich, -ich (-g-, -ch-)   § 128

beuc *roar*	beucaich f.
bùir *bellow*	bùirich f.
geum *low*	geumnaich f.
glaodh *cry*	glaodhaich m.
ràn *roar*	rànaich f., rànach

-aidh   iarr *ask*   iarraidh
-ail (-g-l-) anacail *protect*   anacail f. § 184
              adhlaic *bury*   adnacal m.

  with metathesis—
              tiodhlaic *present*   tiodhlac m.

-ail (-glā-) § 128.
              gabh *take*   gabhail f., gen. gabhalach,
                                         earlier gabāla, gabālach
cpds. §184 cum *hold*   cumail f.
              fàg *leave*   fàgail f.
              faigh *get*   faghail f., faighinn f.
              tog *raise*   togail f.
also   leag *lay low*   leagail f.
but   fuaigh *sew*   fuaigheal m. *seam*
              beuc *roar*   beucail f.
              ràn *roar*   rànail m.
              srann *snore*   srannail f.
-eil   leig *permit*   leigeil m., leigeadh m.
              lean *follow*   leanail, leanailt f.
              tilg *throw*   tilgeil f., tilgeadh m.

-idh   old Inf. cpds. of saig-   § 127
              asgaidh f. *gift*   ionnsuidh m. *attack*

    Ipv.   Ipf.   O.G.
igh   éirich *rise*   éirigh f.   éirge
-m-   tuit *fall*   tuiteam m.
              iomair *row*   iomram m.

  Inf. of obsolete verb: greim m. *hold*

-mh   àireamh *number*   àireamh m.
              caith *spend*   caitheamh m.
              càraich *mend*   càramh m., caradh m.
              dean *do*   deanamh m.
              feith *wait*   feitheamh m.
              iomair *row*   iomramh m.
              seas *stand*   seasamh m.
              tuit *fall*   tàmh m.

  Inf. of obsolete verbs:
  agallamh m. *conversation*
  gnìomh m. *deed*

-n old Inf. of

    (1) ag- § 132

        aoin f. *rush*

cpds.   iomain f. *drive*

        tàin f. *drove*

    (2) org- § 132, 2

        orcain f. *hacking*

	Ipv.	Inf.
cpds.	teasairg *save*	teasairginn f.
	easorgain f. *contrition*	
	tuargan m. *discontent*	

	Ipv.	Ipf.	O.G.
-sa, -se	earb *trust*	earbsa f.	erbud
	tairg *offer*	tairgse f.	taircsin

-t The following consonantal stems add -**t** for the Inf. :

    Ipv. beir *bear*   Inf. breith f. *bearing* § 138

cpds.   dìobairt m. *betrayal*

        eirbhirt f. *hint*

        iomairt f. *plying*

        tabhairt, toirt f. *giving*

        tairbeart f. *isthmus*

        tòbairt f. *flux*

        toirbheart f. *efficiency*

cpds. of

  cuir   tachairt f. *happening*

  gair   agairt f. *claim*

        bagairt f. *threat*

        tògairt f. *banishment*

        fògairt f. *banishment*

        freagairt f. *answer*

        tagairt f. *pleading*

        togairt f. *desire*

  scor   casgairt f. *slaughter*

  Inf. of simple stems § 141, § 184

        bi *be* bith f.

        labhair *speak* labhairt f.

        lomair *shear*, lomairt f.

        màgair *crawl* màgairt

        saltair *trample*, saltairt f.

-d   tiag *go* adds **-d** (O.G. **-t**) for Inf. :
             teach-d f. *going*

cpds.   imeachd f. *going about*
             tiuchd f. *coming*

for **-ts**   after **-d** e.g. meas m. *esteem* § 138

-tinn Some monosyllabic stems form the Inf. by adding **-tinn** (**-tuinn**, **-tainn**, after a guttural, **-duinn -uinn-ainn**) § 158, § 138, 3, to a final **-n** :

bean *touch*	beantuinn m.
buin *belong to*	buntuinn m.
can *say, sing*	cantuinn m.
ceil *conceal*	ceiltinn f.
cinn *grow*	cinntinn m.
cluinn *hear*	cluinntinn f.
fairich *perceive*	faireachduinn f.
fan *stay*	fantuinn f., fanailt f.
geall *promise*	gealltainn m., gealladh m.
gin *beget*	gintinn m., gineamhuinn m.
lean *follow*	leantuinn m., leanmhuinn m.
mair *exist*	maireachduinn f., maireann
meal *enjoy*	mealtuinn m., mealadh m.
pill *return*	pilltinn f., pilleadh m.
seall *look*	sealltainn m., sealladh m.
teirig *fail*	teireachduinn m.
tig *come*	tighinn m., O.G. tichtu

After gutturals :

faigh *got*	faighinn f.
feuch *see, try*	feuchainn f.

after **-s-** the Inf. Suffix **-tinn** becomes **-sinn** by assimilation :

faic *see*	faicsinn f. § 138

This form of the Inf. Suffix spread, by analogy, to the followin g

beir *bear*	beirsinn m.
creid *believe*	creidsinn m.
goir *crow*	goirsinn f.
mair *exist*	mairsinn m.
ruig *reach*	ruigsinn f.
saoil *think*	saoilsinn f.
tairgsinn *offer*	tairgsinn
tréig *forsake*	tréigsinn m.
tuig *understand*	tuigsinn f.

The termination -**tinn** survives also in the Inf. of verbs otherwise obsolete :

> eiridinn m. *nursing the sick*
> faotainn f. *getting* § 138, 3

§ 177.   **THE SUBSTANTIVE VERB.**

THA

Tha *is*, may be used alone to express existence :
> Mu'n robh Abraham ann, Tha mise—
> *Before Abraham was, I am* :—John viii. 58

1. but **tha** is generally used with **ann** :

(1) To express the idea of existence :
> Is mise a tha ann—*I it is* :—Math. xiv. 27

(2) With the prep. **an** + the possessive pronoun, before a noun, used predicatively to express as one of a class the state or occupation of the subject :

> Tha e 'na chlachair—*He is a mason*
> Is ann 'nad lethsgeul féin a bhitheas tu—
> *You will be your own excuse* :—McKay 39
> Tha na fàrdaichean 'nam fàsaich—
> *The dwellings are wildernesses* :—An t-Oran. 270.

This construction does not express complete identity, e.g.
> Tha e 'na athair dhomh—*He is (as) a father to me* : but cf.
> Is e as athair dhomh—*He is my father* :—C.S., McKay 40

(3) This construction is frequently used as an extension of the subject or predicate of other verbs where some part of **tha** is to be understood, probably **gu bhi** :

> Thug se e féin air ar son 'na thabhartas agus 'na ìobairt
> deagh-fhàile do Dhia—*He gave Himself for us an offering and
> a sacrifice to God for a sweet-smelling savour* :—Eph. v. 2·
> Dh' orduicheadh mise a ghlacadh 'nam phrìosonach—
> *I was ordered to be taken prisoner* :—McKay 39
> Chaidh a chur 'na rìgh orra—*He was put as king over them* :—ib.
> Cinnidh mi 'nam bhàta—*I shall become a boat* :—ib.
> Leum e 'na tharbh—*He changed rapidly into a bull* :—ib.

§ 178.

2. **Tha** is used with **ag** :—

   (1) To denote possession :

      Dad a tha agad— *Anything thou hast*

      Am pòsadh tu Ceit na'm biodh airgiod aice ?—
      Would you marry Kate, if she had had money ?

      Cha ghabhainn i, ged bhiodh beinn òir aice—*I would not have*
        her, though she had a mountain of gold :—Munro 108

    (2) To form (in any mood, Active or Passive) with the verbal
noun of a verb, a corresponding Continuous tense of that verb :

      Pres. Continuous : Tha mi ag iarraidh—*I am asking*

      Past   ,,   : Bha mi ag imeachd—*I was going*

      Pres. Con. Pass. : Thathas a' togail an tighe—
                      The house is being built
                      Thathas 'gar marbhadh—
                      We are being killed

3. **Tha** is used with **air** to form the Periphrastic Past. §170, 4, (2).

§ 179.

 Relatively :

   1. For direct statements the absolute form of **tha** is used :

      Is muladach a thà mi, no a bhitheas mi—
      Sad I am, or I will be

      Tha mi mar a bha mi riamh—
      I am as I always was :—McKay 38

   2. For (a) oblique statements and (b) interrogative and ne-
     gative, the conjunct is used :

     (a) An t-eilean far am bheil mi—*The island where I am* :—ib. 2
        An obair ris an robh mi—*The work at which I was* :—ib. 2
        Am fear do an robh i 'na mnaoi—
        The man whose wife she was :—ib. p. 40

     (b) Am bheil e ann ?—*Is he there ?*
        Nach 'eil ?—*Is he not ?*

        Cha n'eil fhios am bi e—*I do not know whether he will be* :
         —ib. 2

        Mur h'eil airgiod agad, cha n-fhaigh thu am bathar—
        If you have not money, you will not get the goods :—
        Munro 108

§ 180. **THE COPULA VERB.**

Is.

I. **Is** is used to bring forward part of the sentence, generally either the subject or the predicate, for emphasis.

Subject and predicate are readily distinguished by the formula :

Is + predicate
Is e + subject

If the part so brought forward be (1) the simple subject (or object), or (2) a simple adjective predicate, the main verb follows in the relative form :

(1) Is e Dia a dh'oibricheas annaibh—
God worketh in you :—Phil. ii. 13
Is mise a b' fhearr a rinn—*I did best* :—Arab. I. 28
Is mi a tha duilich—*I am sorry.*
Is mi nach 'eil gu math—*I am not well* :—Munroe 130
Is e a bhitheas dorcha an nochd—
It will be dark to-night :—ib. 128

(2) Is ann gu làidir a bhuaileas e an t-iarunn—
It is strong(ly) that he strikes the iron.
Is ann gu minic a theirear e—*It is often that it will be said* :—
McKay 26.
B' aotrom a thog e an t-eallach—
It was light(ly) that he lifted the burden.

(3) If an oblique or complex expression is brought forward as predicate, the principal subject, whether noun, pronoun, or verbal noun, follows immediately after this expression :

Is le Criosd sibhse agus is le Dia Criosd—
Ye are Christ's, and Christ is God's :—1 Cor. iii. 23
Is dual dà sin—*That is natural to him* :—McKay 15
B'fhearr leam a fhaicinn na a chluinntinn—
I had rather see than hear it :—ib.
Is luaithe deoch na sgeul—
'Tis a drink before a story :—N.G.P. 263
Is cuinge brù na biadh—
Capacity is narrower than food :—ib. 225
Is fearr sìor-obair na sàr-obair—
Steady work is better than hard work :—ib. 249

(4) If **is** be construed with **ann,** or **co**? the same construction results :

Nach ann duinn a dh' éirich?—
Is it not to us it happened?—A' Choisir 22
'S ann orra tha am bàinedh—
It is upon them is the furore :—Teachd. I. 5

or with **co** :

(Co) fhad 'sa ruitheas uillt gu cuan—
As long as streams run to ocean :—cf. Clar. 19

§ 181.

1. When the subject or object (or both) consists of a substantive group or phrase, **is** (negative **cha**) is used to introduce the predicate, the subject being,

(1) indefinite, one of the species :

Is bean tighe i sin—*She is a housewife* :—Z.C.P. VII. 441
Is eun sgarbh a thig bèo air iasg—
A cormorant is a bird that feeds on fish :—ib.
Is duine còir e, 's na iarr a chuid—
He is a fine man, but don't ask of him :—N.G.P. 229
Cha duine tàillear, is cha duine dhà dhiubh—
A tailor is not a man, and two of them are not a man.

(2) definite, a definite person or thing, further defined or compared in (a) a definite predicate or by (b) a predicate defined by a following noun, Inf. phrase or Rel. clause.

In both cases **is** must be followed by a third personal pronoun agreeing with its noun.   The definite article is often omitted when the subject is made definite by the noun, or relative clause following :

Is E do bheatha (*God is thy life*)—*welcome!*
Is i sin bean-tighe—*She is the housewife* :—Z.C.P. VII. 441
Is mise do bhràthair—*I am thy brother* :—Z.C.P. VII. 441.

(a) Is e deireadh gach cogaidh sìth—
The end of every war is peace :—N.G.P. 232
Is e Diluain iuchar na seachdain—
Monday is the key of the week :—ib. 232
Is e mo charaid caraid na cruaidhe—
My friend is the friend in need :—ib. 233

Is i an àilleantachd maise nam ban—
Modesty is the beauty of women :—ib. 255
Is i an oidhche an oidhche, na'm b'iad na fir na fir—
The night is the night, were the men the men :—N.G.P. 257

(b) Is e am bròn as fhasa fhaotainn—
Grief is easiest to come by :—ib. 229
Is iad na h-eòin acrach as fhearr a ghleacas—
The hungry birds fight best :—ib. 257
Is e sgeul an àigh a b'àill le Pòl—
'Tis a lucky story that would please Paul :—ib. 233
Is i ghaoth tuath a ruaigeas an ceò—
'Tis the north wind drives away mist :—ib. 256
Is e ath-thilleadh na ceathairne as miosa—
The return of the rievers is worst :—ib. 232
Is e farmad a ni treabhadh—
It is emulation that makes ploughing :—ib. 232
Is e bean fortan no mìofhortan fir—
A man's wife is his fortune or misfortune :—ib. 233

§ 182.   RELATIVELY.

(1) In direct statements the relative form of **is** is used :

Dad **as** leat—*What is thine.*
Am fear **as** rìgh an Alba—*The man who is king in Scotland.*
Am fear **as** aithne dhomh—*The man whom I know.*
Is e an Tighearn **is** Dia ann—*The Lord is God* :—McKay 36
Is e Cailean **as** mò—*Colin is the biggest* :—ib.
Mar **is** faide chì mi—*As far as I can see*:—ib. 29
Mas breug bhuam e, is breug chugam e—
I am telling what I was told :—N.G.P. 305

§ 183.

(1) In (a) oblique Relative clauses
     (b) negative clauses
     (c) interrogative sentences
     (d) **ge** clauses and
     (e) some other instances

is (but not **bu**) is included in the rel. or interrogative particle :

(a) Am fear **d' am** bean i, 's **d' am bu** bhean i—
  The man whose wife she is, and whose wife she was.
  Am fear **leis am** fuar, fuaigheadh e—
  He that is cold, let him sew :—N.G.P. 19
  Innis dhomh ciod e an dòigh **anns an** fhearr leat am bàs
    fhulang—*Tell me in what way you prefer to suffer death* :—
    Arab. I. 37

(b) Cleas **nach** aithne dhomh—*A trick I know not.*
  Am fear do **nach** léir a leas—
  The man who does not see his own advantage.
  Cha mhòr **nach** fhaic sinn—*We almost see* :—Cos. 47
  Cha nàir leis bràithrean a ghairm diubh—
  He is not ashamed to call them brethren :—Heb. ii. 11
  Cha n-fhearr leam—*I had rather not* :—Brah. Seer 29
  Is truagh **nach** bu cheàird sinn gu léir an diugh—
  It is a pity we were not all tinkers to-day :—N.G.P. 293

(c) Có i ?—*Who is she ?*—D. Ban 208, 32
  An n-e sin e ?—*Is that he ?*
  Nach spioradan frithealaidh iad uile ?—
  Are they not all ministering spirits ?—Heb. i. 14

In a paratactic construction with **co** the past tense is expressed by a pronoun, not **bu** :

  Na'n robh fhios aige **co mi** is docha gu'n rachadh e as a chiall—
  *Had he known who I was, he would probably have gone out
    of his mind* :—Arab. ii. 46

cf. the non-paratactic construction :

  Cha d' innis mi idir dha gu'm bu mhi Agib—
  I did not tell him that I was Agib :—ib.

(d) Also after **ge** :
  Ge fad' a bha 'n acaid—
  Though long was their pain :—S.O. 152[a]17
  Ge beag an t-ubh, thig eun as—
  Though small the egg, a bird will come out of it :—N.G.P. 194
  Ge b'e as miosa—*Whoever is the worst* :—McKay 14

(e) Also **ni**, **na** (*than is*), **ciod**, **ged**, **masa**, **gur**, **mur**—include the copula, and are followed by a noun, a pronoun, or a relative clause :
  Nì h-e neach eile—*It is not another* :—Job xix. 27
  Ciod e an duine—*What is man ?*—Heb. ii. 6

Ciod e cosmhalachd ?—*What is a parable* ?—Cos. 1.
Ciod is crìoch àraid do'n duine ?—*What is the chief end of man?*
Ciod is suim do na deich àitheantaibh ?—
What is the sum of the ten commandments ?—Catm. 1, 42
Gidheadh—*Though it be it, nevertheless.*
Ged is e an tigh, cha n-e a mhuinntir—
Though it be the house, it is not its people :—N.G.P. 199
Mur tu Criosd—*If Thou be not Christ* :—John i. 25
Neo-air thaing **mur** an robh companaich gu leòir aige—
No fear but he had companions enough :—Cos. 119
Gur muladach tha sinn—*Sorry are we* :—D. Ban 122, 1
Masa fìor a ta an fhaistinn—
If the prophecy be true :—S.O. 45ᵇ36, 41
Mas e bhur toil e—*If you please* :—Arab. ii. 67

(2) Non-relative **is** is often omitted :

A phobull sinn—*We are his people* :—Metr. Ps. 100
Sgiolta na connspuinn An tòiseachadh bhàir iad—
Trim heroes they At the beginning of a fray :—S.O. 152ᵇq
Stròiceach le lannaibh iad,
Dòrtach air falanan—
Cutting to rags with their blades are they,
Shedding streams of blood :—S.O. 152ᵇw
So agaibh e—*Here you have it.* :—Z.C.P. VII. 447
Coma leam e—*I don't like it* :—Z.C.P. VII. 447
Sin i agad a nis, 's urram na h-uaisle do'n choigreach, gabh
    air t' adhart—
There you have it now. The honour of precedence to the
    stranger, go forward :—L.C. 80
Dualchas a chumadh iad—
It is hereditary disposition that they would show :—S.O. 153ᵃ21

§ 184. EXAMPLES OF VERBAL STEMS COMPOUNDED WITH PREVERBS.

1 O.G. stem **ag**- *drive*, L. ag-ō		Inf. áin f.
G. denom. stem		Inf. aoin f. *rush*
imb-	Ipv. iomain *drive*	Inf. iomain f.
to-		Inf. tàin f. *drove*
im-ad-to-		Inf. iomadan m. *restlessness, discomfiture*

2 O.G. **al-** *nourish, bring up*, L. alō   Inf. altram, G. altrum,
                                                         oilean, eilean

                       con-   Inf. conaltradh m.
    G. altrum m. denom. ⎰   *conversation*
                       inn-   Inf. ionaltradh m. *pasture*
                    ess-com-   Inf. asgailt f. *retreat, shelter*

---

3 O.G. stem **an-** *remain, rest, cease*   Inf. anad
    G. stem.   Ipv. f-an- *stay,*   Inf. fanadh m., fantuinn,
                                            fanachd, fanailt,
                                            fantail f.
      com-od-ess-   Inf. cumsanad m. *rest*
      fo-od-ess-   Inf. fuasnadh m. *tumult*
      od-ess-   Inf. osnadh m. *sigh*

---

4 O.G. stem **anag-** *accompany, protect*   Inf. anacul
    G. denom. stem Ipv. anacail *pro-*   Inf. anacladh m.,
                              tect   anacail f.
      ad-   Ipv. adhlaic *bury*   adhnacal m., adhla-
                                          cadh m. *burying*
      to-ess-   Ipv. teanac *deliver*
                           ward off   teanacadh m.,
      to-ind-   Ipv. tiodhlaic   tiodhlac m.,
                          bestow   tiodhlacadh m.

---

5 O.G. stem **and-** *kindle*   Inf. andod *beginning*
                                             annudh
    G. ad-   Inf. adhannadh f.
                                            kindling
                                            adhnadh m.
      for-od-ess-   Inf. fursan m. *flame of*
                                          fire, O.G. forsunnadh

---

6 O.G. stem **arco, arcu,** *ask*, L. posco, precor,
    G. ath-com-   Ipv. athchomhairc *shout again*
      com-arc   Inf. comhairc f. *outcry,*
                                  forewarning, mercy
      fris-com-   Inf. freagnairc f.
                                  conversation

7 O.G. stem (1) **beg**- *break* ; with to-aith- *dissolve,*
                                       Inf. taidbech, taithmech
   G. fo-aith- Ipv. faothaich *relieve, alleviate,*
                                       Inf. faothach m.
         (2) **bo-n-g** *break, reap*   Inf. buan
   G. stem Ipv. buain *reap*   Inf. buain f.
       com-   Inf. combach m. *breach,*
                                     cumach m.
       to-   Inf. tobhach m.
                                     wrestling, compelling
       ess-   abs. asbhuain f. *stubble*

8 O.G. stem **ben**- *strike*   Inf. béim, G. beum m.
   G. stem   Ipv. bean *touch*   Inf. beantainn m., beanail,
                                     beantail, beanailt m. ;
                                     in cpds. -be, -p
      aith-com- Ipv. athchum
                   shape anew Inf. athchumadh m.
      to-air- Ipv. tearbain *sever* Inf. tearbhadh m.
      ad-for-   Inf. oidhirp, oirpe f. *an*
                                     attempt, endeavour
      con-   Inf. (O.G. cuimbe
                                     destruction) cuma, cumad
                                     m. *shape*
      to-ess- Pret. theab, L. concidit, *failed, nearly did* ;
                    teab *flippant person's mouth* ;
                    teabaid f. *taunt*
                    teabad m. *stammerer*
      fo-di-   abs. O.G. fodb. G. faobh *spoils, booty* ;   hence
             denom. Ipv. faobhaich *strip, despoil*
      im-ad- Ipv. màb *vilify*
      to-fo-air-ess-   abs. tuairep m. *turbulence*
      air-   eirbhe f. *fence, wall*
      to-aith-bheum   toibheum m.

9 O.G. stem **ber**- *bear*, L. fer-ō   Inf. breth, breith f.
   G.   Ipv. beir *bear*   Inf. breith f. beirsinn m.
                                     § 176
      air-   Ipv. eirbhir *ask*   Inf. eirbhir f., eirbhirt
                indirectly, hint

aith-od- Ipv. ìobair *sacrifice* Inf. ìobairt f.
com- Ipv. cobhair *help* Inf. cobhair f. cobhradh m.
di-od- Ipv. dìobair *desert,* Inf. dìobairt m.,
         betray dìobradh m.
di- Ipv. dìobhair *vomit* Inf. dìobhairt f.,
                               dìobhradh m.
ess-(later ad-)
      Ipv. abair *say* Inf. (ràdh) m.
frith- Ipv. frithbheart *contradict, object*
imb- Ipv. iomair *play, ply* Inf. iomairt f.
fo-imb- Ipv. fimir *must*
to- Ipv. tabhair *give* Inf. tabhairt f.
in- Inf. eibir f. *report, calumny*
com-di-fo- Inf. cunnart m. *doubt,*
                               danger

com- abs. conbhair *brow*
        antlers of stag
fo-od- Inf. fobair f. *undertaking,*
                               advancemant, rencontre
fo-air- Inf. foirbheart f. *help*
for- Inf. forbairt f. *increase,*
                               profit, emolument
ind- Inf. inbhar, ionbhar m.
                               confluence
to-od- Inf. tobairt f. *flux*
to-air- Inf. toirbheart, tairbheart
                           f. *efficiency, bounty*
tarm- Inf. tairbeart f. *isthmus,*
                               peninsula
ti- Inf. tiort m. *accident*
mì-ess- Inf. mì-abairt f. *mis-saying*

---

10 O.G. stem **bert**- *prepare*
  G. air- Ipv. eirbheirt *move, carry* Inf. eirbheirt f.
     ess-ro- Ipv. arbhartaich *dispossess*
     to-air Ipv. teirbheirt *harass*

---

11 O.G. stem **bidg**- *start* Inf. bidgud
  G. Ipv. bìog *gripe, start* Inf. biog, bìog m.

di-   Inf. dibhirce f. *endeavour*
                                 adj. dibhirceach *diligent,*
                                 violent
                                 Inf. dibhfhearg f. *vengeance,*
                                 wrath

---

12 O.G. stem **bo-n-d** (1) *proclaim* (2) *deny* Gk. πυ-ν-θάνομαι
                                 Inf. apad, abad
  G. stem od-   Ipv. ob *refuse*   Inf. obadh m. *utterance*
          ad-   Inf. abadh m. *syllable*
          ro-   Inf. rabhadh m. *warning*

---

13 O.G. stem **brenn-** *well out,* L. ferveō
  G. to-ess-   Inf. tiobarsan m. *springing*
                                 tiobart *well*
     to-od-   abstr. tobar m. *well*

---

14 O.G. stem **bronn** *spoil, give, spend* hence cognate
  G.   Ipv. brùth *bruise*   Inf. brùthadh m.
     con-   Ipv. comhbhruth   Inf. comhbhruthadh m.
                   bruise

---

15 O.G. stem **can** *sing,* L. canō   Inf. céol n., cétal n.,
                                 cantain f.
  G.   Ipv. can *sing, say* Inf. cantuinn m.
     for-   Ipv. foircheadal *teach* Inf. foircheadal m.
                                 instruction
     to-air-ro-   Inf. taircheadal m.
                                 prophecy

---

16 O.G. stem **car** Ipv. *love*   Inf. (sercc) f.
     ad- abstr. acras m., ocras m. *hunger*, adj. an-acrach *sick*

---

17 **cel-, cell-,** here two, if not three, roots are almost inextricably
     confused :
  1. cel- *hide* < kel, L. cēlo
          Ipv. ceil *conceal*   Inf. cleith f. *secrecy*
     co- Ipv. coigil *spare*   Inf. coigleadh m.
     for-   abstr. faircill m. *a cask-lid,*
                                 pot-lid

2. ciall f. *sense*, W. pwyll
   - air-   Ipv. airchill *watch*,   Inf. airchealladh m.
           listen   *sacrilege, theft*
   - fo-   Ipv. foichill *provide*
   - co-   abstr. coigill f. *thought*
   - di-   abstr. dìchioll m. *diligence*

3. tim-chioll *go, move round* : *quèl, L. -colus, Gk. πόλος,
                       Sk. carati

18 O.G. stem **ci-** *weep*   Inf. cói, cái, cúi, G. caoidh *kei,
                        L. quaeror *kues, kueis
   - G. air-   abstr. oircheas m. *pity, charity*

19 O.G. stem **ci-** *see* < ces, Sk. caks, L. quaero (=quaeso)
   - G. ad-   Ipv. f-aic *see*   Inf. faicsinn, faicinn, f.
   - pf. chunnaic, earlier chunnairc
   - O.G. ad con- dairc, hence
   - G. stem darc
     - ad- fo-   Ipv. amhairc   Inf. amharc
     - ro-   radharc, f-radharc m. *sight*

20 O.G. stem **cing-** *go, march*   Inf. ceimm n. *pace*
   - G.   Inf. ceum m. *pace*
   - to-   Inf. toicheum f. *slow pace*

21 O.G. stem **clad-** *dig*, L. clādēs,   Inf. claide, cf. class
   - G. to-   Ipv. tochail *dig*   Inf. tochailt f. *quarry*
   - ro-od- Ipv. ròcail *tear*   ròcladh m. *mangling*

22 O.G. stem **clech-, clich-**   cf. cluiche *play*, cless *feat*,
                             clechtaim *I use*
   - G. com- adj. cugallach *precarious*, O.G. cuclige cuclaige
                            a shaking, swerving

23 O.G. stem **clo-** *vanquish* cf. Gk. πολεύω *turn round*, Inf. cloud
   - G. stem   Ipv. claoidh *vex, oppress*   Inf. claoidh f.
   - com- imb- Ipv. caochail *change, expire*   Inf. caochladh m.

24 O.G. **crin-** ar-a-chrin *perish* cf. G. crìon *shrivelled*
   - fo-ess   abstr. feascradh m. *shrivelling*

25 O.G. stem **cuir-** *put* (*invite*)   Inf. cor m.

    G. stem   Ipv. cuir- *put*   Inf. cur m., cuireadh m. *invitation*

      air-   Inf. urchair f. *cast, shot*

      ath-   Inf. athchur m. *banishment, wear-resisting property*

      di-   Inf. deachair f. *separation*

      frith-   Inf. freacar, freacur m. *use, practice*

      imb-air-   Inf. iomarchur m. *tumbling, straying, errand*

      to-ad-   Inf. tadar m. *provision, plenty*

      to-aith-   Inf. tàchchur m. *refuse, overflow*

      to-ind-ad-   tionnacair m. *tongs*

      com-   Ipv. comh-chuir   Inf. comh-chur m. *apply, compose, arrange*

      di-od-   Ipv. diocuir *drive*   Inf. diocuireadh m. *expulsion*

      eadar-   Ipv. eadar-chuir   Inf. eadar-chur f. *interpose*   *interjection*

      imb-   Ipv. iomchair *bear,*   Inf. iomchair m. *behave*

      in-   Ipv. eagair *set in*   Inf. eagar m. *order, row* *order*

      to-in-   Ipv. teagair *collect*   Inf. teagar *provide, shelter*

      to-   Ipv. (1) tachair *meet*   Inf. tachairt f. *happen*   (2) tochair *invite*

---

26 O.G. stem **dāl-** *apportion* cf. W. gwn-ddol *dowry*

                                      Inf. dáil

    G. stem   Inf. dàil f. *share*

      air-com-   Inf. earnail f. *share*

      to-for-ess-   Inf. tuarasdal m. *wages*

      ess-   Inf. eudail f. *press, profit*

27 O.G. stem **dam-** *suffer*   Inf. deitiu
    G. denom. stem   Inf. deid f. *obedience, care*
       ad-   Ipv. aidich   Inf. aidmeach m., aidmheil
           (=aidmhich) *confess*   f. *confession*
      denom. of aidm-each :
            abs.   oidheam m. *secret meeting*
       de-ad-   deatam m. *anxiety* ; adj. deatamach
       fo-   foidheam f. *inference, rumour*
       frith-   frideam m. *attention, sufficiency*
       to-   taidheam m. *import*

---

28 O.G. stem **di-n-g-** *press down,* cf. L. fingō, Inf. dinge
    G. com-od-   Inf. còmhdach m. *covering, dress*

---

29 O.G. stem **do-** *singe, burn,* Gk. δαίω
    G. stem   Ipv. dòth *singe*   Inf. dothadh, m.
    ad-   Inf. f-adadh m. *kindling*

---

30 O.G. stem **ell-, la-** *go, set in motion,* Gk. ἐλαύνω
    G. com.   Ipv. comhail *join*   Inf. comhal m.
                     together
      frith-   Ipv. fritheil *attend*   Inf. frithealadh m.
      ind-   Ipv. innil *prepare*   Inf. innileadh m.
                              cf. inneal m. *instrument*
      to-ad-   Ipv. tadhail *visit*   Inf. tadhal m.
      to-in-od- Ipv. tionail *gather*   Inf. tional m.
      com- (to-
      in-od)   Ipv. comh-thionail   Inf. comh-thional m.
                assemble   *congregation*
      tre-   Ipv. triall *proceed*   Inf. triall m. *journey*
      fo-ind-   Inf. fainneal m. *ignorance,*
                              being astray
      to-fo-ind-   Inf. tuaineal m. *stupor*
      imb-ad-   Inf. iomadhall m. *sin,*
                              iniquity
      imb-ro-   Inf. iomrall m. *error,*
                              wandering
      far-   Inf. farail, forail f. *visit,*
                              enquiry for health

sechm-	Inf. seachmhal m. *passing over, forgetfulness*
to-	Inf. (1) tall m. *theft* (2) talladh m. *lopping*
to-ess-od-	Inf. taisdeal m. *journey*

---

31 O.G. **fiad-**, **ad-fiad-** *narrate*, cf. **find-**, **finn-**, *know*, M. W. gwnn ;
    Pf. with pres. or pf. meaning, 1 & 2 s. fetar, 3 s. fitir.
    Inf. fius, g. fessa ; G. fios, g. fiosa m.
  G. from 3 s pf. Ipv. fidir *know, consider*
                         Inf. fidreadh m.
                         abstr. fideadh m. *suggestion*
  Denominatives from fius, a -**u**- stem :

aith -aith -air- Ipv. atharrais *mimic*,	Inf. atharrais f.
air-, ir-	abstr. iris f. *description*
aith-	aithis f. *reproach*
aith-ro-	aithris f. *relating*
co-co-	coguis f. *conscience*
com-aith-air-	caithris f. *watching*
fo- ro-	foras, forfhas f. *research*
ro-fo-	ruais *rhapsody*
ro-fo-imb-	ruapais *rigmarole*

Denominatives from a related -**n**- stem :

ind-, inn-	Ipv. innis *relate*	Inf. innseadh m.
fo-ess-ind-	Ipv. faisneis *detect*	Inf. fàisneis f. *speaking, whispering*
ess-ind-		abstr. aisneis f. *rehearsing, tattle*

---

32 O.G. stem **em-** *protect*, cf. L. emō (comō, demō, sumō ; emptiō,
              sumptus)

G. com-	Ipv. coimhead *watch*	Inf. coimhead m.
frith-com-		freiceadan m. *watch*, f. dubh *Black Watch*
di-		Inf. dìdean f. *protection, fort*
imb-di-		Inf. imdhidean m. *protection*
fo-		Inf. faotainn f. *keeping, getting*
air-fo-		Inf. eiridinn m. *nursing, attendance on sick*

33 O.G. fáisc,   Ipv. *squeeze* (fo-osaicc, L. obsequium P.H.)
    G.   Ipv. fàisg *squeeze*   Inf. fàsgadh m.
    to-   Ipv. taoisg, taosg *drain, overflow*

---

34 O.G. fich-, fech- *fight*, L. vi-n-co   Inf. cpd. with gal *valour*,
                                      Gk. χολή
    G. denom. air-   Inf. iargall f. *skirmish,*
                                          battle
      di-   Ipv. dìoghail, dìol,   Inf. dìol m. dìoghaltas m.
              revenge, avenge   dìoghailt f.
      fo-   Ipv. foghail *raid*   Inf. foghail f.
      ess-   Inf. easgall m. *storm, wave*

---

35 O.G. fuin- *going down* (*of sun*)   Gk. νέομαι
                                    Inf. fuined, G. fuin f. *end*
    G. fuinne m. *setting of the sun,*   *the West*
      to-   Inf. toineadh m. *thaw,*
                                         thawing
      to-air-   Ipv. teirinn, teàrn   Inf. toirneadh m. *respect,*
               descend   *deference*

---

36 O.G. stem **gaib-** *take, sing* L. cap-io, habeo
                                     Inf. gabál f.
    G. stem   Ipv. gabh *take, sing* Inf. gabhail f.
      air-ro-   Ipv. earghabh   Inf. earghabhail
               arrest   f. *miserable captivity*
      con-   Ipv. cum *hold*   Inf. cumail f.
      di-in-   Ipv. diong   Inf. diongbhail f. *repel, be*
                                       match for, effect
      fo-   Ipv. faigh *get*   Inf. faghail f. faighinn
      fo-ad-   Ipv. fàg *leave*   Inf. fàgail f.
      to-od-   Ipv. tog *raise*   Inf. togail f.
      to-ro-od- Ipv. trog *raise*   Inf. trogail f., but cf. § 64
      ath-   Inf. aichbheil f. *reprisal,*
                                       revenge
      di-   Inf. dìoghbhail, dìobhail m.
                                       taking away, loss
      frith-in-   Inf. freasgabhail f. *ascension*
                                       to heaven

imb-im-   Inf. iomghabhail f. *shunning, reducing, conquering*

inn-   Inf. ionghabhail f. *managing, reputation*

in-   Inf. eugmhail f. *harm, evil*

to-in-   Inf. teagmhail f. *occurrence, disease, danger, strife*

to-for-   Inf. turghabhail f. *course, journey* (esp. of *sun*)

to-for-ess-   Inf. tuairisgeul m. *description*

di-ess-   Inf. deasghabhail f. *ascension (day)*

---

37 O.G. stem **gain-** *be born*, L. gignō, Gk. γίγνομαι
          Inf. gein, G. gin f. *anyone*
 G. stem Ipv. gein, gin *beget*, Inf. gintinn, gineadh,
      produce   gineamhuinn m.
 O.G. Pf. s. 1. ro-genar, 2. ro-genar, 3. ro-genair, pl. 1. ro-gennamar, 3. ro-gennatar. With **mad (ma, mo)** *well*; **mo-genar** *well am I born*; Ir. moighéanar hence abstr. (mo ge)near-acht, **nèarachd** *luck*, **nèarach** *happy, prosperous* § 143

---

38 O.G. stem **gair**—*call*, L. garrulus, Gk. γῆρυς, Inf. gairm n.

G.	Ipv. gair *call*	Inf. gairm f.
ad-	Ipv. agair *claim*	Inf. agairt f.
air-	Ipv. earghair *forbid, prohibit*	Inf. earghair f.
fo-	Ipv. foghair *make a noise*	Inf. foghair f. *tone*
fo-od-	Ipv. fògair *denounce, banish*	Inf. fògairt f., fògradh m.
for-	Ipv. forghairm *provoke*	Inf. forghairm f.
frith-	Ipv. freagair *answer*	Inf. freagairt f.
imb-ad-	Ipv. bagair *threaten*	Inf. bagairt f. § 8, III.
to-ad-	Ipv. tagair *plead*	Inf. tagairt f.
to-imb-	Ipv. tiomghair *ask*	Inf. tiomghaire f.
to-od-	Ipv. togair *desire*	Inf. togairt f., togradh m.

com.   Inf. conghair f. *uproar*, comhghairm f.
              convocation
etar-   Inf. eadar-ghaire f. *divorce, separation*
for-com-   Inf. fornair m. *command, offer*
to-   Inf. taghairm f. *echo, divination*
to-air-com-   Inf. tairngaire f. *promise*, hence denom.
              from tairgneachd
       Ipv. targair *foretell, prophecy*   Inf. targradh m.

---

39 O.G. stem **gat**- *steal*   Inf. gait
   G.   Ipv. goid *steal*   Inf. goid f.
      tre-   Inf. treagaid f. *darting
                                       pain, stitch*

---

40 O.G. stem **gel**- *graze*, L. gula   Inf. gleith, geilt
   abs. fo-   fòghlach, fòlach m. *manured grass*
      inn-   ingilt f., inilt f. *pasture*

---

41 O.G. stem **gell**-, **gill**- *pledge, promise*   Inf. gellad
   G.   Ipv. geall *promise, wager*   Inf. gealladh m., gealltainn m.
      for-   Inf. foirgheall m. *pledge for protection, proof*

---

42 O.G. stem **glaid**-, with ad-, *address*   Inf. accaldam f.
   G.   Ipv. glaodh   Inf. glaodhach, glaodhaich
   G. ad-   Inf. agallamh, agalladh m.
                                  conversation
      imb-ad-   Inf. iomagallaimh f. *counsel,
                                  advice*
      for-   Inf. forglad m. *commotion
                                  caused by person coming in
                                  unexpectedly*

---

43 O.G. stem **gleann**- *glean*
   G. di- Ipv. dìoghluim *glean*   Inf. dìoghlum m. *gleanings*
      fo- Ipv. fòghluim *learn*   Inf. fòghlum m.
      ess-   Inf. eaglam *discussion*

---

44 O.G. stem **gni**- *do*, L. gignō, Gk. γίγνομαι
                          Inf. gním *deed*, G. gnìomh m.

G. di-   Ipv. dean *do*   Inf. deanamh m.
di-ro-   Ipv. deàrn *do*
fo-   Ipv. foghain *suffice* Inf. fògnadh m.
air-   Inf. eargnadh m. *quickness of*
                                 apprehension
com-   Inf. còngnadh, còmhnadh m.
                                 aid
in-   Inf. eanghnamh m. *prowess,*
                                 liberality §142
ɪrith-   Inf. friochnadh m. *care,*
                                 diligence
mi- (late)   Inf. mi-ghnìomh m. *evil deed*
ad- abstr. aigne f., aigneadh m. *nature, mind, temper* §146, 1

---

45 O.G. stem **gni-n-** *know*, L. noscō, Gr. γιγνώσκω
O.G. etar-   Inf. etargne, etarcne n.
G. eadar-   Ipv. eadraig *interpose*   Inf. eadraiginn f.
            Ipv. eadar-gnàth *know*,   Inf. eadar-gnàth m.
            distinguish   *ingenuity*
fo-aith-   Ipv. faighnich, foighnich Inf. faighneachd f.
            ask
aith-   Inf. aithne f. *knowledge*
ess-   Inf. eigne, eagna, *knowledge, wisdom*
in-   Inf. eanghnàth m. §142 *prudence, clever-*
                         ness, L. ingenium

---

46 O.G. stem **gon-** *wound, kill*, Gk. φόνος *murder*   Inf. guin n.
G.   Ipv. gon *wound*   Inf. gonadh m., guin m.
                                   pain
imb-   Ipv. iomghon *wound* Inf. iomghonadh m.
            severely
iar-   Ipv. iarguin *deplore* Inf. iarguin f. *sorrow, pain*
aith-   abstr. ath-ghointe *wounded again, severely wounded*
com-   comh-ghuin f. *compunction*
for-   forghuin f. *sharp pain*
imb-   iomaguin m. *anxiety, distress*

---

47 O.G. stem **grenn-**, L. gradior,   Inf. greim *authority, power*
G.   greim m. *grasp, morsel*
con-   congraim f. *cunning, clothing*
inn-   inghreim m. *persecution, clutching*

K

48 O.G. stem   **gu-, go-** *choose,* Gk. γένομαι, L. gustus
   G. di- (dí-gu) diugha, diùbhaidh m. *refuse, the worst*
     ro- (ro-gu) roghadh m., roghainn m. *choice, the best*
     to- Ipv. tagh *choose*.   Inf. taghadh m.

49 O.G. stem   **guid-** *ask, pray,* Gk. ποθέω *wish* θέσσασθα *pray for*
                       Inf. *guide* f.
   G.   di-   Inf. (O.G. dígde *urgent prayer for par-*
                        don), dighe f. *help*
        fo-   Inf. faighdhe, faoighe f. *begging for aid*
                        in kind, thigging
        air-ni-   Inf. ùrnuigh f. *prayer*

50 O.G. stem   **icc-** *come* cf. anag-, L. nanciscor *I reach,* Gk. ἔνεγκον
                 I brought
     to-air-   (O.G. *come,* Ipv. tair, G. tàir, tàrr mar a thàrradh
             H.B.)
           Ipv. tairg *offer*   Inf. tairge, tairgse f.
     to-in-com- O.G. tecmaing *occurrence,* G. teagamh m. *doubt*
     ro-   Ipv. ruig *reach*   Inf. ruigheachd f.
     com-ro-   Inf. còmhrag f. *combat*
                         Inf. comh-riachdain f. *en-*
                         gendering (v. ro-saig-)
     to-   Ipv. tig *come*   Inf. tighinn m.

51 O.G. stem   **láim-** *dare*   Inf. folmaise *attempting,*
                              coming near doing
   G.   Ipv. làmh *dare*   Inf. folmhaise f. *advan-*
                              tage, opportunity

52 O.G. stem   **leg-** *melt,* E. *leak,*   Inf. legad
               N. leka *drip*
   G. Ipv.   leagh *melt*   Inf. leaghadh m.
     di-   Inf. dilgheann m. *des-*
                             truction

53 O.G. stem   **leig-** *leave, let go, allow,* L. linquo,   Inf. leciud
   G.   Ipv. leig *let, let go*   Inf. leigeil, leigeadh m.
     to-ad- *yield to, caress, hush*   Inf. tailciud, talgud

air-　　Ipv. airleag, *lend, borrow*　Inf. airleagadh m.
de-air-　　　　　　　　　abs. dearlaic f. *gift*
od-ess- (and ess-od-)　O.G.　Inf. oslucud *opening*
　　　Ipv. f-osgail *open*　　　Inf. fosgladh m.
to-fo-inn-　Ipv. tuanlaig, tualaig, tuanag, tònag *loose*
to-od-ess-　Ipv. tuasgail, fuas-　Inf. fuasgladh m.
　　　　　　gail *loose*
iom-fo-od-ess-　Ipv. iomfhuas-　Inf. iomfhuasgladh m.
　　　　　　gail *relieve*
to-　　Ipv. tilg *throw*　　　　Inf. tilgeil f., tilgeadh m.
to-od-　Ipv. tulg *rock*

---

54 O.G. stem **len**-, ess-len *defile*, L. ob-linō,　Inf. aéllned
　　do-for- (?)　O.G. druailned *corruption*
　　G. denom　Ipv. truaill *pollute*　　Inf. truailleadh m.

---

55 O.G. **li-n**-, abstr. lie *a flood*　Sk. pr-nā-ti *fills*, * plē-nā-mi
　　G.　　　　Ipv. liòn *fill*,　　　Inf. lìonadh
abs.　fo-　　fuilleadh m. *reward*
　　to-fo-　tuilleadh m. *addition, more*
　　　　　lia, lighe f. *flood*
　　to-od-　tola *superfluity*
　　to-　　　tuil f. *flood*
also　fo-ro-od-　forail *excess*
　　di-ro-od-　dèarail *poor, mean*

---

56 O.G. **ling**-, **leng**- *spring, leap*　Sk. lañghati *springs off,*
　　　　　　　　　　　　Inf. léim n.
　　G.　　　　　　　　　Inf. leum m. *leap*
　　to-air-　　　　　　　Inf. tairleum m. *leaping
　　　　　　　　　　　　　on, overwhelming*
　　ath-　　Ipv. athleum *rebound*　Inf. athleum m. *second
　　　　　　　　　　　　　leap*
　　to-ar-fo-　Ipv. tuirling *descend*　Inf. tuirling f.
　　　　　　alight
　　do-air-fo-　　　　　abstr. doirling f. *promontory, beach*

---

57 O.G. **lo-n-g**-, fo- *support, sustain*　Inf. folog, fulach, fulang
　　G.　　　Ipv. fulaing *suffer*　　**Inf.** fulang m.
　　　　　　endure

com-fo-in-   Inf. cuallach m. *tending*
          cattle
imb-fo-   Inf. iom-fhulang m. *patience*
          long-suffering
in- eallach f.m. *burden, cattle, furniture*
in-to-fo- eatualaing f. *injury*

---

58 O.G. **losc-** *burn*, L. lūcēre, Sk. locana Inf. loscud
  G.   Ipv. loisg *burn*   Inf. losgadh
   ess- (O.G. abstr. aelscud, aeilscud *longing*)
  G. aolais f. *indolence, sluggishness*
   fo- falaisg f. *moor-burning*
   in- eallsg f. *scold, shrew*

---

59 O.G. **lothraig-** *wallow in mud*, G. loth, L. lutum,
             Inf. lothrugud
  G. denom Ipv. loirc *wallow* Inf. loirceadh, cf. lodraigeadh
             m. *sousing*

---

60 O.G. **lú-** *move*, Gk. πλέω *I sail*, Inf. lúud *driving*, fo-lúamain
                flying
  G. lùth m. *strength, agility*
   ess- Ipv. èalaidh *creep, watch*, Inf. èalaidh, èaladh m.
         stalk
   fo- Ipv. falbh *go, depart* Inf. falbh m.
   im-   iomlaid f. *exchange*

---

61 O.G. **luaid-** *move, mention, express, sing of,* Inf. luad
  G.   Ipv. luaidh *mention*   Inf. luaidh m.
   imb- Ipv. iomluadh *speak often,* Inf. iomluadh m.
      or *too much*
   com-   colluadar m. *party, conversation*

---

62 O.G. **luig-**, fo-ad-   Inf. falgud *cut down,*
              causat. of laig
  G. di- Ipv. diolg *dismiss, forgive* Inf. diolgad m.
   fo- Ipv. falaich *hide*   Inf. falach m.

---

63 O.G. **mag-**, to-for-, tòrmach m. *increase*
  G. Ipv. tormaich *magnify* ; tàrmaich ***produce, originate, dwell***

64 O.G. **maid-** *break, burst* Gk. μαδάω, Sk. madati Inf. maidm n.
   G.   Inf. maoim f. *eruption, panic*
      ind-   O.G. Inf. indmat *wash hands*,
                                    also indlat
          Ipv. ionnlaid *wash*, Inf. ionnlad m.
              bathe
    to- -od- tum *dip, bathe* Inf. tumadh m.

---

65 O.G. **maith-** *pardon* denom. maith *good* Inf. maithem
   G. maith *pardon*   Inf. maitheadh m.
    to-   Ipv. tomh *offer, threaten* Inf. tomhadh m.

---

66 O.G. **mel-** *grind*, L. molō, Gk. μι'λλω, Inf. mlith, bleth
   G.   Ipv. bleith *grind*   Inf. bleith f.
    to-   Ipv. tomhailt *eat*
    com- abstr. cuimhealta *bruising*
    fo- -in- abstr. foimeal m. *consumption*
    to-ad-   tàmailt f. *disparagement*

---

67 O.G. **mesc-** *mix, confuse*, L. misceō, Gk. μίσγω, Inf. mescad
   G. misg. f. *drunkenness*
    com- cumasg f. *tumult*
    to-ro- Ipv. toirmisg *hinder*,   Inf. toirmeasg m.
           forbid

---

68 O.G. **mid-** *judge*, L. medeor, Gk. μέδομαι, Inf. mess
   G. ess- Ipv. aom *incline, decline* Inf. aomadh m.
    fo-ess- Ipv. feum *need, must* Inf. feum m.
  Denominatives :
          Ipv. meas *consider, judge* Inf. measadh m.
    ad-   Ipv. amais *aim, hit*   Inf. amas, amasadh m.
    air- Ipv. eirmis *find, out* Inf. eirmeas m.
    to-   Ipv. tomhais *measure*, Inf. tomhas m.
            compute
    com-   abstr. comas m. *power*
    com-   „ cuimse f. *aim, mark* (denom. from p.
                 part. pass)
    in-com-ad- „ eugmhais (*absence*), as eugais *without*
    to-in-com-ad-   teagmhais f. *accident, guess*

```
di-od-        abstr. diomas m. pride
imb-ro-         „    iomarbhas m. sin, punishment
to-air-         „    tàrmus m. dislike of food
to-ro-          „    tarmas m. affront
```

69 O.G. **moin-, muin-** *think*, Sk. manjate, L. reminiscor
  G. air-   Inf. airmid f. *honour, worship*;
                               oirmhid f. *decency, credit*
  con-   abs. cuimhne f. *memory*
  for-   abs. farmad m. *envy*
  di-ro- Ipv. dearmad, Inf. dearmad m., dearmaid *neglect*

70 O.G. **ness-**, ad-ness- *reproach*, Gk. ὄνειδος, Inf. áinsem
  G.   abs. ainnis f. *poverty*
  di-   dinnseadh m. *contempt*
  to-   tuinnse, tuimbreadh m. *blow*
  aith-com- achmhasan m. *reprimand*
  to-air-com- tarcuis f. *contempt* : O.G. tarcuisne, tarcusul

71 O.G. **neth-**, with air- *await, expect*   Inf. irnaide
  G. to- abstr. tuineadh m. *abode, possession*

72 O.G. **nig- neg-** *wash*, Gk. νίξω,   Inf. nige
  G. Ipv. nigh *wash*   Inf. nigheadh m.
  di-   abstr. dineach m. *salutary draught*
  to-   tonach m. *bath*

73 O.G. **no-**, with ad-, n.p. anai *riches* L. ad-nuō
  G. ana *riches*
  to-imb-ad- Ipv. tiomain   Inf. tiomnadh m. *will,*
              bequeathe   testament
  aith-   Ipv. àithn *command* Inf. àithneadh m., àithne,
                      f. *command*

74 O.G. **org-** *kill, destroy*   Inf. orcun
  G.   Ipv. orc *kill*   Inf. orcain f., orcadh m.,
                        f-airgneadh m. *hacking*
  di-   Ipv. tiorc *save*   Inf. tìorcadh m.
  to-ess- Ipv. teasairg *save*   Inf. teasairginn f.

to-imb- Ipv. tiomairg *gather*   Inf. tiomargadh m.
ess-   Inf. easorgain f. *contrition*
to-fo-   Inf. tuargan m. *discontent*,
    tuargnadh m.
to-   Inf. turguin m. *destruction*

---

75 O.G. **rå-** *row*, L. rē-·mus, Gk. ἐρετμός
  imb- Ipv. iomair *row*   Inf. iomram(h) m.
    abstr. iorram m. *boat song*

76 O.G. **råd-** *speak*, Got. rodjan *speak*,   Inf. råd
  G.   Inf. ràdh m.
  imb- Ipv. iomraidh *mention, report* Inf. iomradh m.

---

77 O.G. **reg-, rig-** *bind*, L. rigēre, rigidus, corrigia
  G. ad- Inf. àrach m. *tie, bond, stall-collar*
    com- Ipv. cuibhrich *fetter*   Inf. cuibhreach m.
    fo- Ipv. fuirich *stay, delay* Inf. fuireach m.
  com-fo- Ipv. comh-fhuirich *wait together*
    Inf. comh-fhuireach m.
  adj. righinn *tough*

---

78 O.G. **reg-, rig-** *stretch*, L. regō, pergō, ērigō, surgō Inf. hi rigi
  air- abstr. uirigh f. *couch*
  G. aith-air- (O.G. aithirrech n. *repetition, amendment,*
    aithirge f. *repentance*)
    abstr. aithreachas m. *repentance*
  ess- Ipv. éirich *arise* Inf. éirigh f.
  ess-ess- Inf. eiseirghe, aiseirgh f. *resurrection*
  imb-ess- O.G. immirge, immirce
  G. Ipv. imrich " *flit* " Inf. imrich f.
  to-ess- Ipv. teirig *fail, be spent* Inf. teireachduinn m.
  di-   adj. dìreach *straight*
  di-di-fo- tuirginn f. *flood*
  to-di-fo- adj. tudraig *vigorous* H.B.

---

79 O.G. **re-n-** *sell*, Gk. πέρνημι,   Inf. reic, reicc
  G. Ipv. reic *sell*   Inf. reic m.
  di-   Inf. dire f. *tax, tribute*
  ess-   Inf. éirig f. *ransom*

80 O.G. **reth-** *run*, Lit. ritù *I roll*, L. rota, Inf. riuth, rith
   G.   Ipv. ruith *run*   Inf. ruith f.
   fo-   Ipv. fòir *help*   Inf. fòir f., fòirinn f., foirich-
                                   inn f.
   ind-   Ipv. ionndruinn *miss* Inf. ionndruinn m.
   t-air- Ipv. tàrr *overtake*
   to-od-   abstr. tòir f. *rout*
   for-   forradh m. *helping one's self, foraging*
   to-iarm- abstr. tairmrith, tailmrich f. *bustle noise*
   for-   Inf. foiridinn f. *pursuit*
   di-   abstr. deireadh m. *end*
   fo-ind- abstr. faondradh m. *wandering*
   to-   toradh m. *fruit*
   to-air-od-   turus m. *journey*

---

81 O.G. **riad-** *ride, travel*, Gall. rēda *waggon*, G. réidh *smooth*
                                        Inf. réimm
   G. réim f. *course, power*
   imb-   denom. Ipv. imréimnich *go about*
   to-ro-   abstr. torradh m. *burial*, O.G. torruma

---

82 O.G. rim-, with fo-, *set place*, Gk. ἠρέμα *still, gentle*,
                                     Inf. fuirmed
   G. fuirmheadh m. *seat, foundation*

---

83 O.G. **rím-** *count*, denom. of rím *number* Inf. rím
   G. ad-   Ipv. àireamh *number*   Inf. àireamh f.
   di-   dirim *innumerable, numerous, plentiful*
   to- air-   Inf. tuaiream f. *guess*
   to-ind-   Inf. tionnriomh
                                     conclusion

84 O.G. **said-** *sit*, L. sedeō, Gk. ἕζομαι,   Inf. suide
   G. suidhe m. *seat*
  O.G. imb-suide *obsession*
   G. imb-   impidh f. *intercession, prayer*, L. ob-sess-io
   ni-   nead *nest*, ni- *down*, cf. air-ni-guide, ùrnuigh f. Ped.

---

85 O.G. **sàid-** *thrust* causat. of said-   Inf. sáthud
   G.   Ipv. sáth *thrust*   Inf. sàthadh m.

86 O.G. **saig-** *make for*, L. sagiō, Gk. ἥγεομαι *lead*, Inf. **saigid**
   G.   Ipv. saighead *dart forward* Inf. saigheadh m.
   com-   Ipv. connsaich, comhsaich, cothaich, *dispute*
                  Inf. connsachadh m., comhsachadh m.
  iarm-fo- Ipv. feòraich (fiafraigh) Inf. feòraich f.,
             enquire   feòrachadh m.
  to-ad- Ipv. taisg *deposit, hoard* Inf. taisgeadh,
                          tasgadh m.
  to-od- hardly different from to-ad-
         abstr. toisg f. *opportunity*
    ad-   ,,   asgaidh f. *gift, boon, present*
    di-   ,,   O.G. i ndegaid, G. an deoghaidh *after*
    com-di-   ,,   cuinge f. *solicitation, entreaty*
    aith-com-di- ,, athchuinge f. *prayer, petition*
    ind-   ,,   ionnsuidh m. *attempt, attack*, prep. a
                  dh'ionnsuidh *to, towards*, hence denom.
        Ipv. ionnsaich *learn* Inf. ionnsachadh m.
  fo-con- abstr. fochaide f. *disease, disorder*
  ro-   ,,   rochduin f. *reaching, arriving at, assent*
  to-   ,,   toichead f. *arrest*

---

87 O.G. **samal-** *liken*, L. simulō, Inf. samail
  G. samhuill f. *likeness*
    di-   O.G. diamhlad, G. diamhladh m. *place of retreat*
          or *refuge*
          denom. Ipv. diamhlaich *make dark*
    in-   abstr. eisimeil f. *imitation, dependence, obligation*
    ind-   ,,   ionnsamhuil f. *similitude* ; adj. *comparable*
    to-ind- ,, tionnail f. *likeness of person* or *thing*

---

88 O.G. **sc-**, L. secō, G. sgian
  to-in- (to-ess ?) Ipv. teasg *cut, cut off*, Inf. teasgadh m.

---

89 O.G. **scann-**, with fo- *toss, winnow*
  G. fasgannadh, fasgnadh m. *winnowing*, fasgnag f. *corn-fan*
    ind-   abstr. innsgin f. *mind, courage, vigour*
    to-ind- ,, tionnsgainn f. *beginning*, tionnsgal m.
              ingenuity ; hence denom.
        Ipv. tionnsgail *invent, devise*. From sgail as a
        new base :
  mos-sgail Ipv. mosgail (*early-toss*) *awake, arouse*, Inf.
    mosgladh m.

90 O.G. scar- *sever, separate, cast down*, Ger. scheren, E. *shear*
  G. Ipv. sgar *separate*   Inf. sgaradh, sgarachduinn m.
    con-   Ipv. casgair *slay, butcher*   Inf. casgairt f.
    eadar- Ipv. eadarsgar *separate, divorce*
              Inf. eadarsgaradh, eadarsgarachdainn m.
    imb-   Ipv. iomsgair *separate*
              Inf. iomsgaradh m. *excommunication*
    to- + epenthetic -r- Ipv. trasgair *overwhelm*
                      Inf. trasgradh m. *abrogating*
    ess-   abstr. eascar m. *fall*, easgar m. *plague*
    di-   ,,   diosgar m. *mob, rabble*
    od-   ,,   oscar m. *leap, bound*

---

91 O.G. scart- *cleanse*, cf. cart-
  G. air-   ursgartadh m. *sweeping clean*

---

92 O.G. sceul-, with to- *reveal*, denom. of scél, Inf. toscélad
  G. taisgealadh m. *report, news, prognostication*
    taisgeal m. *finding of anything lost*
    taisgealach m. *spy, betrayer, discoverer, reporter*

---

93 O.G. scuich- *depart, come to an end, remove, change* Inf. scucht
  G. Ipv. sguch *move, stir ; sprain* Inf. sguchadh m. *sprain*
    di-ro-od- Ipv. deàrrsg *polish, burnish*
                Inf. denom. deàrrsgnachadh m.
    deàrrsadh m. *splendour*, deàrrsgnaidh *polished*

---

94 O.G. sech-, L. in-seque *say thou*, Gk. ἔννεπε,, with to-ad-
            abstr. tasg *announcement*
  G. tàsg m. *report, news, character*
    com-   Ipv. coisg, caisg, *check, stop*
                      Inf. cosg, casg m.
    ar-com   Inf. archuisg f. *experiment*
    to-in-com- Ipv. teagaisg *teach* Inf. teagasg m.
    di-od-   Ipv. dùisg *awaken* Inf. dùsgadh m.
            abstr. sg-eul m. *story*
    in-com-   ,,   aogasg, aogas f. *face, appearance*
    ind-com-   ,,   ionchosg m. *impediment, desire, in-*
                        struction

air-in-	abstr.	aireasg f. *apple of the eye, vision*
aith-in-	,,	aitheasg f. *admonition, advice*
to-aith-in-	,,	taitheasg m. *repartee*
ro-	,,	rosg m. *eye, eyelid*
aithi-	,,	aithisg, f. *report, intelligence*
im-	,,	imisg f. *sarcasm, scandal*
in-	,,	inisg f. *reproach, bad name*
inn-	,,	insgne f. *gender, speech*
to-in-	,,	toinisg f. *understanding*
to-ind-com-	,,	tionchosg m. *instruction*
for-to-in-com-	,,	foirtheagasg m. *rudiments, intro-duction to a branch of knowledge*

95 O.G. **sech-** *follow*, L. sequor, Gk. ἕπομαι, Inf. sechem
  G. prep. seach *by, past*, adv. seachad *past*, O.G. sechut *past thee* § 120
  Ipv. seachain *avoid*   Inf. seachnadh m.
  fo-aith- Ipv. faisg *pick off vermin*

96 O.G. **sel-**, with com-, *go (away)*, cf. sil- *drop*, siubhal *walking*
  G. to-fo-com- abstr. toichiosdal, tòstal m. *arrogance*
  to-do-   Ipv. tuisill, tuislich *fall, stumble*
       Inf. tuisleadh adj. tuisleach *stumbling*

97 O.G. **selb-** denom. from selb, *possession* with ad-
                   Inf. asseilbiud
  G. to-ad- Ipv. taisealbh *personate*, Inf. taisealbh m.

98 O.G. **sem-**, with to-ess- *pour out*, Lit. semiu *I create*, Inf. teistiu
  G. to   Ipv. taom *pour out, empty*, abstr. taoim f.
       bilge-water
  to-od-   abstr. tuisdeach m. *parent*

99 O.G. **senn-** *play*, L. sonāre, abstr. senim
  G. Ipv. seinn *sing*   Inf. seinn f.
  to-   Ipv. tabhainn *bay, bark* Inf. tabhann m.
  imb-frith- abstr. imreasan m. *dispute, controversy*

284

100 O.G. **ser-** n- *spread*, L. sternō   Inf. sreth
  G.   abstr. sreath m. *series, row*
    com-   ,,   cosair m. *feast, bed*; hence caisil-chrò
                      bier (bed of gore) L.C. 52
    ess-   ,,   easrad m. *ferns or heather to litter cattle*
    fo-   ,,   fosradh m. *grazing of cattle when
                      tethered*
    inn-   ,,   innsreadh m. *effects, furniture, plenish-
                      ing* :—Arab. ii. 76

101 O.G. **sét-** *blow* sweizd, Cym. chwythu
  G.   Ipv. séid *blow*   Inf. séideadh m.
    air-   Inf. oirfeid m. *music, melody*
    to-   taifeid m. *a bow-string* hence
                fead f. *whistle*

102 O.G. **seth-**, with to-ind- *blow*, L. spī-r-āre, Inf. tinfed *aspiration*
  G. abstr. fèath m. *calm, gentle breeze*
      ,,   onfhadh, anfadh m. *blast, raging of the sea.* Adj.
          ainbhtheach, *stormy*
      ,,   seathan m. *panting, hard breathing*
  fo-   ,,   fafann m. *gentle breeze*

103 O.G. **sir-** *seek* G. Ipv. sir *seek, ask* Inf. sireadh m.
  G. to-fo-   Ipv. tùr *devise, invent*
             abstr. tùr m. *understanding*

104 O.G. **siss-** *stand*, L. sisto, persistō, subsistō, Gk. ἵστομαι,
               ὑφίσταμαι, Inf. sessam
  G.   abstr. seasamh m. *standing*
    air-   ,,   iris f. *handle of basket* or *shield, hen roost
              or perch*
    to-air-   ,,   tairis ! *dairymaid's call to cow at milking,
                "stay!" "bide!"*
    fo-   ,,   (1) faoisid, faosaid f. *confession*
             (2) faosadh, faoiseadh m. *protecting, relief*
    imb-   impis, an impis *almost, about to*
    fo-ro-imb-   farpuis f. *strife*

105 O.G. **slí-**, with fo- abstr. fuillem *usury*, Gk. ἑλεῖν *take*, cf. sealbh
  G. fo-   abstr. fuileadh m. *increase, profit, gain*
    to-   Ipv. toill *deserve, merit*   Inf. toilltinn m.

106 O.G. **slig**- *strike, stroke,* E. *sleek,*   Inf. slige f.
G. ad-   Ipv. aslaich *request, persuade*
Inf. aslach, aslachadh m.
air-   Ipv. airlich, fairtlich *baffle*
Inf. fairtleachadh m.
fo-air-   Ipv. fùirlich *overcome*   Inf. fùirleachadh m.

---

107 O.G. **sluind**- *designate,* O. Cym. istlinnit = profatur,
Inf. slondod, slond
G.   Ipv. sloinn *surname, trace pedigree*
Inf. sloinneadh m.
di-   Ipv. diùlt *refuse, deny*   Inf. diùltadh m.
ad-   Inf. aslonnadh m. *discovery, telling* ; adj. as-
lonnach *tattling*

---

108 O.G. **sní**- *spin, turn, fatigue one's self,* L. neõ, Gk. νέω
Inf. sním *spinning, trouble*
G. denom.   Ipv. snìomh *twist, twine, spin,* Inf. snìomh m.
spinning, sadness
com-   Ipv. coisinn *win, earn, gain*   Inf. cosnadh m.
com-im-   Ipv. caomhain *spare, save*   Inf. caomhnadh
ad-com-   Ipv. asgain (ascnaim) *I go, enter, ascend*
Inf. asgnadh m. *climbing*
fo-ar-   fàrsan m. *travelling for gain,* S.O. 279b22
to-ess-ro- Ipv. tèaruinn *escape*   Inf. tèarnadh m.
to-fo-   tuainig *unloose*
to-air-ess-   tarsuinn, tàirsinn *obtaining, getting off safe
home,* S.O. 151b6 ; P.H. 6462
to-   Ipv. toinn *twist*   Inf. toinneamh m. *twisting,
multure, the miller's share of meal for grinding
it.*
com-to- Ipv. comh-thoinn *convolve*

---

109 O.G. **snig**- drop, rain, L. ningit, nix, Gk. νίφα, Sk.snihjati,
Inf. ac. snigi
G. Ipv. snigh- *fall in drops, ooze in drops*
Inf. snighe, snigheadh m.
to-   abstr. tòineag f. *little drop of spirits*

110 O.G. **so-** *turn*   Sk. sávati *drives on*   Inf. soud
   G.   Ipv. sobhaidh *turn, prevent*
   ess-ro-   Ipv. eur *refuse, deny*   Inf. euradh m.
   ess-od-ro-   Ipv. sòr *hesitate, grudge, shun*   Inf. sòradh m.
      § 8 III.
   G. denom. imb-   Ipv. iompaidh (iompaich) *turn, convert*
         Inf. iompachadh m.
   to-ind-   Ipv. tionndaidh *turn, alter*   Inf. tionndadh m.

---

111 O.G. **sreng-** *draw, drag* :   denom. from sreang f. *string, cord*
   G. to-   Ipv. tarruing *draw, pull*   Inf, tarruing f.

---

112 O.G. **suid-** with ad- *hold fast*, from said *sit*,   Inf. astad
   G. Inf. fastadh m. *stopping, hiring, binding as a servant for a
      stated term*

---

113 O.G. **ta-** *is, exists* from sta *stand* : -bí and -ben *be*, from √ bheu
   to-ess-   Ipv. teasd *die*   Inf. teasd
   in (ad)- com- O.G. pres. 3 s. ad- cota *obtains* ; with loss of
      unaccented first syllable, cothachadh m. *earning, support*

---

114 O.G. **-bí, -ben**
   cét- ceudfadh f. *sense*   § 143   Inf. buid f.
   ess-   abstr. easbhuidh f. *want, defect*
   fris-   freapadh m. *medicine*
   for- (with part.) foirfe *perfect*
      ess-pe, es-bae, eas-ba m. *want, defect*
   to-r-be   to-r-bae, tairbhe f. *profit*

---

115 O.G. **tech-** *flee*, Sk. takti *shoot*,   Inf. teicheadh m.
   ad-   Ipv. ataich *entreat, request*   Inf. atach m.
   com-ad-   Ipv. coitich *press to take something*
         Inf. coiteach, coiteachadh m.

---

116 O.G. **tiag-** *go*, Gk. στείχω,   Inf. techt f., also *messenger*
   G. téid *shall go, goes*   Inf. (dol) m.
   for-   Ipv. furtaich *help* Inf. furtachadh m., furtachd f.
      comfort
   imb-   Ipv. imich *go*   Inf. imeachd f., imtheachd f,
      depart

to-air-   Ipv. tuir *go over,* Inf. tuireadh (O.G. tuirthecht)
          relate

ess-   Inf. eisteachd f. *death*

frith-   Inf. fritheachd f. *coming and going, returning*

com-in-   Inf. cuideachd f. *company*

com-imb-   Inf. coimh- imeachd f. *marching, walking together*

to- denom. Ipv. tiochd, diùc, *come, be continued in,*
         Inf. tidheachd, tigheachd f. *coming,*
         t.Chriosd S.O. 177ᵇ38

inn-   abstr. innteach m. *way, road, gate*

rem-   ,,   reimheachd f. *arrogance, forwardness*

---

117 O.G. **tib**- *laugh*
  G. fo-ad-   abstr. faite f. *smile*
    fo-com- abstr. fochaid f. *scoffing, mocking*

---

118 O.G. **tluch**- with ad- *thank,* L. loquor,   Inf. attlugud
  G. Ipv. altaich, *salute, thank, say grace,* Inf. altachadh m.

---

119 O.G. **tóis**-, tuais-, with air-, *hears,* cf. tó *silent,* Inf. erthuasacht
  G. abstr. tosd m. *silence* (-sd-for-ts-)
  G. com-   Ipv. caisd *listen,* Inf. caisdeachd f.
    in-   Ipv. éisd *hear*   Inf. éisdeachd f.
    com-in-   Inf. f. còisdeachd f. *hearkening, listening*
    fo-in-   abstr. foisdin, foistinn f. *taciturnity, government of the tongue*
    to-   ,,   todhas m. *silence*

---

120 O.G. **to-n-g**- *swear*   Inf. luge ; -tech
  G.   Ipv. lugh *swear, blaspheme,* Got. liugan *wed,*
               Inf. lughadh m.
    com-   Ipv. comhdaich *allege, prove*
                Inf. comhdachadh m. comhdach m.
    ess- ἐηί Ipv. eitich *abjure, forswear, deny, lie*
                Inf. eitheach m.
    frith-   Ipv. freitich *forswear, vow to keep from*
                Inf. freiteach m.

121 O.G. **tracc**- With di-fo- *wish*   Inf. dúthracht
    G. abstr.   dùthrachd f. *earnestness, goodwill*

---

122 O.G. **tuig**- *cover*   Inf. tuige
    G.   Ipv. tugh *thatch*   Inf. tughadh m., tugha
                                    f. *thatch*
      in-   Ipv. aodaich *clothe*   Inf. aodachadh m.
                                    aodach m. *clothes*
      denom. Ipv. éid *dress, accoutre*   Inf. éideadh m. *garb*
      aith-in-   Inf. atach m. *worn-out*
                                        clothes

---

123 O.G. **tuil**- *sleep*, phps. Goth. þulan, Gk. τλῆναι, Sc. thole
    G. com-   Ipv. caidil *sleep*   Inf. cadal, m.

---

124 O.G. **tuit**- *fall*, cf. L. tundō   Inf. tothim, tuitimm ;   tatham,
                                    tám *sleep, death*
    G. tàmh m. *rest, sleep* ;   aith-   aiteamh m. *thaw*
    com-   abstr. cudam m. *scar on head, fault in the hair*
    to-ar-ro-   ,,   torrthaim, toirchim f. *accident, fit*

§ 185.   **PREPOSITIONS.**

I.—Simple Prepositions.

1. Prepositions governing the dative are :

a, as *out of*	(gu *with*)
aig, ag *at*	le *with*
air *on*	mu *about*
an, ann *in*	o *from*
de *of*	os *above*
do *to*	ri *against, towards*
fo *under*	roimh *before*

2. Prepositions governing the accusative are :

    eadar *between*   gun *without*
          seach *past*

3. Prepositions governing the dative without the article, and the accusative with the article, are :

    gu *unto*   mar *as*

4. Prepositions governing the genitive are :

thar *over*

tre, trid, troimh *through*

5. A preposition usually causes no change in a noun which itself governs the gen. :

> aig bean Bhaldi—*with B's wife* :—MacCor. 75
> gu bean a' bhaile—*to the goodwife* :—ib. 77
> aig crìoch an sgeòil—*at the end of the story* :—F.C. 254
> air son saoghal as fheàrr—*for a better world* :—ib. 211

§ 186.

a, as *out of, from* : with dat. : L. ex. ; the final -s-, even when dropped, prevents aspiration. **S** is retained before the art., and the personal and possessive pronouns, and **gach** :

> a baile—*out of town*
> as an tigh—*out of the house*
> as a chéill—*out of his senses* :—H.B. but cf.
> cha mhòr nach robh e as a chiall—*He was almost out of his senses* :—Arab. I. 33
> as leth Dhia (as a leth)—*for God's sake* :—Cuairt. 27, 66x

The prepositional pronoun 3 s., §120, is used adverbially to express extinction or removal—*out, off, away* :

> Chaidh as dà—*He is gone*
> Leig as sin—*Let that go*

Mas tu tha ann, is tu chaidh as—
If it be you, you are sadly changed :—N.G.P. 313

§ 187.

1. **aig, ag** (1) *at* ; (2) *near, with* ; (3) *by* ; with dat. : G. **ag-us,** L. anguste :

> (1) aig an tigh—*at the house, at home*
> aig a chois—*at his foot*

The form **ag** is used only (a) with verbal nouns and (b) in prepositional pronouns :

> (a) B'ionmhuinn leam ag éirigh, 'san òg-mhaduinn—
> *Methought it joyful, arising*
> *In early morn* :—D. Ban 168, 121

ag before verbal nouns has the following variations in form, §5, 1 :

between two vowels, **'g**, e.g. Tha mi 'g imeachd—*I am going*
between two consonants, **a'**, e.g. Tha sinn a' falbh—*We are off*
between a consonant and a vowel, **ag**, e.g. Tha sinn ag imeachd
—*We are going*
between a vowel and a consonant **ag** is omitted, e.g. Tha mi
falbh—*I am off*

(b) Théid agad air thu fhéin a chumail suas— *You will succeed
in supporting yourself* :—Arab. II. 5

(2) Dh' fhàg e beannachd aig an duine fharmadach—*He left
a blessing with the envious man* :—ib. 21
Thu bhi aig na Gaill 'gad chàradh—*That thou shouldest
be with the Lowlanders refreshing thyself* :—S.O. 59ª16

(3) 'S bàrr mo shròin' air a lùbadh
Aig garrach glas—
*And the bridge of my nose bent
By a pale starveling* :—Clarsach 12

2. Also with **tha** to denote possession § 178 :

(a) compounded with pronoun :
O nach robh mac **aige**—*Since he had no son* :—Arab. II. 20
'S e na ' revivals ' a bhitheas **aca** orra, mur bi na 's miosa—
It is revivals they will (have upon, i.e.) dub them, if not worse :—
Cos. 138

(b) with the art., a construction increasingly used for the
possessive pronoun :
As a' bhad gheal a bh' air an earball **aige**—*From the white
tuft that was on his tail* :—Arab. ii. 19
Air an aghaidh **aige**—*On his face* :—ib. i. 64

(c) with a poss. pronoun referring to the subject of the sen-
tence, a verbal noun is passive :
'S an cridh' **'ga** fhàsgadh asd' le bròn,
And the heart wrung out of them with sorrow :—Là Bhr. 378

3. In idiomatic uses :
Nach fhaca a h-aon aca riamh roimhe—*That not one of them
had ever seen before* :—Arab. I. 61

Aig na rinn thu thrusadh á crainig—*Notwithstanding (what you gathered from a hedgehog)* i.e. *your hedgehog's gathering* :—S.O. 46ᵃw

Thug an ceòl agus an t-òran toileachadh anabarrach mòr do'n rìgh **aig** cho math 's cho dùrachdach 's a chluich 's a sheinn i—*The music and the song gave the King extraordinary pleasure, such was the excellence and expression with which she played and sang* :—Arab. I. 101

§ 188.

air 1. *on, upon* ; 2. *for, over* ; 3. *behind, after* : with dat. : a fusion of **ar, for, iar,** n- § 148.

1. air, Lat. prae, E. *fore* : aspirates a following consonant § 142.

air thùs dhiubh—*in the van of them* :—S.O. 287ᵃ24

turus **air** choigrich—*a journey abroad* :—Cos. 165

Gu'm b'anns' a bhi **air** chosg an tràth—*I had rather spend the time* :—Clarsach 22

Tha iad toirt am bóidean air gach dùil—*They swear by every element* :—ib. 18

Thuit mi ann an gaol air—*I fell in love with him* :—Arab. II. 78

With idiomatic usage :

air chinnt' ged tha thu bòidheach—*Notwithstanding the certainty that thou art beautiful* :—S.O. 286ᵇb

Ach **air** cho grad 's gu'n tug an taillear a chasan leis—*But how quickly soever the tailor fled* :—Am Fear-Ciùil 330

2. L. s-uper, Gk. ὑ-πέρ, E. *for* : does not aspirate, § 142.

Sgeul air Calum, sgeul air Donnan, sgeul air Pàdruig—*A tale of St. Columba, a tale of St. Donnan, a tale of St. Patrick* :—Guth na Bliadhna X. 4, 430

Air na pìobairean uile

B'e MacCruimein an rìgh—

Over all the pipers

MacCrimmon was King :—S.O. 148ᵃy

O ! guma buan **air** t' aiteam thu ! *O ! may thou be long over thy people* :—ib. 279ᵃu.

air mo theangaidh—*on my tongue, by heart* :—Arab. II. 1

air leith shuil—*one eyed* :—ib. 53 w :

air an là, **air** an oidhche—*by day and by night* :—ib. 52, 3

mach **air** aon de na h-uinneagaibh—*out of one of the windows*
—Waifs III. 128

Thàinig e a stigh **air** an luidheir—*It came in at the chimney* :
—ib. 12

Chaidh e steach **air** a' gheata—*He went in at the gate* :—
Arab. I. 63

3. **iar n-**, * eperon, compar. of Gk. ἐπί : does not aspirate
a following consonant, § 142

Tachaireadh math-ghamhuin, **air** call a cuilean, air duine—
Let a bear robbed of her whelps meet a man :—Prov. xvii. 12

O ! nach robh mi riamh **air** t' fhàgail—*O ! that I had never
left thee* :—L.C. 20

Ach laidh thu sìos **air** cùl a' chuain—*But thou hast set
behind the ocean* :—Clarsach 82

A leanadh ruaig **air** Cataich fhuara—*Who would follow a
rout after the cold Sutherlandmen* :—S.O. 286ª15

Cha robh sinn ach **air** ruighinn—*We had only arrived* :—
Arab. I. 110

Gu'm bheil an t-aont' a bh' aic' **air** ruith—*That her lease
is run* :—Clarsach 18

Bha ghealach ag éirigh (air) cùl na beinne—*The moon was
rising behind the peak* :—L.C. 14

(1) **air** *on*, referring to a date, a day, etc., is often to be understood :

Ma mharbhas tu beathach Di-haoine bi ruith na h-Aoine
ort am feasda—*If you kill a beast on a Friday, the
Friday fate will follow you for ever* :—N.G.P. 305

Feasgar Luain—*On a Monday evening* :—S.O. 285ᵇ2

Bheirinn m' fhalt a mach Dior-daoin,
'S dheanainn m' ìnean maol Di-luain—
*I would cut my hair on a Thursday,
And pare my nails on a Monday* :—N.G.P. 59

An obair a thòisicheas Di-luain—*The work that begins on a
Monday* :—ib. 33

In instances like the following, the preposition is not used :

Ris na dhealaich mi 'n dé moch la Càisge—*From whom I
parted yesterday morning, Easterday* :—S.O. 47ª27

Rinn thu mhoch-eirigh Di-dòmhnaich— *You rose early on Sunday* :—ib. 39ᵇ5

(2) But if the date be emphasised, the preposition is expressed :

Ach chaidh an t-saighead am chridhe **air** an oidhche sin— *But the arrow entered my heart that night* :—L.C. 14

Air Di-dòmhnaich 's còmhlan leam— *On (a certain) Sunday, company being with me* :—S.O. 282ᵇr

Chrìochnaicheadh a' choinneamh **air** an ath Dhi-luan— *The Assembly was closed on the following Monday* :— Cuairt. 40, 92

Air Di-luain so chaidh— *On Monday last* :—C.G. 24

(3) Idiomatic uses :

Air cho faoin 's gu'm meas sinne an t-aobhar— *However slight we deem the cause* :—Am Fear-Ciùil 168

Air cho fuar 's gu'm biodh an oidhch'— *However cold the night might be* :—An t-Oran. 167, § 97, 3

Ged bu rìgh mi **air** a' chrùn— *Though I were a crowned King* :—Clarsach 66, 96

Toimhseachan nach b' urrainn di fhuasgladh **air** a geurad — *Riddles she could not rede for all her sharpness* :— Mac Cormaig 89

Ach **air** sinead an sgeòil 's **air** cho tric 'sa chluinnear e— *But however old the tale, and however often one hears it* : —F.C. 262

Air ghlainead an tobair bidh salachar ann— *However clean the well, dirt is in it* :—N.G.P. 7

Air mheud nam beus a bhios 'na chorp— *However great the virtues that are in his person* :—ib. 19

§ 189.

an, ann an *in*, L. in, E. *in* ; with dat :

anns, before the art. **an**, before the rel. **an**, and before **gach.**

In the simple preposition the -n- becomes -m- before labials :

am measg— *among* ; a's mi '**m** péin— *and I in pain* :—Ross 48, 9 :

Ma tha e **an** dàn domh dol gu mòd eile— *If I am fated to go to another Mod* :—F.C. 326

'S trom leam m'osnaich **anns gach** là— *Heavy methinks are my sighs every day* :—S.O. 283ᵃ1

Mar bha an fhaoineis an dàn dhomh— *As the foolishness was fated me* :—Clar 12

gu'n éirighinn **'nam** sheasamh a chur fàilte ort—*I should rise to my feet to welcome you* :—Arab. I. 65

cf. Thuit mi as mo sheasamh—*I fell off my feet* :—C.S.

Ach bàs **'na** naoidheachan beag—*But (his) death as a little child* :—S.O. 148a20

Bu mhise agus Sacar **'nar** n-ònar an dithis nach b'fhiach— *Sacar and I were the only two that did not deign* :—Arab. I. 35

Compounded with the art. the unstressed preposition is dropped in current phrases, and the art. alone remains, § 87 :

Anns an toiseach, **'San** toiseach—*In the beginning*
an cor anns am bheil e, an cor **'sa'** bheil e—*The condition in which he is.*

Idiomatic use with subst. verb, § 177 fol. :

Cha n'eil **annad** ach an dearg shlaoightire—*You are but an arrant knave* :—Arab. I. 39

B'e aon de na mnathan-sìthe a bha **anns** a' mhnaoi agam— *My wife was one of the fairy women* :—ib. 28

Na bi **'nad** dhuine na's mò ach bi **'nad** mhoncaidh—*Be a man no longer, but be a monkey* :—ib. II. 22

An m(o)—*in my*, gives **am,** and **an d**(o)—*in thy*, gives **ad.**

To these forms an -**n**- is sometimes prefixed **'nam**, **'nad**, e.g.

Dhiuchd an comas sin **nam'** chàil—*That power has come to my life* :—Stewarts 480, 3

Hence the erroneous forms, § 114 :

Cupid ga **nar** tàladh—*Cupid alluring us* :—Stewarts 121, 5

Chaill sinn **nar** càil agus **nar** treòir—*We lost our appetite and our vigour* :—R.C. 34, 157

Thoirleum **nar** n-inntinn—*overwhelming our mind* :—S.O. 151as

§ 190.

de *of, off, from* : with dat. : O.G. de, di, L. dē, di(s) : often confused with do, § 4 II. 2 :

de is used

(1) with nouns to express a partitive genitive :

Rinn e dà leith dhith— *He made two halves of her* :—Arab. I. 81

Geàrr sgonn dheth so dhomh—*Cut a slice of this for me* :—
Munro 157

Thoir pìos dheth sin do Niall—*Give a piece of that to Neil* :
—ib.

(2) with the adjj. gann *scarce*, falamh *empty*, lom *bare*, beag
small—e.g. gann **de** bhiadh—*scarce of food*.

Also with the adjj. làn *full*, buidheach *thankful*, sgìth *tired* ;
and with the nouns mòran m. *much*, beagan m. *little*,
tuilleadh m. *more*, when they govern a genitive with the
article.

2. Idiomatic uses :

Ach air mo shon-sa **dheth**—*But for my own part of it* :—Arab.
I. 28

Gu'n robh iad mòran na b' fhearr **dheth** na bha iad—*That
they would have been much better off than they were* :—ib. 27

Rinn i eilid **de** m' mhnaoi—*She turned my wife into a hind* :—
ib. 24

Tha de dhaoine 's de dh' eich ann,
Tha de bhreislich 's de smùid ann—
There are so many horses and men there,
So much racket and smoke there :—Clarsach 12

Na tha dhaoine 's de dh' eachaibh
Air fastadh Rìgh Deòrsa—
All the horses and men
In the service of King George :—D. Ban 178, 271

Dean **de dh**' fhàbhar gu'n éisd thu rium—
Show so much favour as listen to me :—Arab. I. 18 (31)

Ma ghabhas sibh **de** dhragh—*If you will take so much trouble* :—
ib. 52

Chunnaic mi nach d' rinn mo chomhairle **de dh**' fheum dhi
ach a fàgail na bu raige na bha i riamh—*I saw that my
advice did her no service but to make her more headstrong
than she was before* :—ib. 72

Cha robh **de** lùths ann na chairicheadh as an ionad an robh e—
*There was not strength enough in him to move out of the place
where he was* :—ib. 34

§ 191.

do *to, for, by* : with dat. : Eng. *to*, Ger. *zu*

Gur cobhartach **do**'n bhàs gach feòil—*That all flesh is a prey to death* :—Ross 18

'S bidh mise a' teàrnadh sìos **do**'n ghleann— *And I shall be descending to the glen* :—Clarsach 82

Chrìosda dh' fhuiling am bàs **duinn**—*O Christ, who hast suffered death for us* :—S.O. 50ª1

'Us b' fhearr **dhomh** fhéin nach robh i ann— *And better were it for myself that it had not been* :—Clarsach 83

Ged nach d' fhuair me e **dhomh** fhéin—*Though I have not got him for myself* :—An t-Oran. 167

Is peathraichean **dhomhsa** an dà ghalla dhubh—*The two black bitches are my sisters* :—Arab. II. 71

§ 192.

eadar : with acc. (1) *between*, generally non-aspirating ;
(2) *both*, aspirating without the art.

(1) So na tha de dhealachadh **eadar** thusa agus do bhean— *This is the extent of the difference between you and your wife* :—Cos. 128

Eadar mo làmh 's mo thaobh—*Between my hand and my side*: —F.C.

Eadar a' chlach 's an sgrath—*'Twixt the stone and the turf* :— N.G.P. 171

Eadar a' chraobh 's a rùsg—*Between the tree and its bark* :—ib.

Eadar an long nodha 's an seann rudha—*Between the new ship and the old headland* :—ib.

'S bochd an sgeul **eadar** bhràithrean—*It is a miserable tale among brethren* :—Turner 44

(2) Bha iad an so **eadar** bheag agus mhór—*They were here both small and great* :—L.C. 62

§ 193.

fo (1) *under*, (2) *along, amidst* : with dat.: aspirates : O.W. guo, W. gwa-, go- ; Gk. ὑπό ; Sk. úpa, cf. L. s-ub

(1) **fo** chomaïn *under obligation* :—Arab. II.

gu dhol **fo** chìs—*to go under tribute* :—S.O. 286ª24

fo chaol mhala—*under a slender eyebrow* :—ib. 285ᵇ22

(2) **fa**, originally only before slender consonants, has **spread**:
fa leth *severally*, fa làr *on the ground*, fa dheireadh *at last*
In O.G. fo, fa with numerals were used as multiplicatives:
fo dí, fa dí *twice*; fo thrí, fa thrí *thrice*. Hence fo, fa
are in G. inextricably confused with mu, ma:
Chuairtich e mu h-aon agus chuairtich e mu dhà e—*He went
round it once and he went round it twice* :—Waifs II. 98
fa'm chòir—*in my presence* :—S.O. 285ᵇ37
'S i 'n tìr fo thuath dha mòr mo luaidh-sa—'*Tis the land
in the North which I love much* :—ib. ᵇ5.   In this sentence
the original phrase an tuath *from the north* was written
successively o thuath, bho thuath, fo thuath, mu thuath.
Chuireadh fonn **fo** na creagan—*Which would send a tune
along* (or *among*) *the rocks* :—S.O. 148ᵇu ;
fo fheasgar—*before evening*, H.B.

§ 194

gu *with* : with dat : O.G. co n- : L. cum.   Its uses being met
by gu *to, unto*, and le *with*, it is now obsolete except in the
phrases gu leth—*with a half, and a half* ; mu thuaiream dà
mhìle **gu** leth a dh' astar—*about two miles and a half
distant* :—Am Fear-Ciùil 294 ; and **gu** mac ic Alasdair 's
Lochial :—H.B. ;   A' Choisir 25

§ 195

gu *to, up to* : with dat. : with the art. **gus**, accus. :   O.G.
co, cu, § 48
O thigh **gu** tigh—*From house to house*
A chuireas leam gach cùis **gu** crìch—*Who by me will bring
every affair to an end* :—Metr. Ps. lvii. 2 ;   a' teannadh
gu crìch—*drawing to an end* :—Am Fear-Ciùil 265
Gus a' chrìoch—*to the end* :—Dan. vi. 26, Matt. x. 22, 1 Cor.
i. 8, Heb. iii. 6, 14 ; vi. 11 ; Rev. ii. 26
but also dat. :—**Gus** a' chrìch, John xiii. 1
Both forms are used in governing a clause :
Gu mis' ùmhlachadh air ball—*To humble me immediately* :—
S.O. 286ᵃ30
Gu esan a bhrath—*to betray him* :—Cos. 15
Gus coinneachadh ris—*To meet him* :—Cos. 132
Gus an talamh a chladhach—*To dig the earth* :—Arab. II. 43

§ 196.

> **gun** *without* : with acc. : aspirates §20, 4 : O.G. cen, cf.
> L. cis *on this side*
>
> **Gun** phiuthar, gun bhràthair—*With no sister or brother* :—
> L.C. 15
>
> Duine **gun** chiall— *A madman* :—D. Ban 432, 84
>
> **Gun** tuar, **gun** chiall—*Without merit or sense* :—Clarsach 59
>
> A bhoirionnaich **gun** chiall—*Senseless woman !*—Arab. I. 72
>
> A shluaigh **gun** chiall thug miann do'n òr— *Ye senseless folk
> who set affection on gold !*—Là Bhr. 181

But, metri causâ, **gun** chéill is used : e.g. D. Ban 168, 126 ;
326, 24 ; Metr. Ps. 49, 20 ; Clarsach 59

With clauses :

> Tha mi guidhe ort **gun** smaoineachadh tuilleadh air—*I pray
> you not to think of it further* :—Arab. I. 7
>
> 'S **gun** againn ach sinn fhéin—*With none but ourselves* :—ib.
> 105
>
> Agus **gun** a stigh ach mi fhein—*With no one at home but
> myself* :—ib. II. 84

This preposition is repeated instead of a conjunction :

> **Gun** stiùir, **gun** ràmh, **gun** phort—*Without rudder, oar, or
> port* :—S.O. 50 ᵇ12, 16

los see under **os**

§ 197

> **le** (1) *with*, (2) *by*, (3) *down*, (4) *belonging to* : with dat. : from
> leth *side*, * let, L. lat-us
>
> **le** coinneil—*with a candle* :—Arab. II. 76

(1) Fann **le** bròn 's **le** bristeadh cridhe—*Weak with sorrow and
> heart-break* :—ib. 50
>
> B' fheàrr dhomh teicheadh **le** m' bheatha na fuireach ri m'
> mharbhadh—*It were better for me to fly with my life than
> stay to be killed* :—ib. 41
>
> Slàn **le** Albainn (eadar) ghleann is chnoc—*Farewell to Scot-
> land, both glen and hill* :—L.C. 75

(2) Na meallar thu an so **le** bréig—*Be not thou deceived here
> by a lie* :—Clarsach 9

Mo rùn cha n-fhaicear **leam**—*My love is not seen by me* :—
ib. 113

'S do dhùthaich fein 'ga mort **le** nàmhaid— *And thine own country massacred by an enemy* :—S.O. 59ᵃ18

(3) Ach thriall na laithean air falbh mar shruth **le** gleann—
But those days have passed away like a stream down a glen :—
Clar. 111

Thuit e car ma char sìos **leis** a' bheinn—*It fell bounding down the mountain* :—Arab. II. 41

Thilg iad **leis** a' chliathaich sinn—*They threw us over the ship's side* :—ib. II. 82

(4) Thaisbein e gu'm bu duine **le** Dia e—*He showed that he was a man of God* :—L.C. 49

Bu **leam** gach ni—*Everything was mine* :—Arab. II. 84

Is **leat** MacPharlain nan cliar,
Bha aig fir t' àite riamh—
Thine is MacPharlain of the poets,
Who was with the men of thy place hitherto :—S.O. 48ᵇ13

Leis cho glic, gleusda 's a bha e—*Owing to his being so wise and clever as he was* :—Arab. II. 44

§ 198.

mar, dat. : but with art. or possessive pronoun, acc. : **aspirates** :

(1) *as* : M.W. mal, O.G. amal, L. similis—unaspirated -**m**- and final -**r**- derived from (2) by analogy

(2) *about, as, within*, M.G. immar, im-mar

(1) Cha n-ann gus thu bhith agam **mar** mo shearbhanta ach **mar** mo bhean—*Not that thou shouldest be with me as my servant but as my wife* :—Arab. II. 82

Cha robh sin aige **mar** a chuid féin— *He had not that as his own portion* :—F.C. 309

Mar an dearcag— *As the berry* :—Clar. 13

Thug i mise **mar** mhnaoi do dhuine—*She gave me as wife to a person* :—Arab. II. 84

Mar mhnaoi ri saothair— *As a woman in travail* :—Rom. viii. 22

(2) 'S nach ruigeadh **mar** réis an glùn— *And that would not reach within a span of the knee* :—D. Ban 284, 72

A chaochail beatha **mar** sheachduinn da chéile—*Who died within a week of each other* :—Turner 377

mar bheagan mhìltean do bhaile-mòr Pheairt—*within a few miles of the city of Perth* :—Cuairt. 27, 68

Na's mó **mar** àird' a' chinn— *Higher by a head* :—H.B.

Mar cheud— *A hundred times* :—S.O. 37ª26, 281ª1

Cha robh e **mar** mhìle dhomh— *He was not within a mile of me* : —H.B.

Mar bheagan cheudan slat do thìr—*within a few hundred yards of land* :—MacCor. 98

Mar là 'us bliadhna do dh'aois chàich—*within a year and a day of the age of the rest* :—Waifs III. 122

Is e a's fhaisge **mar** dhà mhìle—*It is nearer by two miles* :— H.B.

Ged nach biodh tigh na duine **mar** mhìle dh' astar dhaibh— *Though there was no house or living soul within a mile of them* :—Am Fear-Ciùil 317

As conjunction—*as, how* : in comparison—*the . . . the* :

Mar thà—*as it is, already* :—Arab. I. 25

Dh' innis mi dhi **mar** a fhuair mi a mach far an robh i—*I told her how I had discovered where she was* :—II. 7

Cha tuig thu **mar** a dh' fhàsas càrn— *You cannot understand how a cairn rises* :—Clar. 9

Mar is dlùithe a leugh e, 's ann is dìriche a ghluais e—*The closer he read, the straighter he walked* :—Cuairt. 27, 62

Mar bu mhò a bheirteadh de chomhairle oirre, is ann bu mho a bha i cur roimpe gu'm faigheadh i a toil féin— *The more advice was urged upon her, the more was she resolved to get her own way* :—Arab. I. 116

'S ann **mar** as fhaide a chaidh neach 'sam bith anns an olc, 's ann is **mò** gàirdeachas a bhitheas air gu'n deachaidh a leithid a theàrnadh—*The further one has gone in evil, the greater his joy that such as he should have been saved* :— Cos. 139

Bha i **mar** uidhe thrì no ceithir do mhìltibh o Ghrianaig— *She was within a voyage of 3 or 4 miles from Greenock* :— L.C. 149

§ 199

mu *about* : with dat. : aspirates : O.G. imb. imm, Gaul. **ambi**,
W. am, ym-, A.S. ymbe, Sk. abhi
cf. Gk. ἀμφί , L. amb-

Mu ar piuthair eile— *About our other sister* :—Arab. II. 73
Mu ar deidhinn— *About us* :—ib. 54
Sùil **mu**'n t-sròin— *Eye to nose* (i.e. a straight talk, blurt out) :
N.G.P. 350
Cha truagh leam cù 's marag **m'**a amhaich—*I don't pity a dog
with a pudding round his neck* :—ib. 133
Bhiodh òran an sin aig fear **mu** seach—
There would be a song there by each in turn :—Mac Cor. 52

In the following, cf. the use of fo §193 :

Mu mo choinneamh—*To meet me* :—S.O. 285ᵇ18
Mu d' chòir—*In thy presence* :—286ᵃ2, fa m' chòir :—Ross 28

§ 200.

o *from, by* : with dat. : aspirates : O.G. 6, ua : 3 s. **uad—rests
on od, ud**

O cheann gu ceann—*From end to end*
O bhaile gu baile—*From town to town*
Clann a bha aig m'athair **o** mhnaoi eile—*Children my father
had by another wife* :—Arab. II. 72
O'n mhnaoi chòir a bha 'san Arthar—*From the good wife
that lived in Narrachan* :—D. Ban 228, 66
'S an té **o** 'n d' fhuair mi i 'n toiseach— *And the woman from
whom I got her at first* :—ib. 234, 155

§ 201.

O'n is used as a conjunction : *since, after*
O'n a bha fios aige—*Since he knew* :—Arab. II. 4
O'n a dh' fhalbh mi—*Since I went away* :—I. 26

§ 202.

os *above* : with dat. : O.G. ós, uas, W. uch, *up §139 uachdar
m. surface,* s-uas *upwards*

os bàrr *on top*
os cionn *overhead, above*

'S na beanntan gruamach **os** an cinn—
And the gloomy peaks above them :—Clar. 153

cf. ios O.G. *ìs*, W. is, isel *low*, iochdar m. *bottom*, s-ìos *downwards*

os àrd—*openly*

os ìosal—*secretly*, with the alternative forms

os n-ard, os n-iosal, which seem corruptions of the rel. **as** *which is*, with the rel. eclipse retained § 13, I.

§ 203

ri : with art., **ris** : with dat., sometimes with acc. without art. : v. fris, frith §142

1. *to, against*

Is tinne e anns an t-slabhraidh a tha ceangal aobhar **ri** buil—
It is a link in the chain that joins cause to effect :—Am Fear-Ciùil 168

Bha dà chòmhlaidh **ris** a' gheata—*There were two leaves to the gate* :—Arab. I. 63

'S bidh tuilleadh **ris** an àireamh— *And there will be an addition to the number* :—Clar. 135

Thiormaich mi m' aodach **ris** a' ghréin—*I dried my garments in the sun* :—Arab. II. 82

Bha thu gu glé chaoimhneil **rium**— *You were very kind to me* : —ib. I. 29

Rì là gaoith', is uisg', is dìle— *Against a day of wind, rain, and flood* :—D. Ban 64, 30

Ach tha corruich mhòr orm **ri** do bhràithrean—*But I am very angry with your brothers* :—Arab. I. 29

A dol **ri** bruthach—*Going against* (i.e. ascending) *a bank* :— Munro 158

Mar shruth nach till air ais **ri** sliabh—*Like a stream that will not turn back up a hill* :—Clar. 121

Cha dubhairt mi gu'm b' olc **riutha**—*I did not say it was wicked of them* :—Arab. I. 27

Tha e ghnàth aghaidh **ri** aghaidh **ris** an dorus ghlaiste sin air son nach d' fhuair e an iuchair—*He is always face to face with (up against) that shut door for which he had not got the key* :—Am Fear-Ciùil, 209

Aig an robh mac **ris** gach té d'a mhnaibh—
Who had a son by each of his wives :—Waifs III. 112

Tha 'n là dlùthachadh r'a chrìch—*The day groweth to an
end* :—Judges xix. 9

Thoir an aire co **ris** a tha thu bruidhinn—*Mind who you are
speaking to* :—Arab. I. 43

Gach cliù a' **fàs riut**—*Every reputation being added to you* :
S.O. 285ᵇ38, w

'S an tric a shuidh thu **ri** mo ghlùin—*In which thou didst often
sit against my knees* :—Clarsach 83

Bha e là a' bruidhinn **ri** bean-uasal—*He was one day talking
to a lady* :—Cos. 125

2. *exposed*

A dh' fhàg **ris** an cinne daonna—*Which left mankind exposed*:
—D. Ban 432, 104

B' éiginn di a bràighe a leigeadh **ris**—*She had to expose her
neck* :—Arab. I. 101

Leig mi **ris** dha—*I showed him* :—116

Thàinig a' ghrian **ris** gu briagha—*The sun came out beauti-
fully* :—II. 37

Bha sealladh déistinneach air a leigeil **ris** da nis— *An awful
sight now presented itself to him* :—F.T. 232

3. *at, engaged in, occupied with* :

Bha sinn **ri** òl, 's **ri** ceòl, 's **ri** dannsa—*We were occupied with
drinking, music, and dancing* :—Arab. II. 68

Tha e **ri** brògan—*He is engaged in making shoes* :—Munro 158

Bha e **ri** h-ùrnaigh—*He was engaged in prayer* :—ib.

Car son a bha iad **ris** an obair ud—*Why they were engaged
in that work* :—Arab. II. 54

A dhuine gun chiall ! Ciod a tha thu **ris** ?—*Senseless man !
what are you at* ?—Am Fear-Ciùil 159, 219

Chai h e earrann eile d'a ùine **ri** speuradaireachd—*He spent
another portion of his time at astronomy* :—ib. 202

Mo mhàthair bhochd 's i **ris** a' bhàs—*My poor mother at
death's door* :—Clar. 57

Thòisich sinn **ri** marsantachd—*We began trading* :—Arab.
I. 25

A tha **ri** bròn—*Who are in sorrow* :—Math. v. 4

Gu tosdach balbh mar neach **ri** bròn—*Silent and dumb like
one in sorrow* :—L.C. 71

'S mi **ri** uallach nam bó— *And I tending the kine* :—Clar. 116

Bha Alastair **ri** farchluais aig cùl an doruis— *A. was listening at the back of the door* :—Waifs III. 113

4. *with*

Mu'n do dhealaich i **rium**— *Before she parted with me* :—Arab. II. 83

A' sùgradh 's a' beadradh
Ri rianadair feadan nan gleus—
Sporting and flirting
With the tuner of drones :—Ross 49

Confused with **le** :
Ri leathad bruaich—*Down the slope* :—F.T. 232; § 9, 3

5. *during, while*

'S mi 'ga dìth **ri** m' bheò— *And I without her while I live* :—S.O. 286ᵃ8

C'àit am faigh i **ri** beò do leithid-sa ?—*Where, while she lives, will she find the like of thee* :—Stewarts 302, 12

Gu'm bitheadh tu deònach
A rithist mo phòsadh **ri** ùin'—
That thou wouldst be willing
Again to marry me in course of time :—Ross 48

Bidh mi cuimhneachadh **ri** m' mhaireann—*I shall remember as long as I live* :—Clar. 80

6. *to be* (with Inf., as gerundive)

Gu mór **ri** mholadh—*Greatly to be commended* :—Arab. I. 54

Bha **ri** fhaotainn 'san Roinn-Eòrp—*That was to be found in Europe* :—S.O. 285ᵇ34

7. *as* (co-relative of cho, aon, § 95, 4)

Cho caoimhneil **ris** na faoileagan— *As kind as the seagulls* :—C.S.

Aig an aon bhord **ris** fhéin— *At the same table as himself* :—Arab. I. 42

§ 204.

roimh *before* : with dat. : aspirates : O.G. re n-, rem-, remi- hence riam *(p)ri(s)ami, L. primus (prismus)

Le eagal **roimh** theine—*With fear before fire* :—D. Ban 164, 55

A prepositional pronoun formed from this preposition and of the same person as the subject of the verb, follows verbs of motion :

Choisich mi **romham** re iomadh latha—*I walked on for many a day* :—Arab. II. 3

Gabh **romhad**—*Proceed* :—C.S.

Lean **romhad** mar a tha thu—*Continue as you are* :—Arab. I. 71

Na'n leanadh e **roimhe** air an obair a bha aige—*If he should continue in his present conduct* :—Arab. I. 116

Is ann bu mhò a bha i cur **roimpe** gu'm faigheadh i a toil fhéin—*The more was she determined to get her own way* : —Arab. I. 116

§ 205

seach *past, in comparison with* : with acc :

Seach a' chlach—*past the stone* :—Gillies, Gr. 134

Is sean Anna **seach** Mòr— *Anna is old in comparison with Sarah* :—Munro 156

Gun fhathamas do dhuine **seach** duine—*Without partiality to one man more than another* :—H.B.

Is trom a' chlach **seach** a' chlòimhneag—*The stone is heavy compared with the down* :—Stewart, Gr. 132

Nis tha oibre Dhé mòr **seach** oibre dhaoine—

Now God's works are great compared with men's works :—Cos. 57

§ 206

thar *over, beyond* : with gen. : aspirates :

Ciod a tha sibh a deanamh **thar ch**àich ?—*What do ye more than others ?*—Math. v. 47

Thar na còrach—*Beyond what is right* :—H.B.

Bha thu maiseach **thar** nan ceud— *You were fair beyond hundreds* :—A' Choisir 9

A' shnàmhas **thar** a' chaolais—*Who swims through the Kyles* :— ib. 11.

Cha deach Caluinn **thar** mo chinn— *A New Year (Hogmanay) has not gone over my head* :—Mac Cor. 17

Stuadhan na sean eaglais a bha tilgeil a faileis **thar** nan uaighean—*The walls of the old Church which threw its shadow over the graves* :—ib. 92

Thar nan cluas ann an ainbheach—*Over the ears in debt* :—
Am Fear-Ciùil 199

Na muillionan **thar** chunntais—*The millions beyond counting* :
—ib. 213

Am Famhair mòr a chuireas drochaid **thar** na h-aibhne
ann an aon oidhche—*The big giant that puts a bridge over
the river in one night* :—ib. 281

§ 207.

tre *through* : with gen. : aspirates :

tre mo chléith—*through my casement* :—H.B.

tre uisge is tre theine—*through fire and water* :—Stewart,
Gr. 132

ach **tre** nan aitribh (*read* aitreabh) 'san robh mise—*But
through the abodes where I was* :—L.C. 4

§ 208

trìd *through* (*through him* or *it*, old prep. pronoun 3 s. of tria, tre) :
with gen :

trìd Fir-saoiridh—*through a Redeemer* :—Catm. 20

trìd na fìrinn—*through the truth* :—Cuairt. 40, 97

Seadh ge do shiubhail mi **trìd** ghlinn sgàile a' bhàis— *Yea,
though I walk through the valley of the shadow of death* :—
Ps. xxiii. 4, ed. 1807

§ 209.

troimh *through* : with gen. : aspirates :

'S a dhìon **troimh** 'n ghaillinn iad beò— *And which guarded
them alive through the storm* :—Clar. 98

troimh m' chnuaic—*through my costard* :—Am Fear-Ciùil 286 ;
but also with dat. :

ré a thuruis **troimh** an t-saoghal—*during his journey through
the world* :—Am Fear-Ciùil 285

Bhrist e **troimh** an dorus— *He broke through the door* :—ib. 300

'Us rachainn féin **troimh** thonnaibh breun— *And I myself
would go through rank waves* :—A' Choisir 11

A' coiseachd troimh 'n mhuir—*walking through the sea* :—
Waifs III. 15

tromh thuill, tromh na h-uillt—*through bogholes, through
water courses* :—ib. 123

§ 210.   II.—COMPOUND PREPOSITIONS.

1. Compound Preposition are phrases containing a noun, and
hence govern the genitive :

a bhàrr *down from*
a chòir *near to*
a chum *in order to*
a dh' easbhuidh *in want of*
a dh' fhios *to the knowledge of,*
    to, for
a dh' ionnsaidh *towards*
a dhìth *for want of, without*
a los *in order to*
a réir *according to*
a thaobh *regarding, as to*
air bheulaibh *in front of, before*
air cheann *against* (a certain
    time)
air chùlaibh *behind*
air fad   ⎫ *throughout,*
air feadh ⎬ *among, through*
air ghaol   ⎫ *for love of*
air ghràdh ⎭
air muin *on back of*
air sgàth *for sake of*
air son *for the cause of, for*
air tòir *in pursuit of, after*
am bun   ⎫ *at foot of,*
an cois   ⎬ *near*
am fianuis ⎫ *before,*
am fochair ⎬
an làthair ⎭ *in presence of*
am measg *among*
an aghaidh ⎫ *in face of,*
an aodann ⎬ *against*
an àite *instead of*

an caraibh *in grips of, near*
an ceann *at end of, within*
an còmhdhail ⎫ *to meet*
an coinneamh ⎭
an cois *at foot*
a chois *hard by*
an dàil   ⎫ *to meet,*
an déidh   ⎬ *after,*
an deaghaidh ⎭ *in consequence*
an éiric *in requital*
an lorg *in track of, in conse-*
    quence of
an taice *in support of, beside*
as eugmhais *without*
as leth *in behalf of, for*
cleas *a trick, like*; cleas nan
    damh *like the oxen* :—Cos.
    127 ; cleas na binne nach
    maireann *like the late judg-*
    ment :—S.O. 38ᵇ9
fa chomhair *opposite to*
fa chùis *by reason of*
mu choinneamh *opposite*
mu dheidhinn *regarding*
mu thimchioll *about*
mu thuaiream *about* (as a guess)
o bhàrr *from top of*
os cionn *overhead above*
ré (O.G. fri ré) *during, for*
tar éis *over track of, after*
trid *through, by means of*
thun *to, unto* :   M.G. chu-ind
    chu-inn *to vertex* or *end*, § 13

2. But gu ruig, gu ruige (O.G. corrici, with acc.) *till thou reach, to,*
is a conjunction containing a verb and governs acc. :

   Gléidhidh mi do shlighe gu ruig a' chrìoch—*I shall keep thy*
       way unto the end :—Ps. cxix. 33, 112, Catm. No. 36
   Gu ruige Bagdad—*to Bagdad* :—Arab. i. 119, ii. 68, 102

XVI.

§ 211.   **ADVERBS.**

Adverbs qualify verbs, adjectives, and other adverbs, and
are of three classes—adverbs of

    I.—Manner.
    II.—Time.
    III.—Place.

I. An adverb of manner is formed by prefixing **gu** (before
vowels **gu h-**, § 48, 2) to almost any adjective, except pronominal
and possessive adjectives.

cinnteach *certain* ; **gu** cinnteach *certainly*

 Do chreagan **gu** h-uaibhreach
 Mar challaid mu'n cuairt dhut—
 Thy crags proudly
 Like a fence round thee :—Clarsach 26

The adverbial particles **glé, ro-**, and monosyllabic adjectives
qualifying an adjective of manner are placed between **gu** and
the adjective :

 gu glé mhath—*quite well* ; **gu ro** dhàna—*extremely bold*
 gu fìor ghlan—*very purely* ; **gu h-anabarrach** gasda—
           exceedingly nice

But **gu** is frequently omitted.

In a series of adverbs of manner, the conjunction is omitted,
and **gu** is placed before the first word of the series only :

 Gu binne, boidheach, seòcail, ceudach,
 Ceòlmhor, eutrom, éibhinn, àluinn—
 Sweetly bonny, stately, prime,
 Tuneful, joyous, light, and splendid :—D. Ban 342, 31, 2

§ 212. **ro**—*very, too* : aspirates :

    I. ADJJ. ; II. NOUNS.

1. Ach cha bhi 'n àilleachd
 No 'm blàth **ro**-mhaireannach—
 But neither their beauty nor their bloom
 Will be very lasting :—Clarsach 114
 'S mo chridhe fann air fàs **ro**- thròm—
 And my faint heart has become very heavy :—L.C. 70

Chuir sin am bàrd bu ghlaine beus
   Ro thràth fodh 'n lic—
That put the bard of purest life
   Too early under the stone :—Clarsach 130
Ach a nis fhuair e ministreileachd as **ro** fhearr—
But now hath he obtained a more excellent ministry :—
                                                    Heb. viii. 6

2. As a pre-noun **ro** sometimes takes the stress, and conveys
either of two shades of meaning.   § 142.

(1) *good*

Air mheangain ard nan **rò**-chrannaibh—
   On the high boughs of the stately trees :—S.O. 280ᵇ6
Bha Safi ag éisdeachd le **ro**-aire—
   Safi was listening with keen attention :—Arab I. 96 ;
   Lk. xix. 48
Am barraibh **rò**-chrannaibh shuas—
   In the foliage of the stately trees above :—Ross 14

(2) *untoward*

Ro-chùram an t-saoghail so—*The cares of this world* :—Mk.
   iv. 19 ; Lk. xii. 11.
A ghearradh goirid a **rò**-sgeul—*To cut short his exaggerated
   tale* :—Am Fear-Ciùil 218, 250, 289
Cha **rà**-sgeul bréig' e—'*Tis no romantic lying tale* :—S.O.
   51ᵃ31
Cha n-e an **ro**-chabhag as fhearr—*Great haste is not best* :—
   N.G.P. 107
Cha n-iad na **ro**-chléirich as fhearr—*The very learned are
   not the best* :—ib. 119
'S e sgar mi o m' chiall **ro**-mheud do cheanail—*It deprived
   me of my wits—too much of thy kindness* :—A' Choisir 15

§ 213.   I.—ADVERBS OF MANNER.

ach beag—*save a little*
ach neo-ni—*almost*
a   dh'aindeoin—dh'aindeòin—
   in spite of :—Am Fear-Ciùil
   294
a dh'aon obair—*purposely*

a dh'aon fheum—*at one stroke*
an aon fheachd—*in one time*
a dheòin, do dheòin—*willingly*
a dhìth, do dhìth—*a-wanting*
a mheud—*inasmuch*
a n-asgaidh—*freely, gratis*

a rìreadh, do rìreadh—*really*

a rìribh, do rìribh—*truly*

aill air n-àill ⎫ *willingly or*
aill n'air n-àill ⎭ *unwillingly*

air alt ⎫ *so that, in order that,*
air acht ⎭ *in such a way that*

air aineol—*among strangers, abroad*

air aird—*in order, in trim*

air ais—*backwards*

air bhiorsadh m.—*keenly impatient*

air a chuthach m. ⎫
air bàinidh f. ⎬ *in a fury, mad*
air bhoile f. ⎭

air a h-uile cor, ⎫ *at all events*
air gach cor ⎭

air a bheul fodha m.—*face downwards, upside down*

air a cois bhig f.—*peat set on small end, footed, to-dry*

air a lìonadh m.—*filling, flowing* (tide)

air a lethstuic f.—*inclined, leaning*

air a tharsuinn—*obliquely, getting off by skin of teeth* (S.O. 151ᵇ6)

air a thraoghadh m.—*ebbing*

air an dallanaich f.—*blind drunk*

air an neo-chomraich f.—*free from protection, heedless, careless*

air allaban m.—*wandering*

air fàrsan m.—*roving, journey :*—S.O. 279ᵇ 22

air fhiaradh m.—*transversely*

air bhanaltromas m. ⎫ *engage-*
air bhanaltrachd f. ⎬ *ment at nursing*

air bhogadan m.—*wagging, bobbing* D. Ban, 194, 524

air bhogadaich f.—*shaking, waving*

air bhrath m. ⎫ *to the fore,*
air sgeul m. ⎭ *to be heard of*

air bhuil ⎫ *(for use)*
air fhaotainn ⎬ *to be found,*
air ghléidheadh ⎭ *safe*

air chàs m.—*on condition*

air chumha f.—*provided that*

air cheatharnas m.—*acting the freebooter*

air choilltearachd f.—*acting the wood-wanderer,* i.e. *outlawed*

air cheart m.—*all right, in ordinary health*

air chòir f.—*in a proper arrangement*

air choltas m. ⎫ *like to,*
air choslas ⎭ *likely to*

air chall—*lost*

air chonfhadh m.—*raging*

air chor-eigin—*somehow :*—MacCor. 89

air chor 'sam bith—*anyhow*

air chosnadh m. ⎫ *on a foray,*
air fòghnadh m. ⎭ *outlawed*

air chumadh m.—*shaped like, like*

air chuairt f.—*on a circuit, sojourning*

air chuimhne f.—*in remembrance*

air clab a' chraois m.—*(the door) wide open*

air deargan a chuthaich m.—*stark mad*

air dhìth céille m.—*out of his wits*

air dhìobhail céille m.—*mad*

air dìchuimhne f.—*out of re-membrance*

air éiginn f.—*with difficulty, hardly*

air éis f.—*backwards, behind*

air eutromas céille—*light-headed*

air fad—*altogether*

air faoighe f.—*thigging*

air faondradh m.—*wandering, adrift, left to shifts*

air fhorradh féin m.—*helping himself, foraging, left to shifts*

air fògradh m. ⎫ *in exile,*
air fuadach m. ⎬ *in elopement, abduction*

air gleus m.—*in trim, in order*

air iomadan m. ⎫ *adrift,*
air siadan m. ⎬ *rocking, swinging*

air iomradh m.—*in report, in memory*

'san iomradh—*spoken of, to the fore*

air ionndruinn m.—*a-missing, lost*

air lagh m.—*in order, trimmed, ready for action*

air leth m.—*apart, one by one, separately*

air lodragan m.—*waddling,* cf. loirc, lothrugud § 184

air luaireagan m.—*sitting in embers* or *ashes*

air luasgan m.—*rocked, moving about*

air iomrall m. ⎫ *in error,*
air seachran m. ⎭ *astray*

air mhàgaran m.—*on all fours*

air mhaireann m.—*alive, to the fore*

air mhearaichinn f.—*in madness, delirium*

air mhi-chéill f.—*in madness*

air mhire-chatha f.—*in battle frenzy*

air mhì-alt m. ⎫ *ill-accommodated,*
air mhi-dhealbh m. ⎬ *not comfortably*
air mhi-dhreach m. ⎭ *situated, in disorder*

air saod m. ⎫ *on a journey,*
air siubhal m. ⎬ *in order, in health*

air sunnd m.—*in glee*

air seòl m., air dòigh f., air rian m.—*in order, arranged, pleased*

air sgròban m.—*on providing*

air thapadh m.—*on one's luck, outlawed*

air thuarasdal m.—*on one's wages, hired, engaged*

air tulgadh m.—*rocking*

air udal m.—*tossed to and fro*

a mhàin—*only*

amhuil ⎫ *as, like as, even*
amhluidh ⎭

am bitheantas, bithdheantas m. —*habitually, generally*

am feabhas m.—*in a better condition*

am fealla-dhà, *in jest, for fun*; eadar fheala-dhà 's da-rìreadh—*between jest and earnest*:—Am Fear-Ciùil 283; feala-dhà, cf. feala-trì f. *earnest*:—H.B.; fala-dhà—*feud of two,* cf. Accall. Index

am malairt f. ⎱ *in barter,*
⎰ *exchange*
an suaip f. *in swop*
am miadh m. ⎱ *in respect*
am pris f. ⎰ *in estimation*
an car, an caraibh ⎫ *near,*
⎪ *about,*
an gar ⎬ *in grips*
⎪ *with*
an comhair ⎫ *well nigh,*
⎬ *almost,*
an coinneamh⎭ *nearly*
an coinneamh a chinn—*head-long, precipitately*
an comhair a chùil—*backward*
an déidh air, ⎱ *enamoured of,*
an geall air ⎬ *excessively*
⎰ *fond of*
an iarraidh—*middling well* ;
also gun iarraidh
an imbis, an impis, an imis—*almost, nearly* §184, 104
an làthair f.—*present, truly, verily*
an tòir—*in pursuit* ; hence *Tory*
araon ⎫ *as one,*
faraon ⎬ *together,*
maraon ⎭ *both together*
as a chéile—*asunder, disjointed*
as an aghaidh ⎱ *outright*
as an aodann ⎰
as ùr—*anew, afresh*
as 'us as—*out and out*
caoin air ascaoin—*inside out*
car *a turn* is used to qualify
adjj. :
car obann *somewhat suddenly* :—
Am Fear-Ciùil 206
car blàth leis an deoch—*somewhat warm with drink* : ib. 223

car air char—*rolling, tumbling over and over*
car mu char—*round and round, over and over*
car mu chnoc—*hide and seek*
car mu seach—*heads and thraws, topsy-turvy*
car son—*why, wherefore*
casa-gobhlach—*astride*
cha—*not* (ní co-n) §7 III.
cha mhor (it is not much i.e.)
—*almost*
cheana—*indeed, truly* §121, 9
còmhla, mar chòmhla—*together*;
Ir. cómhlámh, *hand to hand*
cuide ri—*together, along with,*
cuitir with *gen,* Wb. 3ᵈ6
cf. W. gyd a *together with,*
tir cyd *land held in common*
cuideachd—*in company*
dìreach—*just so, exactly*
do rìreadh—*really, actually, indeed*
eadar-dhà-lionn—*between sinking and swimming*
fa leth—*severally*
feadh a chéile—*mingled together*
fo chàrn, ⎫ *put to the horn,*
⎬ *outlawed,*
air chàrn ⎭ *on a cairn*
glé—*clearly, very*
gu beachd—*evidently, clearly,*
Ir. beacht, adj., *perfect*
gu dearbh—*certainly*
gu deimhinn—*surely, verily*
gu diachadaich—*especially*
gu h-inbhe—*to size, maturity*
gu léir—*altogether, wholly, entirely*
gu leòir—*enough, sufficiently*

gun amharus ⎫
gun ag ⎬ *without doubt*
gun teagamh ⎭

gun chàird—(a) *without partiality*, (b) *quickly*
le chéile—*together*
leth mar leth—*half and half*
mad—*well*, W. mad § 143
mar an ceudna—*likewise*
mar sin—*in that manner*
mar so—*thus*
mar sud—*in yon manner*
mu làimh—*indifferently*
mu réir—*free*
mu seach—*in turn, alternately*,
O.G. ima sech § 199

mu sgaoil, fa sgaoil—*dispersed*
os aird ; os n-aird—*openly* § 202
os iseal, os n-iosal—*secretly* § 202
os làimh—*in hand*
os barr—*besides*
ro-(L. pro)—*very, excessively*
roimh a chéile—*too hastily*
seachad—*past* § 120
thar a chéile—*mingled together*
trasd—*across*
troimh a chéile—*in confusion*
theagamh—*perhaps*
uidh air n-uidh—*gradually* :—
    Am Fear-Ciùil 316

2. A few short sentences are used practically as adverbs :

cha—*not*
cha mhòr—*it is not much, almost*
ni h-e ⎫
ni h-eadh ⎬ *it is not*

'S e ⎫
'S eadh ⎬ *it is, 'tis* (so)
ma dh' fhaoite—*it might well be,
    perhaps* §143
ma ta—*it is well, well !*

3. A few adverbs are used loosely (1) as prepositions with gen.,

Mu'n àm 'san robh Mànus a' tarruing a luinge **trasd** an
    fhearainn aig an Tairbeart Cheinntrich—
*About the time when Magnus was dragging his ship across
    the land at Tarbert, Kintyre* :—Am Fear-Ciùil 200

(2) with verbs of motion governing a cognate acc. : § 154

Shnàmh i **trasd** an Caolas Diùrach—
She swam across the Sound of Jura :—ib. 298
a' dol **seachad** an t-sràid—*going past the street* :—Arab. II. 68
dol seachad an uinneag—*going past the window* :—MacCor 17
Theirinn i sìos am bruthach—*She went down the bank* :—ib. 113
Na'm faodainn fuireach shìos an gleann—*If I might stay
    down the glen* :—Clarsach 133

§ 214. II.—Adverbs of Time.

1.—Present.

a nis, a nise, nis (O.G. ind-ór-sa
—*this hour*, indosa, Ir. anois)
now

air a' mhionaid—*at this moment*

air an àm—*meantime*

air an uair—*just now, directly*

air ball—*on the spot*

an ceart uair (angeartair)—*just
now, presently*

an diugh—*to-day*

an nochd—*to-night*

an tràth so, an dràsta—*this
time, the present, just now*

2.—Past.

a chianabh—*a little while ago* :
—Waifs II. 222

air tùs—*at the beginning, at first*

an dé—*yesterday*

an earar (compar. of air *before*,
O.G. airther *east*, Ir. am an
oirthear, um an oirthear
Din.)—*the day after to-morrow*

air an là-na-n-earar :—Am
Fear-Ciùil 325

an eararais, an earardhris, an
treastar—*the second day after
to-morrow*

an raoir, a raoir—*last night*

an toiseach—*at first*

an t-seachdain so chaidh—*last
week*

an uiridh (O.G. on nurid, Sk.
parut, Gk. πέρυσι, πέρυτι)—
last year

fòs—*still* (O.G. beos)

mar thà ⎫ *already,*
mu thràth ⎭ *so soon*

moch thra—*at dawn*

o chian—*of old, long ago*

o chain nan cian—*ages ago*

o chionn aimsir—*long ago*

o chionn grathain ⎫ *a short*
o chionn ghoirid ⎭ *time ago*

3.—Future.

a chlisge (from a start)
—*suddenly*

a chaoidh (O.G. caidche, coidche
co aidche, G. gu oidhche *till
night*)—*ever, for ever*

a rìs, a rithist (a fhrith + éisse,
his track)—*back again, again*

a so suas—*henceforward*

air chionn—*by the time, to meet it*

am feasda (O.G. am feachd-sa)
—*for ever*

am màireach—*to-morrow*

an aithghear ⎫ *in a short time,*
an athghoirid ⎭ *soon*

an caise, ⎫ *precipitately,*
an gradaig ⎭ *quickly, soon*

an tiotan ⎫ *in a moment*
an tiota beag ⎭ *in a little while*

do shìor—*ever, for ever*

fo dhéidh ⎫ *after,*
fo dheoidh ⎬ *at length,*
fa dheireadh ⎭ *at last*

fathast (fo ?-fecht-sa)—*yet*

gu bràth—*for ever*

gu dìlinn (*till the deluge*)—*for
ever*

gu là bhratha—*till the judgment
day*

gu là luain (*till Monday*, the
Celtic world ends on a Sunday)—*for ever*

gu minic) often,
gu tric) frequently
gu sìor) for ever
gu sìorruith)
gu so)
chuige so (thuige) thus far
so))
ri h-ùine—in time, bye and bye

4.—INDEFINITE.

a h-uile uair—every time, always
am feadh—whilst
an còmhnuidh—always
an tràth—when
an ùine—whilst
aon uair—once
aon uair 's—when once
car ùine—for a time
cath—continually
cia liuthad uair) how many a
) time,
cia lìon uair) how oft
cia minic) how often
cia tric)
comh luath agus—as soon as,
    whenever

dé an uair—what time, when ?
do là, a là—by day
do dh'oidhche, a dh'oidhche—
    by night
do ghnàth—customarily, always
fo dhéidh) after,
fa dheòigh) at length,
fo dheireadh) at last
fo fheasgar—before evening
gach bliadhna—every year
idir—at all
mu dheireadh—eventually, at
    last
'na thràth—in its proper time
'na uaireannan) at times,
air uairibh) sometimes
ré seal—for a time
ré tamaill—for a while
'sa' bhliadhna—a year, L. per
    annum
'san là—in the day time, a-day
tràth—early, when
uair eigin—sometime
uair air chor-eigin) some time
uair no uair-eigin) or other
                       —Mac Cormaig 60.

§ 215.   III.—ADVERBS OF PLACE.

	Where ? (rest in)	Whither ? (motion to)	Whence ? (motion from)
air E. fore, **ear** f. East	ear in the East	s-oir eastward	a n-ear from the east
all (over)	th-all	a n-ull (O.G. inn-onn) (inn-unn) (ind-shund)	a n-all
iar after ; f. West	iar	s-iar	a n-iar
ìos down	sh-ìos	s-ìos	a n-ìos
os, uas, above	sh-uas	s-uas	a n-uas

		Where ?	Whither ?	Whence ?
deas f. *south*		'sa deas	deas,	an deas,
			gu deas	a deas
tuath *north*		'sa tuath	gu tuath	a tuath,
		tuath		bho 'n tuath
				bho thuath S.O.
				300ᵃv §193 (2)

aird-an-ear f. *the direction from the East, the East*

aird-an-iar f. *the direction from the West, the West*

A sabaid ris a' chuan-an-iar—*fighting with the western ocean* :—
Clarsach 32

le gaoith a tuath—*with the wind from the North*:—Clarsach 57

'S an déidh do chuairt bho 'n ear gu 'n iar— *And after thy course
from East to West* :—ib. 81

Dol uair gu deas 'us uair gu tuath—*Going sometimes South and
sometimes North* :—ib. 81

Gu'n dùisg thu 'm màireach anns an ear—*That thou wilt wake
to-morrow in the East* :—ib. 82

2. *Where ?*

bhos—*on this side*
cian—*far, afar*
fagus—*near*
faisg—*near*
far (O.G. bale)—*where*, rel.
ioras (air-ìos)—*down below*
sin, an sin—*there*
so, an so—*here*
sud, an sud—*yonder*
tarsuinn—*across*
uthard (O.G. for ard)—
    on high

3. *Whither ?*

The 3 s.m. of the prepositional
    pronouns : §120
    ann—*in*
    as—*out*
    deth—*away*
    fodha—*under*
    chuige, thuige—*to, towards*
    leis—*with, down*
    uaidh—*away*
    ris—*against, up*
    roimhe—*forward*
    thairis—*across*
    troimhe—*through*

4. *Where ?*

a thaobh—*aside, past*

a stigh—*inside, within*
a muigh—*outside, without*
air déidh—*last, behind*

5. *Whither ?*

a leth taobh—*to one side, aside*
a mhàin—*downward*
a steach—*inwards, within*
a mach—*outwards, without*
air aghaidh—*forward*

Where ?	*Whither ?*
air deireadh—*last*	air adhart (O.G. ar-airt, L. prorsum)—*forward*
air dheireadh—*behind*	air ais—*backward*
air fasgadh—*to leaward*	
air fuaradh—*to windward*	
air thoiseach—*foremost*	
an céin—*far*	fad as—*afar off*
an còir—*near to*	fad air astar—*far away*
an cois—*along with*	fhad—*lengthwise*
am fad—*far*	
an gar—*close to*	
an laimh—*in hand*	
an sàs—*in custody*	
an taice—*in support*	
	ceana—*whither ?*
càit ? càite ?—*where*	cia an taobh—*whither ?*
chuig' agus uaith—*to and fro*	c'ionad—*whither*
mu'n cuairt—*around*	le lethad—*downward*
mu thimchioll—*around*	ri h-aghaidh ⎫ *against*
ri port—*wind bound*	ri h-aodainn ⎭
ri taobh—*alongside*	ri bruthach—*upwards*
ris—*in an exposed state, uncovered*	ris 'us leis—*up and down*
shios-ud—*down yonder*	seachad—*past*
shuas-ud—*up yonder*	
thall-ud—*over yonder*	
urad-ud—*up, above yonder*	

§ 216. CONJUNCTIONS.

I. Simple Conjunctions :

1. ach—*but, except only*, Gk. ἐκτός *without*
   agus, 'us, is—*and, also, as, but*, L. angustē
   an, am—*whether*, L. an, Goth. an § 144
   co, cho—*so, as*, L. cum
   far am, far an—*where*, O.G. bale am, baile an § 215, 2
   gar—*though not* (ged nach)
   ge—*though*, O.G. ce
   gu'm, gu'n—*in order that, that*, O.G. co n-

gus nach—*until* . . . . *not*

ma—*if*, O.G. má, ma § 145, 3

mar, *as—like as*, O.G. amal, W. mal

mu'n—*before*, independent form of

mus—*before*, G. moch, much, L. mox § 145, 4

mur—*unless* § 145, 4, mu'n—*lest* :—Is. vi. 10

na—*not*, O.G. na, L. ne § 144, 2

na—*or*; *neve, *newe, W. neu, O.G. no, Ipv. at-noi *entrust*, W. ad-neu *deposit, pledge*, L. nū-men, ad-nuo

nach—*that not* § 116, 4

na'm, na'n—*if* (with Ipf. subj. and false supposition) § 145, 4

nara—*or not* (neo nach)

neo—*otherwise, else*

o, o'n, bho—*since, seeing that* § 145, 6

oir—*for, since*, Ir. óir, the ó of which tends to shorten ; O.G. hóre, gen. of uair, L. hōra

2. with **is** :

ged—*though* (it be) *that*, O.G. ce-ed

ged nach—*though* . . . . *not*

ge h-e—*though* (it be) *he*, O.G. cia, ce, ci

giodh e—*though it be he*, O.G. cid, 3 s. pres. (or past) subj. of *is*

gidheadh—*though it be* (or *were*) *that, nevertheless*, O.G. cid ed

gur—*that it is, that it may be*, pres. subj. of *is* with *ro*

guma—*that it might be, oh that !* O.G. co mbad

mas e 's—*if so be that, if*

nach—*that* (it is) *not*

'seadh—*it is that, yes !* O.G. is ed

3. with **ta** :

ged tha, ge ta—*nevertheless*

ma tà, *well*

§ 217.   AGUS.

with co-ordinate words or clauses :

1. Eadar mi fhéin, 's e fhéin—*between myself and him* :—Arab. I. 116.

Thig Dia ré airc 's cha n-airc an uair a thig e—*God comes in distress, and distress goes when he comes* :—N.G.P. 366

2. When the second clause is not stronger than a relative clause :

Tha cuid ann agus tha iad ealamh a ràdh—
There are some who are ready to say :—Cos. 107
Tha Famhair Mòr agus dà cheann air—
There is a big Giant with two heads :—Waifs III. 129
Bha cuid, 's cha mhòr nach robh iad 'nan tosd—
There were some who were almost silent :—Cuairt. 27, 63
Bha mise uair 's gu'm faca mi—
I have seen the time :—S.O. 150^{a}v

adding a strong adj. clause :
An fhuil àrd 's i gun truailleadh—
The lofty blood (which is uncontaminated) :—S.O. 49^{b}p.

adding a co-ordinate adj. clause with emphasis :
Ars an t-iasgair 's e dol air aghaidh leis an naigheachd—
Quoth the fisherman, while he went on with the news :—
Arab. I. 51.
Thuirt Sobaide agus i mar gu'm biodh gruaim oirre—
Said Sobaide, she being, as it were, in displeasure :—I. 87
Bha Sobaide 'na suidhe . . . agus i glé sgìth—
Sobaide was seated . . . being very tired :—I. 100
" Ni mise sin glé thoileach," ars Aimini, agus i breith air
an inneal-chiùil—" *I shall do that very willingly,*" *said
Aimini, taking hold of the instrument* :—ib. 101
" Oh ! fhathaich," ars an t-iasgair ! " 's e freagairt—
" *Oh Giant* " *said the fisherman in answer* :—ib. 39
Chunnaic mi ise 's i coiseachd comhladh ri firionnach—
I saw her while she was walking with a man :—ib. 69
Agus mi cho aoibhneach—*I being so glad* :—ib. 24
Móran sgalann 's beagan ollainn, mu'n dubhairt Muisean,
's e lomairt na muice—*Great cry and little wool, as the
Devil said when he sheared the sow* :—N.G.P. 319
Bha na beannta arda Mòrchuanach, 's iad uaine gu'm
mullach—*The high hills of Ardnamurchan stood green
to the summit* :—L.C. 61

3. As an adversative or arrestive conjunction :
Taing do Dhia a dh' òrdaich pailteas do m' mhanaich,
agus mi 'gam fàgail—*Thanks be to God who has provided
plenty for my monks, though I am leaving them* :—L.C. 51

Nach tioram an talamh agus na rinn e dh' uisge ?—
Is not the ground dry, considering how much it has rained ?
Munro 74

Is math a dh'fhimireadh an dàn a dheanamh, 's a liuthad
fear-millidh a tha aige—*The poem would need to be
well made, since it has so many spoilers* :—N.G.P. 271

Ghabh e t' oighreachd at antoil,

Thar do cheann, a's thu d' bheò-shlaint—
*He seized thine inheritance against thy will, over thy head,
notwithstanding that thou art alive and well* :—S.O. 46ª21.

Is duine còir e, 's na iarr a chuid—*He is a fine man, but
do not ask anything of his* :—N.G.P. 229

Na bi mear, no marbh 's tu òg—
Be not reckless or dead while thou art young :—L.C. 295

'S trom m' aigne 'S nach éighear mi'n caidreamh nam
bràithrean—*Heavy is my heart since I am not called
into the fellowship of the brethren* :—S.O. 47ª23

Fìor chruaidh gun bhogachadh

'S obair air làrach—*Very hard, with no softening, while
there is work to do on a battle-field* :—S.O. 153ª11

Ciamar a b'urrainn domhsa t' aithneachadh 's tu cho
truagh coltas 's a tha thu ?—
*How could I recognise you, since you are so wretched in
appearance as you are ?* :—Arab. I. 25

4.   AGUS—*as*

used as co-relative of cho, ionann, aon, cuidhte, corr, a mheud :

Na bi cho diombach dhiom **agus** m' fhàgail mar sin—
Do not be so angry with me as to leave me like that :—
McKay 32

B'ionann éirigh do m'aigne

'S leum a' bhradain am bùrn—*The rise of my spirit was
like the leap of the salmon in fresh water* :—S.O. 42ᵇ23

Cho beag '**s** gu'n dean sinn air son sìth—
However little we do for peace sake :—Clasrach 58

Ach ged a fhuair mi cuidhte '**s** an dul a bha mu'm mhuineal—
*But though I got quit of the noose that was round my
neck* :—Am Fear-Ciùil 229

'S mise taingeil faotainn cuidhte '**s** i—
I thankful to get quit of her :—ib. 324

Ach fhuair sinn cuidhte 's na trioblaidean sin uidh air
   n-uidh—
   But we got quit of these troubles gradually :—ib. 198
Cheannaich i còrr is fichead seòrsa—
   She bought more than twenty kinds :—Arab. I. 85

5. Closely associated words and ideas are conjoined by **'s, is**
e.g. tusa **'s** mise—*you and I*.

   Gu inbhe fhear **is** bhan—
   to men and women's estate :—Am Fear-Ciùil 257

But when a distinction is drawn, or emphasis is desired,
agus is used :

   Firionn **agus** boirionn bithidh iad—
   They shall be male and female :—Gen. vi. 19
   Am firionn **agus** am boirionn—
   The male and his female :—ib. vii. 2, 3
   Chruthaich Dia an duine fear **agus** bean—
   God created man male and female :—Catm. No. 10.

6.   **Agus** is omitted :

   (1) in a series of adjj. or adverbs :
   'S bachlach, duallach, cas-bhuidh, cuachach,
   Càradh suaimhneis gruag do chinn
   Gu h-aluinn bòidheach faìnneach òr-bhuidh—
   '*Tis crook-shaped, folded, yellow-curling, cupshaped
   Heaping up pleasure, the hair of thy head
   Beautiful, pretty, ringletted, golden-yellow* :—S.O. 285[b]s

   (2) between pairs of epithets :
   Tha mais' a's féile, tlachd a's ceutaich—*There is beauty
      and grace, charm and gracefulness* :—S.O. 285[b]36

§ 218.

gar—*though . . . not* for **ged nach**, corrupted into **gad nach,
ga nach, gara** e.g. **gara mi, gara bheil** for **ged nach mi,
ged nach 'eil** :—Munro 129

For the disappearance of -**ch**- in **nach** cf. **neo** § 150, 7 ;
and for -**n**- becoming -**r**- cf. mur § 145, 4

M

The relative sense being lost with the disappearance of the -ch- a pleonastic rel. pronoun was evolved to express the sense :

Is ioma marcaiche stàteil
Gar an àir' mi ach cuid diubh—
There's many a stately rider,
Though I shall (not) mention but a few of them :—S.O. 42ᵇr
Gar an téid mi g'a innseadh
Tha mi cinnteach a' m' sgeul—
Though I shall not go on to mention it,
I am certain of my tale :—ib. 37ᵃ 27.
Mo thogair **ged nach** till—
I care not if he come not back :—N.G.P. 52
Mo thogair **gar an** till :—C.S.

§ 219

mu'n *before, ere* ; **mu** is the independent form of the O.G. preverb mos- (now **mus**, L. mox, G. much, moch) *soon*, O.G. mos-riccub-sa—*I shall soon come* :—Wb. 28°9

Both forms are still in use :

Mus tàinig an dìle o nèamh—
Before the flood came from heaven :—Stewarts 481
So agad trusgan as fheàrr na trusgan Adhaimh mus do thuit e— *Here you have better raiment than that of Adam before he fell* :—Cos. 160
Mus robh e 'na mhinistear—
Before he was a minister :—ib. 33, 42
Chaidh e air seachran an cridhe **ma's** d' thug (=tug) e aon cheum follaiseach air falbh— *He went astray in heart before he had made a single overt step away* :—ib. 116
Fada **mus** d' fhuair iad rìoghachd Dhé ann an Criosd— *Long before they found the Kingdom of God in Christ* :—ib. 42
Bha mi glé sgìth **mu'n** d'ràinig mi talamh tioram— *I was very tired before I reached dry land* :—Arab. II. 50
Agus e 'na chruthachd nàdarra mar a bha e **mu'n** do chuireadh fo na geasan e—
He being in his natural shape, as he had been before he was put under the spells :—ib. I. 79

Ach 's cian **mu'n** lìonar rìs na glinn—
But it will be long ere the glens be filled again :—L.C. 74
Mu'm fuirich i sàmhach—
Before she stay quiet :—D. Ban 326, 48
Ach **mu'n** robh bheag de sheanachas eatorra—
But before there was much conversation between them :—
Am Fear-Ciùil 265

Na's lugha na—*less than (unless)* is used erroneously for mu'n :

Na's lugha na tha aon de na daoine glice sin a làthair—
Unless one of those wise men is present :—Am Fear-
Ciùil 240

§ 220.

Nara—*or not* (neo nach)

Thigeadh nara tigeadh e—*Let him come or not* :—Munro
162 n.

§ 221.

Neo, air neo—*otherwise, else, quite,* O.G. ciarniu, ciarneo—*for what, wherefore* ?

niu, neo, more usually neoch, d.s. of ni n. *thing* :

Cia ar neoch dorrignis ?—
For what hast thou done it ?—Sg. 217ᵃ5.

Gabh am mach as a' chaisteal agus na tig air ais gu bràth
tuilleadh, **air neo** ma thig, cha bhi 'n tuilleadh saoghail
agad—*Begone from the castle, and return no more for
ever, otherwise if you do, you will not have length of days* :
—Arab. I. 79

Cha bhi 'n sean fhacal claoite
Air neo 's claon théid a thogail—*The proverb will not be
falsified, else it will be wrongly construed* :—S.O. 46ᵇ3.

Is e mo chomhairle dhut gun an còrr cheisdean a chur
oirnn, **air neo** ma chuireas, caillidh tu do shùil dheas
air a shàillibh—*My advice to you is not to put more
questions to us, else if you do, you will lose your right
eye on the heels of it* :—Arab. II. 54

Cha n-e Iain bàn a th' ann co dhiùbh, **neo** bheireadh e
cheud aghaidh air tigh athar—*It is not Ian Bàn that
is present at all events, otherwise he would direct his first
gaze to his father's house* :—MacCormaig 104

Contaminated with **nior**, § 144 II. 2, **air neo** suffers metathesis
and becomes **neo-air-**, retaining the meaning of **nior** :

Bha so 'na bhuille glé throm do dh' Omar, 's bha e air a
leantainn le buill' eile, **neo-air**-thaing cho trom—
*This was a very heavy blow to Omar, and it was followed by
another blow quite as heavy* :—Am Fear-Ciùil 206

§ 222. **II. Conjunctive Phrases.**

1. A number of phrases are used to connect either words or
sentences :

A bharr, os barr—*moreover*
a bharrachd—*besides*
a chionn gu—*because that*
a chum 's gu—*in order that*
a chum 's nach—*in order that . . . not*
a dh'aon chuid—*anyway, nevertheless* :—L.C. 14
a dh' aon chuid . . . no—*either . . . or*
ach co dhiubh—*however*
ach coma—*nevertheless*
ach coma co dhiubh—*well then*
air a shon sin—*for all that, nevertheless*
air an aobhar sin—*therefore*
air chor agus—*so that*
air chor 's—*in such a way that*
air chùl—*besides*
air chùl 's—*over and above*
air eagal gu—*for fear that*, d' eagal gu, eagal 's gu—*lest*
air neo—*otherwise, else*
air son gu—*because that*
an dà chuid . . . agus—*both . . . and* :—Mac Cormaig 40
do bhrìgh gu—*by reason that*
gun fhios an, am—*not knowing but*
gun fhios nach—*in case that, as perhaps*
ionnas gu—*insomuch that*
ionann 's gu—*so that*

mar gu—*as if, like as if*
mar nach—*as if...not*
mar sid agus—*so also, so*
mar sin agus—*likewise*
mar sud agus—*and also*
sol mu'n, sul mu'n—*before, ere*
tuilleadh eile—*another addition, moreover*
uime sin—*therefore*

2. In some cases the conjunction is omitted, and by parataxis the sentences are placed side by side, leaving the Relative connection to be inferred

Cò a tha daoine ag ràdh **is mise** ?—
Whom do men say that I am ?—Mk. viii. 27, §27
   cf. Tha sibhse ag ràdh gur mi—
    Ye say that I am :—Lk. xxii. 70.
Ciod **bu** mhiann leam a ràdh—
What I wished to say :—Arab. I. 101
Tha uirid agus uirid eile is a ta iad ag ràdh, **thiuntaidh**
   Mac a Phersoin—
There is as much and as much again as they say
   MacPherson translated :—H.S. Report p. 39

The Interrogatives become conjunctive adverbs : § 144
An sin dh' fheòraich Fionn deth **cia** as a thàinig e—
Then Fionn enquired of him whence he had come :—
   Waifs. III. 9.
Mas aithne dhuit **co** iad—
If you know who they are :—Teachd. I. 5

In the case of **is**, the Sequence of Tenses may be departed from, e.g. a Past is followed by a Present cf. § 161, 4 :
Cha d'innis e dhomh **co i**—
He did not tell me who she was :—Arab. I. 110.
Dh' innis mi dha gu saoir soilleir **co mi**—
I told him freely and frankly who I was :—ib. II. 4, 5.

§ 224.   **INTERJECTIONS.**

Interjections are of two kinds :
   1. Words exclusively so used, generally either mono-syllables, or monosyllables reduplicated or compounded.

a—*ah ! oh !*

a hath—*aha !*

abab—*fy*

abù !—*war-cry of the Gael*

ach, ach—*ach ! alas !*

adad, atat—*hold, take care !*

bo, bo bo—*strange ! wonderful !*

cuist, uist—*hush !*

faire faire—*ay, ay ?*

faireagan faireagan—*bravo !*—MacCormaig 75

fich, fuigh—*fy*

fise faise

ha, ha, hà-à-à, ib. 53, 75 ; ho, hó, ib. 74

haoi orra, ho ro !—*ha hà !*

ho, ré-é-é, ib. 52 ; ho-ré, ib. 27—*hurrah !*

o—*oh !*

obh, òbh—*dear me* :—Teachd. I. 5 ; MacCormaig 45, 94

och, och och—*alas*

ochan, ochan, ochan, ò—*alas ! oh !* :—ib. 93 ; Arab. II. 7

ochòin, ochòin—*alas !* :—MacCormaig, 59

thalla, thalla—*well, well !* :—Mac Cor. 33, 73

thisd—*hist, hush*

thud, thud—*tut, tut !* :—ib. 58 ; tud, tud ! :—ib. 48

u ! hi-hi-ì—*hee, hee,* :—ib. 48

ud ! ud !—*tut, tut !* :—Am Fear-Ciùil 131, 261

2. Phrases are used in considerable numbers as interjections, e.g.

a chiall !—*oh dear !*

a dhuine !—*dear man !*

a dhuine chridhe !—*dear me !* :—MacInnes, Còmh. 28, § 21

a rìgh, rìgh !—*O King, strange !*

air nàile !—*for shame !*

air t' ais !—*stand back !*

air t' athais !—*avast !* :—Teachd. I. 5

an eadh !—*would you !*

an gille !—*the hero !*

bo thugad !—*take care !* :—Am Fear-Ciùil 162

da rìreadh—*verily !*

deis dé—*halt ! barley !*

eudail—*dear !*

faic, feuch, seall !—*behold !*

fhir mo chridhe !—*my dear sir !*

Firein, firein, obh! obh !—*Hush, hush, little man !* :—
F.T. 104

ma seadh !—*verily !*

matà !—*well !*

Mhoire 's buidheach, a Dhia, ort—*Marry ! I am thankful,
O God, for thee* :—S.O. 39ᵇ9.

mo chràdh ! *my anguish !*

mo chreach !—*my destruction ! alas !*

mo chreach léir ! —*My utter ruin !* :—MacCormaig 84, 98

mo mhasladh !—*my disgrace !*

mo nàire !—*my shame !*—L.C. 67

mo thruaighe !—*my sorrow ! alas !* :—MacCormaig 97

O ! cia mòr a mhaitheas !—*Oh ! how great is His goodness* :
—L.C. 18

och ! mo chreach !—*Oh my destruction* :—ib. 71

seadh !—*yes !*

so, so !—*here here !* :—MacCormaig 55

suas i !—*up with it !* :—ib. 52

suas i rithisd : suas i !— *Up with it again ! up with it !* :—
ib. 56

thugad !—*Take care of yourself !*

———————

List of Annotated or Classified Words

(The Numbers refer to the Pages).

I.—GAELIC INDEX.

II.—WELSH INDEX.

III.—OGHAM INDEX.

ADDITIONS AND CORRECTIONS.

1 *his cow*; 5 solais làn; MacCor.; 6 a *his*; a *her*:; a *who* (relative); 8 àirde; bhàrr; **a** *her*:; a *who* (relative); A. K. McCallum, Laoidh 292; 9 W. chwedl; W. deigr; cf.; 10 G. cat; shifted; 11 **a bhos**; 14 tòrr; Glen Urquhart; -rubha, Tobar-; 18 éces; fáitsine; préisg E.; 19 often-used; an t-sùil; 24 **an** in; dell; cf. MacCor.; tàillear; 25 brugh; 28 r'a chuid; **bu**, §27;

32 **Bu** aspirates all consonants except dentals, and (occasionally) **s**: Bu **s**inn, bu **s**ibh—*'twas we, 'twas ye*:—Stewart 100. The consonant group in sinn, sibh resists aspiration §19, 2, §121, 3. Otherwise aspiration of **s** is almost universal:

> A mhac a bu shine—*his elder son*:—Lk. xv. 25.
>
> Bu shearbh a' dol sìos—*It were bitter going to battle*:—S.O. 148b32, Bu searbh, is still heard in C.S.

33 71, §20; ceannfhionn; eilthir §100, aliter §139; 34 **gach, iomadh, liuthad**; 36 caochladh m.; flath; òlte; 37 fasgnag; fiùthaidh; Am Fear-Ciùil; 38 spliug; E. *store*; 39 fann *weak*; 40 diphthongised; 41 brèagh, èaladh; 42 cnead; 44 ceàrd; ceàrr; deàrrsadh; geàrr; 45 seabhag; 46 ciont; tiugh is short like fliuch; 47 fàisg = fashg; ìomhaigh; 48 aigeantach; aillse; gaire f. *nearness*; tànaiste; meidh; 50 tuagh; 51 suipeir; **eòi**; 52 spliùig; 53 *age; birds; to, against*; gàbhaidh; ri **h**-ùrnaigh; 54 *growth*; πέρα; *fresh, new*; epero-n; cf.; 55 W. celwrn; seàrr; 57 Schwester; E. *peacock*; 58 fairis,; ionraic; 60 bantrach; 61 sùitheach *sooty*; **-l**; 62 com m.; Eigg; lìnn m. *age*; 63 a lìnn; diphthongised; nèamh; As-pirated, like Eng. -**n**- in *net, nit*:; tàillear, dàillear; 64 an t-snàtha; cluinn-idh; léithne; 65 2 before or after -th-:; pronnasg; fòs; 67 fairsinn, better fairsing, for-ess-ang *over-un-narrow*; 68 *spoil*; 70 Sandhi; Arab I. 66y; 71 *l.* ùb**a**raid; 73 *rank, condition*; 74 (m.) (m.); 75 reath, reithe; **coileach**; earb f. *roe*; 76 giuthas; 77 nèamh; dat. taigh; 78 ἵππου, Thess. ἵπποι; àrann; 79 2 a meaningless termination -**a** is also used:

> n.s. a' chuideachd**a** phìceach—
> *the antlered band*:—S.O. 221b41.
> Gur e sgeul**a** na creiche—
> *It is a tale of woe*:—ib. 24b41.
> d.s. (uirsgeul) air cuideachd**a** cheir-ghil—
> *A romance of the white-tailed* (§ 106) *band*:—ib. 24b3.

82 càrnaibh; *splinter*; 83 (pl. spuing and spogan); 84 O.G. cinél; **ia** into **eòi**; 85 mas. -**io**-; 87 **a** into **oi**; 89 Boeot. βανά; mas. -**a**- stems; (pl. & clobhan); 90 còrsan; 91 tràgha; (O.G. g.s. fádha); fiacaill, older fiacail; 92 eàrr; *fairy bull*; 95 D. Ban 4, 1; aireach; 97 tràgha; 99 **Di- beatha; car-a' mhuiltein; eadar-dhà-shian; taigh-fo-thalamh; fheala-dhà 's da-rìreadh**; 101 written also dòrn; 102 spùtan; 107 *l.* Màrt; 110:—Is. lix. 10; 111 as **cumhachdaiche a tha ann**; 112 Cha robh; 113 (& moich); 120 Gillies Gr. 71; (m.); (f.); 123 Waifs III. 10; 124 *These little three*; *Those big four*; 126 *l.* troighean; an t-sèatamh; 128 **cheathrar**; 129 **Ochdnar**; 130 bó-choinneal; 131 (*barr*); (*mullach*); 132 m., O.G.; Svarabhakti:; (*sporran*); 133 (*fàileadh*); fem.; *maid-servant*; 134 (*ceann*); *black martin*.

136 Ciod e a' ghnè dhuine so:—Math. viii. 27, ed. 1902; cf. Lk. viii. 25; Ciod a' ghnè leinibh:—Lk. i. 66; Ciod an coslas duine:—Jas. i. 24; Ciod a'

ghnè dhaoinc :—I. Thes. i. 5, 2 Pet. iii. 11—These examples are Adj. Cpds. Ciod a' ghnè bàis :—John xxi. 19 ; Ciod a' ghnè gràidh :—1 John iii. 1, ed. 1902, are Descriptive Cpds. § 114, 3.

cf. Dh' fhalbh thu féin 's do chuid mac—
Thou art gone, thyself and thy sons :—S.O. 52b17.

l. creithleagan daoine.

137 innt', ; ghaoith ; wet feet ; 138 nighean (contracted to ni) ; 139 Sally, the Dairymaid ; Ri lìnn ; In this example, for an athar ? 141 farmer of ; Strathmashie ; 142 —To life everlasting ; 146 MacAlister ; 147 Conacher ; (a black Gaul) ; MacKerras, Kellas ; God-, N. d with stroke across stem ; 148 -bjórn bear, or -ólfr ; (Ogham TOVISACI) ; Askell, *As-Ketill ; 149 Mac Cerdai, Mac Cearda (v. K. Meyer, Macgnímartha Finn §7) is the regular genitive sing. The forms in the text are folk-etymologies ; or Gutt-ormr ; Mac buidhe ; 150 riabhach (brindled) ; Mac Guaire ; ljótr ; 'Ivarr ; 151 gen. Duibhne ; 152 Sumar-lidi, Thor-módr, N. d, with a stroke across the stem ; 155 S. Tennent's ; 156 Cainnech, L. Canicus ; 157 Eigg ; 158 (Wigtown-shire) ; now Ecclefechan ; 159 (red) ; i.e. Cill-ma-ghlais ; 160 Mac Eòghann ; Kilmalemnoc ; Mungo ; 162 (Patrician) ; (well-born) ; (Warrior) ; Teampull Ronaig ; Lewis ; 163 Sts., l. Sometimes ; 166 shaoil mi ; 61 z, ; Possessive Pronoun ; 170 ad- ; 171 §116, 2, (add) Far am bheil ar dìlsean—Where our kindred are :—ib. 78, Far am=O.G. baile, bale i, with rel. ; 172 as fheàrr, b'fheàrr 230, 246, 247, 295, 296, 309 ; 174 pàirt ; 176 Indo-European ; comparative ; 177 7. 3 pl. m. : Indo-European ; 178 rìghre, O.G. ríg-rad ; 179 Diminutives ; manikin ; 180 nun ; tòiseach m. ; Ogham ; 2. -i- klo- ; 182 better, caoibhneas ; 183 nèamhaidh heavenly ; nèamh ; Ml. 33c2 ; 184 càrnal, càrn ; fràg ; W. gafl ; 185 delete Loth R.C. xiv. xv. ; 186 -ad ; crepitus ventris ; 187 duómi ; edn, ; -a-no- leathann ; 188 Samhuinn ; Br. kroc'hen ; O.G. rígan ; 189 fàistine ; enuein ; dùileamh m ; 190 aimsireil ; Br. glac'har ; triùir, O.G. triar ; 191 Ir. cilornn, W. celwrn ; fàistinn ; 192 Sk sútu- ; 194 but otherwise cf ; eu-crinn-teach ; 200 treamh-laidh H.B. ; 202 § 143 (add) glaodh do mhna muinntir—the wail of thy wife :—S.O. 25b15 ; 225 do-gní, do-ní ; 228 Perf. t-uc ; 229 The stems tha-, bi-, bha- are long, but are seldom written with the accent ; 233 away over there ! ; 237 dh' éireas ; woe's ; 238 3 s. Fut. Indic. ; An t-Oran (with accented O). 239, 241, 255 ; 2. Periphrastic ; AmFear-Ciùil 232 ; 240 Similarly in the Passive ; 243 (2) condition . ;—Ach ; 246 his father met him and not his brother first ; 247 MacC. ; 249 bruith ; 251 tairmesc ; 252, 253 Ipv. Inf. O.G. ; càirich, càradh ; 253 delete tògairt ; speak, ; crawl, ; 254 -duinn -uinn -ainn ; following ; tairg offer ; 257 Munro ; 259 better, Mar is fhaide ; 261 An tòiseachadh blàir ; 263 toibheum m. reproach ; 264 inbhear ; tòbairt ; 266 ad-con-dairc ; perish, ; 267 tàthchur ; iomchar ; meet, ; W. gwaddol ; 268, 27 dam- with fo-, foidhidinn p. 197 ; for- ; 269 finn know ; G. from 3 s. pf. ; 270 fàisc-, ; fich-, fech- ; fuin- ; 271 eugmhail, teagmhail trs. to icc- 274 ; 272 tairngire ; treaghaid ; 273 fòghnadh ; eadar-ghnàth ; 274 θέσσασθαι ; 275 G. denom. ; descend, ; suffer, ; 276 patience, ; 277 μύλλω ; misg f. ; find out ; 278 tuimhseadh ; tiorcadh ; 281 saighead ; samhuil ; sc- cut ; 282 scel ; 283 selb f. possession ; sem- G. to- ; 285 snig- drop, rain, ; 287 diuc ; altaich salute ; (-sd- for -ts-) ; ἐπί is postulated by Ped. as preverb in ei-tich ; 289 L. ex ; 290 §187, 2 (c) This rule is general ; 291 (What you have gathered from a hedgehog, i.e.) ; iar n- ; 300 better, Is e as fhaigse ; is ann bu mhò ; 303 Chaidh ; 305 across the Kyles ; 306 troimh but also with dat. (add) or acc. after verbs of motion ; water-courses ; 307 overhead, above ; 309 prenoun ro- ; 310 to dry ; 318 ge h-e—though (it be) ; ma tà well.